RUM, ROMANISM, & REBELLION

RUM
ROMANISM
&

REBELLION
THE MAKING OF A PRESIDENT
1884

MARK WAHLGREN SUMMERS

The University of North Carolina Press   Chapel Hill & London

Manufactured in the United States of America

Set in Bodoni and Madrone types by Keystone Typesetting, Inc.

The paper in this book meets the guidelines for permanence and durability
of the Committee on Production Guidelines for Book Longevity of the
Council on Library Resources.

Library of Congress Cataloging-in-Publication Data

Summers, Mark W. (Mark Wahlgren), 1951–

Rum, romanism, and rebellion : the making of a president, 1884 /
by Mark Wahlgren Summers.

p.   cm.

Includes bibliographical references and index.

ISBN 0-8078-2524-7 (cloth: alk. paper). –
ISBN 0-8078-4849-2 (pbk.: alk. paper)

1. Presidents–United States–Election–1884.   2. United States–
Politics and government–1881–1885.   I. Title.

E695.S9   2000

324.273'084–DC21   99-34238

CIP

04   03   02   01   00   5   4   3   2   1

Contents

Acknowledgments, ix

Introduction, xi

Prologue: Judgment Day, 1

Chapter 1. No Business To-Day Other Than Politics, 13

Chapter 2. The Dispirit of '76, 27

Chapter 3. The Bloody Shirt—In Hoc Signo Vinces, 41

Chapter 4. The Politics of Personality, 59

Chapter 5. O Temperance, O Mores! 77

Chapter 6. The Protection Racket, 91

Chapter 7. The Democrats Rise from the Dead, 108

Chapter 8. The Passing of Arthur, 124

Chapter 9. We Love Him for the Enemies He Has Made, 143

Chapter 10. The Public Be Crammed! 162

Chapter 11. Love's Libels Lost, 179

Chapter 12. Windypendents' Day, 197

Chapter 13. Ireland Sold for Gold! 210

Chapter 14. Sideshows, 223

Chapter 15. Carrying the War into Africa, 240

Chapter 16. Local All Over, 255

Chapter 17. Clerical Errors, 272

Chapter 18. Lord! But We Skirted the Edge! 289

Chapter 19. Justice at Last! 304

Notes, 317

Bibliography, 353

Index, 369

Illustrations

"Another voice for Cleveland" xii

"The Blaine tariff fraud" 3

"His own Destroyer" 5

"Death at the polls and free from 'federal interference'" 32

"Mr. Tilden's body-guard" 39

"This puts me in the devil of a position" 53

A cartoon of what Democrats thought Readjuster rule meant 56

"Rival rag-pickers" 57

"The *magnetic* Blaine" 63

"A grand Shakespearian revival" 69

"A Big Job" 74

"Her platform going to pieces" 105

"Senator Bayard strikes his grand attitude on the tariff question" 110

"Cleveland the celibate" 117

"Made harmless at last!" 120

"Blaine leans towards Logan" 130

"Phryne before the Chicago tribunal" 137

"He courts the mother and means the daughter" 153

"He can't beat his record" 174

"Those dogs won't fight—they are dying of starvation" 183

"*He* instituted the ordeal. Can he stand it himself?" 187

The writing on the wall 199

"The mistake of a lifetime" 201

"The Blainiac programme" 213

"The spread of American ideas" 215

"Helping the rascals in" 226

Prohibition's pet. St. John" 231

"A magnetic statesman" 258

"Ready for business" 276

"Belshazzar Blaine and the Money Kings" 287

"Out of a job once more!" 297

"Men may come, and men may go; but the work of reform
shall go on forever" 305

"A dead failure" 310

Tables

Table 1. Republican Losses, New York, 1882, 71

Table 2. Ohio Prohibition Party Vote Totals, 85

Table 3. Democratic and Republican Shares of the Vote in the Five Ohio Counties with the Largest Democratic Gain, 88

Table 4. Democratic and Republican Shares of the Vote in Ohio's 1883 Gubernatorial Race, 90

Table 5. Republican Share of the Vote, by Section, 290

Table 6. Democratic Share of the Vote, by Section, 291

Table 7. Where Republicans Gained Most and Lost Worst in the 1884 Presidential Election, 291

Table 8. Party Gains and Irish Votes in Troy, New York, 1884, 293

Table 9. Upstate and Downstate Margins in New York, 295

Table 10. States in Which Blaine Had the Lowest Share of the Vote, 1884, 300

Table 11. Number of Deep South Counties with Black Majorities Carried by Each Party, 1884, 301

Acknowledgments

Acknowledging favors done feels rather like a caucus race: everybody has won, and everyone deserves prizes. Rare the archivist that was less than helpful, though the folks in the Manuscripts Room at the Library of Congress, as always, deserve special kudos. Those at the State Historical Society of Wisconsin and at the University of Pennsylvania Library delved with passionate intensity as well. Kiwanis groups and Rotarian banqueters in Cincinnati and Louisville heard the gist of the book and helped me figure out what point I really was trying to make. Geoffrey Blodgett offered cryptic and sound suggestions. Colleagues at the University of Kentucky, notably William Freehling, heard me out at lunch-bag colloquiums and offered sage advice. Others kindly read the manuscript through: David Hamilton, Tom Cogswell, Philip Harling, and Robert Flynn. Once again, Tom and Dave did ace work, Dave with skepticism about some of my arguments and good counsel about the focus, and Tom with bemusement and reassurance. It is to fond memories of years of Tom's friendship that this book is dedicated, and to the dear memory of that indispensable and commonsensical lady, the very soul of our department and an inspiration for our best work, the late Darlene Calvert. To Mary Caviness, for her expert editing, too, much is owed. I owe the most to my parents, Clyde and Evelyn Summers, who, as ever, pored over every page, questioning everything from the premises to the prose. No one did more than they; in terms of shaping this book, they were indispensable campaign managers.

Introduction

The presidential election of 1884 was one of the gaudiest in history, the campaign itself nearly legendary: Democrats, after twenty-four years out of power, nominated the straight arrow governor of New York, Grover Cleveland; Republicans chose that shifty charmer, former Speaker James G. Blaine, the "Plumed Knight" from Maine; the Mugwumps, a band of civic-spirited Republicans, walked out of their party and onto Cleveland's side. Dirt flew. Blaine was accused of every roguery from shaking down a railroad to guano speculations. Cleveland was exposed as the father of one Maria Halpin's illegitimate child. Cartoons showed the Plumed Knight, a blushing courtesan stripped to his shorts and tattooed with his offenses, and New York's governor plugging his ears to "another voice for Cleveland." Crowds marched the boulevards yelling:

> Blaine! Blaine! James G. Blaine!
> The con-tinental liar from the state of Maine!

Or:

> Ma! Ma! Where's my pa?
> Gone to the White House! Ha, ha, ha!

In the end, New York decided all. There "an ass in the shape of a preacher" cost Blaine the Irish vote and the election by damning Democrats as the party of "Rum, Romanism, and Rebellion." When Cleveland squeaked through by barely a thousand votes, demonstrators sang:

> Hurrah for Maria, hurrah for the kid!
> We voted for Grover, and d—d glad we did![1]

Historians touch at their peril any election so captivating. What killjoy would break a butterfly on the wheel of research (or, for that matter, mention that all three of those war chants occurred on the same day—*after* the election)? Perhaps this is why most scholars have given 1884 no more than a glance, often leering. After all, in Morton Keller's words, the contests of that decade were "not grand confrontations over national issues so much as contests for control of the federal patronage that might go either way." Some modern accounts do the campaign justice, certainly, the best being H. Wayne Morgan's fifty-page narrative and Geoffrey Blodgett's essays about Cleveland and Mugwumpery. Looking elsewhere, however, casual readers are likelier to come upon accounts that treat the election as a near-meaningless moment,

"Another voice for Cleveland"
(Frank Beard, Judge, *September 27, 1884*).

unpolluted by debate over serious ideas, where personalities dominated because the parties were Tweedledum and Tweedledee, and that, in the end, did
what politicians meant it to: it promised the people nothing worth having—
and delivered just what it promised.[2]

If the skeptics are right, this book is all wrong; for I would suggest that
1884 was not just laden with pleasures and personalities, but with issues, that
it revealed many of the strengths as well as the weaknesses of the political
system, and that the weaknesses went far deeper than the precious nonsense
that popular versions of the campaign dwell on.

Those raised on the simplicities of Matthew Josephson's *The Politicos*,
where personality drove factional wars of Stalwart and Half-Breed Republican, where the issue of a free ballot perished with Reconstruction's end, and
where Democrat and Republican mouthed meaningless nostrums while
chasing after the approval of the well-to-do, none of this account will make

sense. Nor will it to those who have taken too literally the historians' reminder that most states were undebatable ground.³ Politicking was not done for public entertainment but to tear away or confirm votes that seemed in doubt. Far from a system in which the two parties, each secure in its domination of many states, battled for control of a few, both sides sensed a political system breaking apart, or, perhaps from the "outs'" perspective, a new political order congealing. Until the end of the 1880s, as one partisan put it, Iowa would go Democratic the day Hell went Methodist. But already in 1884 there must have been religious stirrings in Hell; there certainly were political ones in Iowa. Across the country, the press heralded the news of revolutions no less plausible for the fact that the revolutionaries, at the critical moment, forgot to show up.

If there was no realignment this year, if, indeed, neither side lost or gained more than a smidgen, and if the smidgens canceled each other out, we may have the real explanation backward: Republican and Democrat stuck by the old cause not because the two parties had turned indistinguishable, but because there was still such an obvious gap between their beliefs. Voters did not cast a Democratic ballot because they had grown used to doing so, nor a Republican one because their parsons preached them there. They voted in light of what they had seen the parties do and what they promised; habit and culture helped them decide what promises to believe, and what events to heed, but they knew what later stereotypes of the Gilded Age overlooked: politics mattered because winning meant power to do things or keep them from being done. They knew because in Atchison and on the streets of Danville they had seen that power used.

That is why this book sprawls across the map and over eight years. The campaign was a culmination. Gilded Age politics was not so much national as federal, a crowd of state elections, each with its own specialties. Rum and Romanism—or, to put it more precisely, disputes over how far the state could regulate behavior and see to society's moral upkeep—made a mess of party plans outside Washington. The topics only seem worlds apart from national issues. In fact, the two could not be separated. When a Democratic presidential nominee declared the tariff "a local issue," he knew half of it. Local idiosyncrasies had repercussions that stopped only at the water's edge, and every little mudslinging had a meaning all its own, connecting as it did with "real" issues.

At the same time, elections can define the ideological movement within parties. They can foreclose possibilities in organizations moving contradictory ways. They can serve as a revealing moment in the long-term shift in politics itself. For Democrats, who had long been able to define themselves differently in different places, the campaign showed how far they had come from their old conservatism, even as it forced them to take as their chosen leader the epitome of a new and not universally accepted kind of conservatism, less friendly to the radical strains that many a "demagogue" at the state level had been trying out. For Republicans, haunted still by the war's aftermath, the campaign allowed them to redirect an old faith and to grope for ways of controlling moral impulses that were tugging the party apart. It permitted them to frame their ideas in terms related more to livelihood and family, rather than to wartime loyalty and soldierly manliness. In a sense, this campaign was the defining moment in the tempering of the very masculine tone of Civil War politics, with its party armies and "Boys in Blue." But 1884 also revealed to Republicans how strongly the old themes resonated, and how perilous it would be to cut themselves off too far from their ideological traditions.

If in the making of the president, 1884 shows political managers in a new way, coping with grassroots democracy at its most persnickety and issues raised by those that the political system shortchanged or excluded—women and blacks especially—it has a more disturbing message about Gilded Age politics. For Americans in general, the election demonstrated how far from democratic the political rules had made representative government. Again and again, those who ran the party system, from ward heelers to presidential nominees, did more than react to issues. They shaped and defined them to suit their purposes. Intentionally or not, they set the bounds of discussion, just as those with power set the terms on which minor parties (and in the South major ones) could exist. The election may not have been won, after all, in New York in the two weeks before election day, but across the South in the eight years since Reconstruction had come to a formal end.

The 1884 campaign, then, is worth writing about. Those who thought they knew the basics will find surprises. The Mugwumps will be shoved off center stage and into minor supporting roles, though not because I think their case against the political system irrelevant. On the contrary, the insurgents deserve more credit than some historians of our own day have given them. One might argue that, outside New York, they carried no state for Cleveland—rather like saying that, aside from the fire, October 1871 was a month like any other in Chicago. But historians have been all too generous in giving their role attention (and blame). On those grounds alone, the Mugwumps need to be remanded to the background, as one force among many. At the same time, areas fit for a line or two in traditional accounts loom large. One reason is that nearly every history leaves the perfectly obvious unsaid: without a Solid South, Democrats could not have won, and fraud, threats, and legal tricks helped make it solid. Another reason is that often what could have happened and didn't tells as much as what did.

Scholars with greater knowledge of Gilded Age politics may find suspicions confirmed, though even those who know the campaign best may chance on the unexpected, both as to why things worked as they did and what actually happened, from the selling of St. John to the fractured nature and ineffectiveness of interest-group partisanship.

Indeed, this account may look like an acquaintance in a fun house mirror, too big and too small in the most outlandish places. My hope, rather, is that my account will serve more as corrective lenses for those long accustomed to seeing things a little askew—and that it will give everyone what the topic deserves most, a sight well worth the seeing.

RUM,
ROMANISM,
&
REBELLION

Prologue: Judgment Day

Election day, 1884, put a proper finish on the dirtiest presidential campaign in living memory: from Chicago to the New England coast, storms rolled eastward, flushing the city gutters and turning every country road into a mire.[1]

Ahead of the front, Republicans glanced at lowering clouds uneasily. By tradition, wet days boded ill for Republicans. Some analysts explained that urban Democrats turned out rain or shine. Republican farmers living down mud-choked country lanes stayed home and saved themselves a soaking. Or, some surmised, Republicans thought too hard and Democrats too little: the former told themselves their votes were not needed for victory, while the latter, used to losing anyhow, showed up out of pure cussedness, whatever the weather. Either way, the darkening sky meant bad news for James G. Blaine, the Republican nominee. As everyone knew, he entered the final stretch with hardly a vote to spare.[2]

Take them then as they were on this November 4: what choices did the electorate really have? They could vote, if they wished, for three minor parties: woman's rights, Prohibition, or labor. For all intents and purposes, of course, the first was simply a publicity gimmick for equal suffrage. Whatever her talents as a lawyer, nobody took Belva Lockwood's campaign seriously. Even her public image relegated her to a sideshow curiosity, her campaign posters showing her astride her three-wheeled bicycle. Those who put woman suffrage first favored Blaine. Lockwood did, herself.[3]

Slightly more serious were the two nominees of long-standing third parties. The Labor or People's Party carried on the radical program that the Greenback Party had promoted in two elections past and ran the squinting political veteran General Benjamin F. Butler.

> Rare old Ben of the bunting-mill,
> Running for office, time to kill,
> Indepe-Democrat-Republican-
> Anti-monopoly-workingman-
> Labor-reformer-communist-
> High-License-Prohibitionist-
> Greenbacker-all things to all men,
>> Rare old Ben!
>> Rare, and turned over![4]

People hated, loved, or laughed at him, and had ever since his days as a rough-tongued lawyer before the war. Sent to New Orleans with occupying forces, he had decreed that any woman showing disrespect to a Union soldier would be considered a woman of the streets and punished accordingly. Angry Southerners called him "Beast" and accused him of stealing gold from the city banks and silverware from the aristocrats. Ever after, hecklers would interrupt his speeches by yelling "Spoons!" They hardly dared do worse: Butler was tough and delightfully cheeky. Once when some unfriendly listener hurled an apple at him, he broke off speaking to catch and eat it. Ten years as a Republican congressman made him a host of enemies, who knew him to be a bully and suspected him of being a thief. He mocked the merit system as a way of selecting civil servants and defended highly placed rascals. As far as political influence could swing contracts and special laws his friends' way, Butler had used it to the limit. Those friends, though, included the vast crowd of the economically powerless, factory workers and Irish Catholic immigrants in the Bay State, and persecuted blacks down south. No matter how often Butler changed parties, he never swapped principles. Election day would close his public career; beyond the working-class wards in Northeastern cities, his party had little hope.[5]

One could predict better for the Prohibition Party. Of all parties, it was the only one that could count on active support from women, and especially from the churchgoing ladies of the Women's Christian Temperance Union. Wherever there were Protestant churches in the North, the WCTU was likely to have its organizers, and wherever the temperance message had gotten across, there were likely to be some evangelicals so touched with the faith that they would put in work for the one party not tied to brewers and dis-

"The Blaine tariff fraud. Chorus of workingmen: 'Duped, by gosh!' "
(Thomas Nast, Harper's Weekly, *November 1, 1884). Ben Butler is a mask for Blaine.*
Behind him lurks the notorious robber baron, Jay Gould.

tillers. Prohibitionists had been running presidential candidates since 1872, but only in the last four years had their movement grown prodigiously. Never before had they run a candidate as prominent as former governor John P. St. John, the nemesis of the liquor traffic in Kansas.

Put together, Butler and St. John might carry one vote in twenty. The rest would go to the major party nominees, Blaine and his Democratic rival,

Grover Cleveland. The country could have done worse, though partisans might not have thought so. Forged affidavits, purloined letters, and bad character references from adulterous ministers and indicted grafters all "proved" Blaine a shakedown artist ready to cash in on official position and Cleveland a lifelong bachelor with one child too many. "Mr. Blaine is externally a gentleman, which Mr. Cleveland is not," one editor pointed out. "Mr. Blaine loves his children and their mother, Mr. Cleveland hates his. Mr. Blaine's conversation is refined and scholarly, Mr. Cleveland's is limited to that of a pot-house."[6] Readers of the Republican press were invited to feel horror that a onetime sheriff from Buffalo, New York, should fill the chair of Washington, and, what was more, a sheriff who twice had stood on the gallows to spring the trap under convicts.

"He's blowing now through a tin-trump / The words of deepest knavery," Democrats replied of Blaine,

> To aid the rich, to skin the poor
> Down to the depths of slavery!
> With voices loud, with one accord,
> We shout the battle-call:
> The world for Stalwarts ne'er was made—
> The world was made for all!

Subscribers to Joseph Pulitzer's freshly overhauled *New York World* learned sensational facts about Blaine's private life: how one of his brothers had skipped bail and fled a forgery indictment, and how the candidate was a dying man, moving through the last stages of Bright's disease, an infection of the kidneys. Doctors could be found ready to swear that Blaine could not live through his term, or to give horrible details of the symptoms. Of course Blaine seemed vigorous. Those afflicted were often the last to know. (Journalists should have practiced their amateur medicine on President Chester Alan Arthur. He, not Blaine, was the one dying of Bright's disease.)[7]

Sensation and scandal would be the one great memory of 1884, and yet a case could be made that the two major party nominees typified American public life at its best. Glance first on Blaine, well seasoned from a generation at the center of policy making, one of the most supple minds in the self-proclaimed "party of moral ideas," a politician "bright as a foil, engaging as an actor": erect and animated, flushed in face and boyish in enthusiasms, hair and beard "exquisitely white," sparkling black eyes full of life, a stride, in one observer's phrase, "with the strength of a steam engine."[8]

His temperament fitted the public man: a plucky fighter for his party and a magnificent tactical maneuverer. Raised in Pennsylvania, he taught school as

"His own Destroyer"

(F. Graetz, Puck, September 24, 1884). "Guano statesmanship" refers to Blaine's meddling as secretary of state in the war between Chile and Peru; it was widely alleged that his family had a financial interest in the guano fields at dispute.

a young man in Georgetown, Kentucky, where he wooed and won a Harriet Stanwood, a schoolteacher from Maine. Fitting well enough into Southern society to have folks call him "Major," he found his true calling in Harriet's native state, as a journalist. By 1860, he worked as one of the master-spirits of the legislature. Two years later, he entered the House. In 1869, Republicans elected him Speaker, the ablest since his old hero Henry Clay's day. Even Democrats lauded his fairness and memory for precedent. Since that time, he had been senator, secretary of state, and twice the favorite of his party's rank and file for the nomination.

Blaine was loved as no other politician of his time would be. The country was full of "Blainiacs." "Had he been a woman," one acquaintance wrote, "people would have rushed off to send expensive flowers." They may have felt simply as if they were returning affection. Breezy with journalists, effusive with intimates, he earned his nickname "the magnetic man" on just about every contact. He would put his arm around a caller, ask about his family, and, with very few exceptions, the man was lost to Blaine's charm. Callers were astonished that every circumstance of a casual meeting years past stayed with him. Later, when partisan enmities from 1884 had cooled, a speaker at a Democratic rally mentioned Blaine's name. To his surprise, the audience whooped and cheered. "Blaine seems to have more friends here than he had at [the Republican National Convention]!" he joked. Back came the reply, which set the applause going again: "We are all his friends!"[9]

Now, with the same generous glance, look to his rival, the Democratic governor of New York, Stephen Grover Cleveland. Imagine "a very stout, exceedingly well-groomed looking gentleman, of medium height, with a full florid face, . . . a soldierly-looking gray moustache and a pair of gray-twinkling, friendly eyes." Casual observers might have mistaken him for a banker or vestryman. In fact, he was a Presbyterian minister's son. Though he went into the law and enjoyed a good drink—or several—cigars, a pinochle game, and unrefined male company, his religious upbringing never left him. Righteousness and duty drove him to do brave things in power, not to mention stupid ones. "I have tried so hard to do right," he would murmur in 1908 as he lay dying. Even those who hated him would grant him that much. Nothing gave him more pleasure than hard work behind his desk, unless perhaps it was the stern lecture to legislators who failed to see their duty as clearly as he saw his own. Cast into politics and lifted ever higher on successive reform waves, he offered the Democrats their best chance of replacing an embarrassing party heritage with a fresh start in public life.[10]

Just as the two candidates stood out brighter than the campaign rhetoric of 1884 made them, so the issues driving most voters to the polls were deeper, more substantial than the ephemeral street cries. For both parties, the past defined their present purpose and future mission. To Republicans, theirs remained the good old cause that had brought them into existence thirty years before, of putting a stop to the spread of slavery. Under their leaders, the Union had been saved from secession and three million blacks brought out of bondage and into citizenship. Those who wanted monuments to the Grand Old Party, as it was already known, could look to the national banks in every major city, the land-grant colleges and transcontinental railroads built with government aid, the hundreds of thousands of farmers settled on lands given them for a nominal fee under the Homestead Act, and the three great Reconstruction amendments underlying the promise—still not wholly fulfilled—of equality under law for men of all races. A government with the power to make Americans better and leave them better off, a hearty nationalism with no place for distinctions of class, race, or section, heir as much to Alexander Hamilton and Henry Clay as to Lincoln: these were the ideals that continued to give Republicans their reason for being.[11]

No such bright record marked Democrats' contributions to the statute books. Theirs was the party of liberty (white, anyhow) and localism. Southern Democrats looked back to the "Lost Cause," Northern Democrats to the government of limited powers that Thomas Jefferson and Andrew Jackson had given them. An authority strong enough to do things for Americans, they warned, usually did things to them. In wartime, it shut down presses and arrested dissenters, as Republicans had done. In peace, it used tax-gathering machinery to pluck money out of farmers' and workers' pockets and fill the already bulging pockets of the monopolists, already given advantage over smaller competitors by government favoritism: a national bank charter, say, coupled with a killing tax on banknotes from state-chartered concerns. It imposed Yankee notions of race equality on white Southerners, and hayseed crotchets like a Protestant Sabbath on city dwellers old enough to decide for themselves how to spend Sundays. Republican allegiance lay beneath every ism from feminism to Prohibitionism to miscegenationism, and the "party of moral ideas" always trusted lawmakers to put crank causes onto the statute books.

Anyone standing in the rain that last weekend before the election and watching the processions pass by would have no doubt that real issues still held sway. For every reference to Cleveland's child, a thousand brought up the tariff, the outstanding symbol of Republican nationalism and the idea of a protecting government. Speakers invoked wartime memories, living injustices against blacks in a Democratic South, the need for pensions, and the scraping clean of an administrative system too long in one party's hands. On all these issues, voters knew that the election of a Democratic or Republican president would make a difference.

But now the torches were extinguished, the banners folded away, and there was nothing that Cleveland's will nor Blaine's charm could do. Voters must decide. "Election day at 7:30 a.m.," R. W. McMurdy wrote from New York City to Republican vice presidential nominee John A. "Black Jack" Logan, "I went to Nat. Hd. Qu.'s supposing every arrangement perfect." Instead, he found the front door shut and ward heelers frantic, because at many polls, nobody had gotten around to sending the tickets or setting up the booths. Some had been given bunches of mutilated ballots, with bits of the presidential electors' names clipped off. McMurdy had to handle matters on the spot. Naturally, the reverend suspected treachery; everyone knew that the powers running the state committee had backed another candidate for the nomination, their old boss, president Arthur. Republican committee offices stood deserted in Indianapolis, too, but more because everything seemed so well in hand. Regular reports reached headquarters throughout the day, exit polls by party workers checking off the names of reliable Republicans as they cast a ballot at the polls and hazarding guesses at how their own turnout compared with Democrats'.[12]

Cleveland had returned to Buffalo two days before the election for some rest and the company of old friends. Strolling to the polls during a break in the storm, he voted in a Blaine and Logan assembly hall, amid a crowd of well-wishers, many of whom tried to shove ballots into his hand. Cleveland dismissed them amiably. His was already prepared, and "a fellow can't cast but one, you know." Reporters wondered about Tammany Hall. As the strongest Democratic machine in New York City, its influence and nothing else could give the party a margin big enough to make up for the expected Republican majorities north of the Harlem Bridge. But boss John Kelly was known as a good hater, and Cleveland had given him plenty to hate. With more hope than confidence, the governor assured newspapermen that Kelly would do right by the whole ticket.[13]

Polls closed at sundown in many places, but not all. Then came the tabulations. Now party headquarters filled, and crowds gathered outside, waiting for good news. Most interested people moved downtown to the major newspaper offices, where telegrams would be posted, informing them of the results.

Party managers waited restlessly. This year, for the first time, they could get early reports over the telephone, but local leaders still sent most of their information over the wires, and Western Union did a heavy business. At the Associated Press, large tables in blank had been drawn up a fortnight before, covering every precinct in a state. A grid of lines provided blanks for each party's present vote, and next to it, the returns four years before, already filled in. From these, the men at the wire service and the Republicans in close contact with them could make instant comparisons ward by ward, district by district, of how well Blaine was doing this year, compared to James A. Garfield in 1880.[14]

Returns came slowly. All through the evening the telegrams reached the Republican high command, now optimistic, now cautious; the national committee sent the candidates its latest information, all of it tentative. Indiana and Virginia seemed out of danger, committee secretary Samuel Fessenden wired Logan. New York stayed uncertain, "but improving." Other insiders put the Republican margin there at fifteen thousand.[15]

In Augusta, Blaine waited, nervous and cautious. His friends talked of possible cabinet nominations but without the candidate's blessing. "I'll talk about Cabinets when I'm elected," he told them, and on that last point he had his doubts. In the library, a special wire brought in the latest news.

Blaine paused there. "If I carry New York by only a thousand votes," he told his secretary, Thomas Sherman, "they will surely count me out. I'm going to bed. Don't disturb me unless something decisive comes in." Nothing did.[16]

No special wire ran to the Governor's Mansion in Albany, where Cleveland had returned late in the day. All afternoon, messengers had delivered premature telegrams of congratulation. Now Cleveland and his friends waited by the telephone for the latest word, but the downpour had knocked out the wires. Every now and then the household received a dispatch, some local return that could be compared with the results from 1882, when Cleveland had won the governorship in a walk. It was evident that no landslide was in the making. There might be no margin at all. Brooklyn's machine was delivering a whopping majority, but across the East River, Cleveland held all too modest a lead. With each new report, the governor's secretary, sleek, unobtrusive Dan Lamont, and the frail, well-seasoned operator Edward Apgar, had to draw their estimates anew. Every minute narrowed Cleveland's projected lead: now seven thousand, now five. Worried, the governor's friend Colonel William Gorham Rice went down to the local Democratic newspaper office for more up-to-date information, which was more worrisome still. Cleveland took matters calmly. He had a quiet supper and at midnight bade everyone good night, adding, "If you stay up much longer, you will be counting me out."[17]

Rice, Apgar, and Lamont had quite different ideas. Returns from the Republican counties seemed suspiciously slow. It would not be the first time that one party had withheld its announcement of the total vote until it could see how big an opposition majority it had to overcome. Democratic leaders all over the state must be advised to keep a sharp lookout, and at once. The governor's friends got busy at the local telegraph office. Local managers were ordered to send in immediate estimates of the probable figures, the better to compare with what Republican returning boards tried to certify later. To make the request stick, the aides signed Daniel Manning's name. Manning had administered the party upstate for some years. If anyone's word was law, his was. Perhaps two thousand telegrams passed across the wires from Albany, and many hundreds more came back, asking for further instructions and sending the latest information. The skies were lightening across the Hudson River by the time Apgar and his friends stumbled into the open air to buy a morning newspaper. Then they returned to send on more messages: the returns in county clerks' offices must be watched until an official count had been filed. Local leaders must send certified copies of the vote to Albany by special messenger at once.[18]

For, as any newspaper could have told them, the returns *were* close. The

Great Plains, the prairies, had gone for Blaine. So had Pennsylvania and most of New England. All that was to be expected. Nearly balancing it off, a Solid South put Democrats within reach of victory. Four Northern states held the key. Indiana, New Jersey, and Connecticut had fragile Democratic leads. Of New York's outcome the morning papers knew nothing.

Or, rather, every one of them knew too much. Both sides claimed it for their own. Pension commissioner William W. Dudley, one of the Republican organizers in Indiana, not only claimed that state and New York, but Florida and possibly Virginia. The brains behind the Republican National Committee, Stephen B. Elkins, thought Connecticut safe and put Blaine's New York lead at ten to fifteen thousand votes. Other Republicans put it at a third as much. But as the count continued, the forecasts projected an ever-tighter race. By the next morning, with only thirteen districts unaccounted for, Blaine was ahead by just 988 votes in the preliminary count.[19]

A day before, some newspapers had felt confident enough to run editorials explaining just what Blaine's election signified. Plainly, Americans preferred "a statesman to a puppet," "a gentleman to a blackguard," "brains to beef," the *Oneida Dispatch* boasted. Republican victory, the *Indianapolis Journal* assured readers, ended the Solid South forever. There were no boasts by November 6.[20]

Both sides still claimed victory. That Thursday, Republican National Committee chairman Benjamin F. Jones made the remarkable announcement that every Northern state but two (New Jersey and Connecticut) had gone Republican, along with Virginia and West Virginia. Other Southern states, he added, were "in doubt." Two days later, he revealed "information" that Butler's votes had been counted for Cleveland in four counties—none of which he could recall for reporters. Republican spokesmen declared that they had uncovered Democratic attempts to "tamper" with New York's returns and that by no honest count could the state be taken from them. Prompted by advice from the New York headquarters, Blaine issued a statement to the press that there had been "frauds committed" in New York and that the state was his by rights. "Though the defeated candidate for the Presidency is at the head of the election machinery in this State," the GOP headquarters added darkly, "the Democratic party . . . will not be permitted to thwart the will of the people." Insiders believed it, too, even though the Associated Press, the source on which they relied for their statement of a Blaine plurality, gave Cleveland the lead late on Friday night. Already, attorneys had begun readying for a challenge to the official returns, as the national committee secretary promised to "bring out some startling facts."[21]

To Democrats, it all sounded so familiar. Victory had been snatched from their fingers eight years before in just the same way, with allegations of fraud and assertions of an "honest" majority to prepare the public mind. Above all, that suspicion must have struck home with Democratic vice presidential candidate Thomas A. Hendricks, who had been defeated by the "steal" of 1876. "We will not submit to being counted out this time," he told an Indianapolis crowd. Cleveland took the same tone. "I believe I have been elected president," he announced to the press, "and nothing but the greatest fraud can keep me out of it, and that we will not permit." Daniel Manning's statement, issued after an emergency meeting of the New York Democratic state committee, was still more aggressive, hinting at inaugurating Cleveland by force. Even mild-mannered Dan Lamont's eye flashed fire at the prospect of a stolen election. "We have won this fight, and by the living God, we'll hold it!" he exclaimed to a friend.[22]

Mobs collected outside Republican newspaper offices and traded blows with opponents in the Indianapolis streets. There was talk of violence against the vote stealers—assuming there were any. Rumors spread that the real returns were being suppressed by Wall Street speculator Jay Gould. His support for Blaine was common knowledge. So was his career, a series of notorious moments: the grinding out of illegal stock in the Erie "railroad war," the 1869 Wall Street panic caused by his cornering the gold market, and the crushing of a telegraphers' strike, among others. As head of Western Union, he could be withholding returns, either for his own profit or until Republicans could "fix" them. The street outside Western Union headquarters seethed with angry Democrats, waving fists and making threats. Crowds marched past the millionaire's house on Fifth Avenue, singing, "We'll hang Jay Gould to a sour apple tree." For his own sake, Gould sent Cleveland a telegram and released a copy to the press, congratulating him on having won. A big crowd in Central Park roared as they got the news. "I tell you, boys, there isn't one of them [the election stealers] who would have lived long enough to eat his Sunday dinner," one Democrat shouted.[23]

Both sides were quicker to rattle their sabers than draw them. Under the energetic leadership of Senator Arthur Pue Gorman of Maryland, Democrats picked an all-star team of lawyers to attend the official count before the state board of canvassers. Gorman spent many sleepless nights, and his efforts added to the national committee's expenses: usually, the headquarters closed right after the election, instead of running for two more weeks to coordinate efforts. But vigilance could not be stinted. By November 8, Republicans were admitting that the returns, on their face, put Cleveland ahead.[24] They would need proofs of fraud to overturn it, but the promised affidavits from Butler voters swindled out of their franchise never made their appearance. Those thousands of "irregularities" dwindled into a handful of clerical errors, evenly distributed between the two parties. "It looks here very much as though we were laid out cold," one Treasury agent conceded on Sunday. "The gloom around the Custom House could be cut with a knife." The following Saturday, as canvassers finished re-counting New York City's votes, even the most diehard Republicans gave up hope.[25]

To the Blaines, the final disappointment brought relief. Those "trying days" were "all a horror" to Harriet Stanwood Blaine, who had spent the first two after the election persuaded that her husband had won. Blaine himself had expected the worst since the Friday after the election—and did not find it so bad, after all. To Grover Cleveland, reporter William Hudson hastened with the news that the leading Republican newspaper had conceded the Democrats' election. "I am very glad to hear it," the governor responded. "I am more than glad that they yield peaceably." His face hardened. "For in any event, I should have felt it my duty to take the office of the president of the United States on the fourth of next March."[26]

All this may have been no more than stage thunder. Still, the public's readiness to jump to conclusions poses disturbing questions about the Gilded Age party system, far more disturbing ones than those involving the issues of fornication and prevarication leveled at the two major candidates. What lay beneath the tinsel of 1884 politics and the issues, real and false? How far had chance, inadvertent fair play, and political manipulation brought about the result? What events, what partisan tradition, could have wakened so strong a belief that somebody was cheating somebody somehow, somewhere? And, finally, what meaning did the making of a president in 1884 hold for the transformation of Gilded Age American politics?

No Business To-Day Other Than Politics

From the perspective of the late twentieth century, politics one hundred years past may seem quite refreshing. Its charm is its peril. Seeing so much apparent democracy in action, we may so appreciate a system that worked that we pass lightly over the question, *worked for whom?* Yet the question is essential if the tumult and billingsgate of 1884 is to be understood, and the best place to begin finding an answer is with election day itself.

Election day was the last ceremony in a campaign of spectacle. Rain or shine, parties got most eligible voters to the polls between dawn and dusk. They always had, as long as most active politicians could remember. In closely contested states, the usual turnout was immense; in Louisiana, it often was thousands more than the registered vote—and, in Republican parishes, always translated into mammoth Democratic majorities. Most places, three voters in four showed up. Any state of electoral consequence could do that in a presidential year, and only five summoned less than half their eligibles.[1]

A few states set taxpaying, literacy, or property qualifications. Foreign-born inhabitants just about everywhere had to take out their "second papers." Still, only Rhode Island demanded a residency long enough to disfranchise the majority of the foreign-born for more than a few years, and Pennsylvania asked just ten days. Many places had no statewide registration system at all. Republican legislators often applied registration to the cities exclusively. Democrats there, they knew, would cheat every chance they got by all the time-tested ruses: "colonizing" (bringing in outsiders to vote), "resurrectionism" (voting the dead), and "pudding-tickets" (where one ballot had folded within it several other lighter "tissue ballots"). Besides, going to the polls twice in two weeks, once to register and once to vote, would burden Democratic factory workers more than Republican silk stockings.[2]

Safeguards existed, of a sort. Federal law let the government police an election with deputy marshals. Given adequate funding and sufficient public backing, the government might have protected a fair turnout down south. Instead, supervisors concentrated their efforts in Northern cities, where, the victims complained, every ten-dollar-a-day patriot the authorities hired had the same "defiant 'ye-can't vote-here-if-ye're-a-dimocrat' expression of countenance." Black voters in Northern cities faced a barrage of Democratic challenges; whites, unable to tell one black man from another, inclined to assume them imported from some other state. West Virginians located the "colonized" vote as Marylanders, Ohio and Indiana blamed Kentucky, and Virginians saw North Carolina blacks everywhere. Republicans, who generally depended on blacks to vote their way, took special care to furnish affidavits or produce witnesses to back up their case.[3]

All these barriers against a full vote were less sturdy than they looked, especially with party organizers applying whatever stimulants they could find. Where voters had to pay a poll tax before voting, like Virginia and Delaware, the parties shelled out the money for needy men in their own ranks. Emissaries showed up on election day with handfuls of tax receipts, to hand out along with the right kind of ballot. Friendly judges could turn out naturalization papers in jig time. One of them in New York City was able to naturalize two applicants a minute for eight hours at a stretch.[4]

And both sides produced money. Some of it went to buy voters. A dollar (sometimes as much as five, in a close race) thrust into one hand and a printed ballot pressed into the other could be depended on in ways that a real secret ballot never could. Voters whose loyalty was never in doubt still might expect payment, say, "two dollars for time lost in going to the polls." Some of the payoffs were just tokens of gratitude, like the yellow tickets Democrats once passed out in downtown Philadelphia, inscribed, "Good for a drink." Altogether, contemporaries estimated that one New Hampshire voter in ten expected payment, and a later historian put the total in New Jersey at one-third or more.[5]

Vote buying was simple to arrange because there was no official ballot. Each party printed its own, with an exclusive list of their official candidates. Every precinct had its variations in shape and color, within the general requirements of state law as to print and size. Disgruntled local pols might print up alternative versions; it sometimes happened that some citizens' group drew up a hybrid version, with several from one party, some from another. Still, even with the impossible—strict party loyalty—each party printed up far more ballots than were used. In St. Louis, with some fifty thousand votes cast, Democrats printed up twelve times that many "tickets" for 1884, and all the other organizations together prepared another 700,000. Extrapolate that ratio nationwide, and twenty-six million ballots accommodated one million voters: eighty-five freight cars' load, 1.7 million pounds of paper.[6]

Inefficient as the system seemed, it allowed an array of possible choices wider than anything in generations yet to come. Any group with a printing press could mount a local challenge. Inhabitants unable to read could exercise their rights as freely as their better-schooled neighbors. There was no need to choose between confusing names, which, to the illiterate, might as well have been in Sanskrit. Instead, voters could exercise their choice the way one elector did in the Indianapolis twelfth ward, not knowing whether he was depositing a ticket or a tax receipt.[7]

Convenience came at the price of confidentiality. A few vest-pocket voters came ticket in hand, but most equipped themselves at the polls. The moment they approached a party peddler, they gave their preferences away. With acquaintances close at hand, voting wrong might bring embarrassment. It might even be dangerous. Parties knew well how intimidating unofficial poll watching could be. That was one reason that they urged their followers not just to turn out but to stick around until the polls had closed and why black voters down south often chose to stay home. "Never mind business," a New York editor urged the faithful. "There will be no business to-day other than politics. Give the whole day to the cause."[8]

Standing among the ticket distributors in most towns, the unwary voter also might meet the con-artists of partisan politics. They might be peddling "Republican" tickets with a full list of *Democratic* presidential electors, or the name of the Republican congressman from the district one county over, or any number of endless other ruses to dupe the undesigning. That was one reason that partisan newspapers issued to their readers regular warnings of tricks in the offing, even when there were no tricks, and dinned into their brains the full names of the candidates, from president down to probate clerk.[9]

Every step in the process was designed to give the parties as much input as possible. The verdict of the people took extensive stage-managing, down to the hiring of carriages to carry infirm supporters to the polls. Party envoys manned the polling places, ideally with two poll watchers per precinct. They bought ballot boxes of regulation make and paid for polling clerks, arranged for printing up of the ballots, and challenged as many votes cast by the other side as possible. Every county, most towns, and some states had official "returning boards" to count the votes and certify the returns, but the board members were dedicated partisans. That was one reason that the law usually required representatives from both parties among the election officials, and one reason that both sides tried to find somebody pliable (or illiterate) to represent the other side. That was also one reason that, on this particular election day, Republicans in New York City were scrambling to get fresh ballots into their supporters' hands. At the last minute, they had discovered misprints that Democratic judges could have used to disqualify them all.[10]

A "quiet" election day in Kentucky, as the joke went, saw half a dozen killings, which, in 1884 was not a joke; most places performed their election rites more calmly than did Kentucky. In cities, there usually would be trouble in some working-class ward, but as often as not, it had nothing to do with the presidential candidates. Formal challenges of electors' credentials or right to vote could slow the balloting considerably and cut down the votes of their opponents, who would not have enough time to cast them. Now and again, some voter showed up drunk, but the law usually closed the saloons for the election, and arrests for intoxication dropped—at least until the polls closed.[11]

Voting, then, could be everything that flag-waving orators said of it: democratic process distilled and an affirmation of faith in the people's right to rule themselves. But "could be" stood pretty far from "is" in Gilded Age America. Where no competitive party system was possible or dominant partisans determined to have their way, election day offered one last chance to show how ruthless and selective the political process could be.

Outside of Wyoming and Utah Territories, the first Tuesday after the first Monday in November was a day for men only. It was generally agreed that the "fairer sex" was naturally more virtuous than men—all the more reason to keep it from being polluted by exercising political power. Women should have a say in running the household, and that allowed them a hearing on issues related to preserving the family and raising children. Petitioning or getting out the vote to pass laws against saloons or to keep the Sabbath holy suited femininity perfectly. Some places, women even voted in school board elections. They were useful, even necessary, to grace party rallies, and newspapers loved to note the appearance of comeliness softening the coarseness of political events. Showing up, they gave parties a certificate of good character, testimony that the men were fit guardians for virtue. They could wear campaign ribbons or give money, discuss some of the issues, even run Belva

No Business To-Day Other Than Politics

Lockwood for president, as the Woman's Rights Party did in 1884. But they could not vote for her, and she could not vote for herself.[12]

Finally, most pervasively, where national office was concerned, the whole political process worked to limit the real choices open to the voters. At the local level, third and fourth parties could muster the resources to make a game fight, but only a major organization could make a strong showing everywhere. That took money in sums beyond insurgents' command. Printing up tickets and distributing them even on a citywide basis took deep pockets. When New York City's Irving Hall Democratic faction wanted to issue ballots this fall, it had to employ 250 typesetters, pressmen, and counters. Women and children from three hundred families lugged away large baskets of tickets to their tenement homes for folding; other young women bunched the tickets in sets of eight. None of this came cheaply. One newspaper calculated that each New York City faction paid $12,000 to $60,000 that fall on printing alone. Modified for partisan advantage in Thomas Jefferson's day, the electoral college had become a winner-take-all system, where a bare plurality of the popular vote in each state carried with it a unanimous slate of presidential electors. Voting for a third-party presidential candidate might do as an assertion of some great principle, or as a way of penalizing one of the two major parties. Beyond its ability to shift the outcome toward Republicans or Democrats, a third-party vote was a vote thrown away.[13]

Participatory politics, like election day, was shaped to suit the major parties, for whose active members winning mattered more than playing the game fairly. They could justify themselves easily by pointing to deathless principles on their own side and deadly enemies on the other. The appeal to partisanship was just about universal. Indeed, for the two major parties, any other outlook was unnatural, and they equated it with perversity. "Mr. president, the neuter gender is not popular either in nature or society," Senator John J. Ingalls would sneer in 1886. Independents were "effeminate without being masculine or feminine; unable either to beget or to bear; ... doomed to sterility, isolation and extinction."[14]

All across the calendar, Americans imbibed political awareness with their morning papers. If a reader subscribed to a daily, politics very likely stood on page one. Awareness, certainly, did not necessarily mean partisan commitment. By the 1880s, every city had its Independent journal, fed by advertising. The best metropolitan papers were expanding their local reporting, and all of them had taken up a regular, extensive sports coverage that just ten years before barely existed. A big-city paper could survive, even thrive, without taking sides in politics, but that did not discourage it from covering political events. If anything, the richer a newspaper was, the more it could afford to spend covering Americans' favorite participatory sport. "Events," whether in Washington or Westminster, generally meant *political* occurrences: bills, intrigues, elections, and which statesman had which other statesman on the hip. And while the big-city journals could afford a dozen special correspondents and extensive Associated Press wire services, newspapers elsewhere filled up their columns with politics, because it was easier and cheaper to get, and because they could not afford to do otherwise.[15]

Whether they rooted for one team or the other, more Americans then than later could name the players. Many of them knew the leading figures so well that, until the 1880s, Thomas Nast, the greatest cartoonist of his day, never bothered to label them. Readers of *Harper's Weekly* would have to know the faces of a dozen, or even close to a hundred party eminences, though any child could tell which ones were Democrats. Their every defect, moral and physical, pilloried them. Nast's rivals, Joseph Keppler and Bernhard Gillam of *Puck*, peopled their color lithographs with public figures by the dozens, well aware that New Jersey congressmen and Manhattan editors were, for the magazine's readers, very nearly household words.

Most of the time, the press tried to impart the mainstream parties' point of view. Nonpartisanship dwindled beyond city limits, just as commercial advertising did. Often as not, the local postmaster edited one of the papers in town. The administration had given him the job to flush more money into the press. County governments needed printing done, states needed their laws published, and sheriffs had to issue advertisements for public sales and foreclosures. In each case, the authorities preferred to throw business their friends' way. Take all those resources away, and a newspaper lived a struggling existence. Even metropolitan editors could not afford to break the partisan tie. Just about every town of consequence had two newspapers, if not more. Big cities had anywhere from five to eight. In a competitive market, "independence" sold, but so did partisanship.[16]

Outside of the South, most towns had two party "organs," each grinding out the news to its own distinct tune. That tune was often set in a strident key. Its political friends could do no wrong, and a charge against them appeared only indirectly, when the editors published a complete refutation. Newspapers were so used to the party rhetoric that their very phrases had a soothing inevitability. Any veteran they ran for office had a "gallant" war record, every arraignment of the opposition was "terrible," every charge against them a "campaign lie," every bondholder "bloated." Distortions were selectively applied, of course. A newspaper's own side apparently held only magnificent rallies, and the other side had difficulty even attracting half a dozen children and a stray dog.[17] The party banner flew at the masthead and

No Business To-Day Other Than Politics

with it the approved ticket. Readers could follow half a dozen columns of political speeches, so carefully transcribed that they even covered material that the speakers wished they had said—and applause the audience doubtless wished it had given. Editorials might overlook foreign affairs or current events, but never the duty of party faithful to turn out for processions and turn up for election day, and, win or lose, to explain why victory perched on their banners—if not there, then somewhere.

With such persistent inducement, Americans did not just inhale politics once a campaign got under way. They exhaled it, in cheers and chants. Paraders might stick to catchphrases or shout out poetry specially made for the occasion:

> Now don't you see—
> Take one from two
> And that leaves three?
> Which proves it true,
> The more you're taxed
> The richer you'll be.

Evidently, as one editor joked, both sides assumed that the one "that can make the most noise and display" had "the inside track."[18]

Politics often began in childhood. Enrolled in the endless ranks of campaign clubs, schoolboys found a chance to stay out late and skip classes when they marched as "escorts." But party managers were thinking of more than swelling a procession when they enlisted them. "Every step a boy takes when in the Republican line of march, every cheer he gives, makes him a stronger and better Republican, and makes him less inclined to follow off after strange gods," the *Des Moines Register* explained.[19]

Habit and heritage bred deep partisan loyalties, even if a willingness to act on that faith often took constant stirring up. Children voted as their fathers had, and veterans often claimed to have voted "as they shot" (which meant, in the South, a big turnout of Confederate veterans for the Democratic Party, and in the North, a host of Union soldiers who kept on fighting the war by rallying around the Republican flag). Most participants were Republican or Democratic, without wavering. With a few feeble presses, a financial pittance, and no patronage to dole out to followers, minor parties collected handfuls of votes. They could swing a result in closely contested states. But their organization fell apart when the polls closed, and when it was revived, it never quite had the same shape as before. As for pure, Independent voters, swerving from one side to the other, they were a rare phenomenon. Changes depended more on those newly enfranchised than on converts. Restive party members simply stayed home. Asking for an opposition ticket with party associates standing by took considerable moral courage. Even when a partisan simply "scratched" nominees off his own party's official ballot, he might attract unwelcome attention.[20]

Later onlookers could only envy the show that either party, in full form, put on a thousand times in a single campaign—the special trains, bringing in partisan clubs from outlying villages, the brass bands, the bouquets tendered to the featured speaker, the "Hussars," "Zouaves," and "Plumed Knights" in their costumes, marching under the flare of torchlights, the floats where young women represented states or personated the Goddess of Liberty, the mottoes and posters, the homes along the parade route illuminated with candles, the orators' platform embellished with evergreen boughs, flags, and eagles, and the hours of ready-made oratory. Politicians certainly knew how to swell a crowd. They hauled in loyalists from the next county or even the next state. They hired marchers and helped pay for the uniforms, themselves a powerful inducement for young men to enlist in the ranks. But all those preparations together built on a partisanship and an interest in political spectacle already there. Onlookers clearly had a good time, and expected to be entertained. They brought their families and picnic lunches, fed on barbecues thrown by the party hosting the affair, cheered, and went home smelling of coal oil, as the kerosene in the torches was known, and feeling as if they had taken part in a dramatic event. If they were lucky, the rally ended with a fireworks display.[21]

To assume that the politicians were simply trying to earn their bread by giving the people a circus, though, would be to miss the essential point. Like the party press, hoopla strengthened participants' sense of being part of something important, and of serving a cause larger than themselves. Divisions of class, gender, and sometimes of race, melted away, at least on the line of march. To a later reader, the orators' phrases may have seemed threadbare, clichés worn smooth from overuse, or even cant-phrases meant not so much to convince listeners' as to prompt a convulsive twitch of partisanship. But at their worst, they served a crucial purpose, to carry their audiences to the polls by way of a trip down memory lane. They revived the old traditions, stirred up the recollections of earlier campaigns, and set out in plain language the partisanship that for many had receded into a vague, unexplainable instinct. Popular politics inspired and reinforced a faith in party and in politics itself.

The dazzle of those torchlights may blind an outsider to the harsher realities of how Republican and Democratic loyalties were made. Americans' partisan bent was not simply a natural reaction to events as they occurred. As has been suggested, partisan zeal lived on artificial stimulants. Bringing out

No Business To-Day Other Than Politics

the marchers, organizing the clubs, raising the money to man the polls, swelling the registration rolls, canvassing neighborhoods, and counting which voter was sure, which doubtful, and which hopeless was the special work of a large, active set of party workers. Editors, contractors, placemen, and professional politicians knew better than to trust the people. Partisan loyalty alone could not bring out a heavy vote nor fill the war chest. "Modern politics means the science of organization," one Democrat reminded his liege lord. "No idea however good or bad can be made to prevail now-a-days in politics without . . . systematic organization."[22]

With active, well-heeled partisan workers so important, government remained in 1884 what it had been for sixty years, not just an engine of policy but a preserve full of political places to reward services on the winning party's behalf. Arguments that "to the victor belongs the spoils" had been around since the 1830s, and the practice dated far earlier than the preaching. Partisans spoke of "rotation in office" and argued that public servants "fresh from the people" kept the bureaucracy responsive to the popular will. But patronage did not, in fact, hand public office to the public. It simply allowed the local politicians to get their friends the pickings. It prodded the politically active to work harder. Most of all, it created an army of loyalists, paid for by public funds, whose influence could be thrown to the party's side during the campaign.

Putting a premium on loyalty did not create a system of absolute incompetents or scoundrels, but it hardly offered a safeguard against unfit appointments. As long as partisans saw the offices as rewards, they would turn them to profit for themselves and the party. Into the early 1880s, every federal employee could expect an "assessment," usually a percentage of his or her salary. The law insisted that the payment come voluntarily, but as long as superiors did the collecting and could fire underlings at any time, it was easy to strong-arm a handout. Federal clerks went home to vote, to man the local party bureaus, or to pack conventions for ambitious politicians. Those who refused a request to do so would find themselves going home anyway, never to return.[23]

Politics, plainly, could be a rough trade, and insiders practiced it to serve themselves. They gerrymandered legislatures to assure party advantage, changed voting requirements to reduce the opposition's vote. Properly handled, party conventions were stage-managed events, where the professionals wrote up the slate of officers in advance, gave special weight to candidates able to pay their own (and party workers') way in the coming campaign, arranged the committees, and gave delegates the chance to vote on pre-packaged platforms of principles. At best, they mediated dissensions within the rank and file and worked out the differences; every party, after all, had its ideologues and fanatics. At worst, the pols assembled what one newspaper called "an omnium-gatherum made up chiefly of antiquated political hacks, tin-horn statesmen and patriots for plunder." Even then, conventions were an improvement on many a local primary. To judge from some of them, the only time any Republican brightened to see a Democrat was when he helped pack a Republican caucus.[24]

The culture of partisanship coarsened politics in more overt ways. Getting out a full vote encouraged just such campaigns as 1884, where every issue was pitched in apocalyptic terms and the public was alarmed unnecessarily about risks that simply did not exist. Winning might take campaigns of forgery, deceit, and last-minute shockers, all of which the partisan press broadcast wholesale and refuted only when party advantage required it. Every coalition between a minor party and the opposition was a "bargain and sale," and many of them were the first steps toward revolution.[25]

But that same partisanship made victories illegitimate. Neither side believed that the game had been played fairly in 1876 or in 1880. Each of them suspected the other of cheating its way to victory. "Republican arguments—barrels of flour and ten dollar notes," one banner read in the 1880 campaign. For years, a controversy over control of Maine's legislature allowed Democrats and Greenbackers to roar about Republicans' effort to "steal" the state with greenbacks, Gatling guns, and gin, while Republicans waved the raw head and bloody bones of "revolution." As blacks fled the South for better treatment in 1879, Northern Democrats saw a Republican-run plot to colonize them in Indiana and make the state sure.[26]

Politics had run pretty much by these rules for fifty years, but in the Gilded Age the process was beginning to show its age. One sign of substantial change was the growth of third- and fourth-party challenges, still not large enough to win—just big enough at times to swing the victory to one side or the other. In off-year elections, the electorate was volatile, sharply so in choosing congressmen. Voters who went Republican in presidential years were likelier to break ranks and support a "sideshow" party or to stay home. When that happened, congressmen lost by the dozens.[27]

Increasingly vocal critics wondered whether the old system made any sense. Among the most visible were the liberal reformers, who came to be known as "Mugwumps." Later judgments have often been as harsh as partisan critics were at the time. The "unco' guid," Senator Roscoe Conkling of New York had called them, too high-minded to soil themselves with the realities of winning power, but always forward with unsolicited advice to the winners about what to do with their mandates.[28]

No Business To-Day Other Than Politics

Much about liberal reformers might seem provoking. Mugwumps always seemed to stand apart from the pleasures of participatory politics, and, indeed, from the dynamic world of a rapidly industrializing America. Many of them were proud to distance themselves from the moneygrubbing and materialism that they saw around them. Later generations, accustomed to think of Theodore Roosevelt as the epitome of American manliness, would marvel at the impression that the Manhattan assemblyman and his followers left on regulars in the national convention: men who had "their hair parted in the middle, banged in front, wore an eyeglass, rolled their r's and pronounced the word either with the i. sound instead of the e." They applauded by clapping "with the tips of their fingers, held immediately in front of their noses."[29]

Civil service reform had never been the exclusive sport of the Ivy League elite. It did not take a snob to resent a thief. Merchants angry at the mulcting spoilsmen taking their cut out of customhouse duties and politicians shut out of the patronage had their own reasons for joining the cause. But there was no question that when reform spoke, its accents were those of high society, of professionals more than industrialists, of the upper class more than those below, and of the college-educated minority who deplored rule by the underpropertied and ignorant in the big cities. They were likelier than the ordinary run of politicians to speak of gentlemanly behavior, and far likelier to point to England as a model for what America should be doing in revenue and civil service reform. And naturally, they were far more inclined to belong to the one "respectable" party, the Republican Party.[30]

Heading the pack was Edwin L. Godkin, editor of the *New York Evening Post* and the *Nation* and for a generation the self-proclaimed oracle of liberal reform. No editor could match him for sarcasm, irony, crisp style, and the ability to discredit any viewpoint by simply restating it. He was utterly dauntless, the terror of the *Post*'s business office. "I don't care anything about the handful of Mugwumps who read [the *Post*]," a New York politico complained. "The trouble with the damned sheet is that every editor in New York State reads it."[31]

More through him than anyone else, the very term "reform" had been tempered into something covering the honest, efficient administration of government, and not much more: a platform better written in a ledger than on a broadside. When Godkin spoke of the "people," he meant "respectable" people, usually middle-class or better; when he used the term "citizen," he often confused it with propertied men and, where the South was concerned, white ones exclusively. Labor legislation to Godkin and liberals like him, was not "reform." It was "class legislation." So were tariffs. Humanitarian crusades, struggles for women's suffrage or to protect civil rights, for example, so often classified as reform before the war, were either fanaticism or political opportunism. By no means did all reformers ascribe to Godkin's beliefs. But that distrust for measures helping those in need, that readiness to see legislation on behalf of those who soiled their hands with hard labor as demagoguery, was palpable.[32]

At their least attractive, the liberal reformers make easy targets. So does any group at its least attractive. Detractors pinned the term "Mugwump" upon them, which jokesters would later ascribe to their place on the fence, with their mugs on one side and wumps on the other. At the time, allegedly, it hearkened back to an Algonquin word meaning "Great Man."[33]

In fact, there was much more to Gilded Age liberalism than invocations of pallid do-goodism. Liberals argued sensibly that government at its best should not be a patchwork of laws, inconsistent in basic principle with one another and consistent only in their readiness to please powerful groups. If its spokesmen deplored "special interest" and "class" legislation, the terms also covered the grabs to serve the upper classes, the hungry railroad corporations demanding subsidies, and the tariff tinkerers putting local advantage ahead of national good. "When we fought for free trade we fought for labor," one of Godkin's associates wrote later; "when we fought for the purification of our political life, notably our civic life, we fought primarily for the workingman." Spoilsmen, as reformers pointed out, made even the poorest city dweller pay in rotten service, "foul water, dirty and ill-paved streets, poor and high-priced gas, inefficient policemen," and businesslike responsibilities handled "upon a political basis."[34]

An age of increasingly complex public responsibilities needed a professional civil service, one in which workers put their administrative duties ahead of partisan ones. Presidents needed a system of appointments that freed them from the clatter of thousands of supplicants after office in an administration's opening days and from the demands of congressmen and senators thereafter. But civil service reformers would have argued that more was at stake than making the government machinery run smoothly and cheaply. Spoilsmanship united personal and partisan advantage to create a system in which the main purpose was winning office rather than doing anything with it. It impeded a party's commitments to causes in which there was no immediate political payoff and resisted any changes that would interfere with "public office as a private snap." Lowering the moral tone of government service, partisanship was virtually unable to distinguish between public and private advantage, and hard put to discipline wrongdoers who had

No Business To-Day Other Than Politics

been of service to their party. It invited corruption, collusion, and incoherence.[35]

That corruption sometimes grew, sometimes diminished, but it never vanished entirely. It couldn't. Power brought many rewards, from the chance to hand out printing and advertising contracts to the inside information that could bring politicians into promising concerns for no money down. It was for their influence that a railroad construction firm, the Credit Mobilier, invited leading Republican congressmen to invest. The profits were stupendous; Credit Mobilier overcharged its parent company, the Union Pacific, many times over. The government had provided the funds in the first place, and to critics, the stock options distributed on Capitol Hill were hush money, awarded to prominent Republicans to keep their minds friendly to the firm and their eyes shut.[36]

A merit system and an end to assessments would not solve all America's problems. Still, they were a first essential step before government could be entrusted with new responsibilities. Appointed commissions could master the intricacies of their field in ways that no party-packed body could. Government *for* the people might indeed be possible only by making it less one *of* and *by* the people.

Mugwumpery in action could be a nuisance for established politicians, but there were other groups equally uncomfortable with politics-as-usual. As businesses grew, their ability to use their money and influence grew as well. Lobbying became more professional. Instead of the jack-of-all-trades agent in Washington or Albany, companies put emissaries on their payrolls to work for them exclusively. They learned how to mount petitioning campaigns and to call out letters by the score. All of this put officials under a pressure that often worked against the party line; but then, businessmen could not afford to carry their firms into partisan politics. They contributed as individuals; with strong supporters of both parties on the board of directors, a corporation president would have plenty of explaining to do—perhaps in court—for diverting company funds to one side on partisan grounds. Businessmen did not control politics, and in most cases they knew that politicians could control them, and would, if a certain bill won them votes or would bring company representatives running to pay for having it dropped. That was one reason that Credit Mobilier's representative on Capitol Hill shared the wealth with Republican leaders and that Southern railroad projects listed top partisans among their privileged incorporators. To many a businessman, politics was a dirty, unpredictable business, very much in need of reform.[37]

The minor parties shared that sense of politics' illegitimacy. Their founders saw no hope inside the two-party system. Purity of purpose lay with a new organization, founded for specific goals, not for winning office.[38] Outsiders could not break the main parties, but, like the Mugwumps, they could complicate a close race. To neutralize the sideshow parties and to stanch the future flow of votes in their direction, Republican and Democrat would have to adjust their programs to suit outside demand.

None of this made democracy the worse. Perhaps it improved matters. If anything, the many-partied system was more flexible, more open to pressure than a two-party America would have been. But from all these groups and from the rant of each party against the other came the same message: there was something seriously wrong with politics as it was practiced. At the heart of a system that seemed to run so well, hidden from the untrained eye by the glare of torchlight and the strong colors of partisan bunting, something rotten lay.

No Business To-Day Other Than Politics

The Dispirit of '76

Imagining a plot to cheat the voters, as happened after the 1884 campaign, did not take paranoid delusions. It just took memory. Indeed, without understanding the "stolen election" of 1876, we cannot understand the shape of politics in 1884. On Republican and Democratic organizations alike the past laid a smothering weight.

Not since before the war had the two parties stood so evenly matched. What little support there had been for the Republican governments in the South that Reconstruction had fostered had gone; hard times and political scandals had offset Republican Party achievements. Closing ignominiously, Ulysses S. Grant's administration had shed one cabinet member after another, as proofs of corruption and incompetence came out.[1] Worst of all, the Democrats had nominated what seemed the ideal candidate.

Wisps of greatness clung to Samuel Jones Tilden. His admirers told his story fetchingly, of an idealist, stirred in youth against Southern dominance of the Democratic Party to join the antislavery Free-Soilers. They passed quickly over the lesson that Tilden seemed to have learned from flirtation with principle, never to get angry about slavery or the sectional conflict again. They praised his cool temperament, which in an impassioned age applied itself to corporate law. While others broke up the Union or fought to preserve it, Tilden made himself an expert in railroad receiverships. Shunning publicity, he had become the impresario of New York's Democratic organization.

From personal experience, Tilden knew how the party benefited from the money and votes that Tammany Hall's machine could deliver. Yet at just the right moment, he joined the war on the Tweed Ring, Tammany's reigning plunderers. The ring was broken. Tilden got all the credit he was due, and more besides. As a legislator, he offered reforms to prevent the grafters taking hold again. As a politician, he put Tammany in cleaner hands and helped revive the Democratic Party. New York elected him governor in 1874. From the Executive Mansion, Tilden "waked up snakes" bringing Tweed's cronies to book and nabbing grabby canal contractors upstate as well. Enemies like the Canal Ring and "Honest John" Kelly's Tammany Hall won the governor a national reputation.[2]

Other, less inspiring qualities made Tilden an even more attractive nominee. He was well-fixed. Democrats could always use "Uncle Sammy's barrel," as it came to be known. With New York's patronage in his grip, he could deliver the one state the party needed most. Observers pointed to his organization with branch offices in every school district. As Tilden ran for the nomination, insiders spotted the other innovations, among them the first coherent publicity agency, a "Literary Bureau" that collected information from hundreds of newspapers and sent prepared campaign material to as many more. "He carries on a campaign in politics like a merchant manufacturer," one state senator marveled.[3]

Caution pervaded Tilden's every utterance. Callers met a courtly, well-cultivated old bachelor, with a memory as precise as a Swiss watch and conversation every bit as carefully calibrated. Legend fixed on him as the great American wire-puller, too clever to leave trails behind him, either of damaging remarks or of crooked dealings. It was said that the catchphrase "See you later" was Tilden's creation, his way of evading a direct answer and ridding himself of a pesky caller.[4]

Those who saw the ultimate politician actually overestimated the man. Tilden was secretive even when he had no secrets, crafty when it thwarted his own purposes. So cunningly did he devise his own will and with such characteristic indecision that it assured a court battle. Just as the 1876 campaign got under way, one of Tilden's closest associates, William C. Whitney, called at Greystone, the candidate's mansion in Yonkers. He and others had come for pointers on how to run the campaign. After a long delay, Tilden appeared. He beckoned to Whitney and led him up a winding staircase. Flattered that he was about to learn secrets too confidential to share with the other guests, Whitney waited expectantly. Lowering his voice to a conspiratorial whisper, Tilden told him, "You can see Staten Island from here." There was a long silence, but nothing followed. As the governor started down again, it was all

The Dispirit of '76

Whitney could do to keep from kicking him down the stairs. Others seeking guidance had similar experiences.[5]

Adopting Tilden as standard-bearer, the party committed itself to a politics as pallid as the nominee's and "reform" as risky as pointing out Staten Island. What he proposed threatened neither the pillars of the state nor of property. Reform in the federal government, to Tilden, meant spending less and driving out the swindling contractors. The old Democratic solutions of Jefferson and Jackson's day, with small government and states' rights, would set everything else right. Of those other strains in Jacksonian Democracy, such as democracy itself, Tilden had not a word to say.[6]

Playing it safe, Tilden was playing to win. For too long, Republicans had used wartime memories to alarm the country about the Democrats. It would take special work to alarm anybody about Tilden. Altogether, he presented Rutherford B. Hayes, the GOP nominee, with a formidable challenge. Wise observers predicted a close contest.

Nobody knew how close until the morning after election, when Republicans claimed victory by a single electoral vote. They owed it all to their friends in the three Southern states still "unredeemed." Partisan returning boards in South Carolina, Louisiana, and Florida threw out enough Democratic votes to count Hayes in—and their own state tickets, as well. Democrats, who had bullied, cheated, and killed their way to a near majority there and elsewhere in the cotton South, were furious and a little terrified. "Liberty is '*done for*'—played out—on this continent," one Democrat mourned. From the most angry rose the cry, "Tilden or Blood!" In fact, there was no reasonable chance of either. Republicans held the army, the presidency, and the Senate. But House Democrats could impede Hayes's inauguration by stopping the count. Hounded by investigations, fending off impeachment resolutions, the president-elect's job would not be worth holding. Both sides had done things to win that could not stand exposure; both could use a face-saving way out. Midway through January, they struck a deal, a special Electoral Commission of fifteen to decide how to count the three disputed states. By eight to seven, a strict partisan majority gave Hayes every single electoral vote.[7]

Sensing certain failure, Southern Democrats angled for the best deal they could from the incoming administration, in return for their cooperation in speeding up the count in the House. They had opened lines of communication with Hayes's friends long since. Promises had been half made on either side. Only one really mattered. White Southerners wanted guarantees that federal troops would not be used to prop up Republican governments in

South Carolina and Louisiana. There must be a "New Departure." Nothing was set to paper, but the Democrats involved were satisfied, and a diehard filibuster broke down.[8]

Hayes could hardly have done otherwise. In eight of the ten Reconstructed states, Republican rule was history, and in several of them, rather ancient history. With rival "Redeemer" governments already running the courts and collecting the taxes in the two disputed states, Republican officers' authority barely ran beyond the doorstep of the buildings in which they sat. Without funding, there would be no army to back up Republican officials or anything else: the Democratic House held the purse strings. For all of its achievements, and they were far greater than even most Northern Republicans would admit, Southern Reconstruction had failed to bring peace or prosperity to the South or to make blacks' fundamental rights secure.[9]

Against such bitter realities, Hayes set some illusive hopes. There had been guarantees, voiced through emissaries, that the fair treatment that Reconstruction had been designed to promote would not end. There were even hints that white Southerners interested in a New South, veterans of the old Whig Party, were just looking for the chance to join the Republicans. With so respectable a leadership, the Republican Party might revive. That was blacks' best hope; indeed, as Hayes saw it, their only hope.[10]

Hayes therefore had very little room to maneuver. His actions brought an outpouring of good will from his enemies. It may have fostered that spirit of reunion between North and South for which he had been hoping. Not just in his Southern policy but in his fair words (if faltering actions) against the use of government offices for the rawest sort of partisanship, the president gave reform-minded Republicans new reasons to stand by the party. When he stepped down four years later, the presidency stayed in Republican hands, an outcome better than anyone dared hope in 1877. "He has done so well," one Democrat quipped, "that I sometimes almost wish he had been elected."[11]

Hayes's New Departure failed where it mattered most, in salvaging something for black Southerners from the wreckage of Reconstruction. Indeed, insofar as equal rights depended on strong Southern Republican parties, the New Departure actually made things worse. Letting hollow Republican governments collapse and renouncing the use of a military power that no longer was within the administration's means was one thing. Starving the Southern Republican parties by taking away their patronage and larding it onto Redeemer Democrats without getting any specific benefits in return was another. Halfhearted enforcement of the federal election laws on the books simply encouraged Democrats to bulldoze Republican voters wholeheart-

The Dispirit of '76

edly. Even many party members who backed Hayes did so tentatively, treating the New Departure as an experiment. Doubting, they still hoped that some good might be salvaged from it. Other partisans minced no words: the policy was doomed and dishonorable to those who had risked life and reputation for Hayes's sake. "The foundations of this new policy are cemented in our blood," a South Carolinian cried; "the corner-stone is laid in black ingratitude."[12]

The pessimists were right. The so-called Redemption of the Republican South proved to be a great tragedy, the retreat from equal rights. The change was not total, immediate, or comprehensive. Conditions, both political and economic, remained better in the Upper South than in the Lower. But the change had begun, because the balance of power between Republican and Democrat, white and black, had tilted so far in one direction. Along with the tax cuts were cuts in service. There was less money for asylums, prisons, and schools, especially black schools. Merchants and planters changed the laws to strengthen their lien on tenant farmers' profit and to limit the exemption on foreclosures against debtors' property. New statutes made it harder for sharecroppers to change employers and widened the definition of vagrancy to permit landowners to round up forced labor at harvest season. Only in the late 1880s did states begin writing segregation into law, but the discrimination by custom hardened almost at once. "The niggers know their place," a Louisiana Democrat told one reporter. "There is a nigger in this town right now, that has been in the state legislature, and I can tell him to come and black my boots, or to go and hitch up my horse, and he'll do it, and thank me if I give him a dime for it."[13]

That promised Whig-oriented Republican Party never happened. Shut out of employment by conservative men of property, denied the patronage essential to their survival, Mississippi Republicans disbanded their party in the summer of 1877. There would be no state ticket in Alabama, Arkansas, Louisiana, or the Carolinas the following year. Nominations would simply cost Republican lives, and winning was out of the question.

Local Republican organizations made nominations and joined forces with disgruntled Democrats who for one reason or another were up in arms against the Redeemers. But the fix was in, as blacks found almost at once. Party organizers were warned not to call mass meetings. Several speakers who ignored the advice were thrown in jail on trumped-up charges until election day. In Louisiana, some fifty Republicans lost their lives. That November, Natchitoches parish reported 2,811 votes cast. Not one was Republican. In upcountry South Carolina bullies manhandled federal marshals and broke up party gatherings, on explicit direction from the Democratic

"Death at the polls and free from 'federal interference'"
(*Thomas Nast*, Harper's Weekly, *October 18, 1879*).

state chairman. Red-shirted "militias" kept such good order at the polls that no black got within ten feet of the ballot box. In black precincts, Redeemer-stacked returning boards and election officials rejected thousands of black votes but made up for it by inserting thousands more onionskin Democratic "tissue ballots" after closing time.[14]

These were states in which guarantees had been made. But the New Departure's hopes had gone beyond assuring fair play in two enclaves. They applied to the South generally, and, generally speaking, the 1878 elections told the same dispiriting story. Where Independents ran, they were attacked as "Radical emissaries in disguise" and accused of attempting racial equality

The Dispirit of '76

and planning the forced marriage of white and black. Where Republicans votes were the thickest, polling places were closed. Assuming that blacks could find the remaining ones—and the boards often kept their location as an election-day surprise—they confronted a host of Democratic challengers, abetted by friendly authorities. It scarcely mattered; the real election began after all ballots were cast, and, as Alabama Democrats had been jeering for months, "You can outvote us, but we can outcount you." They proceeded to prove it.[15]

When the Forty-sixth Congress met in March 1879, the proofs of Hayes's failure were as plain to see as the Democratic majorities in House and Senate. By rights, as the *New York Times* calculated, South Carolina should have elected four Republican congressmen, Alabama three, Louisiana two. In every Southern state, the large black vote or substantial white support should have taken at least one congressional district. But instead of thirteen to twenty representatives from the cotton states, Republicans elected one. For the first time in ten years, there were no black congressmen.[16]

Time diminished the violence, only because Republicans had given up trying in some places and been barred from a competitive canvass by law in others. "It's just this way," a white Louisianian explained. "This is a white man's country, and the white men are going to rule it, and there isn't enough of 'em for two parties." All-Democratic registration boards decided who qualified to vote, and partisan county commissions certified the winners. Georgia's 1877 constitution permitted a poll tax as one requirement for voting. The tax worked harshly on the poor, the black poor especially. Where black voting could not be overcome at the polls, it could be neutralized by changing city charters, gerrymandering legislative districts, and giving Republicans no offices to vote for. Canny redistricting could dole out just enough of the Black Belt to seven congressional districts to insure white conservative control in all, or squeeze riverbank counties into the "shoestring" district and give a state's black majority just one member of the House.[17]

The South's New Departure from democracy was not immediate and never complete. Even in the cotton belt, a black vote persisted. There would be black sheriffs, clerks, assemblymen, and even congressmen for two decades to come. Farther north, Republicans could count on white votes. All along the Appalachians, Democrats had to fight for their victories against well-organized "party-armies" and Independent challenges. Looking at the South over all, indeed, a statistician might even conclude that two-party politics stood poised for a comeback: Republicans' share of the vote throughout the 1880s and 1890s stayed just about level. But there was no comeback, and in the Deep South, the chances of one lessened yearly, as all the scaffolding on which a healthy party must be based vanished. Without rewards for their organizers, newspapers to inspire the faithful or get out the party message, or money to carry on a campaign, and without access to public offices, the Republican Party atrophied, so far that in any fair contest it could no longer match the Democrats on equal terms, even where Republicans outnumbered Democrats.[18]

With the making of a Solid South, national power swung hard in a Democratic direction. So far had the political landscape changed that by 1880, winning the old majority in the North no longer was enough for Republicans. It was true, of course, that twenty years of Republican state-making had left the South in a smaller minority than ever before. All the new states admitted were Northern ones, Republican strongholds from the prairies westward. Without that help, the Senate, not just the House, would have been Democratic after 1875. Hayes could not have won otherwise in 1876, nor any Republican for twenty years thereafter. Yet the margin of safety remained a slim one. Western states had just begun to grow. Nebraska's one House seat could not compare with South Carolina's five.[19]

A strictly Northern party had no chance of holding the House, at least as long as the opposition carried dozens of Northern seats itself. Only with Southern help did Republicans win it in 1881; doubling their Southern contingent put a Republican back in the Speakership in 1889 after six years in the minority. In each case, white districts from the Upper and Border South made the difference: twenty-two of the twenty-five Southern Republicans in the Fifty-first Congress came from there. Even the Senate was a close thing. The last Republican holdovers from the South gave Republicans their majority until 1879, and an alliance of convenience in Virginia brought them the one-vote margin to hold it in 1881.

Control mattered, not just because the party program became a mere wish list without it. Democratic dominance also meant a license for fraud and intimidation down south. Defeated candidates' last hope lay with the Elections Committee. As long as Republicans ran the House, challengers could make their case before a friendly panel. But any black Republican wasted his time appealing there as long as Democrats chose a chairman who himself had been elected by bulldozing. When Democrats chose Georgia's Henry G. Turner to head the committee, they sent an unmistakable message to the light-vote cavalry. Lest anybody overlook the obvious, they reinforced it when Turner retired. Seniority rules were cast aside to give his colleague Charles Crisp the chair. Crisp never had to worry about Republican competition. He hardly even had to worry about voters. Most Northern districts had a turnout of thirty thousand; that would have been enough to elect seventeen Crisps.[20]

Diminishing democracy in the South skewed the representative nature of politics both in Washington and in the nation as a whole. It also had a corrosive effect within the Republican Party itself. State organizations down south that once had represented real sources of political power did so no longer. No longer could they elect governors or congressmen; no longer had they the power to deliver their states. Their active members had dwindled to a handful. They spoke for millions of Southerners, but for all the good it would do on election day, they represented nobody. To a greater or lesser extent, a dozen states had become rotten boroughs. Yet came the National Republican Convention, and there they were, electing delegates and throwing their weight on the side of this presidential nominee or that. To treat them as equals in judgment or influence with, say, the delegation from Ohio would be absurd. Yet their votes counted every bit as much.

Hollowed out within by local attrition, Southern delegations became the playthings of officeholders and patronage brokers. For money and power, they were beholden not to their constituents but to Washington, where a friendly cabinet officer might throw the spoils their way. Their delegates were likelier to be picked by collectors of customs and Internal Revenue commissioners. Delegates worthy of less respect and with no prospects outside of federal preferment were easier to buy, and when they showed up at conventions were treated as marketable commodities. (Black ones got most of the blame for putting their votes up for sale, but, if fickleness of loyalties in the balloting proves any guide, white ones got most of the money.) A candidate who won with their support already began the campaign with a tainted title. A party looking to them for guidance would find its most selfish instincts exaggerated. Not by coincidence, it was a Southerner who rose in the 1880 convention when efforts were made to add praise for Hayes's civil service reform record to the platform. "Texas has had quite enough of the civil service," Webster Flanagan roared. "There is one plank in the Democratic Party that I have ever admired, and that is, 'To the victors belong the spoils.' . . . What are we here for?"[21]

What they were there for, in fact, was to nominate Hayes's successor, and under the terms Redemption had set, terms that Republicans would find as disadvantageous in 1884. The South had 150 presidential electors locked up for any Democratic nominee. To win, their opponents would need a "solid North," more solid than in 1876. Ohio, New York, Indiana, and New Jersey could go either way. Losing two, Republicans would lose the White House. It seemed so unfair, but then, of course, it was. Staying well within the law, Democrats had rigged a national election on their behalf. Without waving around a single shotgun in 1884, they had half stolen a majority in the electoral college already.

It would take more than a generation for Republicans to take this injustice for granted, and certainly not while the wrongs were fresh and the election-rigging as flagrant as under Hayes. Even the president had to admit his New Departure a failure. Southern Republicans would find it easier to get post offices and government jobs in the last two years of his administration than the first, and Hayes addressed some choice words at the bulldozers. His critics spoke even more bluntly. Very likely, some of the machine politicians who waved the bloody shirt against Hayes simply thought it a good pretext; the president's support for civil service reform angered them more. But the sense of betrayal went beyond spoils-seeking and found willing listeners.

It could hardly compare with the sense of betrayal that Democrats felt about the "steal" of 1876. As the Electoral Commission deliberated, letters flooded the Speaker's desk for action—any kind of action—to save the republic. "Tilden must go in if it takes one hundred thousand lives to put him there," one Pennsylvanian wrote. "In God's name do not give up the ship," another begged Speaker of the House Samuel J. Randall. "If you give up now its for all time to come."[22]

They hated the Republicans and they hated themselves. "The cowardice of the democratic party is without example," one diehard raged. Apparently, "weak idiots" ran party counsels. Though the Senate's two leading Democrats, Allen Thurman of Ohio and Thomas Bayard of Delaware, had supported Tilden's side on the Electoral Commission, they refused to break up the commission when it voted wrong. That in itself was enough to condemn them, but Bayard had also been one of the most outspoken supporters of a peaceful solution, even if it cost Tilden the office. Tilden and many of his friends never forgave him. Well into the next Congress, Democrats were still trading charges about which one had done more to sell the presidency, and for what price.[23]

The trauma of having been denied their due had lasting consequences. It hardened the feeling in Democratic ranks that Republicans were capable of anything. "Damn them, they will steal from a pathmaster to a President," one Democrat exclaimed. "I would not trust one of them from a justice of the peace to a judge of the Supreme Court," another exploded. "They are all corrupt."[24] Hereafter, Democrats were likely to suspect the worst when the polls closed.

Those suspicions took renewed strength in 1880. No outlandish Republican fraud elected James A. Garfield president that November. None was needed; Democrats' morale had been shattered a month before the presidential election, when Indiana narrowly elected a Republican governor. The losers were not at all surprised late the following winter when one of the architects of that victory, Stephen W. Dorsey, was given a tremendous banquet at Delmonico's fancy restaurant in New York, and vice president–elect Chester Alan Arthur let the cat out of the bag. "Indiana was really, I suppose, a Democratic state," he allowed, as his listeners laughed appreciatively. "It had been put down on the books always as a State that might be carried by close and perfect organization and a great deal of–" "Soap!" members of the audience shouted, "soap" being the slang term for vote-buying money. When a few years later Dorsey boasted that he had used $400,000 to win the state and that all his work had been done with the presidential nominee's connivance, Democrats swallowed the sixfold exaggeration whole. If they had known the quiet scramble of Republican leaders to find and destroy their national chairman's correspondence after his death, they would have suspected other, dirtier tricks needing concealment.[25]

Democrats had good reasons for feeling outcheated twice in a row. At the same time, the myth of the 1876 stolen election, and to a lesser extent the defeat of 1880, offered the party the powerful consolation that it, and not the GOP, spoke for the electorate. Only rascality deprived them of their due. They had the votes, if only they could get them counted, and get them counted they would. Once cheated, Democrats were resolved not to back down again. So when the returns came in slowly on election night, 1884, to assume that Republicans were about to steal the presidency was the most natural response in the world. Making sure they didn't ran a close second.

Beyond that shared legacy of suspicion that the political process was rigged against them and that shared confidence that in any fair contest theirs was the majority's will, Democrats inherited one great liability from the crisis of 1876 that Republicans escaped. They found themselves saddled with a martyr–and, worse, a deathless one.

The freshness of Tilden's appeal suffered badly from the moment he was nominated. Not only had he failed to run the flawless, well-organized campaign that both sides expected; he chose not to run it at all. Beneath the calculation, Democrats discovered, lay no bold conception and very little force of will. In the confusion just after the election, the party needed leadership more than ever. No personal acquaintance expected a seasoned corporate attorney to summon the masses to the barricades. Still, many hoped for some ringing statement of his rights, some artful solution to the stalemate on Capitol Hill, or even some noble renunciation for the sake of a nation's peace. Instead, there was only silence. "While he was as inanimate as a gorged anaconda," one of his allies raged, "the prize slipped from his grasp."[26]

Others close to him had not been so inanimate. Persuading themselves that there was no dishonesty in ransoming stolen goods, Tilden's friends had opened negotiations to buy the returning-board members before they could make an official decision. Democrats could not come up with enough money in time, but their dealings had been entrusted to coded telegrams that Western Union handed over to Republicans. Among the ringleaders was Colonel William F. Pelton, Tilden's nephew and permanent houseguest. In 1878, the *New York Tribune* published these "cipher dispatches." On the stand, Tilden swore that he had known nothing about the transactions going on downstairs. Some Democrats believed him. More sensible onlookers concluded that he had closed his eyes, "the way a modest lady would turn her back while her husband was changing his shirt."[27]

By then defeat had stripped Tilden of many of his advantages. He had passed the governorship into friendly hands. Never again would he hold office. Never again after the exposure of the "cipher dispatches" could he represent reform in a convincing way. What Tilden represented was himself, and the thwarting of the people's will. He had been badly wronged. How well he knew it, and how well his listeners knew it, on those few occasions when he spoke in public. It was as if the 1876 election had consumed all his energies. Those energies were of the most sparing sort. As governor, Tilden had been in poor health, which worsened markedly. Over time, the sage of Gramercy Park became an invalid, a virtual prisoner in his new suburban mansion, Greystone. One reporter, spotting him at a political dinner in 1877, was shocked at the change. Eighteen months before, he had spoken to a hale man with a sharp blue eye. Now a dry, cadaverous figure stood before him, one eye fixed on nothing, left arm hanging useless at his side, voice nearly inaudible. Tilden had grown old, and, as the Hayes administration edged toward civil service reform, his ideas seemed to have grown old, too. Even his reputation as the one man able to carry New York deserted him when Republicans won the governorship in 1879. After years of quarreling with Tilden, Tammany Hall's Boss Kelly split the Democratic vote by running as a spoiler candidate. What he could do for Tilden's successor at Albany, Kelly made clear, he would be glad to do for Tilden; if Democrats disbelieved him, let them nominate the old man for president and see![28]

Yet the circumstances of the 1876 election ironically made this damaged politician an imperishable candidate. Professional politicians glancing at the returns noted how many Northern states, hopelessly Republican, had gone

"Mr. Tilden's body-guard. On his march to retirement"
(F. Graetz, Puck, June 18, 1884).

Democratic or run the majority party a close race. Democrats had come so close to winning. Indeed, they *had* won. Tilden was the real president, not Hayes. The only way to prove it was to renominate him in 1880 and let the voters right the wrong done four years before. Passing over Tilden would be shrugging off the crime of the century. Vindicating the party, Democrats had to vindicate Tilden, and Tilden never let them forget it.[29]

There was no chance of his assuming the burdens of the presidency, much less guiding an active campaign. Tilden knew that as well as anyone. He never meant to accept a nomination. But his ambition to dictate a nominee once his vanity had been gratified stayed as robust as ever. Well into 1880, he let his friends foster a Tilden boom. Misled as to his condition, deluded as to the former governor's real purposes, his old lieutenants across the country rounded up the votes to control state conventions. Opponents had come to detest "the old paralitic [*sic*] intrigant." All the same, they waged a losing battle against the feeling that, dead or alive, the candidate of 1876 must have the courtesy of first refusal in 1880.[30]

Tilden's ploy very nearly worked. His foes had the votes to prevent his nomination but not to keep him from holding a controlling share of the delegates, or enough to put over any plausible candidate. Everything depended on how and when he took himself out of the running. As so often before, Tilden showed himself too cunning, too secretive. Timing his letter of withdrawal too late and in language too ambiguously phrased, the former governor frittered away his chance. The delegates gave the letter a perfunctory cheer and moved on to serious business. General Winfield Scott Hancock, a solid Union veteran and hero of the battle of Gettysburg, won the nomination with Tilden's devotees scattering every which way.[31] Among the casualties when the convention ended were some of Tilden's most devoted friends.

Tilden got no better. His ailments had gone too far to hide convincingly. Uncharitable Republicans might have dwelt on the neat fit between the man and his followers. To them, Tilden *was* the Democratic Party of the early 1880s: infirm and yet imperishable, crafty yet ineffectual, narrow, selfish, a mass of negatives and bitternesses living on an increasingly remote reputation for positive achievements, a fading presence with no progeny. It was a caricature, of course, as brutal as one of Thomas Nast's cartoons, but, like Nast's, very like the original. Yet the Tilden boom never entirely collapsed. It actually prospered the more new issues pulled the Democrats apart. Tilden's reclusiveness gave him special advantages no active politician had. A man so remote from the issues of the last six years was the one man least likely to divide the party. Instead of facing the present, the opposition could feed on old memories. Those memories lingered. As late as 1883, the *Chicago Daily News* approved of keeping Hayes's portrait on the White House walls, because people needed reminding "that the American navy is not the only thing this republic has to be ashamed of."[32]

These, then, were the legacies of 1876: on the Democratic side, an inextinguishable candidate, unfit to lead and unwilling to do anything else; on the Republican side, a political system weighted against them and against a fair expression of the popular will; and on both sides, the best of reasons for feeling that they were about to be cheated out of their due.

The Bloody Shirt—In Hoc Signo Vinces

From most accounts of the 1884 election, readers might imagine the Southern issue laid to rest. Only once does it stir, in the form of a single foolish word uttered by a clergyman at the close of the campaign. No absence could seem more natural, with the war nineteen years past. The real surprise was that so-called bloody-shirt politics had survived so long.

Conventional wisdom has the story half right. Compared with 1880 or 1876, sectional issues made a paltry display in 1884. But if the South as an issue did not figure largely in the campaign, the South as a political problem figured hugely in the *election*. The comparative silence of the Republicans was not the silence of cynics shamed into abandoning a cant that their own followers no longer heeded. It was the forced silence of politicians who dared not speak plain truths because they wanted to win.

Textbooks never have a good word to say for "waving the bloody shirt." Rousing Northern sentiment against white Southerners for political effect, invoking long-past wartime loyalties (and disloyalties), playing up every crime against blacks as part of some monster plot to put a Solid South in command: pictured that way, the bloody shirt seems a pretty sordid garment.[1]

To judge from the regular reports of progress in settling the "Negro question" and the constant boasts of an industrial New South wiping out the old, the bloody shirt would also have seemed irrelevant by the 1880s. Most newspapers only scoffed when speculators started buying Confederate bonds. The

Confederacy was as dead as slavery. Not even the Redeemers would redeem wastepaper. When General Sherman got a hero's welcome in Atlanta, stay-at-home patriots would need good reasons for showing less charity.[2] It followed that those who waved the bloody shirt were hypocrites, hallucinators, or back numbers.

Senator John A. Logan of Illinois looked like the perfect example of all three. Before the war, "Black Jack" had been a Democrat from "Egypt," the southern-accented end of the state. Race prejudice ran deep there. Logan himself sponsored legislation to punish any black coming into Illinois. Then the war came. Enlisting in the Union army, he made a valiant figure, dashing headlong wherever the fighting was thickest. Wartime service carried him into the House, and in 1871, the Senate, as one of the most radical Republicans. With his long, jet-black hair and handlebar mustache, Logan became one of the most familiar, if not most respected, national figures.[3]

To those who did not share his views, the senator seemed a perfect example of what was wrong with letting wartime loyalties dictate peacetime leadership. His oratory never advanced beyond stump speaking, and then in a narrow range. Financial questions muddled him. He shifted positions as his constituents did. All he wanted from presidents was patronage, and no matter how much he got, he grumbled at not getting more. A casual observer might have suspected that Logan's idea of government was nothing more than a vast pension-granting mill, doling out money to every middle-aged boy in blue. In all, as one newspaper put it, the Illinois senator was as much like a statesman as a "nicely roast pig on the table" resembled "a three hundred pound Poland China boar in a blue grass pasture."[4]

Logan was not, perhaps, the all-powerful boss that his enemies described. Political reverses cost him his Senate seat in 1877. Yet, without a grip on the patronage, Logan made a terrific comeback. As soon as Republicans won back the legislature, they made him senator again. No wonder: for Logan's real strength lay in the veterans, for whom he remained an untarnished hero. As one of the early commanders of the Grand Army of the Republic, the greatest of the Union veterans' societies, and as the founder of Memorial Day, Logan was sure of a warm welcome wherever the GAR had followers. In the 1880s, that was everywhere.[5]

"Everywhere" included political offices from constable to chief executive. From 1868 through 1900, every Republican presidential candidate but one had a military record. Congress was crowded with veterans whose postwar career counted for more than their wartime glories. Some of them despised bloody-shirt tactics, Democratic ex-generals especially. Still, all of them owed their rise in part to deeds on the field. Many of them made a career out of reminding the voters of it. At stirring-up army reunions, no one could outdo wartime's noncombatant calico-seller Governor Charles Foster of Ohio, the *Chicago Daily News* asserted, and who with a better right? "He lost one leg at Shiloh, another at Antietam, another at Pea Ridge, and another at Atlanta."[6]

Warlike words and a wartime spirit outliving its time were not simply ridiculous to liberal reformers. They exposed how out of kilter the political system had become. Bloody-shirt patriotism was not the last refuge of a scoundrel; it was the first. Corrupt politicians were able to keep on stealing as long as voters could see no further than their faded uniforms. But corruption went in both directions. The Logans bought voters with pensions, turning their common heroism into a marketable commodity. A noble past had been taken over by hucksters. Their bombast stirred up sectional hatred and, as long as blacks voted Republican, race hatred, too.[7]

Bloody-shirt appeals stitched out of the whole cloth abounded. Near election time, Republicans could always find someone ready to file an affidavit that some opposing candidate had insulted an old vet or called Union soldiers "Lincoln's dogs." Newspapers gave "positive proof" that the Democrats meant to pension all the old Confederate soldiers and pay for lost slave "property" if they won in 1884: the fact that the national platform never said otherwise. ("A man who stands in dread of that deserves to have holes bored in the top of his skull to let the darkness out," Kentucky editor Henry Watterson commented scornfully.)[8] Yet, in the end, the examples prove far less than they seem. Every true issue has its cant. A strong case can be made in favor of the bloody shirt, not only as a legitimate issue but one of continuing relevance.

Sectional issues were not just the trumped-up device of cynical pols. As any counting up of electoral votes and House seats showed, the Solid South posed Republicans a real political problem. Democracy denied in one part of the country vitiated it everywhere. It hobbled a majority's power to make policy in Washington. The bloody shirt was not a purely Northern fashion, either. White Southerners found it irresistible. Every two years, Democrats exhumed the nastier bits of Reconstruction to wave them before the electorate. Far more often than in the North, Southern voters rewarded candidates with a war record, and would accept no substitutes.[9] Nothing could be more offensive than a Virginian's declaration that he would like to see West Point sold, or Senator Lucius Q. C. Lamar of Mississippi comparing Jefferson Davis with George Washington, unless it was one North Carolina congressman's boast at a dinner reception that he came from "a district where thirty thousand Union soldiers rotted within the city limits." (His reference to Salisbury, one of the Confederacy's notorious prison camps, was an immediate sensation. A Democratic veteran instantly leaped up, grabbed the congressman by the throat, and threatened to "choke the life out of" him.)[10]

There was another point, and one that politicians ignored at their peril. Up to 1884, the bloody shirt *sold*. Certainly over time its appeal must fade. No veteran could live forever. But until the Civil War generation passed from the scene, the issues of war and Reconstruction would matter more than all others to a large share of the electorate. The ones who cared counted for more than their numbers might suggest. If moderate people turned out on election day, the true believers were the ones who inspired them to do so. Party loyalty, ambition, a chance of the spoils—all could make an organizer work his hardest. But so did intense belief, for temperance, say, or equal rights, or the Lost Cause. Men so driven manned the local committees, rounded up the apathetic voters, bullied, cajoled, and contributed to party success. As long as Northerners like that cared about the bloody shirt, it must keep its place in the party appeal.

It must do so all the more because, by the 1880s, bloody-shirt politics was being reinforced by pressure groups outside the party machinery. The march to the cemetery for a last parting with one of the honored dead became more and more frequent. Bit by bit, the remembered past was becoming a recounted one, told by those who were there to the growing number who were not. That change may even have intensified the war's popular appeal, making it more acceptable by transforming it into something less partisan, and making the celebration of the war into something more universal.

As the war receded into the past, a recollection of its horrors gave way to nostalgia. Many middle-aged men recalled it as the defining experience of their lives. As the wartime generation began to pass away, surviving veterans stirred themselves to make sure that America did not forget their sacrifices. Most of the monuments of the war would be built only after 1875; thereafter, veterans' associations grew in number and swelled in membership. Only then did the full-blown civil religion of the Lost Cause and of what could be called the "Won Cause" reach its fullest potential and widest appeal.[11]

The veterans' societies reinforced the parties, Republicans in the North and Democrats in the South, but they also posed a problem for them. In ways that the politicians never quite grasped, the GAR and kindred organizations offered an alternative to the popular politics on which the two-party system was based. Let them call their gatherings encampments; they looked like conventions, with moderators and elected officers, delegates chosen by states, and platforms of resolutions. The parade, the campaign button, the cheers, marching songs, and elaborate rituals, the keynote speakers, all pro-

The Bloody Shirt—In Hoc Signo Vinces

vided a movement culture strikingly like the partisan experience. As the veterans' organizations applied themselves to building homes for their indigent members and raising statues to their heroes, they gave their members a shared sense of purpose that any Republican partisan would have understood perfectly. Their sense of belonging was enriched by a special exclusiveness that Republicans never shared (a Confederate *could* join the GOP, after all—and General James Longstreet did). But in another way, the veterans' societies had a wider appeal than either major party. Some of them had active women's auxiliaries. Others worked in concert with sister societies. For the widows, wives, and daughters of veterans, the organizations found tasks that needed doing and the honor of sharing a common cause.[12]

Allegiance to the veterans' societies therefore provided a nonpartisan option for many Americans wanting to serve some higher end than their own advantage and seeking a sense of belonging in a disorienting, industrializing world. Those energies could be directed to a party's benefit, but there was no necessary reason that they would be. The veterans would need some sign that the parties remembered them. Theirs was, ever so slightly, a conditional partisanship—which, as will become clear, was an increasing character of the American political system as the third American party system aged.[13] As more groups put their own agenda first, party loyalty could no longer be taken as much for granted. Prohibitionists, Mugwumps, tariff reformers, and industrialists all shared in the new attitude. So, too, with veterans. To reach the old soldiers, the two parties must find some way of making the Civil War a touchstone for present policies.

The bloody shirt, then, expressed genuine, legitimate concerns, but its survival was not due simply to the persistence of old political attitudes. New events and conditions kept it aloft. As times changed, so did its character. Generally overlooked, the point about transformation is vital. Whether waving the bloody shirt really was demagogic and hypocritical depends on whether its users were pointing to threats that no longer existed or to promises they never expected to keep. That question, in turn, depends on just what bloody-shirt language meant from year to year.

Clearly, when Hayes left office in 1881, the threat that Southern supremacy and Democratic majorities posed was very different from when he came in, and the hope for changing things far less. Renewing the two-party system of Reconstruction days was out of the question. Patronage could feed Republican organizations again. It could not restore them. Setting up partisan newspapers that had starved to death for lack of public funding would cost far more than keeping existing ones going. Four years of discouragement and unfriendly state legislation had imposed formidable barriers. In the

Deep South, the GOP might win locally under its own label. Only in the Upper South, especially in white counties where Democrats could not use the race issue as effectively, could it expect statewide gains.

Any Republican resurgence would have been resisted more fiercely by Democrats, now more firmly entrenched than ever. For all the talk of sectional reconciliation, the forces keeping alive the passions of war and Reconstruction remained strong after Redemption. If anything, they got stronger. Even the mildest deviation from the official Democratic ticket set off warnings that "Negro rule" would follow. Lynching was on the rise. The most virulent race prejudice had begun to win intellectual backing from Northern universities, as leading scholars offered what purported to be scientific evidence of black inferiority.[14]

The same racial reaction made any action for equal rights less likely to win a following in the North. A few white Republicans continued to resent the injustices done to black Southerners. Some, Hayes included, worked hard to find solutions in black education. But the sympathy as a whole vanished. Even those who waved the bloody shirt came to believe much of the economic hyperbole about a New South and welcomed it. Newspapers that had fed readers on Southern affairs devoted less and less space to them. In *Harper's Weekly* alongside the Nast cartoons, subscribers could see sentimental images of fond masters and former slaves and the comic "darkeys" of "Blackville."[15] As illustrated periodicals proliferated in the 1880s, the spate of these kinds of images turned into a flood, all of them providing a far pleasanter picture of race relations and of the dynamics of New South society. A new literature of sentimentality toward the Old South arose, much of it directed at indicting the false values of the materialistic North. When Henry James's *Bostonians* wanted a fitting rival for the ideologues of women's rights, it picked a Southern aristocrat; Henry Adams's *Democracy* devised just such an ex-Confederate conscience to counter its corrupt and attractive senator (modeled on James G. Blaine, among others). Joel Chandler Harris's recast folktales of "B'rer Rabbit" had a national following, and their African origins were easily obscured by the happy plantation surroundings.[16]

Northern reporters down south were likelier to send back prose poems about quaint customs than investigative reporting. Few of them bothered to interview blacks themselves. Usually, blacks' actions were framed within the stereotypes that Northerners had come to believe, of a simple, happy people, content with the little that a white South gave them. Camp meetings appeared as spectacle, at which Northerners noted everything but the religious devotion: the sister arrested just after her baptism for stealing the white cotton gloves she had worn during immersion, the depredations on "hen-roosts and melon patches" thereabouts, the comical dialect of the preachers, and the pride "the Southern 'pickaninny'" took in being able to rattle off a catechism. Blacks "work only when actually obliged, and display an amount of shiftlessness that is truly amazing," one Republican journalist wrote from upcountry South Carolina. That "shiftlessness," from his own account, in-cluded the creation of churches, temperance organizations, Bands of Hope, militia companies, amateur theatrical and fire companies, and newspapers—conclusive proof of how imitative "colored folks" were, as a race.[17]

The change in attitude stretched all the way into the Supreme Court. The civil rights cases in 1883 overturned federal laws against segregation and discrimination. The Fourteenth Amendment, the Supreme Court explained, had been aimed at state actions, not at what private individuals did. Federal authority could not compel a theater owner or hotel keeper to serve blacks. State law covered such offenses. Blacks reacted with dismay. Dead letter though the 1875 civil rights law had been, Frederick Douglass protested, it had expressed "the sentiment of justice and fair play." Now a Republican court had hauled down that "banner on the outer wall of American liberty." A Republican press expressed only relief. Even the *New York Tribune* dis-missed the civil rights laws as delaying the day when all "unreasonable" race distinctions vanished.[18]

Northern Republicans could have been stirred up by election-day vio-lence, but there just wasn't all that much available anymore. Through quiet pressure and legal trickery, black voters were being denied their rights as badly, or worse, than when bulldozing was at its height. Still, the effect was not the same. One might grow as indignant over a legal mechanism as a mound of corpses, but the disgust, the horror, no longer went with it. The more law did the disfranchising, the less chance there would be of Republi-can interference. Strong-arm tactics might excite the House to refuse a Dem-ocratic contender his certificate, but a gerrymander, never.

The new nostalgia for the war also took a toll on the old-fashioned bloody-shirt argument. The soldiers' courage, not the cause in which they showed it, took an ever greater prominence. It became increasingly bad form to hold the wrongs of the Confederacy against Confederate veterans. Union veterans remembered their sacrifices but were willing to accord respect to those of their adversaries. But the wrongs committed by Confederate soldiers and the atrocities of Andersonville had been one of the essential parts of the bloody shirt in Reconstruction days. Something else must be found to take its place.

Even during Reconstruction the bloody-shirt issue had never covered much beyond the political aspect of the wrongs committed by the South;

now it belabored those almost exclusively. Gradually, what was done to blacks faded from view. Instead, polemicists concentrated on the injury to the rights of the North and of Republicans everywhere. But that change was part of a larger emphasis, not on the obstructive power of the South but on its aggressive tendencies within the Union. Talk of renewed secession died away. In its place was a variant on the old warnings with which Republicanism had begun, of an aggrandizing Slave Power. Unable to ruin the nation, the South meant to rule it again, to wipe out all those innovations that the war had legalized, from the national banks to the protective tariff.[19]

Redemption, in other words, forced the bloody shirt into a defensive key. It became an instrument of conservative values rather than radical ones. It promised not reform so much as the preservation of values and institutions already in existence. It protected gains already made rather than advancing new ones. Republicans were doing their best to position themselves as supporters of "progress," but that "progress" was one in which promotion of economic development played a far more important part than the advancement of democratic institutions. Republicanism was friendly to banks, businesses, and landholders. It protected the just rights of labor without interpreting those rights more broadly. It was the party of order, of law, and of middle-class values. Instead of being the vanguard of human rights, it described itself as the preserver of the Union.[20]

The change did not begin in 1877, to be sure. But events that year, including the great strike on the railway system, strengthened the image. By 1879, Democrats had been typecast as a new kind of subversive, intent not on dividing the Union so much as undermining a stable, established national order. Instead of teaching Northerners to fear the Confederate sword, propagandists pointed to the insurrectionists' torch.

Southerners gave them plenty of grounds for alarm. By 1879, the danger that the army would enforce order at the polls down south was remote at best. The federal election laws remained on the books and, except in the North, rarely reached the level of a minor nuisance. But the Forty-fifth Congress, spurred on by Southern hotheads, determined on a showdown and the repeal of federal election laws. When President Hayes balked, they threatened to stop government entirely. Without passage of the general appropriations bill, the president would have to call an extra session. There, for the first time in twenty-two years, Democrats would have a majority in both houses. By attaching repeal as a rider to spending bills, they could force Hayes to submit.[21]

Southern Democrats underestimated the president and the Republicans. They had seen his conciliation as weakness and the party's retreat from

The Bloody Shirt—In Hoc Signo Vinces

Reconstruction as a failure of nerve. Instead, Hayes vetoed the appropriations bill and every bill that followed with a rider attached. Even defenders of his New Departure spoke like "Stalwarts" now. What Democrats were attempting was "revolution," *Harper's Weekly* warned. They would destroy "all the checks and balances of our political system," turning Congress into the supreme power and making the subordinate states as sovereign as if no war had settled the issue.[22]

With each veto, Hayes's support across the North grew. As Republicans warned of "a new rebellion," Democrats retreated. Having first compared themselves to the Parliaments that fought King Charles I (which, since Charles ended up being deposed and put to death, was an unfortunate choice of analogies), their leaders tried to pretend that they had never meant to impose conditions at all. One spending bill after another passed without the riders attached. Putting the best face on the debacle, Henry Watterson urged House members to declare a moral victory, pass the bill funding the army, and adjourn. They had made their point about the injustice of using the army in politics. Three days later, the editor made his point plainer. "Come home, you suckers," the leading article screamed at Democratic lawmakers. "Come home, you chuckleheads. Come home, you knock-kneed, bandy-shanked, bow-legged, web-footed and red-haired varmints. C-O-M-E H-O-M-E!!"[23]

By then, it was too late. Now even moderate Republicans blanched at the idea of a Democratic victory in 1880. At the very least, the White House must stay in safe hands, to hold the rebel brigadiers at bay. From the Stalwart end of the party the cry mounted that a "strong man" would be needed in the White House, someone with the will and experience to control a "half-subdued" Southern spirit. Many of them rallied behind a third term for Ulysses S. Grant, not as the preserver of Reconstruction but as the protector of a republic in peril.[24]

The emphasis toward a conservative direction was intensified, and the change in bloody-shirt language was hastened by the pressure-group politics of the veterans' organizations in the 1880s. They no longer wanted vindication—every Northern party lauded the veteran—but recognition. They wanted pensions, and yearly the appeals grew louder.[25]

So the agenda of the bloody shirt changed. Restoration of Southern Republican rule turned into a general appeal for "a full vote and a fair count"; talk about the party's reform of Southern political backwardness was tempered into language about Republicanism as the bulwark of property, progress, and Southern economic development; and defenses of equal rights gave way to discussion of the benefits that a solid North could give to the former soldiers. Pension legislation set up a standard for "loyalty" that the economy-minded Democrats would find harder than Republicans to meet. But pensions were also seen as one of the last installments on a debt contracted in wartime, a personal and human debt, no less sacred than the government's pledge to the bondholders. To refuse pensions was not just coldheartedness. Such a rejection could be seen as intended to discredit the sacrifices of the war and belittle the significance of the war itself as the defining moment in American life, when a union of nearly sovereign states was welded into a nation—with broad leeway for state power and wide jurisdiction over subjects that the national government must not meddle in, but a nation, all the same.[26]

By emphasizing pensions and the preservation of the postwar settlement, the Republican Party also positioned itself to handle the most difficult problem: how to attract Southern votes and still use the bloody shirt to bring out its Northern enthusiasts. As long as many Northerners responded better to the sectional appeal than any other, as long as Republicans wanted a touchstone to the party's heritage and its traditions, the party might well lose more votes than it gained in the North by putting the bloody shirt away. But even then, it would not be enough to create a solid North; and without that, the Republican Party would still be badly handicapped. For better than a national stalemate, the Solid South must be broken.

In its modified form, the bloody shirt could keep its Northern appeal without giving Southern allies too much to explain away. But could those allies be found? Even as the Hayes administration fostered hopes of a new Whig Party down south, Southern Republicans tried other possible combinations. With luck, indeed, the party might rebuild itself in the South on terms that would mute the sectional issue. In 1878, Republicans in many Southern states joined forces with any dissidents out to challenge the Redeemers. Four years later, President Arthur's administration embarked on the policy of applying patronage to whatever groups it would do the most good: disgruntled Democrats, Greenbackers, and Independents.[27]

Dissidents came in every form, united only in their opposition to the so-called Bourbon Democracy, which, like the old French royal family, forgot nothing and learned nothing. In some states, they included former Confederates and bulldozers like James R. Chalmers of Mississippi. In Alabama and Texas, they drew on enemies of the national banking system and proponents of an inflated money supply, like the Greenbackers. In Arkansas and Tennessee, Republicans aligned with the sternest advocates of paying the state debts. In North Carolina, Republicans combined with Democrats opposed to Prohibition legislation and called themselves the "Liberal Party."[28]

It only sounded cynical. Ideological consistency lay in the larger question of how free the South should be to make a fair choice between political alternatives. Whatever their background, all dissidents had felt the oppression of a system rigged for Democrats' benefit. All wanted "a full vote, a free ballot, a fair count." Marking out more common ground could wait, but coalitions offered the promise of overturning an entrenched party and opening the way to a political system in which more common ground between Democrats' enemies might be found. Even as Republicans gave up their separate identity, they made Independents give up the color line. To win, dissident movements had to mute their prejudices. The biggest group of disaffected Southerners were black Republicans. Beyond the hill country of eastern Mississippi and the white counties along the Appalachians, there would be no chance of beating the Bourbon Democrats without them. When the insurgents came into power, there were good reasons for hoping that they would expand their program in ways serving Republican interests.[29]

Anyone wanting confirmation of that hope need only look to the half-won revolution in Virginia. Other Southern governments had contracted vast debts, though usually they solved the problem by altering state obligations and repudiating great swaths of bonds outright. Virginia delayed readjustment longest and in doing so set off a political explosion. Pleading that the state's honor was at stake in keeping its financial promises to the last penny, the Democratic-Conservatives resolved to sacrifice everything to debt payment.[30]

Honor, as expressed under the Funding Act of 1871, came at bitterly high cost. A tremendously regressive tax system doubled its burdens on small farmers. Spending on asylums, roads, and schools was cut drastically. Even then the state ran a deficit. When the governor vetoed a school appropriation in 1878, explaining that free public education was a mere "luxury," the disaffected banded together in a movement to readjust the terms of the state debt and the terms by which Virginia spent public funds.[31] In 1879, the Readjusters and Republicans carried the state House and put General William Mahone into the Senate. Two years later, Readjusters took the legislature again, and the governorship with it.

"The ogre of Democratic Virginia," as one reporter called him, Mahone was a remarkable character. Short, slender, with long flowing hair and beard, he looked light enough to blow away. One foe taunted the little Democrat for weighing only 110 pounds. "True," Mahone shot back, "but 80 pounds of the 110 pounds is backbone." The debt-paying so-called Funder Democrats had always known that. They remembered him as the bold Confederate soldier and the pushing railroad promoter, whose political skills won more than one state election. What they had not noticed so clearly was Mahone's faith in a

New South based on public schools and industrial development, of a kind that Funders' notion of "honor" would smother.[32]

Enemies explained the general's advance on his iron will and ruthless use of patronage. Mahone certainly was not a safe man to cross. His political machine handed out every place of preferment in the commonwealth to Readjusters, whether they were gentlemen or not. Even teachers and charitable institutions worked for the machine. Mahone's accomplishments rested less on bossing than on balancing. From the first, the movement was an unlikely and uncomfortable coalition of disparate interests: Democrats, Greenbackers, many whites with no love for racial equality, some blacks, and a large chunk of the white Republicans. Only a leader gifted in concession and in flexibility could keep it together and redefine it to catch the most votes from one year to the next.[33]

At the heart of "Mahoneism's" appeal lay its ability to deliver results, not spoils. Once in power, the Readjusters did not just set up new terms for the state debt. They shifted the tax burden away from small farmers and levied it on the canal and railroad companies. The legislature found money to reform and expand the University of Virginia, to reopen the public schools, and to widen their benefits. Black schools doubled, and the state set up its first state-supported black college. Under the Conservatives, anyone who committed a crime punishable by whipping lost the right to vote. The law fell hardest on blacks, and thousands more had been disfranchised by the poll tax. Readjusters eliminated both qualifications. With Mahone's blessing, they spread the offices across the color line. A Readjusted Virginia had black clerks and policemen, school board officials and jurors.[34]

Mahone's victory set the example for a host of Independent movements in other states in 1882. North Carolina "liberals" picked up several House seats and gave Democratic managers a scare. In Texas, the Republican-Greenbacker coalition carried the Galveston congressional district. The most promising ground seemed to be that in Georgia, where the "Triumvirate" that controlled Democratic politics had exasperated upcountry farmers. Insurgent Democrats led by William and Rebecca Felton welcomed Republican help in breaking the people's bondage "to machine politics and insolent and presumptuous Ringmasters." Hopes ran high that a "liberal" movement could put former Confederate vice president Alexander Stephens into the governorship.[35]

So far, so good; but so far was nowhere near enough to do the national Republican Party much good. Independent movements grew to a point far below majority strength, and then they broke or were broken. Many of the insurgents had local concerns—the "court-house ring" at the county seat, or

The Bloody Shirt—In Hoc Signo Vinces

"This puts me in the devil of a position"
(Stur, Puck, May 25, 1881). General Mahone finds himself caught between parties on the
Readjuster platform. Redeemer Democratic senators Wade Hampton, Joe Brown, and
Ben Hill look on scornfully.

the grievances of hill-country farmers against the Black Belt planters. Beyond their local confines, they did poorly. As long as they could not win a statewide majority, the election machinery would stay in Bourbon hands, and the odds against their winning remained as bleak as ever.

A statewide coalition would take closer ties to Republicans than most Independents dared try. They might share the same concerns. In Georgia, Independents denounced the convict-lease system and efforts to starve black schools out of existence by funding them exclusively from black taxpayers' contributions. Alabama insurgents tried to protect blacks' right to sit on juries. But there was a clear limit in how far even the bolder Independents were prepared to go, and the one charge they feared the most was that they were acting as equal partners with the black party. Always, the Feltons had to prove their Democracy by showing that they had never accepted Republican funds in the past and that if any black had come to make speeches in the Independents' favor, it was done without their consent. Even in the Old Dominion, the foremost Mahone paper pitched its arguments in a Southern key. The Funders, it warned, were tools of Wall Street brokers and the money power that Republican legislation had created. What business was it of outsiders to dictate terms to Virginia? Those true to a state's right to decide matters for itself would stick by Mahone. When even the *Richmond Whig* tried to galvanize Readjusters by ranting about racial intermarriage, the chances of a lasting coalition across race lines took on the aspects of a mirage.[36]

The earth shook beneath Democratic leaders' feet, but in most places they kept their legs under them better than in Virginia. Power was worth a few concessions. Losing the Tennessee governorship to a Republican when their party split over funding the debt in 1880, party managers adjusted much faster than Virginia's Funders had. Within two years' time they had taken up a compromise settlement that brought everybody back into the ranks except a few blue-sky conservatives bent on giving the states' creditors a better deal. Arkansas Democrats never drove their "readjusters" out. Voters ratified debt repudiation and elected Democratic nominees by the same overwhelming margins. Greenback uprisings dwindled as Southern Democrats stormed against Wall Street bankers and clamored for an inflated money supply.[37] In Georgia, Stephens won, but as a regular. Having gotten the Democratic nomination, he refused any other. The insurgents were utterly demoralized. "He, with his usual Jesuitical cunning, has completely deceived them, and placed their whole enterprise so flatly on its back, that it has no chance whatever to rise again," a straight-out Republican wrote bitterly. "The only result attained by this 'syndicate' so far, is to have Union soldiers turned out of office & in this they have been very successful."[38]

Richmond, Petersburg, and Lynchburg might have energetic dissident newspapers to present the case against Bourbonism, but farther south, every daily and most weeklies hewed to the Democratic line. Challengers might be quashed by a complete news blackout on their activities. Their speeches, rallies, conventions, and programs all might go unreported. Editors limited their notice of the most important insurgents to ridicule and abuse. Most of all, they made sure that racial fears never faded from the voters' minds. If Republicans in one part of Mississippi ran James Hill, a black, for Congress, Greenbackers in other counties would never hear the end of it. They became the associates of "saffron Jim," and their party simply "a fence for the rads to climb on." Any white who voted for Hill should expect to be shunned "as a social leper," one newspaper warned. Hill lost in 1882, and only the presence

The Bloody Shirt—In Hoc Signo Vinces

of federal deputy marshals in another Mississippi district saved the white independent James Chalmers from being bullied and counted out as well.[39]

Mahoneism thus proved more a fluke than a model. Even in Virginia, the fluke did not last. With the readjustment of the debt, the strongest reason for eastern farmers to support Mahone vanished. Even as the Readjuster legislature put through major reforms, Mahone found himself with less and less room to maneuver. His every accommodation with Republicans gave his Democratic followers more excuse to abandon him. At the same time, Mahone found limits to the number of Republicans ready to follow him. Readjustment got poor reviews among Northern bondholders and party workers who saw themselves cut out of the patronage to make room for Mahone's crowd. It was precisely because Republicans were such a strong presence in Virginia politics that the regulars could recruit prominent support up north, and they got the biggest name outside the administration to make their case: James G. Blaine. Blaine had personal reasons for joining a growing outcry against Arthur's policy, but he also spoke for views many principled Republicans found irresistible, that no lasting party raiment could be made out of Democratic shreds and patches. Old Ku Kluxers and debt repudiators would never make a New South along the lines Republicans wanted. Only more Republicans would do that, and first and foremost, the party ought to keep faith with those already in the ranks and use its basic ideals to look for converts.[40]

By 1883, Mahone had played to the end of his string. Democrats had repositioned themselves to accept the debt adjustment, had advanced fresh leaders less tainted with Bourbon reputations (but nearly as tinctured with Bourbon thinking), and had welcomed the lost legions back into the ranks. The one issue now, party spokesmen cried, was Negro rule. Mahoneism meant mixed marriages and integrated schools, with black teachers wielding the rod on white parents' children. Virginia would be "Kansasized" with a civil rights code. Let families look to Danville for the fruits of Readjuster rule! Whites paid all the taxes so that ne'er-do-well blacks could loaf in schools. "*Negro women* have been known to *force ladies* from the pavement, and remind them that they will 'learn to step aside the next time,'" one circular warned. "*In several instances white children* have been struck by grown negroes."[41]

None of the charges susceptible to proof held up, but that did not make this circular any less effective, and just before the election, Democrats had a real "outrage" to publicize when a scuffle in the Danville streets turned into a race riot. Each side blamed the other, but what was undeniable was that at the end, whites had done all the killing and blacks all the dying. The news

A cartoon of what Readjuster rule meant, issued by Democrats in the 1883
Virginia campaign.

spread across the state instantly—so quickly, indeed, that Readjusters suspected the whole incident of having been stage-managed by Democrats to
begin with. White Readjusters were panicked by the news or intimidated by
their more alarmed neighbors into staying away from the polls. In some
neighborhoods, Democrats warned black voters that they would be shot if
they appeared at the polls. Amid charges of corruption and bullying, the
Democrats won a heavy majority in the legislature.[42]

The bloody shirt, Southern-style, had been too strong for Mahone. In-

The Bloody Shirt—In Hoc Signo Vinces

"Rival rag-pickers. Republican research and Democratic damphoolery."
(F. Graetz, Puck, April 2, 1884). Illinois congressman William Springer probes for dirt on
Republicans in the Star Route scandal; Senator John Sherman does Democrats the same
disservice in Southern political violence.

stead of taking over the Democratic organization, he found himself an out-
cast, and his followers with him. There was no going back to the old party's
ranks, even if they had wanted to. If Mahone did so, he would have to
abandon his black supporters to their fate and ally himself to a party resolute
against federal spending for the internal improvements and schools that
Virginia so needed. The following spring the Readjusters turned from Republicans' allies into Republican recruits.

Mahone could not have done otherwise, but in doing so, he gave every
Democrat a club to use against any Independent movement: that they were
fronts for the Republicans, or had been, all along. There could be no faltering in the ranks, no searching for alternatives, no flirtation with sideshow
movements, as long as a strong, seducing Republican Party remained in the
North, always ready to exploit divisions among white men, always ready to
find some traitor like Mahone to lead unsuspecting Democrats into their own
ranks.

Mahone's defeat renewed the sense that, without a vigilant North, the
South would not be able to change for the better. A Republican senate
investigated the Danville riot in early 1884 and came up with the usual
appalling material for front-page stories in party newspapers. The story made
a good companion piece to senate revelations about a similar riot and spate

of killings in Copiah, Mississippi. "There are at least two more presidents in the bloody shirt," an editor asserted.[43]

But the "redemption" of Virginia did more than dabble fresh blood on the bloody shirt. It also suggested that Blaine may have been right that Republicans, not Readjusters and Independents, remained the best hope for a two-party South. To win, they must find some appeal consistent with their national party program and less unfriendly to conservative business interests than the debt-readjusting and currency-inflating notions of the Southern Independents.

The Politics of Personality

To casual students of the Gilded Age, the warfare Republicans waged on one another may look so meaningless that anyone could understand it: a clash of personalities for patronage and power, with just a little principle thrown in. And no terms get more use than those of the two great factions of the early 1880s, "Stalwarts" and "Half-Breeds."

See them, then, as popular history ranges them: on one side, the political opportunists and machine politicians. On their lips is the language of sectional hatred, in their minds nothing but a yen for office. Standing before Republican conventions, they direct their sneers at the "man-milliners," all high-flown ideals and "gush." As one heeler boasted, "I am a Stalwart, and I believe in deals."[1] Ranged against them, not quite as sordid, are the politicians for whom machines afford the means to economic ends. They fight for gain, they take what spoils they can get. But when they pick up the bloody shirt, they do so diffidently. One can imagine them listening in the Senate as Stalwarts rant against "snivel-service reform." Their nostrils twitch with impatience. Reformers irritate the Half-Breeds, too, but surely the country has more serious business to perform? tariffs to write and financial measures to perfect, for the benefit of the party's corporate chums?[2]

Look down on the ideal Gilded Age Senate, existing only in the imagination. It is April 1879. Stalwart and Half-Breed eye each other suspiciously. There, among the former, we may miss the black beard and crippled figure of Oliver P. Morton. The ruthless boss of Indiana politics has gone to what, we may suspect, was an even more ruthless afterlife, where no appeals to the flag would avail him. But we can still spot the well-fed, dissolute frame of Matthew Carpenter, the flowing mane and olive skin of "Black Jack" Logan, and the implacable countenance of Zachariah Chandler, whose hard drinking was so celebrated that a distillery in Kentucky named its brew after him. Nursing a hangover, perhaps, sits the brooding junior senator from Pennsylvania, J. Donald Cameron. A fortune made in coal, railroads, and banking never schooled him in political ethics. There is nothing any other boss could teach the commanders of the Cameron machine, and certainly not its future heir, Matt Quay, master of the three great political virtues: addition, division, and silence.[3] Reformers know them, one and all, as a pirate crew, sailing under the banners of the bloody shirt.

But our eyes do not linger long on these Stalwarts, for their leader, proud as Lucifer and as gaudy as a stage Mephistopheles, has the floor. What a magnificent spectacle is Roscoe Conkling, New York's boss! Wasp-waisted with a well-developed chest, he has an actor's flamboyance. One carefully tended lock of blonde-red hair curls down his forehead. Like a good stage actor, his eyes flash, his tones roll. Every syllable has been rehearsed, every one stings. Quite likely the speech's target is President Hayes himself, whose dismissals at the New York customhouse dealt a staggering blow to the Conkling machine. The perquisites and patronage at the collector's disposal are without compare, and so, naturally, irreplaceable.[4]

Now our eye shifts toward the Half-Breeds, again as historical fancy paints them. Representing Massachusetts are two, George Frisbie Hoar, a rosy-faced, censorious figure with a powerful conscience tempered by ambition and a sense of the practical, and Henry L. Dawes, "a cunning, experienced singed-cat kind of man," ready to support civil service reform only in the abstract and a "Chinese wall" tariff in every particular.[5] Two Ohio Half-Breeds lounge at the back of the chamber as guests, James A. Garfield, minority leader of the House, and Secretary of the Treasury John Sherman. There are no reform notions about "the Ohio Icicle," as enemies call Sherman, no misgivings about using the spoils to reward his friends; but his friends don't steal, and the Treasury has never run so smoothly. Petty, grudgeful, secretive, eminently practical, the once and future senator has made financial matters his life's work. His rhetorical closet comes complete with a bloody shirt, but it is not for all occasions; indeed, one might miss sight of it, among the row of tidy business suits that make up his stock in trade. Bankers love him; so do German American voters, but not for his temperament. Folks say that the fire screen in front of his hearth is to keep his personality from freezing the flames.[6]

The Politics of Personality

One Half-Breed towers above the rest, Maine's "magnetic man." Freshman senator James G. Blaine is gray-bearded now but still all energy. In his own way, he may be more interesting than Conkling, and more interesting because of Conkling. The two men detested each other, ever since a debate in 1866 turned into an insulting match. No major law would bear Blaine's name, no compelling, fresh visions of the uses or perils of government emanated from his pen. But he was unsurpassed in the one respect that a partisan culture honored most. As a colleague said of him, "When work is to be done: when the clouds are black & threatening, Blaine strips to the belt, and goes in." He was a dangerous customer to take on. There was a secretiveness behind the frankness, a talent for putting himself in a strong position, hard to strike, that foes discovered too late and to their cost. "Mr. Blaine is a cat-bird in the bush," one reporter summed it up, "always heard squawking, but the worst shot a gunner can get. Where you think he is he isn't, and when nowhere he pops in full sight." Better than other great men of his day, he knew how well it became him at times to have "a few brilliant flashes of silence." He made no speeches without careful prearrangement, burned himself out on no hopeless causes or radical dreams, did favors that the beneficiaries would remember, and dealt blows that the victims would come to forgive.[7]

The senator had a positive talent for vaulting to the front ranks wherever he was. When Republicans lost the House in 1875, they gained an aggressive floor leader, dauntless and unrivaled in his parliamentary talents. Scarcely had Democrats settled themselves into their places before Blaine seized the bloody shirt and turned a debate over amnesty for future Confederates into a rousing discussion of the Union prisoners of war who perished at Andersonville. "Like an armed warrior," the great orator Robert G. Ingersoll told the Republican convention that summer, "like a plumed knight, James G. Blaine marched down the halls of the American Congress and threw his shining lance full and fair against the brazen forehead of every traitor to his country and every maligner of his fair reputation." Only by turning off the gas in the convention hall and forcing an adjournment at a critical moment and by uniting on Hayes for the nominee could Blaine's rivals keep him from carrying off the prize. When the "Plumed Knight" was translated into the Senate in July 1876, he took much of the excitement of the lower chamber away with him.[8]

"Excitement" is a word grave political analysts rarely associate with the statesman. To them, Blaine was the public performer, too proud of his own cleverness to hide the way the trick was done. Instead of a plodding diligence, there was an unsettling emotional intensity. "When I want a thing, I want it dreadfully," he once remarked. That was all too clear. The insecurity, the hypochondria, the streak of fatalism that grew upon him, the petulant moods where self-pity and an eagerness for attention consumed him, all lay outside of the public gaze. That vulnerability might have made him more appealing; for to those who saw the hunger for advancement and financial gain, unalloyed with other traits, Blaine looked positively dangerous. He was, a Democrat explained, the kind of politician who would promise to "paint the moon pink and the first cloudy night he would take the voter out of doors and say, 'There, can't you see that I have done the job.'"[9]

This was politics as the liberal reformers would have seen it, and as clear an indictment of what was wrong with the system as a list of actual crimes. For these men put their own advantage foremost, and, admittedly to a varying extent, issues to them were merely excuses for advancing their fortunes or protecting their fiefdoms. Behind everything lay the true reality of politics: spoils and the financial advantages of office.

Blaine provided a striking example. Back in 1869, when he was Speaker, his help had saved a land grant for the Little Rock & Fort Smith, a Southern railroad project. Grateful, one of the contractors, Warren Fisher, offered Blaine a special deal, selling company bonds on commission. The Speaker was delighted. "I do not feel that I shall prove a dead-head in the enterprise, if I once embark on it," he assured Fisher. "I see various channels in which I can be useful." From a Speaker of the House with plenty of authority to wield "usefully," the words were ambiguous, but Blaine's demands were not. He wanted a special deal as seller of securities and reminded the company of his official service to the railroad in the past. The company submitted. Blaine sold $130,000 in securities to his Maine acquaintances and collected $130,000 of land grant bonds and $32,500 of first-mortgage bonds as his commission. Then when the Little Rock & Fort Smith fell into difficulties and its bonds became practically worthless, Tom Scott, one of the greatest railroad tycoons in the land, bought $75,000 worth of them back from Blaine's friends for $64,000, far more than their market price. Scott knew what he was doing; even as the transaction took place, he was pushing a tremendous land grant bill through Congress to benefit his Texas & Pacific transcontinental railroad plans—a Congress where Blaine was still master of the House.[10]

All this reformers knew, even if Blaine's partisans blinded themselves to the evidence so plainly in view. They knew, too, how when in 1876 a Democratic House got on Blaine's scent, the former Speaker lied about his investments. They knew, too, how an embittered clerk, James Mulligan, had exposed the truth by bringing to Washington copies of letters that Blaine had written Fisher, and how Blaine, cornering Mulligan at his hotel room, had

The Politics of Personality

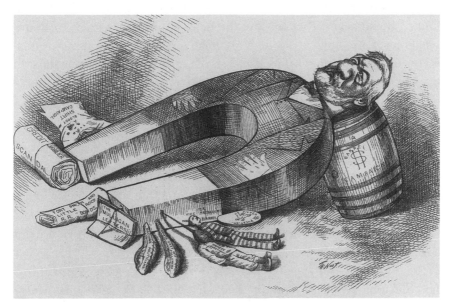

"The 'magnetic' Blaine, or, a very heavy 'load'-stone for the Republican Party to carry" (Thomas Nast, Harper's Weekly, May 8, 1880). Nast's Blaine attracts anti-Chinese demagogues, silver coinage, Mulligan letters, the bloody shirt, and political leeches.

snatched the letters from his grasp, only to vindicate himself before the full House three days later with a dramatic reading of the evidence in question.[11]

Read helter-skelter, the letters sounded innocent enough. In cold print, in the order in which they were written, they showed ethical laxity and suggested influence peddling. But how many congressmen had time to read and reflect? Reformers then could not know that the Speaker also had shaken down Jay Cooke & Co., the nation's premier banking house for a personal loan, and hinted that its own railroad projects would find a friendlier reception if it took some of the Little Rock bonds off his hands. And it wasn't until the 1884 campaign that reformers would find confirmation that Scott had bought the Little Rock bonds at the time they suspected, that his and Blaine's testimony on that matter were lies, and that Blaine had written a letter, comprehensive and false, clearing himself and had tried to induce Fisher to sign it and send it in as testimony of his own. What they did realize by then mattered just as much: that Blaine made office pay and when cornered either would lie or tell the truth in so shaded and partial a fashion that it misled the unwary completely, and that his technique worked magnificently.[12]

Personalities and selfish ends flavored politics. To reformers, it was tempting to think that they defined it, too. With such an outlook, Blaine's nomination for president made perfect sense. Arguably, the cult of personality had blinded Republicans. Partisanship, the husk of loyalty that remained after the kernel of principles was gone, kept those who knew better from speaking out once the convention made its decision. Cast in terms of personality, the real issue in 1884 could be just a simple matter of character, with the public forced to choose between an accomplished mountebank and a rough-hewn reformer.

For dramatic purposes, every bit of the portrait should be true. But it is not true. Machines there were, as were cults of personalities and scrambles for spoils. Yet they explain neither Blaine's appeal nor the battles that followed. In 1879, for all the personal jealousies that set Conkling and Blaine apart, the vying ambitions of would-be presidential nominees, there were no Half-Breeds, only administration Republicans and Stalwarts. In fact, Blaine at that moment was more a Stalwart than Conkling himself.[13]

The solution to this apparent paradox lies in the gap between what historians mean by the term "Stalwart" and what, until early 1881, most Americans understood it to mean. It had relatively little to do with civil service reform or personality politics and everything to do with the one great issue of Hayes's administration. Stalwartism began on March 6, 1877, and it began as a point of principle. Machine politicians would have plenty of reasons to detest the new president. He had filled his cabinet with momentary Republicans like Carl Schurz and unremitting Democrats like David M. Key. Soon it would become evident that he meant to make good on the promises he had made during the campaign, of meting out blows against the spoils system. Hayes promised more than he delivered, though in the case of Senator Roscoe Conkling's New York machine, the blows landed hard. But two days into the term, with civil service reform barely begun, regular Republicans already had grounds for unease on another matter. They only had to glance south.

It was on March 6 that Blaine rose for a brief "defense" of the president, which was, in fact, more in the nature of a warning. He threw back in Democrats' teeth the report that the president meant to sell out the last remaining Republican governments of the South. Later, when it became clear that Hayes would do just that, Blaine issued a protest on behalf of "stalwart Republicans," those firm in the old faith, of protecting equal rights for black voters and Northern interests against an aggressive South; and it was as Stalwarts that Hayes's critics came to be known.[14]

Blaine could not be president, but he could lead. Behind him the critics of Hayes's New Departure, and a large share of the president's other enemies, flocked. The scathing attacks on Hayes's civil service reforms that the *New*

The Politics of Personality

York Tribune carried might be signed by "Gail Hamilton," but the author, Mary A. Dodge, as most knowledgeable politicians were aware, was Blaine's cousin, a semipermanent resident in his home. No one doubted that in this, as in her criticism of the administration's Southern policy, he spoke through her. In the aftermath of the 1878 Southern elections, it was Blaine who called for a Senate investigation. When Congress tried to repeal the federal election laws and wipe out even the symbol of government protection for a free vote and a fair count, Blaine was on his feet, as devastating as ever.[15]

Blaine had far more going for him than the very real fear of a resurgent South, but until Hayes left office, that fear was at the heart of his appeal. He was the Stalwart of Stalwarts, the epitome of bloody-shirt politics. That reputation would never leave him, and for those who supported Hayes's New Departure, it was one of the first and most fundamental reasons for distrusting him.

> There was an old stalwart named Blaine,
> Who hailed from the region of Maine,
> When he felt badly hurt
> He would cry "Bloody Shirt"—
> And slay over the already slain.[16]

Unsurprisingly, presidential speculations always put him among the likeliest prospects in 1880. But another seemed even more likely as the convention approached: Ulysses S. Grant.

As the Solid South hardened into a reality, the voices, at first disparate and tentative, grew more insistent. With unrepentant Rebels in control of House and Senate, the North must meet willfulness with unshakable will. There must be a "strong man" in the White House, seasoned in national affairs, resolute in crisis, impossible to scare or bluff, and free from idealistic illusions about remaking the South on the basis of goodwill tours and Democratic postmasters. Those Stalwarts who detested Blaine—and there were many, among them Conkling and Logan—saw in General Ulysses S. Grant the one figure who could rouse the enthusiasm back home that the senator from Maine evoked and perhaps the only nominee who could rescue their wheezing machines.[17]

With the Southern rotten boroughs at his back and the strong-arm tactics of the Republican machine in Pennsylvania, New York, and Illinois to count every delegate there for Grant, whether they favored Blaine or not, the former president came to the national convention at Chicago with 306 votes. Only Blaine could have brought together a strong enough minority to keep the "political hyenas" from winning outright. With John Sherman's few dozen followers and a bevy of minor candidates, the convention deadlocked for thirty-three ballots. The third-termites' ranks held firm; it was Blaine's that started crumbling in the end. Ironically, the solution seemed to lie in the rotten boroughs of the South, powerful nowhere except in the national convention; there, some hundred Sherman and Blaine backers seemed poised to move Grant's way. By the thirty-fourth ballot, a break was only a matter of time. When the Wisconsin delegation put James A. Garfield's name in nomination, it seemed like the last chance of heading off Grant. The delegates seized it, and Blaine barely had time to release his followers before the last of them clambered aboard the Garfield bandwagon.[18]

Hayes's administration had drawn the lines of conflict between Republican factions before. Now those lines melted; now, at last, Stalwart became a title associated more with men than with measures, the proud possession of those who had followed Conkling, Logan, and the Camerons into the third-term movement. In fact, the new divisions were no more wholly about the scramble for spoils than the old ones had been primarily about it. The new Stalwart faction was a shrinking band, most of its members rooted more in the Civil War issues than in the ones that followed. They came from states where Republicans would have a hard battle to win, or where winning was hopeless. If they showed more concern for spoils than their opponents, it was because patronage was so vital. For Southern Republicans, losing the post offices and customhouses meant virtual extinction as a party. Stalwartism was less than radical Republicanism, but it carried strains of the collective memory of Reconstruction. Some still remembered, nine years after the event, that Blaine and moderates like him had crushed the last serious attempt to enforce fair elections in the South, in the so-called Force Bill of 1875. Convinced that opportunistic alliances with Democrats like Mahone were the only way to restore Republicans to power, they would not forget Blaine's rallying opposition to the policy, a sure way, as many Stalwarts saw it, to keep the party untainted by election. "Sham Republicanism," George C. Gorham called the philosophy, "for years the concubine of the Democratic Turk."[19]

"Sham" Republicans outnumbered the real ones by far. Reconstruction's end dealt a mortal blow to the Stalwarts of the South. Without newspapers, patronage, or prospects of election, they could not fend off challenges from Democrats nor from ambitious newcomers in their own party. Many were forced into retirement, and no one of equal stature remained to take their place. Elsewhere, the Civil War generation was passing. Chandler had died in 1879, Carpenter in 1881. In New York, the Stalwart machine had only barely triumphed over Blaine's friends in the scramble for delegates to Chicago in

The Politics of Personality

1880. Scarcely had the presidential campaign finished than the revolt broke out anew. But this time Roscoe Conkling found himself outmatched. He had been grooming his trusted lieutenant, Chester Alan Arthur, for senator, but when Arthur took the vice presidential nomination, the senior senator had no clear alternative. Stalwart lieutenants vied with one another, and one of them, Thomas C. Platt, rounded up the votes in the Republican caucus by making a secret pact with the Blaine Republicans, soon to be reviled as Half-Breeds. When Conkling could not trust Platt or his own governor, Alonzo Cornell, it would not take much work to knock the Stalwart machine to bits.[20]

Blaine took that task upon himself. For all his zest for battle, he had not found the Senate as congenial a forum as the House. Many of his colleagues were every bit his match in parliamentary skill and his superior for gravity and glittering phrase. Becoming a leader took patient study, not sauciness and dash. When President-elect Garfield tendered his old friend the State Department, the Senate must have breathed a collective sigh of relief. Garfield's feelings must have been more mixed, for Blaine was an overpowering presence and he was resolved to finish off the Stalwart threat for good. The "desperate bad men of the party" should not be "knocked down with bludgeons; they must have their throats cut with a feather." The new president, too, had lost patience with Roscoe Conkling, who was so quick to sneer at those who disagreed with him, sulk when needed in a campaign, and insist on the choicest cabinet posts for his friends. Before the first month of Garfield's term was out, the administration had chosen one of Conkling's enemies, William H. Robertson, for Collector of the Port in New York. Holding the customhouse was not absolutely essential for Stalwarts. They had done without it for two years already. But giving it to Blaine's floor leader in the New York delegation was worse than insulting. It was a death sentence. Conkling stormed "like a bull of Bashan," in one embarrassed colleague's words. When at last it became clear that he could not block confirmation, he resigned his seat, taking Platt out with him. Friends prevailed upon him to reconsider, and he made a desperate, hopeless fight for reelection as a "vindication." Working behind the scenes, Blaine blocked the way, driving the former senator into private life and electing Warner Miller, a Half-Breed pulp manufacturer from upstate.[21]

By then, Blaine's victory had turned to ashes. His career depended on Garfield's. On July 2, as the two men waited at the depot for the train carrying the president to a class reunion, a crackbrained Stalwart office-seeker, Charles Guiteau, fired into Garfield's back. The president spent two months dying, his husky frame wasting away as the nation watched, cruelly deceived by each bulletin of apparent recovery. And when the waiting ended, Blaine found himself with a new master, Conkling's lieutenant, Arthur.[22]

Later historians would rate Arthur higher than his contemporaries did. Despising him as a low politician and resenting him as an aristocrat, pundits never overcame their distaste. "A diamond-stud of the purest water," sneered one Democrat, "a flash of lightning without a cloud, a thunder-peal in a clear sky." It was not just that nobody thought him up to the job. Most knowledgeable Washingtonians believed him "not his own master." They knew whose master he was. "So far as I can see we are *now* in Grant's third term," Senator Thomas F. Bayard of Delaware complained mournfully. The corruption and hangers-on of the past would "be restored as far as possible."[23]

Nothing like that happened. Coming to an office he had never wanted, aware of how deeply distrusted, even hated he was, the victim himself of an attempted assassination, Arthur had no intention of justifying that hatred. Conkling came with advice: Blaine must be shown the door, not allowed to resign at a time of his own choosing. The New York customhouse must go into other hands and the cabinet remade. Arthur was sick of political warfare. He refused to heed his old patron, and the former senator stalked out in a black fury. Their friendship was gone for good. "I will have no trouble with Arthur," Illinois's top Stalwart, John A. Logan, wrote his wife before he approached the president asking favors. The interview over, he came away shaken to have found that "you can get nothing out of him about anything."[24]

Arthur set to work giving the presidency a new dignity and the White House a new coat of paint. Courtly even to his enemies, formal with his old friends, he declined to put himself on display. Reformers were pleasantly surprised when he resisted the demagogues and vetoed a measure closing off Chinese immigration for the next twenty years and dumbfounded that the president's tariff commission, packed protectionists' way, actually called for a big cut in duties. "At times I am almost disposed to applaud him," one of his harshest critics admitted.[25]

Almost. No matter what the president did, he found it hard to stir anyone to more than a tepid appreciation, and Democrats actually tried to assemble proofs that he was foreign-born and therefore ineligible. There were no wars, no crises, no crusades to give Arthur an inspiring backdrop. The Navy Department let out contracts on the first modern steel warships, the ABCD fleet, as they were known from their first initials. In this as in everything, Arthur was supportive but remote. Presidential labors fatigued him and, all too apparently to journalists, bored him. No one could be as impressive as Arthur looked, and certainly not Arthur. "It is said that a wrinkle in his coat

The Politics of Personality

"A grand Shakespearian revival
(which we have but little hope of seeing on the stage of the national capital)"
(Joseph Keppler, Puck, October 1881). President Arthur, as dissolute Prince Hal turned
statesmanlike Henry V, turns away Falstaff (Roscoe Conkling) and his rascally followers
(Star Routers Dorsey and Brady and former senator Thomas Platt). Monopolists
Jay Gould and William ("the public be d–d") Vanderbilt hold the royal train. Black
Jack Logan and General Grant look on mournfully.

shakes him up as would sudden news of a foreign invasion on our coast," one
observer commented.[26] Something vital, robust, and manly seemed to be
missing.

Blaine's friends were quick to suggest what—or rather, who. Later, there
were plausible reports that Blaine never wanted to quit the cabinet. As
Garfield lingered interminably, the secretary had intrigued to have the cabinet declare Arthur president in fact. What later generations would take as
sheer common sense (someone had to govern, and the problem would have
to be faced eventually) enemies then took as proof of Blaine's bid for his new
master's favor, or, worse, for the power to act as Garfield's regent. Dubious
stories would circulate that the new president forced Blaine out with proofs
that "Jingo Jim" had used his official powers to bully warring South American nations so that a company in which his family was involved could make a
killing in guano mining. Simple explanations worked better. While the president urged his secretary of state to remain, neither man felt comfortable in
the other's presence. Before Christmas, Blaine had sent in his resignation.
Frederick T. Frelinghuysen, the coolheaded former senator from New Jersey

who replaced him, began at once to dismantle whatever he could of Blaine's foreign policy. Overarching networks of trade and alliance were dropped in favor of separate treaties swapping special deals on tariff duties with individual countries. The Pan-American conference was left to neglect, and Blaine's handling of Chile and Peru's "guano war" was left exposed for embarrassing public inspection.[27]

Differences over policy need emphasis. Just as with the Stalwarts themselves and the contest over the 1880 nomination, the real story was not just one of thwarted personal ambition driving Blaine on but a sense of a continental vision abandoned by its inheritors. For him, there were issues at stake, issues, admittedly, that the American public cared little about, and the Senate still less; even Arthur's more modest reciprocity treaties went unratified.

Yet the essential effect of Blaine's retirement was to harden the lines within the party between Blaine's friends and Arthur's. Between Arthur and his secretary of state, there was nothing but courtesy, at least, to outward show. Invitations to dinners at the Executive Mansion and visits with the Blaine clan up in Augusta were exchanged, as well as a "very nice letter" or two of thanks and appreciation. Privately, Blaine turned his influence to repaying scores. So as Arthur tried to reach out with increasing weariness, Blaine orchestrated a private campaign of press attacks upon him. His weapon of choice was Whitelaw Reid's *New York Tribune*, the most influential Republican journal of its day. Short editorial paragraphs were drawn up for Reid to print, and their location suggested. Blaine also had time to arrange for insertions damaging his other old enemies in the Stalwart camp.[28]

In New York, Blaine set his friends to work on behalf of Governor Cornell, once Arthur's ally and now estranged from the administration; in Pennsylvania, Blaine's allies helped along a revolt against Stalwart boss Don Cameron. In both states, Republicans tore themselves asunder. When Arthur's secretary of the treasury, Charles Folger, won the New York gubernatorial nomination away from Cornell in 1882, Blaine Republicans sat out the campaign with their leader's blessing. It was they, not the fresh appeal of Democratic nominee Grover Cleveland, that sent Folger to the worst defeat of any candidate in thirty years (see Table 1). In Pennsylvania, Blaine's friends fostered an Independent challenge that helped Democrats rout the Stalwarts at the polls. Blaine made no secret of his pleasure at the president's humiliation.[29]

Blaine's campaign only contributed to the malaise within the party. Half-Breeds, most of whom preferred the name "Garfield Republicans," looked to the former secretary of state to lead them, and they never lacked for reasons to remember that their loss had been Arthur's gain. The issues of Garfield's administration were not interred with his bones. Instead, the newspapers in

The Politics of Personality

TABLE 1. REPUBLICAN LOSSES, NEW YORK, 1882

	Actual Vote	Gain/ Loss	Percentage	Gain/ Loss
Republican vote, 1880	555,544		50.32	
Republican vote, 1882	342,464	−213,080	37.40	−12.92
Democratic vote, 1880	534,511		48.42	
Democratic vote, 1882	535,318	+807	58.47	+10.05
Prohibition vote, 1880	1,517		0.14	
Prohibition vote, 1882	25,783	+24,266	2.82	+2.66
Total vote, 1880	1,103,945		100.0	
Total vote, 1882	915,539	−188,406	100.0	

Source: *Tribune Almanac*, 1881, 1883.

Note: The discrepancy between the total vote loss in 1882 and the aggregate of gain and loss on this table comes from the votes cast for the Greenback and other parties in those two years.

the summers of 1882 and 1883 teemed with newly discovered letters and correspondence unleashed to the press discussing how Indiana had been stolen in 1880, of broken promises to Conkling, and treachery in his administration. To Democrats, this news reinforced their opinion about the rottenness of the Republicans, the illegitimacy of their mandate. To Garfield's friends, it all seemed like a campaign waged by Conkling and his adherents—the president, too—to denigrate the dead man and take vengeance on his name. Indeed, Conkling's enemies traced the murder itself back to him and his president. "For you personally, my dear friend, I cannot be sorry," Garfield's widow would write Harriet Blaine after the election defeat in 1884. "The treacherous foe did not lurk in camp to help elect Mr. Blaine, and with his diabolic hatred then arm the assassin."[30]

A party adrift for new issues, a languid administration, a discredited president, and the persistence of factionalism centering on rival personalities made a dangerous combination. What made it worse was the sense of something gone badly wrong in American ethics. It was not, perhaps, the saturnalia of President Grant's day. But even while Garfield lived, there was a growing sense that the politics of personal advantage had created a shabby, grabby government, nearly incapable of handling America's new problems.

Three issues spotlighted that sense of something gone wrong in the early 1880s. The first was a scandal in the awarding of mail-carrying contracts that broke soon after Garfield came to office. Distance, rough conditions, and a widely scattered population made the desert West a special case. The mail service could not pay for itself there, nor man the field. Congress had arranged to let the work on a four-year contract. Special conditions would earn special pay. The "Star Route" contracts, so called because the agreements had asterisks by the words "certainty, celerity, and security," had subsidized delivery by horse, stagecoach, and wagon. Properly handled, those contracts could be worth a mint. Thomas J. Brady, the second assistant postmaster general, could give the job to the lowest bidder and then raise the compensation as he pleased. So he did, for a share of the take. Contractors without horses or coaches but with excellent political credentials gained hugely. To win preferment, applicants forged petitions and, in one case, took several sheets of signatures from the back of one such appeal and tacked it to one for a route in another state entirely.[31]

Garfield's postmaster general, Thomas James, and Attorney General Wayne MacVeagh broke the Star Route ring. Indictments followed. As the investigation continued, the government netted bigger fish than Brady, including Stephen Dorsey, who had done so much on Garfield's behalf in 1880. With Arthur's elevation, James retired. Convinced that the new president would not give prosecution the support it needed, MacVeagh quit. The new attorney general had full authority to bring convictions. All the same, nothing much happened. The Star Route trials took place, ending in misfires and acquittals in spite of the evidence. Dirt was flung in all directions, with Brady publishing Garfield's letters about the assessment of postal workers during the 1880 campaign, and Dorsey unburdening himself of tales of Garfield's own corruption. Three minor postal employees were convicted. Dorsey and Brady escaped. Democrats accused the administration of sabotaging the legal efforts to protect party bigwigs, though a congressional investigation turned up nothing.[32]

The second defining moment for public perceptions came under Arthur, in the summer of 1882 when Congress fashioned a spending measure to improve rivers and harbors. With the Treasury bulging and credit tightening, editors and businessmen clamored for tax relief. There were plenty of "war taxes" to remove: Internal Revenue duties on tobacco and distilled liquors and duties on imported goods imposed in the Morrill "war tariff." Instead, under the feckless guidance of J. Warren Keifer, the Stalwart Speaker of the House, and the roughshod pressure of George M. Robeson, the Stalwart former secretary of the Navy now in charge of appropriations, the Republican majority put its minds to finding new ways of spending the money. For those who confused retrenchment with "reform"—and for years, polemicists had done just that—any spending beyond the absolutely essential was stealing. Now critics found "a freshet of frauds": fat contracts for naval construction, say, and individual bills to build federal courthouses and post offices on an

The Politics of Personality

opulent scale. "UNPARALLELED REPUBLICAN OUTRAGE!" screamed one Democratic newspaper as the grabbing reached furthest. "A POOR SOUTH CAROLINA NEGRO CONDEMNED TO SIT IN THE HOUSE AND ASSOCIATE WITH ROBESON, KEIFER AND THEIR GANG." (Republican newspapers could be just as scathing. One urged the president to make Keifer America's emissary to the Punjab of Swat; reportedly, people in Swat ate foreign guests.)[33]

The "Big Divide" was in a class by itself. It was the biggest pork barrel bill in history, a $19 million river and harbor improvement measure. Money went for such nowheres as Buttermilk Channel, Cheesequake Creek, and Sheepshead Bay. Abram S. Hewitt of New York knew one such waterway well. He had fished there as a boy. It was seven miles long and never more than ankle deep. The only practical way to improve it, Hewitt guessed, would be to pave it.[34]

Party lines dissolved. Upright men put themselves on record against the "Big Divide" and ducked the final vote to let the bill go through. Northeastern newspapers were almost unanimous against the "stealing," but then the states north of the Potomac got less than a sixth of the take. President Arthur sent in a veto. Chiding the pork barrelers "like a schoolmaster," as one congressman complained, earned him good publicity, though even here, many of his critics suspected posturing: a careful nose count had assured him that Congress had just votes enough to override.[35]

The third great issue was the never-ending scramble for government jobs. Garfield's assassination had given new life to the civil service reformers. An office-seeker's attack ending an administration that had been consumed with the struggle over spoils made as good a proof as any that the system must change. If one overlooked the administration's letting Mahone dun federal departments for contributions and its use of officeholders in New York to raise a corruption fund, reformers could claim that Arthur had given them at least nominal support. The Forty-seventh Congress gave them none. On the contrary, the first session ended with a fresh scandal over the collection of assessments by Jay Hubbell, chairman of the Republican Congressional Committee. "Hubbellism" became a code word for shakedowns. Let no one heed the moral mouthings of Republicans, the *Indianapolis Sentinel* warned. "Those shrieks come from the same leaders that stole a President, bought a President and killed a President."[36]

For all these reasons, the 1882 elections turned into an apparent referendum on public ethics. The Stalwarts were sulky, their ranks sundered, their leaders sick at heart over an indifferent administration. Reformers may not have been more numerous, but they were winning a much wider hearing among Republicans with their own reasons for disliking Arthur and his followers. Independents were so swearing-mad in Pennsylvania that they

"A Big Job. Cameron, the political Aeolus, strives to master the winds"
(Bernhard Gillam, Puck, June 14, 1882). Don Cameron is overwhelmed by the
revolt against his Pennsylvania machine.

spurned the Cameron machine's peace offerings and ran a separate nominee
for governor. Ironmasters and silk stockings from Philadelphia's Committee
of One Hundred made common cause against the bosses—or, at any rate,
Stalwart bosses: Jim McManes, whose "Gas Trust" held a commanding position in Philadelphia party politics, gave them all the help he could. From
western Massachusetts, Independents issued a local appeal that echoed national themes:

> VOTE AGAINST the extravagant River and Harbor and Sundry Civil bills.
> VOTE AGAINST wire-pulling and caucus-packing politicians.
> VOTE AGAINST Keiferism, Mahoneism, Hubbellism, and Robesonism.
> VOTE FOR taking the offices from the politicians and giving them to the people.
> VOTE FOR conducting the Government business on business principles.
> VOTE FOR economy.
> VOTE FOR purity in politics.[37]

Whether the voters did so was an open question. Down south, many of
them voted for alternatives to Democratic Bourbons, if they got the chance to

vote at all. Elsewhere, Republicans posted their biggest losses in eight years. There would be 200 Democrats in the new House, against 119 Republicans, and in the Senate, Republicans would have a four-vote margin. State returns were just as dramatic. Democrats carried every important governor's race in the north. They elected Grover Cleveland in New York, old Ben Butler in Massachusetts, and Philadelphia's reforming city comptroller Robert Pattison in Pennsylvania. Republicans even lost Kansas and Michigan. "We have been beaten, bummeled and pounded and by our own people," complained Congressman Thomas Brackett Reed of Maine.[38]

The most aggressive Stalwart machines of the East were badly damaged, and in New York put out of commission for good. In that sense, Blaine gained more than he lost by the results. No other Republican could take comfort. "Congress is like a pack of whipped boys this winter," Mrs. Henry Adams commented a month later. They were so whipped that they actually tried reform. The Pendleton Act, mandating the merit system to some federal offices and giving presidents power to extend its provisions to others, passed early in the New Year. Republicans anticipating loss of the presidency two years hence were eager to enact anything that would protect their appointees from dismissal. Democrats worrying about a hard fight in 1884 were glad to get any bill making it harder to fill the Republican war chests. Washington still had plenty of patronage to hand out, enough to build machines with. Still, the Pendleton Act was a start in the push for comprehensive civil service reform.[39]

That same outside pressure drove Republicans to search for some way of cutting the surplus. Coupled with tax reductions, the "Big Divide" might not have stirred a storm. Action could be delayed no longer, especially since a Democratic House would have its own ideas and would certainly take the credit for what it did. After months of wrangling, Republicans settled on a compromise, often misnamed the "Mongrel Tariff" of 1883. Mongrel it certainly was, if system and logic were essentials to any thoroughbred measure. With barely a day between the emergence of the conference committee's bill and the session's close, all was confusion for members, journalists, and even economic experts. Days after its passage, Treasury officials had no idea whether the new tariff would bring in more revenue or less. But Congress had not passed a tariff so much as a package. Since House and Senate could not agree on the precise shape of tariff reduction, the Senate had tacked its own tariff bill to the end of the House's Internal Revenue measure. Put together, the two parts of the package did what the Pendleton bill had done, mixing partisan tactics with a down payment on reform. It would be much harder now for Democrats to make a case for "tariff tinkering" or to turn revenue reform into a compelling issue. That was one reason that many Democrats, out of sympathy with their party's commitment to lower tariffs, confined their resistance to the measure to rant and cant.

That matter of partisan tactics offers another way of seeing the significance of the lame-duck session. By passing the Pendleton Act, Congress had done to civil service reformers what the "Mongrel Tariff" did to supporters of tariff reduction: it had taken away much of their motive power. The one difference was that without Hubbellism and an active Stalwart force in politics, it would be hard to restore a sense of urgency to the crusade for the merit system. But the surplus remained, and with it the tariff issue. That issue, if anything, had come into its own.

In the clash between the president and his rival, that was good news for Blaine. Beyond his Republican affiliation, Arthur had never associated himself with the high-tariff cause. Alongside the aggressive nationalism of Blaine's foreign policy, it made a natural fit. At the same time, it added to Blaine's problems with reform-minded Republicans. Among the liberals most inclined to a professional civil service, feeling ran strong against the tariff system. It was, in its own way, a spoils system. Instead of offices being bestowed on local favorites, preferential duties were doled out to serve local interests. Blaine's commitment to protection did not distract his enemy's attention from his ethics; it only stirred the suspicion more deeply. Add to that his record as a bloody-shirt politician in an era when liberals insisted that sectionalism was no longer an issue and Blaine had fixed himself as a symbol of politics at its worst. He embodied evil as much because he came to represent the two great political issues of his time as because of his personal failings.

The history of warring faction in the years leading up to 1884, then, may turn popular accounts inside out. Personality mattered, but for the most part as it attached itself to real issues—as Blaine's would to the Southern question and Conkling and Arthur's would to a professional civil service. Except for passing moments (among them the fight over Robertson's appointment), the Republicans' quarrel was not the struggle of spoilsmen without ideas. It was a battle between conflicting views of how the party should reconcile its future course to its past tradition.

But there were others who offered very different ideas of what the Republican mission must be. True believers in the party rank and file had an agenda that threatened Republicans' hold on power, Blaine or no Blaine, spoils system or reform.

O Temperance, O Mores!

A: It looks like rain.
Q: "Well, what does rain make?"
A: "It makes corn."
Q: "What does corn make?"
A: "Whiskey."
Q: "What does whiskey make?"
A: "Give it up."
Q: "Why, Democrats, of course."
A: "What do Democrats make?"
Q: "Darned fools of themselves every four years."
—two Republicans talking, as reported in the
Des Moines Iowa State Register, September 27, 1884

No successful party can make itself over anew in a generation's time. Not just self-interest but a heritage of memory, of shared experience in battles past, binds its members. Transformation of party doctrines must take place within a narrower confine, in finding new causes that have some consistency with the old.

The only question was, *which* causes? Party tradition did not make a straight path from one goal to the next. It splayed into many roads, some of them leading in dangerous directions. By 1880, Republicans found their main problem not in finding a new crusade connected to the old but in finding the *right* new crusade.

Remove the sectional issue, Democrats had argued since the 1850s, and the Republican Party would vanish. Liberal reformers often agreed. For them, the real Republican Party had outlived its mission when it outlasted its founders. The Union was saved. Slavery was gone. Corruption, love of power, and a talent for duping the voters with dead issues had prolonged the party's reign. They could not do so forever.

Liberals misunderstood the Republican Party's staying power. From the first, it had made itself the haven for those confident that public authority could raise Americans' morals, as well as their incomes. Emancipation and enfranchisement just began government's possibilities to shut pornography from the mails, to force Protestant Bible readings on the schools, or to eradicate polygamy. Though Democrats sneered at "the party of moral ideas," Republicans took that name proudly.[1]

Religion did not define party loyalties. Still, it gave them a powerful nudge. In the rolling farmland south and east of Reading, Pennsylvania, one might come upon Pennsylvania Dutch families, prosperous, thrifty farmers with German dialect flavoring their English and an Old World look to their barns. Outsiders saw the land as all of a piece. Not politicians. For them, Berks and Lancaster Counties were separate worlds. Democrats had always carried the first, Republicans the second. One reason was that Lancaster farmers were likelier to be Mennonites, Dunkers, and Quakers, "peace sects" with long antislavery traditions, while the more hierarchical German Reformed and Lutheran churches of Berks had leaned Democratic. A joke told of an Irish Catholic on his deathbed who asked to be buried in the Protestant Swedish graveyard. As he explained, it was the last place the Devil would look for a Democrat. The more evangelical a church, and the more bent on using the state on morality's behalf, the more intensely Republican its congregation was likely to be.[2]

What governments did strengthened those allegiances. Since the end of the 1860s, the impulse within Republican ranks for enforcing a Protestant morality had strengthened. Anti-Catholicism was as old an instinct in the party as antislavery. School history texts reinforced suspicions, with their images of Protestant martyrs burning at Smithfield under "Bloody Mary," the Spanish Inquisition, and the slaughter of the innocents on St. Bartholemew's Eve. For Republicans, the Catholic Church remained an alien power, unfriendly to democracy, intolerant of dissent, and ruled by Old World ignorance. With some conspicuous exceptions, most Catholics were Democrats, especially Irish Catholics. After years of electing Catholic school-board members, Republicans could stir up nerve storms for the Protestant public school overnight, sending German Lutheran congregations to the polls in a body and bringing out Welsh Methodists to parade under banners protesting, "Yagolion rhad I bawb" (Free schools for all.)[3]

Now and again passions roused by local issues touched national Republican politics. President Grant himself had tried to nudge his party in that direction in one of his annual messages, and the campaign in Ohio in 1875 started out with some pretty flagrant Catholic bashing. "A Vote for [Governor] Allen is a Vote for Priestly Rule!" one newspaper shrieked. As the religious issue warmed up that fall, James G. Blaine briefly tried to make it his own by proposing a national constitutional amendment forbidding the establishment of religion or public funding for religious schools. The Senate expanded Blaine's proposal to shut religious instruction out of prisons and reformatories and to permit Protestant Bible-reading in the public schools. (By then, the presidential nomination convention was over and Blaine had lost interest; he failed to show up when the Senate fell four votes short of the necessary two-thirds required to pass it, and when he wrote his memoirs in 1884, he omitted the affair entirely.)[4]

Done discreetly and confined to certain localities, the strategy of appealing to militant Protestantism worked well enough. It helped elect Hayes in 1875. Not one state had a ban on public money for religious schools in 1870. Six years later, fifteen states did, and by 1890, twenty-nine. By nominating a Irish-born Catholic for mayor of New York City in 1880 Democrats brought Republicans out in force against them. William R. Grace, a very respectable mousy-faced merchant, made it through by a comfortable margin, though it was thousands of votes less than Democrats were counting on, and too little to overcome Republican majorities upstate in the presidential contest going on at the same time. Losing New York, General Winfield Scott Hancock lost his chance at the White House.[5]

On the whole, anti-Catholicism paid. When Republicans moved beyond it to the regulation of personal behavior, the benefits were nowhere near as clear. Not even all Protestants believed that to keep the Sabbath holy, all shops and forms of amusement must be shut down. Many appreciated the "Continental Sunday," where the soul could refresh itself at church and in parks, museums, or beer-gardens. Even when Protestants shared ideas of what was moral and what was not, they disagreed about how far the state should go about upholding moral values. Some considered it government's highest duty. Others agreed with mainstream Catholics that personal morality was a matter best left to the church. And increasingly, the voice of "moral ideas" had a distinct rural accent, hostile to the many cultures of the city and determined to make them conform to Yankee patterns.[6]

Trouble stirred when Republicans strengthened the Sunday laws forbidding rail service and baseball games on Sundays, though quite possibly they inspired more small-town Protestants than they alienated city voters. That was nothing compared to the strains that the temperance crusade carried with it. The Dries' case was more than religious. Workingmen spending money on drink had just that much less to save. Drunkenness caused crime, vice, and poverty. It added to brutality against women and children. It corrupted the police force. Why did fifty buildings rise in Topeka for every one in Leavenworth, one Republican asked listeners. Everyone knew the answer. Whiskey came free and easy from Leavenworth's two hundred saloons. Travelers could smell beer on the air as they picked their way down rotten wooden sidewalks. Atchison wouldn't surpass temperate towns, either, as long as its "notion of sociability is a lot of drunken men spewing over each other."[7]

At the same time, Republicans never lost sight of the partisan advantage. They associated saloons with the "dangerous classes," not with the respectable working-class and sober middle-class values with which their own party was identified. Democrats had always been the protectors of rum sellers, and of the hard-drinking Irish immigrants. The Democratic city machines always rested on a foundation of well-paying saloon keepers. "What spirit *runs* [the Democratic] party today?" asked a Republican circular in Maine during the 1880 campaign. "Answer—The *Spirit* of '*Rule or Ruin*' (as in 1861), Rum and Romanism, Rebellion and Despotism!"[8]

Most Republicans favored some kind of regulation on the saloons, but a vocal minority had no patience with temporizing courses. "They say we cannot get Prohibition, and half a loaf is better than no bread at all," Rev. De Witt Talmadge, Brooklyn's second most famous minister, noted. "That depends entirely upon whether the half-loaf is poisoned or not." If the state could issue licenses to traffic in human misery, why not have the Excise Board post fixed rates for other vices, and, say, suppress anyone who used profanity without paying for it?[9] Taxing liquor turned the state into the distillers' and brewers' partner; as long as they made money, the Treasury flourished. The price of Prohibition would go up: closing down the rum seller would force the legislature to levy new taxes to make up the loss.

Ever since the Women's Crusade sent churchgoers into the streets to pray and plead for help against the saloons in the winter of 1874, temperance forces had been massing their strength. The founding of the Women's Chris-

O Temperance, O Mores!

tian Temperance Union (WCTU) that year created one of the new, formidable presences in the struggle to educate American on the perils of alcohol and to bring the issue back into politics. Evangelical crusades flickered, appearing and then fading. Law and Order leagues were organized, open to drinkers and teetotalers alike who were disturbed at the abuse of the liquor traffic. They were often unofficial posses, there to enforce liquor laws in the big cities, where public officials had no interest in doing so.[10]

Kansas gave new life to the temperance fight. When the Russian grand duke visited the state for buffalo hunting, the lieutenant governor waved at a flag bearing the state's motto. "Duke, them there words is Latin," he explained, "and they mean to the stars after a hell of a lot of trouble."[11] No slogan could have fit the Prohibition crusade better. Until the late 1870s, Kansas had some of the toughest laws on the books and some of the loosest enforcement, especially in the rowdy cow towns where the cattle trade from Texas met the railroads going east. Exasperated with halfway measures, a separate Prohibition party had established itself in 1874. Still nothing changed.

Then, in May 1878, the movement quickened with life. Leaders of various temperance groups joined forces to form the Kansas State Temperance Union. At its head, the KSTU chose a temperance-minded state senator from Olathe, John P. St. John. By pure accident a few weeks later, when the Republican convention deadlocked, it chose him for governor. Temperance voters were not pivotal in his win that fall, if only because they never threatened to withhold their support. For Republicans, taking their votes was like the Dutch taking Holland.

Idealism had carried St. John from the Union army into radical Republican politics and then to the fore of the temperance supporters. He was not yet an outright Prohibitionist. But he was a quick learner, and again events took an unexpected turn. When the new legislature convened, enemies of a stronger local-option law discovered the foolproof way to block it. They would divide the temperance forces by offering a constitutional amendment forbidding the sale or manufacture of alcohol. There was slim chance of it winning the two-thirds needed in both houses, none that the voters would ratify—or so they imagined. They mistook public sentiment. The governor embraced the amendment and helped lobby it through. With his aid and the evangelical skills of the temperance union, the voters were schooled thoroughly. In 1880, they ratified the amendment and reelected St. John.[12]

Saloons closed in the small towns. In cities like Leavenworth, they gave way to drugstores, where customers refreshed themselves on fifty-proof patent-medicines. Anybody could get a drink who wanted it, but the hindrances made fewer Kansans want it. Someone asked Senator John J. Ingalls how the ban was working. "Oh, first rate," he answered. "The prohibitionists have all the law they want; the other fellows have all the whisky they want. Consequently everybody is happy."[13]

The Kansas miracle inspired hope in Dries everywhere. Until now, they had passed laws, not constitutional amendments. Only Michigan and Ohio had gone that far. They forbade the legislature to issue liquor licenses; saloon keepers simply sold without one. Now temperance advocates in every state from Massachusetts west to Nebraska rounded up signatures and peppered the legislatures with petitions for a Kansas-style Prohibition amendment. Local option dried up counties; where states failed to act, high-license laws drove marginal gin joints into bankruptcy; and laws required the schools to instruct in alcohol's evils. Everywhere, the WCTU spread a temperance constituency with new chapters and pamphleteering.[14]

Six states adopted Prohibition during the 1880s. Dries hoped for far more, but in the early part of the decade, anything seemed possible, and many more states put through restrictions of varying intensity on the liquor dealers. Pushing the fight, all the important national temperance groups met in 1882 to give the Prohibition Party new life. The party itself had been an almost invisible presence since its founding in 1869. Now there was a change both in name (to the Prohibition Home Protection Party) and in spirit. In fourteen states, temperance forces ran their own ticket. They gathered 92,821 votes.[15]

That spelled real trouble for Republicans. Prohibitionists were deeply, intensely Republican, which made them the bitterest enemies of a party that had proven recreant to its uplifting traditions. In view of Republican lawmaking, the rage seemed a harsh one, but Prohibitionists looked to enforcement, not to enactment. They pointed to a liquor traffic vastly greater after twenty-four years of Republican rule than it had been under a Democratic president. "Every distillery in the land has greater protection than any home, any school house or any church in the country," St. John protested.[16]

Even as the Prohibitionists summoned the more extreme temperance advocates out of Republican ranks, the rush toward temperance legislation drove other Republicans off in the other direction. Many Americans, especially those in the big cities, loved their liquor and resented Sunday closing laws with every dram they drank. One spacious pleasure spot in New York actually looked forward to police raids as a floor show, and customers laughed as bartenders were hauled away. They had every right to laugh. Law enforcement was the longest-running farce in town. Policemen made a great show of stopping the beer spigots at one end of the counter while taps flowed at the other.[17]

O Temperance, O Mores!

More than a love of liquor was at stake. Distillers were as likely to vote Republican as not, and brewers contributed to party war chests. Without the German vote, Republican majorities would have been wiped out in Cincinnati and Cleveland, and Germans, Catholic and Lutheran alike, disliked any regulation of their private lives. Prohibition aimed its fulminations at the dark saloons, those all-male retreats where whiskey flowed and vice flourished, an establishment light-years away from the *bier-gartens* in the German neighborhoods, where Sunday afternoon outings often took in the whole family, and where the most offensive entertainment available was an ill-tuned German band. Prohibition struck a blow at "personal liberty." Regulating one personal habit, the state earned the right to regulate all. "Why, the next thing they will do will be to say that we shall not eat corn-bread; shall not eat tomatoes," an orator thundered.[18]

Handled clumsily, the issue stirred up religious anxieties in the wrong place, among Catholics more than among their enemies. Prohibition breathed "the spirit of the inquisition," a Kansan reminded secular readers. "It is the spirit of church and state, one and inseparable." Even Republicans who supported a ban on alcohol muttered privately that the crusade dulled citizens' sense of fair play in the use of public authority. They got so used to treating the wicked brewers' property as they pleased that in time, they came to think that they could do that with anyone's—including the railroads'! "Our party went mad on prohibition and would nominate no man for office who was not a crank on that subject," Iowa's James "Ret" Clarkson later complained.[19]

When the issue was drawn so clearly along the lines of Prohibition or regulation, Democrats could hardly lose. They could even hold a share of the moderate temperance vote. They could argue that Prohibition only mixed hypocrisy with drinking. Their representatives in Iowa's legislature proposed a tough alternative to Prohibition, and elsewhere, Democratic support for tougher licensing on saloons allowed them to take the sting out of Republican charges that they were the rum sellers' lackeys.[20]

Kansas showed how much trouble the temperance issue could cause Republicans. If any state should have been secure for the party of moral ideas, it was St. John's. Outside of Atchison and Leavenworth, border towns with Missouri habits, Democrats made a miserable showing. When one Republican orator declared, "A Democrat has no business in Kansas," he was simply stating what seemed an obvious fact. More than Nebraska or Iowa, Kansas had a native-born, Protestant population, and even many of its immigrants were of an evangelical strain, friendly to the idea that government must advance morality.[21]

Yet the drying out of the state upset all calculations. Republicans usually won by tens of thousands of votes. The amendment carried by a scant 7,998. Democrats had never won twenty-seven counties. Prohibition's enemies did. Now some Republican leaders stayed mum, hoping that the whole issue would go away, and St. John with it. Others opposed it openly. Unhappiness over Prohibition was not the only crimp in St. John's bid for a third term. Still, George W. Glick was an outspoken critic of Prohibition. He did what no Democrat had done before or would do again for fifty years to come: he won the governorship.[22]

Results elsewhere in the Midwest were more mixed that fall, though again, debates over sumptuary legislation put Republicans on the defensive everywhere. As soon as Iowa Republicans carried their amendment, they started losing German voters. Democrats in eastern river counties came nearer to winning than they had in years. In Wisconsin and Illinois, temperance anxieties frayed nerves and shaved Republican majorities. It removed it entirely in Indiana, and the votes the Grand Old Party had talked of reaping at "Temperance Harvests" showed up to elect a Democratic congressional delegation. The fifteen hundred true believers that voted for Neal Dow in New York in 1880 swelled to twenty-five thousand (Table 1). Even in New England, restiveness about stricter liquor laws gave Democrats their edge.[23]

But it was Ohio that showed most plainly the risks that Republicans ran. No Republican state took harder fights to hold, most years, and hold it the party must: losing it in a presidential year meant almost unavoidable defeat nationwide. Seventh in the nation in the number of breweries (169) and responsible for producing one-tenth of the country's beer, the state had fifteen thousand liquor sellers. It also had a vigorous temperance movement.[24]

Inspired by events in Kansas, 200,000 citizens signed petitions for a local-option law in 1881. When the legislature failed to act and the GOP convention offered a cautious platform, temperance advocates were furious. A Prohibitionist state convention nominated a state ticket and called on like-minded voters to measure every legislative candidate by his stance on Prohibition.

Governor Charles Foster was ready to brave it out, or thought so. He had never felt much sympathy with the temperance activists. He pledged the bare minimum of what the Dries wanted, a constitutional amendment giving the government power to license saloons. The Brewers' Association had such strong reassurances that it bankrolled the Republican campaign. Foster won reelection, and Republicans carried Ohio that autumn, but the Prohibitionist Party did unexpectedly well. It took sixteen thousand votes, eight times its

O Temperance, O Mores!

TABLE 2. OHIO PROHIBITION PARTY VOTE TOTALS

Presidency, 1880	2,616 (0.36%)
Governorship, 1881	16,597 (2.65%)
Secretary of State, 1882	12,202 (1.92%)
Governorship, 1883	8,362 (1.16%)

Source: Tribune Almanac, 1881, 1882, 1883, 1884

old following (Table 2), and, knowledgeable insiders thought, had the potential to poll four times as many as it did. Most of them certainly were recent Republicans.[25]

Still treading cautiously, Foster called on the newly assembled lawmakers to give Prohibitionists a symbolic victory—let temperance legislation be left to the people—by submitting three constitutional amendments of differing severity. Instead, the legislature passed two laws, the Smith Act closing saloons on Sunday, and the Pond Act, levying a tax on saloon keepers. City authorities, even Republican ones, gave up enforcing the Smith Law almost at once. Within a few months, the supreme court had struck down the Pond Act as unconstitutional, licensing under another name. As a result, Republicans had put through two laws with nothing to show for either. That, Prohibitionists suspected, had been the idea all along.[26]

Even granting Republicans' good intentions, the Pond Act would have done them little good with the more ardent Prohibitionists, for whom taxation seemed worse than no action at all. Stronger overtures would be needed to attract the ultratemperance vote. With that in mind, three days before the Prohibitionists held their convention, Governor Foster made a stunning about-face. He endorsed both the Pond and Smith laws. More than that, he singled out the brewers for attack. The question, to the governor's mind, was simple: would the Sunday laws be enforced, or would the state give in to the "Liquor-Dealers' Rebellion"?[27]

Foster's timing seemed shrewd. From the start, the "temperanceites" had disagreed over whether their strongest influence lay in running a separate ticket or in endorsing those major-party candidates who served their cause the best. A few friendly words from the governor might strengthen the disgruntled Republicans ready to cooperate and weaken the irreconcilables. There was no getting around the Republicans' record anyhow. Making a virtue out of necessity, the party might pick up more "honest democrats" than it lost "bastard republicans." Women would rejoice at the crusade, and, Republican strategists calculated, they were good for any number of husbands' votes.[28]

Many partisans lined up willingly behind the governor. Democratic victory would mean "Free Whiskey and No Sunday!" newspapers warned. German American protests, the *Cleveland Leader* scolded, were simply the ravings of "delirium tremens manufacturers." Other Republican papers called the foreign-born critics "Hessians," hired soldiers for either side, and invited them to go home. There would be no retreat; on the contrary, Foster promised, Republicans would advance the cause when the elections were over by drafting a Prohibition amendment for voters to consider.[29]

Almost immediately, the strategy started going wrong. The Prohibitionist convention, when it met, did not take the bait. If Foster so appreciated their principles, delegates announced, he was welcome to join their party himself. They were not about to be lured into his, not with halfway measures like the Pond Law. Murat Halstead, whose *Cincinnati Commercial* ranked as the foremost Republican newspaper in the state, pleaded that the liquor issue should not enter into the canvass at all, since the real offices at stake were those of congressmen, who could do nothing about setting state policy; let the topic rest until 1883, when a new legislature would be chosen. Senator John Sherman, whose support had always been particularly strong in the German communities, was equally unhappy with Foster's initiative. As one Cincinnati congressman put it, "The Dutch are h−l."[30]

So were the Democrats. To keep the Prohibitionist ranks intact, every Republican hypocrisy became front-page material, from the "whiskey dealers" that temperance-minded Republican papers had endorsed for office to the barrel of beer that the "party of moral ideas" had let its delegates soak at local conventions just the year before. At the same time, Democrats did their best to persuade German voters that "Flopper Foster" meant every temperance word he said. As appropriate mottoes, the *Plain Dealer* suggested that the local party convention put up those choice quotations from the Grand Old Party: "D−n the Dutch," "The Germans should be strung up," and "People who drink beer are hogs." A fresh Pond Law would just be for starters, Democrats warned. Let Ohioans look to what Republicans had done that year in Kansas and Iowa, if they thought Prohibition impossible; and let them keep in mind Republican threats to punish German quitters after the election by drying up the state in earnest.[31]

Corruption, extravagance, and river and harbor steals all entered into the public debate. Even so, the central issue was inescapable. Disgusted or discouraged, contributors closed their wallets. The usual campaign cost $22,000. This year, the GOP could scrape together barely $10,000. Even the postmasters refused to fork over. Their campaign clogged by "Pond lillies," Republicans lost seats in the House. If their legislators had been up for

O Temperance, O Mores!

election, they would have lost the General Assembly as well. "THE DEMOCRACY TRIUMPHANT!" the *Hocking Sentinel* crowed. "SUNDAY WILL OCCUR AS USUAL. CHURCHES AND SCHOOLS WILL CONTINUE. AND WHISKY WILL NOT BE FREE—BUT WILL COST 10 CENTS PER DRINK!"[32]

"What a campaign!" the *Commercial* fumed. "It was a race of idiots for a front seat at burlesque political theatricals." Postmortems assigned the blame beyond question. Voices like that of Rutherford B. Hayes, who claimed that "Sunday School politics" had been a minor reason for Republicans' failure that fall and that "the boss system" was the main culprit, were few. They were also very likely wrong. The big losses were in the larger cities, especially ones like Toledo, Sandusky, Cleveland, and Cincinnati with large German communities (Table 3). Republicans carried Hamilton County (Cincinnati) by some 3,500 votes in 1881; they lost it by nearly 11,000 now. Between 1876 and 1890, Cuyahoga County (Cleveland) went Democratic exactly twice, in 1882 and in 1883. A 6,800-vote lead was changed to a 2,500-vote loss.[33]

The urban vote, or, more precisely, the German vote, was lost to the Republicans. It had no intention of being "Yankeeized" or "Scotch-Irished," one defender warned. If the Republican Party meant to be run for moral meddlers' benefit, and to be "banged in pieces on the question of woman suffrage, and . . . driving our distilleries and breweries to Covington and Newport, . . . and if the great test of morality is to be that each man shall guzzle from his own bottle on Sunday as a religious exercise—why, there should be recruiting stations for cranks immediately established, for in that case the German army has marched out never to return."[34]

Yet there was no retreat. What Foster noticed was the Prohibitionist totals. Without the temperance lean to the party, Foster guessed, the Prohibitionists might have taken fifty thousand votes or more. Instead, their totals were down to twelve thousand, just about the margin by which Republicans lost their state ticket. Fine-tuning the law and some concessions to the friends of a "Continental Sunday" might keep the Dries and even regain some of the German vote. The legislature returned with that cause in mind. It enacted the Scott Law, taxing retail liquor sellers, and left the question of Sunday sales to municipalities. In a concession to German voters, and an open bid to split the distillers and brewers' interests apart, the measure laid only half the tax on those selling beer and wine that it did on those dealing in hard liquor. Four thousand saloons would go out of business in one year, and county treasuries looked forward to two million dollars in new tax revenue statewide. Thinking he knew a winner when he saw one, Foster took credit for putting the Scott Law through.[35]

Democrats thought otherwise. They pronounced the Scott Law an intru-

TABLE 3. DEMOCRATIC AND REPUBLICAN SHARES OF THE VOTE IN THE FIVE OHIO COUNTIES WITH THE LARGEST DEMOCRATIC GAIN

	1880 Presidency	1881 Governorship	1882 Secretary of State	Gain/Loss from 1880
DEMOCRATIC				
Hamilton (Cincinnati)	46.06%	46.37%	59.19%	+13.13%
Cuyahoga (Cleveland)	40.23	40.51	52.64	+12.41
Erie (Sandusky)	46.6	48.72	55.35	+8.75
Lucas (Toledo)	44.11	49.58	52.81	+8.7
Franklin (Columbus)	50.85	50.35	53.74	+2.89
Ohio	47.01	46.25	50.12	+3.87
REPUBLICAN				
Hamilton (Cincinnati) (16.99%)	53.78	52.73	40.72	−13.06
Cuyahoga (Cleveland) (13.74)	58.82	58.17	45.53	−13.29
Erie (Sandusky) (14.96)	51.61	49.14	42.1	−9.51
Lucas (Toledo) (12.27)	52.75	47.63	45.17	−7.58
Franklin (Columbus) (7.03)	48.65	47.24	44.51	−4.14
Ohio	51.73	50.09	47.09	−4.66

Source: Tribune Almanac, 1881, 1883
Note: In no other counties did Democratic gain over 1880 reach 5 percent. Numbers in parentheses refer to the percentage of residents of German birth. The number of German Americans (that is, those with at least one German-born parent) is necessarily higher.

sion and a dead letter, sure to be knocked down by the supreme court just as the Pond Law had been. Even those Dries who accepted the principle of taxation agreed. Only a constitutional amendment would do the job, they warned. Rather than leave matters to shuffling politicians, activists led by the WCTU gathered over 160,000 signatures for one outlawing the sale or manufacture of alcohol entirely. Republican legislators endorsed it and another, explicitly permitting taxation of the liquor traffic. Both of them went to the voters.[36]

If Republicans had believed their own claims that saloon keepers would endorse the Scott Law, they were disabused quickly enough. Brewers assembled and announced that they would buy no more barley until after election

O Temperance, O Mores!

day. Once Prohibition went through, farmers might find their best customers gone for good. Real estate owners feared that Prohibition would bring a drop in property values. Businessmen predicted financial disturbances, even a run on country banks.[37]

Democrats chose a candidate superbly fitted for exploiting the opposition's discontents. A Republican until 1872, Judge George Hoadly had no wartime record to explain, no race-baiting past to justify. He was an urbane, well-paid Cincinnati lawyer who had supported Tilden and reform in 1876 and had come to the front of the fight for "personal liberty" now. Democratic strategy gave Republicans an equally poor target. They embraced temperance by other means: a graduated tax, a licensing system, and certificates of good moral character from all license seekers.[38]

Banking on the Scott Law as a winning issue, the Republicans might have emphasized the taxation amendment and downplayed the so-called second amendment, if the state supreme court had obliged them by striking down the Scott Law as liquor-licensing under another name. Instead, the judges upheld the law. The state needed no new power to regulate liquor sales, it argued. That made the amendment unnecessary. As a result, Prohibition came front and center.[39]

Plainly, Foster left a pretty awkward legacy for the Republican nominee, Joseph B. Foraker. Even as they sold themselves in general terms as the defenders of temperance and protectors of the family, Republicans edged as far as they could from the referendum. They protested it no party measure and touted it as a ploy form smothering the fanatics for good, by letting the people speak their will. But the women of the WCTU, not party organizers, did the proselytizing and showed up at the polls. They rented homes near polling places to decorate with flowers and banners and recruited men to distribute Prohibition ballots. Voters might even see an emblem, children kneeling in prayer, and a motto in terms Prohibition's enemies had tried to make their exclusive property: "Personal Liberty, for God and home and native land; as for me and my house, we will serve the Lord."[40]

Hoadly won, to nobody's surprise. He was the first Democrat in thirty years to get an outright majority. Democrats won the legislature, too. Their margins slipped a little in the cities, rose a little in the countryside. All the amendments failed badly. Republicans were just grateful that they had done no worse. They gave Foraker the credit and Foster the blame. If the party had endorsed Prohibition, John Sherman commented, Ohio would have buried them by fifty thousand votes.[41]

Yet, were there not some promising signs amid the ruins? The Prohibitionists had lost one voter in three from the year before; their party now

**TABLE 4. DEMOCRATIC AND REPUBLICAN SHARES OF
THE VOTE IN OHIO'S 1883 GUBERNATORIAL RACE**

	Democratic	Republican	Democratic Gain/Loss from 1882
Hamilton (Cincinnati)	52.08%	47.92%	−7.11%
Cuyahoga (Cleveland)	50.46	49.54	−2.18
Erie (Sandusky)	60.89	39.11	+5.54
Lucas (Toledo)	56.43	43.57	+3.62
Franklin (Columbus)	53.64	46.36	−0.1
Ohio	50.08	48.2	−1.88

Source: *Tribune Almanac*, 1884

polled just half as many true believers as in 1881 (Table 2). Many who turned out to vote for the amendment stayed to vote Republican. The German revolt did not seem to be as bad in 1883 as it had been in 1882. Republicans still lost the cities, but by nowhere near as much (Table 4). As other states had shown, Wet voters reacted. Apparently, they did not realign. Once Prohibition had been cleared away as an option, many of the fears of the moderate Wets might vanish. So would their newfound Democratic leanings; they had given Democrats "the cold and dirty shake" before.[42]

Democratic forces, then, stood a good chance of coming up against the same limits that confined Republican revival in the South to local, short-lived Independent movements. The party's victories came because it had identified itself with a local political cause that had no equivalent beyond the state level. The issues from the off-year elections gave them conflicting guidance about what direction to go in a presidential year.

Yet Ohio elections offered another hint, easy to overlook amid the "temperanceite" clamor. Democratic gains in Ohio's countryside had less to do with wine than wool. Sheep-raisers were incensed at the lower duties that the 1883 "Mongrel tariff" had put in place. The Democratic campaign promised to restore the old rates. Distancing itself not just from free rum but free trade, the state platform promised protective duties where labor got the benefit. Soon protectionists in the party across the country were talking up the "Ohio idea" as the way to win the presidency in 1884.[43]

That assumed that Democrats knew what was good for them. Did they? As one editor growled, "We have so many infernal fools in our party that any success sets them crazy."[44] How crazy the new Congress, just about to open, would give him indisputable evidence.

O Temperance, O Mores!

The Protection Racket

If moral issues lured and snared Republicans in the early 1880s, the tariff issue threatened Democrats with a like fate. First enacted in 1861, the Morrill "war tariff" became, in one congressman's joke, "a thing of duty and a jaw forever."[1] Its sponsors urged it to help raise revenue to suppress the Rebellion and to push the nation toward self-sufficiency by crimping foreign competition. It still did so, collecting far more money than the government needed. By 1881, the Treasury had a $100 million surplus, and every month the surplus grew. This was no good thing. The more the Treasury took in, the tighter private credit became. So much money lying idle tempted congressmen to use it in lavish new ways and a lot of weary old ones: pork for constituents, private pensions and relief bills, public buildings for two-bit cities. "A surplus revenue breeds extravagance and jobs as naturally as putrefaction breeds maggots," one editor asserted. By 1882, with its "Big Divide," the clamor for tax relief had become too powerful for politicians to ignore. "Revenue reform" found champions in both parties, differ though they might about what "reform" involved.[2]

With very few exceptions, and those being radicals or academics of modest political standing, no genuine free-traders existed. Abolish the tariff and even a skinflint government would go into the red. Practicality required at least a tariff for revenue only, its duties covering government expenses. The question was, should it go beyond that? If it offered protection, how much?

Should it hamper foreign imports or wall them out entirely? And for whom should the protection be directed?[3]

Protectionism was more than blind atavism, even for "Chinese wall" congressmen like William D. "Pig-Iron" Kelley of Pennsylvania, who apparently never saw a duty he didn't like. Spokesmen could make a plausible argument for high tariffs, not just on economic grounds but as part of the Republican tradition. Clay, Webster, Lincoln, and Hamilton hovered over it in spirit. To its defenders, it was nationalism personified, a policy where all paid and all gained. Even as Americans shared the costs as consumers, they shared its blessings as producers. In that sense, it was more than a thousand different rates: it was a *system*, binding farm and town, labor and capital together with a netting of self-interest.

America's industrial progress since 1860 was not just due to the tariff. Machinery, mass production, division of labor, and the creation of a national market had transformed the country. But to defenders of protection, the tariff ushered in all the great advances. As they argued it, the tariff had opened mill and mine and given them the home market to keep them running. The tariff sheltered "infant industries" from large-scale competition until they could fend for themselves. It rebuilt a simple, agricultural economy, dependent on world markets and vulnerable to every change in foreign demand, into something more complex and less easily affected by slumps on the grain or cotton exchanges. Most of all, protectionists insisted, it upheld high wages and steady work, and gave American labor more money to spend on the goods that other Americans made.

To make cheaper goods at lower wages, just to swap the "home market"— really all that American producers needed—for the chance at a wider foreign trade was to trade the reality of one prosperous domestic consumer for the mirage of a mob of foreign paupers. Given all these assumptions, protectionists tried to paint themselves as the only true Americans. Their enemies would sell them out to foreign influences, England's in particular.

Tariff reformers could reply that their ideas reflected a deeper faith in America. They, at least, believed that with protection removed, American industries could still compete with those of the world and with wage levels intact. Cheap labor with sickles could never beat high-priced labor with McCormick reapers. American know-how and high quality were the real secrets of growth, said reformers. Industrialization had begun before protection went into effect, advanced quickly in some businesses where rates were low, and occurred unevenly across a country protected by the same schedules everywhere. If the tariff really made healthy industries, able to fend for

The Protection Racket

themselves, how could a cut in rates close every factory in the country, as protectionists sometimes claimed?[4]

The tax on foreign trade really fell on American consumers, reformers argued. Manufacturers charged more because overseas competitors had to sell their goods with the cost of the tariff built in. The very seamstresses in New York City, sewing coarse trousers at seven cents a pair, paid a 25 percent tax on their needles and an 80 percent duty on thread, Congressman Samuel "Sunset" Cox pleaded.

Did protection raise wages and keep them up? Did it make a shock-proof economy? Anyone remembering the hungry 1870s, the wage cuts, the army of tramps on the roads, and jobless men looking for work knew the answers. The supply of available workers set the wage level, and industrialists made sure that level remained as low as possible. They kept the nation's borders wide open to workers, even if not to products. Child labor worked the protected mines, and "half-clad women" fed the furnace fires. Claiming that raising the duties on one-fourth of all American industries would raise wages for the nineteen workers in twenty who worked in unprotected businesses was, as one critic put it, "like saying that to dam the Hudson River would raise the level of New York Harbor and consequently that of the Atlantic Ocean."[5]

There were just a few things wrong with the reformers' case. Tariff rates and all, prices were going down, not up—protection's doing, according to its defenders. In fact, machinery allowed more products to be made at lower cost; an expanding railroad network let them be shipped at less expense. Protectionists could cite case after case in which goods cost so little that they undersold English goods in London itself, even with shipping costs tacked on. Higher prices did not matter, either, if wages outpaced them. "We used to have to pay a pound of dairy butter for a pound of ten-penny nails," one Republican boasted, "and now we can buy a pound of ten-penny nails for a quart of skim milk."[6]

Reformers could not deny that American wages were the highest in the world. In many industries, they afforded a bare living, but any work was better than none, and most working-class families knew from harsh experience how close to poverty a slump in demand could bring them. If there were not jobs enough for all now, would there be less or more once English "pauper labor" crowded its wares into the market? Revenue reform might open wide enough foreign markets to make up for domestic consumers lost, or it might not. However slight, the risk in competing with "Mongolians" at "nine cents a day" was there.[7] Low prices were all very well, as long as consumers had the money to buy goods; but lower prices and lower wages or work stoppages often went hand in hand.

All the conflicting currents of gain and loss made the tariff an awkward issue to deal with nationally, but an enticing prospect locally, where one or few products had protection and consumers paid duties on many. No one really knew for sure *how* the tariff issue would play, in the end. There were so many variables. Would voters think more as consumers or as producers? Would they feel that the gains from across-the-board tariff cuts outweighed the risks from more specific changes affecting themselves? Who would line up where? Even a hasty survey showed that farmers and businessmen had two minds about protection. Merchants especially liked to import, and imports slowed as rates rose. However keen on keeping out Canadian hops the growers of upstate New York were, brewers just down the road resented paying artificially high prices for their materials. Canada and Australia had wool, Canada its forests, and Nova Scotia its coal. Eliminate the tariff and farm prices would have to fall to world-market rates, too low for Northeastern producers to stay in business. By contrast, farmers on the prairies never felt the impact of protection on their behalf, only in the cost of what they bought.

Because the tariff affected so many interests in varying ways, it had real drawbacks in partisan terms. General Winfield Scott Hancock had blurted out the truth in the 1880 campaign and had been laughed at for his simplicity: the tariff was a local issue. Missouri wanted lead protected, Louisiana cared above all for sugar, Syracuse demanded help for its salt, Troy for his cuffs and collars. Tariff reformers supported schemes of reduction that tiptoed around products from their own neighborhoods.[8]

Localism was the greatest apparent weakness in the tariff and its greatest political strength. Reformers were quite right when they claimed that the system, as it had developed, was a hodgepodge, irrational and unscientific. For years, the Ways and Means Committee refused to consider removing "alkakange" from the schedules. The very thought put its chairman, "Pig-Iron" Kelley, who was unaware that there was no such thing as alkakange, in a pet: it had slipped into an earlier tariff when a printer tried to put together some spilled type into a plausible-sounding word. Every bill invited logrolling and favor swapping. Introducing a measure into Congress, as social critic Henry George gibed, was "like throwing a banana into a cage of monkeys."[9] But the "war tariff's" attention to local interests protected it from serious assault. Any reduction would knock some beneficiaries out of the arrangement and turn them into enemies of the protective system: why should they be taxed, as consumers, to benefit the industries that reform spared? On the other hand, as long as everyone got something, congressmen would never

The Protection Racket

give up their power over the tariff to any independent commission of experts. They would not give the president the untrammeled power to raise or lower rates, either.

The intricacies of tariff-making discouraged any but the most diligent lawmakers from comprehending the tariff as a whole. But it was as a whole that the tariff *issue* emerged in the early 1880s as the solution to many of both parties' problems. For a dozen years after the Civil War, the tariff had remained a muddled territory. Both parties favored revision, and neither party got much of anywhere with it. Tariff reform sentiment ran from the prairies across Ohio. It added force to the liberal reformers' revolt against the Grant administration in 1872. But as long as most Democratic congressmen came from the Northeast, where sentiment for protection was strongest, there could be no united voice on the matter. It was a Republican Congress in 1872 that put through a "free breakfast table," with lower rates for coffee, tea, and sugar, and an across-the-board reduction for other items.[10]

Redemption cleared up some of the muddle between party lines. The Solid South pushed the bulk of Democratic lawmakers into the low tariff camp. Democrats still differed, especially in the industrial Northeast, though the protectionist ones had to defend themselves against an increasing number of associates who called the high tariff "robbery" and "a system of legalised communism."[11] By then, states just across the Appalachians that once had held strong tariff reform sympathies had industrialized further, and Republican reform sympathies there had waned. Within a generation, protection became the Republican orthodoxy just about everywhere.

For Republicans, protection was all the more useful because it allowed them to find a new mission consistent with the old. They could even make a virtue of the tangle of tariff schedules: it fit well their ideal of a society of many interests cooperating rather than competing. The tariff more than anything illustrated how an injury to one would be an injury to all. That nationalism that had saved the Union from Confederates would now save it from John Bull. It was an easy step from protecting black former slaves to protecting wage-earners in danger of being reduced to the slavery of pauperism. English domination had always been an appealing bogeyman to wave about, ever since the Revolution, and Republicans now saw ways of using it to appeal to Irish American voters, until now dependably Democratic.[12] The very term "war tariff" bound present policy with past accomplishments.

Emphasis on the tariff, however, was more than the old party doctrine rewarmed. Republicans could cloak it in the language of family, the language that the temperance crusade had adopted. High rates protected the home, wife, and child. There would be an added benefit, as well. The surplus must be reduced one way or another. What if it were used to build up school-houses? What if, instead of lowering the tariff, Congress took the duty off whiskey? At first glance, this might seem a boon to distillers, the last thing that Prohibition-minded Americans would want. On the contrary, protectionists argued, it would break the "Whiskey Ring." Tax or no tax, the demand for distilled liquor would remain steady. The biggest distillers, the only ones able to make spirits in such bulk that they could turn a profit with taxes in place, would lose their advantage over smaller manufacturers. At the same time, the government would have freed itself from dependence on the revenue that distillers brought in. One of the biggest arguments against Prohibition—its effect on Treasury receipts—would be removed.

It might also break the Solid South and efface the Civil War issues that still marked party lines there. Northern observers had seen a different society in the making, a "New South," where factories and small farms were replacing the plantation economy. Trumpeted by editors like Henry Grady of the *Atlanta Constitution*, the New South had freed itself from dependence on the great cash crops. Railroads rebuilt Atlanta within a year of General Sherman's burning it down. Twenty years more, and open fields in northern Alabama had turned into an ironmaking center, dynamic Birmingham. As lowland rice plantations in the Carolinas decayed, enterprising Southerners imported new strains of rice that could grow in the onetime cotton fields of upland Louisiana. Making money, onlookers asserted, the New Southerners would have no interest in making trouble. Their willingness to abandon fire-eating talk and race-baiting was more than a business decision. With the Old South fading into a memory, the way of thinking that carried so many states out of the Union would fade as well. Merchants, farmers, millhands, and mill owners would put their pocketbook interests first rather than herding together as white men or Confederate veterans. Loyalty to Alabama iron and Kentucky hemp might trump Democratic habits.[13]

The right kind of revenue reform might make it possible. Southern whites, especially in Virginia and North Carolina, detested the Internal Revenue taxes even more than the tariff. Cut the government's intake there, and votes could be made among the orchard-growers, whose fruit went into spirits. *Using* the surplus rather than wiping it out might broaden the Republicans' appeal. Instead of seeing the tariff as a hindrance, voters interested in river and harbor improvements (like Louisiana), or levee construction (like Mississippi), or more generous veterans' pensions (like Northerners) would have a stake in continuing its operation. Late in 1883, Blaine himself offered a revenue-sharing plan. The federal government could keep

The Protection Racket

its taxes high but turn the surplus back to the states, to apply as they saw fit: for building schoolhouses, perhaps, or for property tax relief.[14]

Henry Blair, New Hampshire's senior senator, had a different idea. Building on a long-held dream of radical Republicans, he proposed to have the federal government underwrite public school systems nationwide: 105 million dollars' worth over ten years. Each state would receive a share, based on its illiterate population. The Blair bill appealed to temperance-minded Americans who saw schools as the ideal means of inculcating proper values; indeed, the WCTU supported the bill heartily. So did the Knights of Labor. White Southerners, unhappy about funding black education, would welcome the outside help. Their states would get most of the money. Black voters, disappointed at how little Republicans had done for them at the ballot box, would find their old faith renewed by a measure that would surely give them more and better schools than Redeemers allowed. Wipe out ignorance, partisan Republicans predicted, and government would wipe out Democratic majorities. Give blacks the schoolbook and respectable white Southerners would come to trust them with the ballot, eventually. As an appeal to the South across race lines, then, the Blair bill offered magnificent possibilities, the more so because Northern Democrats were so hotly against the bill and Democrats in the cotton states almost unanimously in favor of it. And, of course, as an incidental benefit, it might make the surplus seem more a boon than a bane, and with it the tariff rates that made a fat Treasury possible. Posing the choice between "Intelligence & Protection vs. Ignorance & Free Trade" would open "the southern strongholds of the Democracy to Republican theories & early supremacy," Blair predicted.[15]

Democrats, too, saw in the tariff issue a way out of their difficulties. Tariff reduction afforded them a platform with national, not sectional support. It reinforced the party's antimonopoly credentials by illustrating how the tax system robbed the poor to give to the rich. "A patent medicine monopolist's bottle of sarsaparilla sold for $1 is taxed four cents," the *Indianapolis Sentinel* raged. "A workingman's woollen undershirt, valued at $1, is taxed 90 cents. Vanderbilt's bank check for $1,000,000 is taxed two cents. A workingman's dollar's worth of rice is taxed 85 cents."[16] At the same time, the crusade brought them recruits among Northeastern importers and scholars in politics who until now had always associated the Republican Party with their own best interests. Many a business might trade protection for itself for a chance at free raw materials. As a way of trimming the surplus, tariff reduction would appeal to firms wanting easier credit: an emptier Treasury put more money in circulation and lowered rates. It also removed the greatest temptation to pork barrel spending and corruption, by making giveaways and subsidies impossible without raising revenue from new means.

All these considerations explain why the tariff had become not just a substitute for old issues but a fitting complement to them. Halfway through the 1880 campaign, with their prospects flagging, Republicans had picked up the tariff issue. Later, a generally unreliable reporter gave Blaine the credit for the brainstorm. "You want to fold up the bloody shirt and lay it away," he told the party chairman. "It's of no use to us. . . . Those foolish five words of the Democratic platform, 'A tariff for revenue only,' give you the chance." In fact, Garfield had come to the same conclusion himself and pressed campaigners to push "the business aspect" harder. Whoever came up with the change in strategy, it worked spectacularly. Stumping Ohio, one Democrat found every manufacturing town littered with posters warning against "Democratic free trade as dictated by the South." Electing General Hancock "meant the closing of mills and foundries, and the 'blowing out' of furnaces." Whatever the realities, protectionists credited the GOP turnaround in the October states to the shift away from bloody-shirt topics. New Jersey and Connecticut went narrowly Republican, and high-tariff spokesmen on both sides knew why.[17]

Revenue reformers insisted that their case had simply been mishandled, and their eyes turned west of Ohio. There the clamor for tax relief sounded to their ears like the cries of an army of consumers, ready to bring the tariff walls tumbling down. To them, the 1882 returns were a mandate for freer trade. "The worms in the new-made graves laugh at the prospect of all-Irish linen shrouds to feed on," a reformer gloated. "The unborn babes are leaping to learn of the gorgeous flannels in store for them." From Iowa and Nebraska, party leaders swore that free trade could redeem their states and give Greenbackers a down payment on Democratic rhetoric about antimonopoly. By 1883, reformers took their cues from Henry Watterson of the *Louisville Courier-Journal*, author of the 1880 tariff plank and the loudest spokesman for what he called "the Star-Eyed Goddess of Reform." Kentucky's Democratic convention that summer set forth the doctrine frankly. And the place for the crusade to begin must be the House, where South and West would dominate.[18]

Even before the Forty-seventh Congress adjourned, the Speakership race for the Forty-eighth had begun. Political observers bruited about plenty of possible candidates, but the only serious, lasting candidates were Samuel S. Cox of New York, John G. Carlisle of Kentucky, and Samuel J. Randall of Pennsylvania.

"Sunset" Cox's candidacy was the most easily disposed of. For all his bright, chaffing humor and quick tongue in debate, he lacked the stature—physically as well as politically—for the job. Having been Speaker in the late 1870s, Randall had to be taken seriously. He was one of the best parliamentarians in the chamber and a rigorous defender of the Democratic faith in cheap government and states' rights. Always present, unfailingly alert with a motion or an objection, his clean-shaven, "Napoleonic" face one of the first that visitors to the gallery recognized, Randall made himself the terror of jobbers. His Philadelphia district ran from the financial marts downtown to the worst slums along the waterfront. What both had in common was an undying faith in protection and in Sam Randall, which, to his working-class constituents' thinking, were pretty much the same thing. No Republican had a chance against him, and the party machine drew district lines to keep him in the House. On the tariff, at least, they would never find a Democrat they liked better.[19]

In every state, there was someone, highly placed in business or politics, that Randall could contact. Many of them owed him favors: a committee chairmanship given, a tariff revision blocked, a public building appropriation ferried through by the Speaker's timely recognition. Veterans of the Tilden organization rallied behind him, and Tilden himself let friends know that Randall was his choice. Increasingly out of step with low-tariff Democrats though Randall was, he could use the Speaker's power to bury the tariff issue until after the presidential election. Industrialist politicians from the New South flocked to his cause.[20]

Far less familiar than either of his competitors, John G. Carlisle was bookish, even-tempered, and comfortingly commonplace. Observers likened his pale appearance to that of a "very proper clergyman," or an invalid, never a politician. Still, when the gentleman from Kentucky rose, members noticed, he always had something to say and the careful study to back it up. What he had to say was, on every issue but one, very much what one might expect from Randall himself; but that exception was the tariff. If the party meant "reduction" when it spoke of tariff "reform," if its promises of change meant the raising of fresh men from a new generation, Carlisle was the only practical choice. In any case, having cast most of the Democratic votes in the House, the South wanted a little recognition: a Speaker from south of the Ohio.[21]

By the time Randall's friends took the Carlisle candidacy seriously, it was too late. Carlisle's friends not only had gotten congressmen pledged to their side; they had the vows sworn publicly. A secret ballot might have allowed enough bad faith for Randall to win, but tariff reformers had no intention of giving double-dealers the chance. On December 1, the caucus met. The result was not even close. The Kentuckian carried the first ballot by more than two to one. Jaw firmly set, his face full of pain, Randall rose and made a game pledge of support for the winner.[22]

Carlisle's supporters read great things into the result. It had broken with the privileged interests, the "bloodsuckers" and tired old political leadership, erecting what one of Cox's friends called "a new brilliant Edison Electric Democratic Light House for the country." For Randall's friends, and for the dwindling band of protectionist Democrats everywhere, the caucus vote came as a shock. Recriminations flew against the whiskey ring and Rebel brigadiers. "Democrats, having obtained a patent right for d–d fools, appear unwilling to suffer any infringement of their right to the invention," stormed one Grange leader.[23]

A perception that the South had beaten the North and meant to dictate terms was an ominous one, though not exactly true. The vote *had* been sectional. Only eight Democrats voted for Randall in the Deep South (Cox got none), and twelve in the Upper South, a far cry from the majority that Randall had been promised. But as one observer put it, the Speakership owed more to a solid West than a Solid South. West of Ohio, Randall found only two supporters. Carlisle should have felt equally uneasy. East of the Appalachians, north of the Potomac, only two representatives voted for him. Many turned a receptive ear to the warnings from Randall's camp that electing a Kentuckian would inflame the North. Quite conceivably, charges of sectionalism did just the opposite among Southerners. By reminding them that Randall's supporters still held them as on probation unless they voted right, it alienated them from the former Speaker for good. Even more potent was the Northeast's uneasiness about a ham-handed "reform" of the tariff. Carlisle's election increased their alarm. Editors who had promised to deliver their congressmen now vowed to destroy them or bring them round next time.[24]

The Speakership fight served as an omen of the drawbacks in adopting tariff reform as a rallying cry. But it also committed the Democrats to action. Having chosen Carlisle, they could not afford to end the crusade there. Within a few weeks, the Speaker had put a reform-minded majority on the Ways and Means Committee and legislating began.

Party leaders never expected success. They wanted to design an inspiring failure. Tariff reform might limp out of the Democratic House; it could never survive a Republican Senate. But Democrats would have written themselves a platform for the fall. They would have shown that the party of obstruction could do constructive legislation. Properly handled, a tariff bill could reassure manufacturers of Democrats' moderation, even as it gave revenue re-

The Protection Racket

formers a down payment on past promises. It would give the lie to the impression, so damaging in 1880, that Democratic rule would bring radicals, agrarians, and free-traders into policy making.

Still, success hung on a few very improbable *ifs*. If Democrats stuck together and Republicans did not, and if tariff reformers kept protectionists on the defensive every step of the way, the bill the House passed might be a failure to be proud of. But that assumed qualities that long years of obstruction and short weeks of public life had not given the new Democratic majority. Some of the oldest members had the oldest grudges, and their skills were not of a kind that might rescue a faltering cause.

Just such a man was William R. Morrison of Illinois, new chairman of the Ways and Means Committee, in whose care any new tariff legislation lay. Gallery visitors might see him pacing the aisles, a brawny, gray-bearded man, looking rather like a crossroads storekeeper, his hands stuck deep in his pockets. He spoke rarely, unmemorably, and awkwardly. For parliamentary law or coalition-building, Democrats had a dozen members more capable and a hundred more tactful. All his merits were quiet ones: integrity, doggedness, and a sense of duty. Morrison did not trim his principles to suit the fashions. He believed in hard money, low tariffs, and administrative reform even before those issues came into fashion among his constituents.[25]

Six years on the sidelines, while Randall ran the House and then led the Democratic minority, made Morrison's passion for tariff reform stronger than ever, but there was an added personal savor to the achievement he had in mind. Randall and Morrison had taken each other's measure long since. Each had blocked the other's advance at one time or another. For years Randall had been able to hedge, voting with the protectionists but feigning sympathy with reform. Now he would be forced on record, his deviance from the party line exposed. Make the tariff issue central to Democratic Party fortunes, and Randall would be out of the running for Speaker for all time to come. There would be no serious negotiations between the former Speaker and his old enemy, no effort to find a common ground.[26]

Tariff reformers shared Morrison's confidence. Confronting Randall, they were sure to gain and he to lose. But this calculation rested on two doubtful assumptions, that Randall could not muster enough Democrats to prevent a vote on Morrison's bill, and that Republican ranks would break reform's way.

Randall had sound reasons for resisting any bill acceptable to Morrison. Pennsylvania's electorate breathed protection sentiments. Rate reductions would slaughter his friends at the polls. A Morrison tariff would be just the platform for Morrison, but it would rule his enemy out as a presidential prospect and might doom any other Democratic nominee in November. But a taste for revenge sweetened the former Speaker's desire for a battle. Apparently, most of the House Democrats had been convinced that they could do without him. They needed a hard lesson, and Randall had just the teaching credentials for the job.

The learning began as soon as Morrison won the chairmanship. Members returned from the Christmas holidays with troubling news. Far from being inspired, voters were worried. Louisianians would not stand for any cut in sugar duties. Mississippi wanted jute protected, South Carolina insisted on guarantees for rice, Alabama for iron. Distillers and tobacco farmers in the Upper South cared less about the tariff than the Internal Revenue taxes they paid. Any tax cuts, they thought, ought to come there. Not "doing something for wool" would cost the Democrats Ohio, Michigan, and California. Pragmatists high in party councils urged that the whole subject be buried until the presidency had been won. Make free trade the issue, Ohio's senator-elect warned, and six Southern states might desert the party. Morrison's own estimates put Randall's followers at forty or more. Without Republican reinforcements, that number would doom tariff reform, and the reinforcements could not be found. Some Republicans favored tariff revision, many more did not, but all could agree that the party that made the tariff originally was the only one that could be trusted to streamline it, and that a season of unsettled economic conditions, one year after the last "tariff tinkering," was the wrong time for action.[27]

With the forces already ranging against them, revenue reformers needed a bill easy to explain and short on detail. Any measure adjusting rates on several thousand items would require weeks of hearings and then fill thousands of pages in the *Congressional Record* with damaging debate. The closer to free trade a bill came, the harder it would be resisted. So Morrison hit upon a solution that Republicans had tried in 1872: a simple bill, reducing all duties by 20 percent. That would be a smaller reduction than the Tariff Commission had recommended, and Morrison's bill had the added proviso that in no case would duties fall below what they had been in the original 1861 "war tariff." The closest thing to real reform was a wide new list of duty-free goods: coal, salt, and lumber among them. By eliminating certain items from the tariff, they knew, "the protectionist chain of mutual interests" might unlink in future revisions. "Put lumber on the free list [now] & Conger & Sawyer [from the timber states of Michigan and Wisconsin] will go smashing everything [in the rest of the tariff]. Salt will sicken Hiscock [who represented the saltworks of Syracuse] & a lot of others."[28]

Tariff reformers tried to mask their disappointment. "How is it possible to defend it?" the head of the *New York Herald*'s Washington bureau protested.

The Protection Racket

"Every argument you make for it, is an argument agst. the tariff entirely." To protectionists, on the other hand, Morrison's "horizontal bill" showed how little the Democrats understood rate-making. Some duties would stay exorbitant, even with a 20 percent cut. Other industries would suffer hugely by any trimming at all.[29]

Even taken on its own terms, Morrison's bill seemed a pretty poor makeshift. Would it really cut down on the Treasury surplus, as promised? If imports stayed steady, a cut in duties would reduce customhouse revenues. But trade did not work that way. Some products had a more flexible demand than others. As rates fell, imports would rise. Revenue collection might actually increase. Real surplus reduction, in fact, might require very different means. Raising rates to prohibitive levels would close imports out of the customhouse entirely; putting goods on the free list would let them bypass it.[30] In both cases, the government would take in less money. Either method, of course, would be economically disruptive, though it would affect fewer industries than any across-the-board plan. And if surplus reduction mattered most, there was an easier way still, the one that Randall's friends proposed, of abolishing or reducing Internal Revenue taxes.

The bill was crude, unscientific, and cautious. Still, as one Republican admitted privately, "it was a *staggering* at something that ought to be done." It was, in fact, more than the Democratic majority could do. When the party caucus met on March 25, members agreed to let Morrison's bill go forward, but, without making it an official party measure. No Democrat needed to fear the consequences of opposing it.[31]

In the weeks that followed, tariff reform leaped from one moment of crisis to the next. Using his power as chairman of the Appropriations Committee, Randall delayed reporting funding bills for weeks. When reported, those bills would take precedence over any others. Timed properly, they could delay discussion of the Morrison bill forever. But as winter changed into spring, it became clear that Randall needed no such expedients. His following in the House held firm. Ohio Democrats had pledged themselves to restoring wool duties. Morrison's forces were able to defeat a special bill, doing so by a mere five votes. Scarcely a week later, the House agreed to consider the Morrison tariff by only two votes, and some of the majority did so purely as a personal favor to the beleaguered chairman. Debate continued, but always with the tariff reformers on the defensive, with protectionists taunting them to bring the bill up for a vote. By now the message from back home was too strong for wavering members to miss. The only constituents who cared about reform were those fearful of its injuring them. "I don't pretend to be a 4,000-horse power statesman," a Missouri congressman allowed, "and I don't find many of that kind in Congress. . . . In my district there are iron works and glass furnaces employing several hundred men; also large lumber interests and various manufacturing concerns. . . . When they write me that they don't want any reduction of the tariff my judgment tells me I ought to vote against a reduction." Morrison's own allies were so dispirited that they started floating alternative measures even before the committee bill had come up for a vote.[32]

Each narrow escape dimmed the prospect of any real reform passing the House. Talk of some "trade or dicker with the Randall side" stilled. By early May, everyone knew the next move. The opposition meant to offer a motion striking out the bill's enacting clause. If it passed, that killed the measure. If it failed, consideration could proceed, but the price of final passage would be a debilitating barrage of amendments on behalf of coal, salt, lumber, wool, and endless other products. The bill that emerged would have been unrecognizable, and, as Morrison himself admitted, worthless. Either way, the vote would be close. California's six Democrats would turn the scale.[33]

They turned it Randall's way. On May 6, with galleries packed to suffocation and backstairs lobbying exhausted, George L. Converse of Ohio made the long-anticipated motion. It carried by four votes. Together, the majority party had been bested by 118 Republicans and 41 Democrats. More than half the Democrats came from Pennsylvania and Ohio; California, New Jersey, and New York provided most of the rest.[34]

Dazed by their defeat, Democratic leaders tried to persuade themselves that something could yet be saved. It took them a week to find out otherwise. New York ironmonger Abram S. Hewitt came forth with a bill of his own, half changes in administrative procedure and half tariff reductions. It widened the free list and imposed a more selective "horizontal" reduction of 10 percent in certain schedules. Southern congressmen conferred about measures ending the tobacco tax and easing the duties on peach brandy and applejack. But none of these measures had a chance of passing Morrison's committee. The chairman was tired and heartsick. He had no intention of reporting another tariff bill and meeting another humiliation. Nor would he give his enemies the satisfaction of cutting the surplus any other way.[35]

Reform had met a mortifying failure. Free-trade theorist David Wells asserted that free trade had advanced further in three months than in the twenty years past. "Perhaps Mr. Wells can tell us what advantage a precocious child has other children if, when it is three months old, it is able to roam at large in the streets and is run over by a milk-wagon," the *Chicago Daily News* responded aptly.[36] Morrison's downfall exposed the gap between "tariff revision" in the abstract and rate reduction in the specific. If a Democratic

The Protection Racket

"Her platform going to pieces"
(Bernhard Gillam, Puck, March 26, 1884). John G. Carlisle and Sam Randall go opposite ways on the tariff. As the crown of shamrocks suggests, Democracy has an Irish pedigree.

House with a seventy-vote majority could not put through a measure as conservative as "Horizontal Bill's," political revolution alone could achieve anything more drastic.

That revolution could not begin without purging the party itself. Already the Democrats had turned on each other. As Randall stepped into the aisle, his face aglow with triumph, a Missouri congressman shoved into his path. "Mr. Randall," he shouted, "in my opinion you are no more a Democrat than Judge Kelley." "Hereafter we must place you as the champion of the worst monopolies and the avowed enemy of the people at large," one partisan wrote him.[37] Tempers cooled, but Randall had reasserted his power in the House by methods that ruled him out as a force in his own party's councils. No man whose strength rested on a working alliance with the Republicans could ever hope to be Speaker again.

Randall's decline as a national figure had only begun. For the first time, the Pennsylvania Democracy was his to command; in contrast to the threats and pistol-brandishing of four years before, there was hardly a flicker of dissent at the state convention that spring. Randall himself wrote the tariff plank.[38] And Randall had made his point. If Democrats wanted unity, they would have to drop tariff reform.

Republicans would not. Their ranks virtually unbroken, they had used the session to float other means of diminishing the surplus. None could get through the House, but all put the party on record, tying the protective tariff to the party's old concerns and its new aspirations. One such bill helped just about every disabled Union veteran who had served ninety days; it contrasted sharply with House Democrats' version, which insisted on proof that the injuries had something to do with the war, and its Mexican War pension bill, which set up no bar against supporting veterans who later rallied to the Confederate service. More cantankerous because it broke party lines on both sides was the Blair education bill, amended to insure matching state funds and with the federal grants limited to $77 million. Most Northern and border-state Democrats opposed it, but those from farther south hailed the idea. Alabama's John T. Morgan stood almost alone in warning that education would make good field hands forget their place and that the millions would be spent better shipping blacks to the Congo. Any measure that would raise four-fifths of the sum from Northern taxpayers and spend three-fourths of the total on the South was hard to resist.[39] On terms such as those, Republicans just might bring out a larger black vote that fall and induce white Southerners to pack away their prejudices.

If the tariff fight complicated Democrats' platform-writing, it simplified the presidential race. Safety dictated a nominee as little associated with the tariff issue as possible. Naturally, that ruled out Morrison, Randall, Carlisle, and Hewitt. But it also worked against Thomas F. Bayard of Delaware and former senator Joseph McDonald of Indiana, each of whom had placed himself too squarely among the tariff reformers.[40]

Most of all, the debates marred Tilden's chances. Low-tariff men never trusted his friendliness to Randall. Now as his associates tried to smother the issue, the "sage of Gramercy's" hand was seen behind every maneuver against the Morrison bill. When a protectionist circular appeared in the Capitol, some reformers ascribed it to the Tilden "Literary Bureau." The

The Protection Racket

closer Tilden and Randall seemed allied, the more controversial nominating either one grew.[41]

The outcome of the tariff fight, then, may actually have enhanced Democratic prospects. It forced the party to look outside of Congress for its standard-bearer and shoved it away from a stance that surely would have cost it the North. By itself, Morrison's failure was more reassuring than the "horizontal bill." When a big Democratic majority could produce nothing worse than stalemate, protected industries would never think Republican victory that fall a life-or-death matter.

Was it, indeed, a life-or-death matter for any of the groups that had feared Democratic revival? What did Democracy mean by this election year?

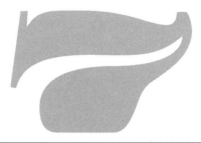

The Democrats Rise from the Dead

To join the Democratic party is to go down among the dead men at once,
and to chain one's self to the dead past forever.
—*New York Tribune*, July 6, 1882.

Take the critics at their word, and the 1884 election would turn on the need
for reform. Only two questions stood out: Could the Democrats deliver? And
what, exactly, *was* reform?

Whatever the definition, some Democrat, somewhere, fit it. Opposition
and the federal system had permitted the party luxuries that only those free
from the national responsibility for running things could enjoy. Taking party
traditions as a starting point, Democrats locally could range not just in any,
but every, direction. They had no need to stick to one opinion on the tariff or
currency expansion, race relations, or even temperance. All they had to do
was put distance between their beliefs and Republicans'. The result was not,
as some suggested, a party with no ideas but rather one with far too many. All
of them pointed to "reform" in the mid-1880s but differed in what direction
and on how far it should go.

Professionals and merchants who supported the "Swallowtail" wing of the
party in New York City shared the thinking of the so-called Bourbons across
the South and West. They emphasized the party traditions of states' rights
and limited government power. The less authorities spent, the better; the
stricter city charters confined the taxing power, the less money "tax-eaters"

would find for stealing. A state that kept order and protected property suited them best, free from all the meddling paternal notions of Republican morals and political economy. Quite a few Democratic leaders not only protected property but amassed it. They included railroad men like James J. Hill of St. Paul, whose empire was stretching toward the Pacific, or railroad and coal barons like George M. Baer and Frank Cowen of Pennsylvania, whose hatred for Republicans never compared with their hatred as "Christian men of property" for labor unions. In Georgia, the party virtually belonged to the "Triumvirate," led by former governor Joseph E. Brown, who owned railroads, coal mines, and factories.[1]

Those who appreciated Democracy at its most austere took as their heroes men like the conspicuously patrician Senator Thomas F. Bayard of Delaware, the kind of public servant that the Founders would have devised: clean-shaven, clean-minded, and "straight [postured] as an Indian." Elected to his father's seat in 1869, he moved through a corrupt time with hands unsoiled by bribes, compromises, or even day-to-day political involvement. Proud to be a gentleman in a vulgar time, Bayard despised spoilsmen and radicalism. His stock in trade, the subject of endless speeches, was the need to get back to constitutional principles and limited government. The senator lived to do his duty and highly appreciated his own purity. No Bayard acted the demagogue, which, as he defined it, was anyone who favored "class legislation" for farmers or workers, endorsed a protective tariff, or wanted a money supply backed up by something other than gold.[2]

He was not, in other words, like the Democratic governor of Massachusetts, Benjamin F. Butler, who claimed as good a grounding in party tradition as all the Bayards. By the time Butler won the governorship in 1882, he had been a radical Republican and a Greenbacker:

> Rare old Ben, with the bias eyes,
> Rare, and tough, and extremely sly;
> Busy all day and up all night,
> Free of speech and quick in fight;
> Up to snuff with your guileless tricks,
> The hold of your high hat full of bricks,
> Scoffed, and hated, and feared of men,
> Rare old Ben!
> Rare, and no gravy.[3]

Butler did like a scrap. He was never happier, as one newspaper put it, than when he could prove that a coal heap was a snowbank, and that black was white. But his career showed a consistent belief that there was nothing wrong

"Senator Bayard strikes his grand attitude on the tariff question"
(Bernhard Gillam, Puck, January 23, 1884).

in using government power to protect the weak against the strong. By the 1870s, his heresies about expanding the money supply and his readiness to use government to enrich his friends made him too hot for Republicans to handle. Even before he left the party, he had joined House Democrats to uncover the rottenness that kept Tilden out of the presidency. A year more and Butler's friends had won him the Democratic nomination for governor.

The Democrats in Massachusetts had been just ripe for a takeover. Outside of Boston and enclaves in milltowns, the party ran short on voters; inside of them, it ran short on leaders with a statewide appeal. For years, the gap had grown between their genteel Yankee leadership and their more earthy, ethnic

The Democrats Rise from the Dead

rank and file. The gentlemen cut the ticket in 1879 when Butler ran for governor, but his showing was astonishingly good. Then, in 1882 a divided Republican Party allowed Butler to win.

His one year in power was not exactly a disaster. It was more like a performance, sometimes outrageous and always entertaining. Butler went out of his way to pick fights, notoriously his attack on the Tewksbury Almshouse, which he accused of selling deceased inmates to Harvard's medical school. Nothing could compare with the sensational charge that the medical students were wearing footwear and carrying wallets made from paupers' skin. Shocked and disdainful, Harvard withheld the customary honorary LL.D.[4]

Which Democrats spoke for the party as a whole? Even in the wake of the 1882 elections, liberal reformers like former secretary of the interior Carl Schurz, E. L. Godkin of the *Nation,* and George William Curtis of *Harper's Weekly* looked at the Democratic Party uneasily. To them it still seemed the party of leftovers and losers, better at nagging the natural party of government for whatever it tried to do than at doing things itself. Its constituencies were the unrespectables, the priest-dominated offscourings that lived in big-city slums, topers and saloon keepers, black-killers and Union-haters. As for the notion of a party of spoilsmen and bosses protecting civil service reform, who would believe it?

Witness the fate of George Pendleton of Ohio. As a wartime "copperhead," inflated-currency spokesman, and railroad attorney who was widely thought to have bought his Senate seat, "Gentleman George" stood for everything the Godkins saw wrong about Democracy. Then, suddenly, Ohio's senior senator became a champion of civil service reform. By the time his bill passed in early 1883, reformers had forgiven him everything. Surely one good term deserved another. Instead, Ohio Democrats could hardly wait to serve Pendleton's head on a platter. Governor-elect Hoadly had the patronage and former congressman Henry B. Payne of Cleveland the "barrel" to beat Pendleton. Payne's money helped make him senator-elect. There would be no newfangled reform ideas about him or the so-called Coal-Oil Democracy. Payne was tied to Standard Oil through his brother Oliver, who sat on the board of directors (which explains the faction's nickname: "coal oil" was the term for kerosene, Standard Oil's leading product). He favored a high tariff and detested the merit system. If Democrats won, he told supporters, they should fire the place-holders en masse. "An Augean stable cannot be cleaned with a toothbrush!"[5]

To most Americans' minds, however, Democratic corruption showed itself most plainly in boss-run New York City, where John Kelly's Tammany Hall controlled the favors. A fraternal society that had become one of the most powerful forces in the downstate Democracy, Tammany appealed to slum dwellers, Irish and Catholic voters, saloon keepers, and purveyors of vice needing protection. It had no patience with civil service reform notions. Its "shoulder-hitters" raised a row at the polls, and its "paint-eaters" consumed every perquisite that municipal office opened to them. For selfishness and corruption, no image was more enduring than that of Tammany's grand sachem in the early 1870s, William M. Tweed. His ring stole $200 million from the city in six years, shook down corporations wanting favors at Albany, milked estates and firms in receivership, and helped along Democratic election totals by wholesale naturalizations and an occasional creative counting. Pilloried by Thomas Nast's cartoons and newspaper exposures, Tweed fled the country and was brought back from Spain to die in prison in 1878.

As far as reformers cared, the tiger had not changed its stripes, only its boss. From 1872 to 1886, "Honest John" Kelly ran Tammany Hall. Twenty years before, he had been sheriff, earning his nickname by raking in nothing more than the fortune that the office's legal fees allowed. A quarrel with Tweed drove him out of office and into exile. After Tweed's fall, the respectable Swallowtails downtown still needed every vote a cleaned-up machine could muster. That required a boss that no grand jury could touch, even a Republican one. "Honest John" seemed a natural. By 1874, Kelly had Tammany running smoothly again, strong enough to elect a governor and mayor. Muckrakers later would describe him as a dictator, crushing rivals and marching his underlings in lockstep. It went without saying that New York was robbed—with a little more discretion, perhaps, than in Tweed's day—and misgoverned.[6]

Such was the image that Democrats would need to counter, then, if they were to be trusted for national office. How they did so became the great legend of later popular history: how in 1882, Republican scoundrelry opened the way for Grover Cleveland, a clean Democrat from upstate, whose war on machine politics—and, more critical historians would say, his usefulness as a corporation tool—made him the indispensable candidate for president. The true picture is much more complex and covers a far wider canvas. Far from the negative outlook that the term "Bourbon" implied, then, or the imagery Thomas Nast fashioned for Democrats, of a conclave of skeletons, representing dead issues, Democracy was alive and, on the local level, could be surprisingly flexible.

Only with the midterm elections did Democrats have the chance to show just how broad and positive a program they could have. Nothing could fit the old party more than its black-hating ways. But for many reasons, in the late 1870s, Northern leaders had begun to change. As long as blacks voted, they

The Democrats Rise from the Dead

were worth appealing to, and former Republicans brought their sympathy with civil rights into Democratic ranks. Nobody much noticed when a Tammany congressman nominated a black teenager to West Point and a Tammany state senator put up the funds to pay his way there; even from a neighborhood where rioters hung blacks from lampposts in wartime, such a gesture could be seen as a local curiosity. But in 1881, when a Democrat offered a bill strengthening the state's civil rights law, every assemblyman on his side of the aisle but one voted it into law. During the war, Leon Abbett had been a race-baiting New Jersey assemblyman. As governor in 1884, he helped enact a civil rights act to replace the national law that the Supreme Court had overturned. Even more noteworthy, when the Hackensack Cemetery Company refused to let a mulatto sexton be buried on its land, Abbett sent lawmakers a special message calling for an end to discrimination in graveyards. Democrats in both houses helped put a bill through. Thomas Waller and George Hoadly, the Democratic governors in Ohio and Connecticut called for civil rights laws, too, and got them with overwhelming bipartisan support. When Rhode Island Republicans offered a similar bill in 1885, Democrats countered with a stronger one, and carried it, too. Ohio's leading black newspaper, the *Cleveland Gazette*, caught the moral plainly: "The world moves, and with it even the Bourbon Democratic Party."[7]

It moved in other ways. Just as the two parties had found ways of connecting their traditional values with opposing views of the tariff, Democrats hearkened back to Andrew Jackson to strengthen their commitment to government action against "monopoly," an elastic term that could cover anything from a dominant railroad to a strike-breaking employer. For many Democrats, Western farmer and New York merchant alike, what needed reform the most was not the administration of federal departments but the way government power helped business interests at workers' and consumers' expense.

Political pragmatism pushed them on. New York's Anti-Monopoly League had touched a nerve the moment it was founded among those who resented discriminatory railroad rates and swaggering corporate bullies. When William Vanderbilt, whose New York Central had given him a base to expand all the way into the Midwest, blurted out, "The public be d—d!" less than a month before the midterm elections, he became a campaign issue. So did Jay Gould, his sometime rival, whose control over Western Union and railroads in the prairie Southwest made him the most hated man in America. When the Republican state convention denied incumbent governor Alonzo Cornell renomination, antimonopolists knew why: he had let a railroad commission pass into law, vetoed a tax giveaway worth $200,000 to Gould, and stopped a bill that would have made Gould's Pacific Mail Steamship Company $90,000 richer. Combine that with Cornell's failure to help out his old master Conkling when the senator tried to win back his old Senate seat the year before and the fact that Conkling now held Gould's legal retainer, and the conclusion seemed obvious. "When Cornell went out," Rev. Henry Ward Beecher exclaimed, "Avarice and Revenge kissed each other." Two days later, so did the Anti-Monopoly leadership and the state Democratic convention. " 'Gould and Conkling,' 'Gould and Conkling'—that is the cry and it seems to set men mad," Republican nominee Charles Folger wrote mournfully after a trip upstate.[8]

Yet Democrats could argue that they rallied to antimonopoly causes because so many of them had been standing there holding the banner to begin with. In denouncing the government-chartered national banks, Greenbackers were uttering true Democratic doctrine; a coalition made perfect sense. In Ohio, Democrats shouted at "the Pig Iron Princes and Coal Kings." On the Pacific coast, they adopted the language of the Workingmen's Party, blending hatred for the Chinese with resentment toward the Southern Pacific Railroad, which dominated the state's economy, charged extortionate rates, and dodged its taxes. "Whenever the Democracy bends the knee to corporate influence, and seeks to harmonize into the party a few corrupt scoundrels with the railroad collar around their neck, then they harmonize me out of it, and I don't care a d—n who knows it," one congressman wrote a friend.[9]

Change for the better, they agreed, could only come once government action restored the imbalances that years of legal privileges and monopoly power had wrought. Even where they protested national interference, many Democrats welcomed state action. Indiana Democrats might object to a federal program to help out schools, but they lauded Indiana's own school system and tried to convince voters that they had always felt that way. Once all the lip service to a government being best that governed least was expressed, its spokesmen had come up with a growing number of things that government would have to do so that society could run smoothly.[10]

Cynics might dismiss it as stage thunder. A party thick with railroad attorneys, all the way up to Tilden, "the Great Forecloser," was simply adopting its sense of outrage for show. In fact, the corporate Bourbons faced a fight just about anywhere that they tried to dominate, and in many places they never got close to putting the party under their sway. Local needs turned Democratic congressmen into spokesmen for trade unions or silver coinage, and nobody could outinveigh Senator Daniel W. Voorhees of Indiana when it came to talk about the "Money Power."[11]

The test of sincerity came when Democrats had power to use. How they used it after the 1882 midterm elections was suggestive. In Connecticut and Pennsylvania, the new executives committed their governorship to political reforms of the kind that liberals esteemed most highly. Connecticut's Tom Waller called for laws to make voting easier and end money contributions to candidates, called for a state civil service reform law, and encouraged an expansion of women's rights along the lines of New York and Massachusetts.[12] Robert Pattison had good practical reasons for breaking machine politics: as Pennsylvania's first Democratic governor in twenty-two years, he also might well be its last. But he also owed his rise to uprisings against the machine in Philadelphia, where he won the city comptrollership, and then statewide. His reputation for rigorous honesty was well deserved—as any number of exasperated Democratic office-seekers would testify gladly. He did what he could to abolish needless offices, replace fees with salaries, trim public spending, and induce a skeptical legislature to consider the merit system.[13]

Pattison and Waller were more than Mugwumps, and Democrats had a program of greater interest to labor than liberals. By the end of his first six months, Pattison had signed bills not just forbidding political assessments on officeholders but also abolishing the prison contract system and guaranteeing safety for bituminous miners. Democratic lawmakers were more advanced than he and joined Republicans to establish an arbitration system for labor disputes and a law against railroad rate discrimination between shippers. If the more advanced Democrats could have mustered the vote, Pennsylvania would also have had an eight-hour-day law and a statute forcing employers to pay wages no later than every other week. Waller, too, got a law against the use of convict contract labor out of an unfriendly Republican legislature. By the time New Jersey's 1884 session adjourned, the state had a tougher child labor statute, an outright ban on convict labor, a law to deal with river pollution, a regulation of the sale of oleomargarine, and requirements that shopkeepers provide seats for their women employees.[14]

There and elsewhere in the Northeast, Democrats also showed how far they meant to go in fighting "monopoly." Pattison urged an end to the practice of depositing state funds in private banks. New Jersey's governor, Leon Abbett, called for radical tax reform to force the corporations to pay their fair share, and actually carried the first serious railroad tax law in state history. Waller himself championed tax reform, but Republican lawmakers refused to go along.[15]

Placed in such a crowd of strivers and achievers, Ben Butler's accomplishments as governor of Massachusetts look far less freakish. The old general certainly liked playing to the galleries, but the role he played was that of a reformer not so far from other Democrats, both in the Governor's Mansions and out. Admittedly, his notions of "reform" showed far more breadth than the most genteel liberal reformers' and an outmoded vision of cheaper government that worked against the kind of bureaucracy that intervention on behalf of the powerless required. Calling for woman's suffrage and an end to the poll tax, shorter hours for labor, a ten-hour day for railroad employees, and an end to the blue laws, Butler championed democracy over efficiency, retrenchment over paternalism, and "class legislation" over business promotion. Republican lawmakers killed his program, and a Republican-stacked executive council blocked most of his appointments. Late in 1883, Butler lost his bid for reelection. By 1884 the Democratic Party was looking for converts in more respectable quarters. Still, Butler's followers persisted. In Boston's Irish neighborhoods and in the milltowns, there were too many of them, self-defined Jacksonians all.[16] When the silk-stocking Democrats finally won the state, they would have to give labor more than lip service.

Clearly, Democrats' ability to raise more than a thicket of negatives showed itself in plenty of other places besides New York; it also demonstrated that the party's refashioning itself had to do with many issues besides the administrative cleanup that Mugwumps defined as "reform." It is in that unnoticed context that Grover Cleveland needs to be seen.

At first glance, the story of Grover Cleveland's rise fits popular legend very well, indeed. Just beginning his second year in the Governor's Mansion at the start of 1884, a beefy bachelor with thinning hair and "a well-fed look," Cleveland looked as if he had been made from rather rough and cheap materials. There was no style to him. His handshake was firm, his greeting bluff and hearty, his appetites of a plain pork-chop-and-potatoes variety. Local residents guessed that of his $10,000 salary, he saved $7,000. As one of them explained, "What would you expect of a Governor who doesn't entertain, doesn't keep a carriage, and even walks to the Capitol on the day of his inauguration?"[17]

Cleveland had had little to take into the world except a good reputation and a rigorous Presbyterian conscience. His parents' raising nine children on less than $600 a year took a frugality that he, the fifth child, never outgrew. When his father died, Cleveland had to drop plans for going to college and had to make a living, at first teaching in a school for the blind and then, when prospects beckoned, clerking and studying law in Buffalo. Long hours agreed with him, and so did attorney's work. Cleveland mastered facts. He had none of the razzle-dazzle of a great courtroom attorney—only a doggedness and thoroughness of preparation that made him a power to reckon with in any court case. If he sent a substitute to war when the draft summoned him, his

The Democrats Rise from the Dead

"Cleveland the celibate"

(Bernhard Gillam, Puck, *April 18, 1884). A cartoon (perhaps inappropriate, all things considered) honoring the governor's diligence.*

reasons did him credit: giving up law would leave his mother and sisters destitute. With the comforts of hunting or fishing in western New York, "Big Steve" played poker, minded his own business, and showed no interest in any job (even a $75,000 retainer from the New York Central Railroad) that would force him to travel much beyond city limits. Except for two years as sheriff in the early 1870s, Cleveland left public affairs strictly alone.[18]

But events did not leave him alone. The Republican machine in Buffalo had grown increasingly corrupt. Business leaders wanted honest men in power, or at any rate, less expensive ones. With a split in Republican ranks looming, Democrats needed someone irreproachable at the head of their city ticket. They chose Cleveland and elected him. The new mayor lived up to his campaign billing. He fought the grafters trying to gouge the city for street cleaning and the pork barrelers on the city council, wielded his pen in some ringing veto messages, and saw to it that professional engineers, not political pros, laid the new sewer system. Uprightness and a great deal of luck had their reward within the year, when the Democratic state convention dead-locked between favorite sons downstate. In the scramble between rival machines, Cleveland looked like the only serious prospect who might bring the followers of both to the polls come November. He alone could draw Republicans disgusted with the backstairs intrigues that had given them Secretary of the Treasury Charles Folger as their nominee. That fall, Republican factionalism swept in the Democrats, but Cleveland's freshness certainly helped.[19]

Cleveland fit an executive suite the way Blaine fit a public forum. Callers got in the way of his work, which went on for fourteen hours or more a day behind an office desk, its red leather surface heaped with papers. Time-wasters, especially ones asking for favors or offices, got a rough greeting and a curt dismissal. Often midnight had passed by the time the governor, laying down his pen, would sigh to his ever-present secretary, Dan Lamont, "Well, I guess we'll quit and call it half a day." Cleveland "eats and works, eats and works, and works and eats," a journalist complained.[20]

Cleveland himself had no big ideas, no comprehensive program to pro-pose. To his way of thinking, governors were administrators merely. They must be judged by what they allowed to happen, not what they made happen. Their job was to prevent the legislature from making its mistakes into law. Within those limits, Cleveland's two years were quite a success. The legislature reapportioned congressional seats, set up a state board of claims, and revamped the state militia's military code. At the governor's behest, Niagara Falls was set aside as a state park, an annual examination of the books of banks and trust companies was made mandatory, and the state charitable institutions were organized on more efficient business principles.[21]

But there were three areas where Cleveland's record mattered most, if he were to have higher political ambitions. Three stereotypes defined Northern Democrats in most Republicans' eyes: bosses, boozers, and Bourbons. In all three, the governor distanced himself from the political typecasting.

Civil service reformers noted the bosses especially. Cleveland quickly won a reputation for what one observer described as a "you-be-damned" quality. State Democratic chairman Daniel Manning grumbled that the governor never consulted him about appointments or anything else. Good men were chosen, but they were not central to the machine and had scant interest in its

The Democrats Rise from the Dead

upkeep. The superintendent of public works had jobs all along New York's extensive canal system at his disposal. A shrewd governor could use that patronage to hire claqueurs, pack caucuses, and control political conventions. Cleveland's choice to head the department was James Shanahan, a professional engineer, who had helped span the Hudson River at Albany.[22]

Tammany Hall had the most reason to complain. Its votes had put Cleveland's nomination across. Now the governor seemed to be spoiling for a fight. When the machine demanded a share of the offices in the Immigration Department in return for passing a bill placing it under a single commissioner with a new set of harbormasters, all picked by himself, Cleveland refused. Instead, he gave the top appointment to Hugh McLaughlin's Brooklyn machine. Nothing could have been more offensive to Tammany Hall. McLaughlin's ethics were no better than "Honest John" Kelly's, though his notoriety as a boss was less. When Cleveland sent in his last batch of appointments under the new system, Tammany discovered that out of three hundred places, it got not "so much as a night watchman at Castle Garden." Furiously, Tammany's state senators joined Republicans to block the nominees' confirmation. Cleveland knew a shakedown scheme when he saw one. "Give me a sheet of paper," he exploded to Dan Lamont; "I'll tell the people what a set of d—d rascals they have upstairs." To unbiased observers, the whole affair said volumes about the governor's bullheadedness and inflexibility; Cleveland's stubbornness threw away the chance of any reform passing at all. To a cheering public, though, the incident said much about Cleveland's pluck, integrity, and independence.[23]

Readers got further proof of headlong righteousness that autumn when John Kelly's protégé, Tom Grady, sought another term in the state senate. Grady had been one of the most outspoken critics of Cleveland's stubbornness. Now Cleveland wrote Kelly, asking him to keep Grady off the ticket. Grady was having trouble anyhow. The rival County Democracy machine would not accept him, and a divided party might lose the district. He withdrew with conspicuously ill grace. It was not Cleveland's doing, but Kelly needed to blame someone for setbacks at the polls, and he had every good reason to feel incensed: Tammany had humbled itself to restore good relations with the governor. Grady even made what sounded like a public apology to Cleveland. Days before the election, the boss released the governor's letter to the press. To Tammany regulars, it looked like intolerable meddling. To the public, it gave one more proof that Cleveland answered to his own conscience and no one else's.[24]

The final evidence of integrity and courage came in the spring of 1884,

"Made harmless at last!"
(F. Graetz, Puck, March 26, 1884). The Tammany tiger (John Kelly) clipped by
Grover Cleveland and Theodore Roosevelt.

when Theodore Roosevelt shepherded bills through the legislature reforming New York City's charter and municipal methods of doing business. Tammany Hall and County Democracy had grown fat on the fees that went with
the big offices of New York county sheriff, surrogate, clerk, and register. Now
two of the offices were put on straight salary, and the fee system was reformed
for the others. The aldermen's power to confirm mayoral appointments had
created an atmosphere of deal-making and mutual back-scratching between
factions technically at war but really in cahoots, where divvying the swag was
concerned. Roosevelt's legislation took that power away and enhanced that
of the mayor. Tammany Hall had been able to elect enough aldermen to have
its way in the past; more often than not, the mayor's office lay out of range,
unless the machine chose someone of known independence and respectability. Together, the reforms hampered not only Tammany but any other would-
be boss, including Hubert O. Thompson, the fat, voluptuous master of the

The Democrats Rise from the Dead

County Democracy organization, whose machine gave Cleveland its surest support downstate. The governor lent Roosevelt his influence and signed the bills promptly.[25]

There was just one exception, a bill to set limits to the terms of the city department heads. In the past, mayors had been plagued with appointees chosen by their lame-duck successors. That might happen again at the year's end. At stake was the patronage-rich Public Works Department, soon to be richer as it doled out contracts for the projected aqueduct from upstate. Hubert Thompson was commissioner and ran it for County Democracy's benefit. The General Assembly put through a measure aimed at ending the commissioner's term soon after that of the mayor's. One month after lawmakers had adjourned, Cleveland pocket vetoed it. Favoritism to a friendly machine, critics later called it. Actually, the bill offended the governor's legal mind. It was sloppy to the point of meaninglessness. A "very shabby piece of legislation, quit unfit to find a place in the statute book," its author admitted. Far from serving County Democracy's interests, Cleveland's action may actually have helped out Tammany's. Without new legislation, the mayor could still appoint a new commissioner. The only difference was that until the end of the year, he would need the Tammany-run board of aldermen to confirm it. As it turned out, he did appoint a new man. Thompson was sent packing.[26]

There was more to Cleveland's administration than honest government. Moral reformers could not complain of vice let loose. Far from opening the state to liquor dealers, Cleveland signed the new, more restrictive law, proposing a higher license for New York's saloons, a bill that Assemblyman Theodore Roosevelt sponsored. He also signed a new, more lenient Sunday-closing law, but one that kept the essential Protestant ban on Sunday business and amusements on the books.[27]

Dealings with labor mattered more to Democrats interested in broadening their working-class appeal. Here Cleveland went astray as often as he went right, and the first incident nearly ruined his reputation. Labor matters began on the worst possible footing when Democratic legislators leveled a blow at "monopoly" by mandating a five-cent fare on the streetcars of New York City. The bill had a strong appeal to workers, stronger still to those who wanted to do something against that sinister railroad tycoon Jay Gould. Cleveland vetoed the measure. A stickler for legalism and the rights of property, perhaps ingrained from long years as a railroad attorney, Cleveland insisted that the bill violated the rights of contract. The streetcars' right to charge whatever fare they pleased lay in their charter, and the terms of the charter could not be changed without mutual consent, he insisted. The governor had taken an unpopular stand. Though he weathered a brief storm of criticism, he never really escaped the lasting suspicion that he served Wall Street interests above all others.[28]

From a longer perspective, Cleveland's record on labor issues looked decidedly better. The Workingmen's Assembly in New York City spoke for organized labor, such as it was. The five-cent-fare bill had not been among their list of desired measures, but six other proposals had been, and Cleveland signed all but one of them. The real fight that labor waged in the 1883 legislature had not been the struggle over streetcar fares but rather one against contract labor in the state prison system. The Assembly wanted it abolished. Cleveland used his influence behind the scenes to help get the bill passed. Another measure ended hat-making in the prisons. Democrats also enacted a law ending the sweatshop conditions in tenement-house cigar-making. Past legislators had turned down the bill as "communistic." Cigar-workers' unions claimed that it was the only practical means of keeping their strikes from being broken by employers relying on take-home work. Cleveland signed it. When the courts struck down the law, he signed a substitute measure. With his approval, New York set up a Bureau of Labor Statistics as well.[29]

Several points about Cleveland's reform record need emphasis. First, his role was more passive than active. He did little to push reform measures. He simply let the public know that he favored them and stood out of their way. Second, his reputation as a machine smasher was slightly misleading. Cleveland fought Tammany. He got along much better with the Brooklyn machine, and if he showed no open friendship for the rotten Irving Hall and County Democracy organizations in New York City, at least he left them pretty much alone. All the same, there was more to the Cleveland record than Mugwumpery, and for Democrats, the governor's image could serve them well. By June 1884, it was possible for thoughtful observers to wonder whether the governor, instead of being an exception to an unregenerate party, might be testimony to how far the Democracy had adapted to suit the times.

That was quite possible, but Cleveland provided an illustration of a weakness that Democrats would not repair in his lifetime. He represented a party remade, but remade in contradictory ways. It would have taken a supremely flexible politician to hold together partisans of clashing ideals for long. Democrats had the good fortune in 1884 to come upon a candidate brimful of a sense of right; for that good fortune, they would pay a ruinous price over the generation to come. It was not just that his strengths carried weaknesses with them: courage and obstinacy, firmness and inflexibility, righteousness and self-righteousness. In elevating Cleveland, they took from the party much of the flexibility that had allowed it the forward motion that made a Cleveland

The Democrats Rise from the Dead

possible. As two terms in the White House would show, there were other issues besides the tariff on which Democrats could find no common ground— and not needing to define themselves in any one particular way was one of the few privileges that their lack of national responsibility had given them. It would be a privilege they would sorely miss before they were done with Cleveland, or Cleveland was done with them.

The Passing of Arthur

A week before the Republican National Convention, editor Murat Halstead of the *Cincinnati Commercial Gazette* was summoned to James G. Blaine's for a talk. Fretfulness was only natural in the front-runner for the nomination, but Blaine seemed almost alarmed. He really feared that he might win, unless Halstead prevented it. "With the South against us, we cannot succeed without New York," he told the flabbergasted editor, "and I cannot carry that State." But someone else could, and Blaine had written him, urging him to accept the party's call: old General William Tecumseh Sherman.

Sherman must not have known whether to be dumbfounded or exasperated. He hated politics, loathed snooping newspapers, and was having the time of his life in retirement, feasting on public acclaim—quite literally, as the guest of countless banquets. Flirtations outside his marriage and Catholic relatives within it were the last items he wanted spread over page one in a political campaign. And here he was, asked to take an office he never wanted, cutting out his brother John, who very much did! He sent Blaine an emphatic refusal. Now Blaine wanted Halstead to arrange a draft. Make Secretary of War Robert Lincoln the running mate, and the ticket "would elect itself. We should have a campaign of marching and song."[1]

Halstead thought it poetry, not politics. By early June, the Blaine delegates were not likely to stand for any such nonsense. But could the gambit have been politics of a craftier sort, by a man eager to look as if he really were not eager for the presidency? That would have fit political protocol. To believe every "reluctant" nominee's protests, one would have thought Gilded Age offices the first peacetime draft in American history. In fact, Blaine was quite serious. He had wanted the nomination badly in 1876; he may have wanted it in 1880; he had very mixed feelings now.

Time changes men as well as parties. The keenness of a youthful middle age had given way to the fatalism of a man well past fifty. The attacks on his character in 1876 may have damaged his confidence, and his physical collapse just before the convention that summer had alarmed him. Never again could he free himself from health worries. By the 1880s, fitful complaints had become chronic hypochondria. Friends laughed at his wearing two overcoats to ward off a chill or his collywobbles about his digestion, minutes before gorging on sweets "that would have tested the hardihood of a young candy-eater." There was nothing funny about it to Blaine himself, however.

Garfield's brief administration had changed his ambitions. His new desire was to be secretary of state again, if any president would take him on. Perhaps the gratification of being able to shake the world excited him. More likely, Garfield's death had undercut his inner confidence further; for Blaine had been at the president's side when the assassin fired. Indeed, Blaine thought the bullet directed at him and imagined that Guiteau had shouted, "My God, I meant to hit Blaine!" How much his response came from fear, how much from guilt for his part in the feuding that led to Guiteau's act, and how much from a sense that the presidency simply was not worth having, there is no knowing. Clearly, though, Blaine believed that something would keep him from being president, or, if he became one, from living out his term.[2]

A word could have punctured the Blaine boom, but Blaine never said it. "I do not desire or expect the nomination," he wrote early in 1884, "but I don't intend that man in the White House shall have it." Bitterness drove him, but so did his dread of the Stalwarts. Patronage could give life to what seemed a field of dead bones, and, as Blaine's friends saw it, the president had used his distribution of offices for just that purpose: across the South, in Ohio, and wherever appointments could do him good. Only Blaine could pull together enough Republicans to fend off an incumbent's bid. The eventual nominee would owe his victory to the man from Maine, just as Garfield had in 1880, and would likely give him the State Department as Garfield did.[3]

Blaine was wrong about the Stalwarts, wronger still about Arthur. Stalwartism was broken beyond recovery. The president led a remnant, even in his home state. Old allies had gone their separate ways. Arthur himself was fatally ill, though only he and his doctors knew it. Even at his healthiest, he disliked the administrative detail of his job and the nosiness of the press. His wife's death in 1880 and Garfield's in 1881 quenched what ambitions he had once had.

Presidential aspirations may have waxed and waned as his health did, and his taste for a fight slackened when it became clear that he must lose. But for all his diffidence, Arthur let administration followers assume that he expected another term. Pride may have kept him from withdrawing. The press would have been sure to read it as the cowardice of a gentleman too dainty to fight anyone stronger than himself or a confession of his own unworthiness. For his officeholding friends' sake, the president must make a token fight, at least.[4] Most of all, perhaps, as Blaine loomed larger, Arthur had to stay in. Only he could keep Blaine from winning, and Blaine was the one nominee whose selection would be read as a rebuke for the president.

Arthur must stand for the office, then, but he could not run, even if he had wanted to. No vice president promoted by the incumbent's death ever had enjoyed the legitimacy that a general election gave. None had won renomination. Worse still, to many Americans, Arthur was the man on whose behalf Charles Guiteau fired two bullets into Garfield, and in some sense the beneficiary of that campaign of partisan hatred that the Stalwarts had been waging. Winning the nomination would only generate new believers that he had been a party to the assassination. Garfield's long, agonizing death by gangrene, as doctors probed suppurating pockets in his body for an unremoved bullet, remained a searing memory. The last thing the choice of what one newspaper called the "Pus-cavity Stalwarts" could do was make an active campaign, using the powers that murder had put into his hands.[5]

So the president let his friends push him for the nomination but gave it so flickering an attention that the initiative always lay with his enemies. Matt Quay, Don Cameron's right-hand man, could do wonders with the Pennsylvania machine, but when he came to ask for favors in return, Arthur could not be bothered. "Black Jack" Logan's friends hinted at some alliance by which the Stalwarts of Illinois and the South would deliver the nomination to Arthur and a cabinet post to one of Logan's chums. The president made no promises.[6]

Arthur could count on the rotten boroughs where no Republican had a prayer come November. He could inspire the business sentiment of New York City as well, but a panic on Wall Street that spring made that a poor selling point. With little popular support, the president had to win New York's delegations the old-fashioned way, by letting federal officeholders do their worst. Later historians would wonder why reformers fearful of Blaine did not embrace the president. There was really no mystery to it. Reform victories

The Passing of Arthur

were not made by packing conventions down south and mustering the ward heelers from the customhouse and navy yard to bring out a big vote in downstate New York.[7]

If Arthur won the nomination, then, it would be in spite of the rank and file, not because of them, and that brought up the most obvious calculation that all politicians had to reckon with: which nominee had the best chance of winning. "Arthur is the very weakest candidate we could nominate," New York assemblyman Theodore Roosevelt protested. "[He] could not carry New York, Ohio, or Indiana; he would be beaten out of sight." Indiana usually went five thousand votes either way. Even a small band of "Garfield Republicans" could hand it to the Democrats. New York was the president's strongest card, assuming he could carry it; but his secretary of the Treasury had lost it in 1882, and by the biggest margin in history. And always, professionals came back to Ohio. Garfield's successor could not carry it in its mid-October election. Lose then, and the national party was sure to lose heart. Then the presidential race was as good as gone. But Blaine was "Garfield's heir," the man who cradled the wounded president as he lay on the railroad depot floor and who gave his eulogy the following spring.[8]

The president's candidacy might not win, but with enough Republicans in the race, it could tie up the convention. The more delegates Arthur won, the more his managers might be able to swing over to some compromise third choice. Such a strategy had a certain promise. Beyond the two leading candidates, the party found room for a host of lesser ones. Senators Logan of Illinois, Sherman of Ohio, and Benjamin Harrison of Indiana all hoped for the nomination. There was some brief talk of choosing Robert Lincoln, Abraham's son, and the tiniest of boomlets for General Philip Sheridan. Sheridan was not interested, and as for Lincoln, he was, as one observer remarked, "a man of prodigiously reserved power," a cold, formal, unimaginative man whom only a parent could love, and then with real difficulty. Putting him on the ticket would certainly bring up questions about his having forced his mother into an asylum.[9]

Reform Republicans touted George F. Edmunds of Vermont. In his fifties and looking past seventy, with the bald head, gray beard, and stern look of an early Christian martyr, Edmunds was made for Senate life. As head of the Judiciary Committee, he made a specialty of constitutional law. Raised to presiding officer in early 1884, he proved a first-class parliamentarian and a nemesis to colleagues trying to stick riders onto appropriation bills. Even Democrats allowed that "St. Jerome" had "one of the clearest brains" in the public service, and honored him for his relentless way of debating. There was no fancy there, no humor, no flowers of rhetoric, nothing profound. Everything was very Yankee and matter-of-fact. His very "aye" or "nay," an un-friendly reporter gibed, sounded "like a silent protest against the wickedness of this world."

Admirers sometimes likened Vermont's senator to those in ancient Rome's most selfless day. If the analogy was accurate, Edmunds was less another Cicero than an American Cato, but Cato without a cause. There was no gainsaying his mark on legislation, including laws against Mormonism and polygamy and the Thurman Pacific Railroad funding act. Still, most senators knew Edmunds more as a master of legal technicality and precision, a fret to lawmakers, a chronic objector and quibbler. As one congressman put it, he could see a fly on a barn door four miles away without ever seeing the barn. It was typical of his severity as Senate president that he paid special attention to grammatical mistakes in enrolled bills. The sure way to get Edmunds's vote against a measure, Senator David Davis quipped, would be to phrase the question in the New England way, "Contrary-minded will say no": Edmunds *always* was contrary-minded.[10]

There was no generosity in him, no forgiveness. His words left welts. Others had to handle the compromises that pushed a bill through both houses. A "congealed pillar of alleged . . . virtue," one observer called him, and one newspaper, playing on his cold temperament, captioned its news story about a killing frost in late spring, "An Edmunds Boom." Reformers tried to make the best of what they could not deny. Part of a courageous president's job was to say no. Chilly? "We believe . . . in the antiseptic qualities of cold," Andrew D. White of Cornell explained, "and we hope to freeze a good many things out."[11]

Mugwumps were not just sotted with negative virtues. Keen-eyed to Blaine's defects, they let their admiration blind them to Edmunds's defects. His fondness for drink was a standing joke in Washington. "See here," one senator exploded. "If there is to be any more of this bossing, [we Western senators] will go over to the Democrats and we'll reorganize the senate, and you'll have to pack up your whiskey jug and get out of the Judiciary Commit-tee room." He chased money as hard as Blaine did, but he did better at catching it, mostly in court as a high-priced corporate attorney. He still collected a $1,000 retainer annually from the Vermont Central Railroad, the most powerful railroad in the state and his political patron, and it was one of his poorer clients. Attending to his private business during the session, Ed-munds often absented himself from the Senate or appeared late in the after-noon to cavil about measures that had been under debate for hours. Enemies suggested that railroads owned the senator, not by bribery, but because they made too valuable clients to offend by public action.[12]

The Passing of Arthur

Most pertinently, Edmunds had scant following beyond the Independent press. Republican crowds never heard him at campaign appearances, and party organizers had no past favors for which to feel beholden. Reformers themselves allowed that the Vermont senator was not a practical choice and that he really did not want the nomination. He was simply a rallying point, until they could mass their troops to march over to someone with a better draw among the rest of the delegates.[13]

Were they any more shortsighted, indeed, than the "regulars" who marched with Logan? He offered an alternative to a president that so many Stalwarts had come to despise. For those hoping to raise the bloody shirt as the party standard, Logan could not have been bettered. In a published interview, General Grant supported his candidacy. As the one outspoken supporter of the Blair educational bill and with his past record on civil rights, black leaders preferred him to any other candidate. "He has a backbone like the Brooklyn Bridge," Frederick Douglass told reporters. Alone among the contenders, he had "spread around the Negro the network of the laws."[14]

Even then, Logan fell far short. His midnight conversion to civil service reform did not convert reformers' own ideas of Logan's integrity, much less his intelligence. Business interests had nothing to do with him. Coteries stirred up sentiment for him in Ohio and Indiana, but east of the Appalachians, his name excited derision, nothing more. By May 1884, the senator had lost all but a faint hope himself. Commenting on a news item about a woman who had swallowed a beetle, the *Chicago Daily News* predicted that when extracted, "the small but pestiferous insect" would turn out to have been "the so-called Logan boom."[15]

Other possibilities had a better chance of uniting the Republican factions and a record more acceptable to regulars and reformers alike. At the head of the pack was Senator John Sherman of Ohio. Having steered clear of the temperance wars, he could be counted on to carry his state; financiers trusted him completely, and his administrative talent was unquestionable. Importers sensed an encouraging tentativeness in his high-tariff talk, and black voters agreed that, after Logan, Sherman cared more about election outrages down south than any other nominee. As for German voters, one editor argued, the "very name would flatter them, G(Sh)erman."[16]

Favorite sons hoped for deadlock, but their hopes were based on the illusion that the tight factions of 1880 persisted still, that neither Arthur's band nor Blaine's would break. But without a General Grant to rally round or a Conkling to capture the spirit of the Stalwarts, the 1884 race took on a wholly different character. Blaine's friends had no national organization. Indeed, until mid-March, many "Blainiacs" assumed that he meant to re-

"Blaine leans towards Logan"
(Thomas Nast, Harper's Weekly, *March 15, 1884).*

main in retirement, letting Arthur have the nomination without a murmur. When they found otherwise, they were astonished and had to make up for lost time. They might write to Whitelaw Reid of the *New York Tribune* for guidance, but Reid was less the manager of the Blaine campaign than its most conspicuous cheerleader. Over time, Stephen B. Elkins, West Virginia's railroad and coal tycoon and the aspiring boss of the state Republican Party, put himself at the center of Blaine's cause. But even he could not work up the rudimentary machinery that modern campaigns have, the press bureaus and central headquarters. Organized from the bottom, each state made its movement catch-as-catch-can, finding money for itself and deciding every

The Passing of Arthur

problem as it arose unaided. As late as mid-May, the movement seemed to proceed half-blind.[17]

Yet proceed it did, carrying all before it. Everywhere, other candidates found themselves buffeted by the Blaine tide. Favorite sons had the advantage on their own ground. Elsewhere, Blaine's friends usually outmatched them. Nine-tenths of his supporters in Iowa believed "that in some way or other either directly or indirectly, Arthur and his men are responsible for the death of Garfield, and the fall of Blaine," a railroad president wrote one of the president's organizers. "Blaine's fight is their personal fight. His God is their God; his country is their country, and they expect to go to him when they die." From the Mississippi to the Golden Gate, the West went for Blaine in a whoop.[18]

Even at home, favorite sons found themselves under siege. Without Ohio solid, Sherman's boom would bust, but from the first, Blainiacs cropped up everywhere. By the time the state convention met, Sherman's handlers were admitting that Blaine had a majority of the delegates and put their hopes on managing the organization. Where Sherman delegates had been elected, they often represented a minority of the rank and file. Sherman's friends had to give ground. "The affair at Cleveland was as near a *good natured mob* as any *Convention* I ever saw," one participant commented. Of the four delegates at large, only two were clearly for Sherman, and one was indisputably for Blaine. In Illinois, Logan had to fight just to win favorite-son status. Senator Shelby Cullom gave perfunctory support to his colleague but, as one observer commented wryly, was unlikely to "wear crepe when Logan is defeated." It took machine tactics to win an endorsement from the state convention. The support at the grass roots for Blaine was too plain to be missed.[19]

In Pennsylvania, the old Stalwarts looked better off, at least from the outside. Cameron and Quay still ran the machinery and meant to keep doing so, whoever Republicans ran for president. Losing the governorship in 1882 had scared them badly. Fortunately, it unnerved the dissident "Independent Republicans" nearly as much. With state patronage lost and city patronage in Democratic hands, the GOP could not afford to lose the federal spoils, too. Machinist and Independent quickly reached an understanding. If Quay could treat with reformers, he was not likely to perish in the last ditch just to beat Blaine or save Arthur.

The uprising for Blaine could be contained but not crushed. Reforms in the means of selecting delegates had taken away much of the machine's power to decree who would attend the national convention. Quay's whim was still law in Democratic counties, where officeholders could pack conventions and primaries. But in Philadelphia, the GOP boss was James McManes, head of the gasworks and a longtime Blaine loyalist. Quay let him have his way; it was better to avoid a battle than suffer humiliating defeat. The Pittsburgh boss, jovial Chris Magee, was friendlier to the machine, but the Blaine challenge was too strong for him to stifle it entirely. Blaine's friends chose a separate slate of delegates and sent them to the state convention, demanding recognition as the true voice of the Smoky City.

With a majority there instructed for Blaine, Quay could not keep him from winning the great symbolic prize, the at-large delegates that the state convention would select. The most he could do was arrange surrender terms. Blaine's backers would get everything they wanted, as far as the national convention was concerned, but the Quay-Cameron machine would be granted mastery of the state committee and Magee's delegation would be the one the state convention recognized. The harmony, one hostile reporter wrote, "was like the peace of a graveyard; it meant death to all liberty of thought in the party."[20]

New York was the administration's last great hope, its must-win state. If anything, prospects there were even bleaker. Old Stalwart leaders were less keen on helping Arthur out than helping him out of office. Conkling scorned to lift a finger. Cornell and Platt were eager to serve Blaine's cause, more eager, indeed, than the Blaine Republicans were to have them: the more allies, the more widely the spoils of victory would have to be shared. Collectors of Internal Revenue, surveyors of customs, city assessors, and postmasters rallied what troops they could for the president. In New York City and Buffalo, administration machinery worked well. In the countryside, Republicans chose anyone but Arthur's friends, and as often as not, they were for Blaine. Even in Brooklyn, the Stalwarts saw their slates smashed and a few of their top men defeated for delegate.[21]

By the time the state convention opened at Utica, Arthur's followers were near despair. Blaine delegates needed only a half-dozen votes for a majority. That half-dozen might be found among the so-called Independents, tentatively for Edmunds, and, just possibly, among Arthur's own loyalists from downstate. Accepting the inevitable the day before the convention met, Stalwart leaders sued for peace. They sent word to Senator Warner Miller, manager of the Blaine forces, that for a symbolic draw, just two delegates-at-large in four, they would lay down their arms.

A smart boss would have taken the offer immediately. Not only would he have won the most vital point—keeping the president from controlling his own state's delegation—but he could have taken the credit as a peacemaker

The Passing of Arthur

in the party. Miller chose to grind his enemies into the dust. Stalwart offers met with an offhand disdain. Edmunds's Independents broached terms of their own. Much as they distrusted Blaine, they detested Arthur rather more. They, too, were prepared to join forces, taking as their share two of the four delegates-at-large. Miller brushed the overture aside. A few hours later, a committee of Independents came with a formal proposal of alliance and received a curt dismissal. One Edmunds man of their choosing out of the four he would agree to, as long as that Edmunds man was friendly to Blaine. That upstart assemblyman Theodore Roosevelt would be quite out of the question. If this arrangement did not suit them, the Independents could do as they pleased.

When the committee trudged back to Roosevelt's rooms to report, their colleagues were furious. They also had news of their own. Minutes before, callers from the Stalwart headquarters had dropped by. Arthur's managers wanted a deal, any deal to beat Blaine. They asked only one delegate-at-large in four. Still waiting word from Miller, the Independents held out. The Stalwarts filed out and then, moments later, filed back in again. Whatever foursome the Independents chose, the Arthurians would take up as their own.

The next day, when the convention opened, the politicians and reformers both saw near miracles: machine politicians who kept their word and stood by the ticket, and political amateurs who not only outmaneuvered the professionals but held together with machinelike discipline. Too late Miller realized his blindness. He offered the Independents all kinds of new deals, each sweeter than the last. Nothing worked. The Independent slate won. Theodore Roosevelt would go to Chicago. Miller would stay home.[22]

The Utica convention loomed large in significance to the politics in 1884. Miller as boss was finished, his judgment discredited. Other, cannier Republican leaders would minister the party's affairs instead—notably the gray, quiet former senator Tom Platt. But there were other worrisome auguries. The reformers had won a little, but President Arthur had nearly lost all. His followers had staved off complete humiliation, nothing more. To Republicans everywhere, it was plain that Arthur could not hold his own state in line. Any hope of imposing New York's will on the national convention was lost.[23]

Blaine's setback did him less damage. He may even have been extremely lucky. Winning might have ended the struggle for the nomination right then and there—or it might have forced the president to withdraw. When that happened, all the elements opposing Blaine, from the White House to the offices of *Harper's Weekly*, might have been set free to join for some less offensive candidate: Sherman, say, or Harrison of Indiana. And, since Blaine himself was driven to seek the nomination so strongly by his own hatred for Arthur, much of his own willingness to push his own candidacy might have gone out of the campaign.

Two other lessons held omens for Blaine's long-term prospects and those of the Independents. On the one hand, the Blaine forces had overestimated their own ability to carry their candidate, without placating reformers. Miller assumed too much about the amateurishness, the disunity among the Independents. That arrogance cost him; a like arrogance would cost his candidate in the months ahead. Indeed, Blaine miscalculated almost at once by launching a strike against Edmunds rather than reaching out to win over the Independents.

Because the second clear point of the convention was that he *could* have won many of them over. It was no accident that made the Independents seek an alliance with Blaine's forces rather than Arthur's. Some Independents liked Blaine, many more opposed his candidacy only because they feared his defeat in November. When the national convention came, there would be many like them who would fight for Edmunds only as the best among acceptable alternatives. If Blaine had spoken early and convincingly for civil service reform, the losses he suffered might have been nowhere near as serious.

Instead, Blaine overreacted badly. Determined to crush the Edmunds threat before it went further, he unleashed his friends. On April 27, the *New York Tribune* published a vigorous defense of Blaine's railroad investments from Congressman William Walter Phelps of New Jersey. The author and the place of publication were a plain tip-off. Phelps was one of the *Tribune*'s stockholders and an intimate friend of Blaine's. Two years before, the former secretary of state had been grooming him for a place on the tail of the presidential ticket. Phelps's defense used facts selectively and proved the falsity of charges never made, but that was standard. What enraged reformers was the *Tribune*'s attempt to prove Edmunds as guilty as Blaine. In April 1869, just when the Speaker of the House helped out the Little Rock & Fort Smith line, Edmunds had backed a bill to restore a lapsed land grant to the Burlington & Missouri Railroad, a firm in which he owned stock. Later, he sold the stock for a profit.[24]

It sounded damning, but Edmunds had no difficulty tearing the allegations apart. He had *not* owned securities in the railroad in question until three months after his vote on its legislation. The bill did *not* restore its land grant or enhance the value of its stock. Unlike Blaine, Edmunds paid cash for stock at full market price and unloaded it at the going rate. Phelps quickly backed down with a quibble. "The boisterous silence of Willie Wallie Phelps, which has suddenly come over the republic like an electric storm on the

The Passing of Arthur

Nebraska prairies, induces the suspicion that Mr. Blaine may have turned him out to grass," the *Chicago Daily News* gibed. He hadn't; Whitelaw Reid of the *Tribune* had. Blaine, not knowing when to leave well enough, tried feeding the *Tribune* attacks on the integrity of Horace White of the *New York Evening Post*, whom he suspected of authoring that paper's revival of the Mulligan letters scandal. Blaine's insert, written under a pseudonym and pretending to have come from Chicago, was framed as a series of damaging questions. Reid wisely refused it, sure that it would do more harm than good. (Four months later, Blaine found a more obliging editor.)[25]

The whole incident was a worse blunder than it seemed at first glance. Reformers saw Phelps as a front man only. "I refer to it as Mr. Blaine's letter," Edmunds told the *Herald*, "as I am familiar with his writings and recognize his style."[26] The poison pen, the cloaked attack, only reinforced reformers' suspicions of Blaine. It did more. By forcing them to compare the two candidates' records, it brought the Mulligan letters into plainer view than ever. Misgivings about Blaine as a nominee now intensified. So did threats that Independents might take a walk in November.

Phelps's venture was not the only reason for the louder protests, admittedly. By the end of May, the Plumed Knight's nomination seemed nearly a sure thing. Of the four top candidates, only he and Arthur had a national constituency, but where Arthur's came from the Democratic South, Blaine's covered the Republican North. In the three Stalwart strongholds of 1880, Blaine controlled a near majority in two, Pennsylvania and New York, and in Illinois he was the clear second choice. Sherman held only half his own state's delegation, and Arthur less than half of his.[27]

The nomination, in other words, was Blaine's to lose. Throughout April and May, his competitors had been working out complex understandings. It was virtually certain that Logan would deliver his support to Blaine once he dropped out. His hopes fading, Sherman still wanted to try his strength; Blaine's backers tried to induce him to withdraw entirely, with the promise that if Blaine's candidacy failed, they would support him on some later ballot. Sherman balked, but by mid-April, he had promised to deliver Blaine the whole Ohio delegation when needed. His only real hope now lay in the reformers and Arthurians rallying to him as a last resort. There were rumors that Benjamin Harrison was negotiating a "treaty" with Blaine, too.[28]

With the prospects of a reform candidate gone glimmering, the Independents tried out new options, among them Postmaster General Walter Q. Gresham. Gresham's integrity and civil service views were beyond doubt. So was his refusal to enter the race as long as Arthur sought a nomination. In any case, he could not carry the Indiana delegation. It leaned slightly in favor of Harrison. The moment he lost it, the delegates would slide to Blaine. Harrison, too, would have suited the reformers, but again, the divided Indiana delegation prevented any forceful action on his behalf outside the state. Neither Hoosier favorite son would give way to the other. "Gresham and Harrison have been throwing spit-balls at each other, and then looking the other way for some time," a reporter explained. With his war record and reform inclinations, Senator Joseph Hawley of Connecticut looked appealing enough, but the puny Nutmeg State made a poor base from which to launch a boom, and Hawley had no delegates elsewhere.[29]

When all the delegates trooped into Chicago at the end of May, nobody had a majority locked up. But the Blaine men radiated enough confidence for all. To believe them, one reporter joked, their candidate had backing from "God and the heavy artillery, Chicago and the darkies, Confederate brigadiers and loyal colonels, the British lion and the Irish harp and the Scotch thistle, the Papist, the Puritan, the publican and the sinner and the populace, native and foreign, young and old and both sexes and all languages."[30]

There was one ominous note. On the morning before the delegates were called to order, ten thousand copies of the latest issue of *Puck*, New York's leading humor magazine, hit the Chicago streets. Usually Independent with a Democratic, low-tariff lean, *Puck* had taken on a national readership. Bad barbers all stocked it, one Texan later commented, because their clients would be groaning so loudly over the jokes that they would overlook the razor's nicks. That spring, *Puck*'s artists had tried out Arthur as a snake charmer, Logan as a wild man of Borneo, and boss John Kelly as a trained pig. Almost incidentally, they had turned Blaine into the tattooed man in Uncle Sam's dime museum. The image took, and now, in a cartoon "Dedicated to the Chicago Convention," Bernhard Gillam drew the former Speaker as a classical courtesan, blushingly unveiled in his underwear. His wrongs were written all over him: "Little Rock RR Bonds," "Mulligan Letters," "Anti-Chinese Demagogism," "Guano Statesmanship."[31]

Delegates cursed the crude versions struck off as broadsheets by the hundreds and passed out in Chicago hotels. Distributors were beaten up and their bundles taken away, but no one beat up *Puck*'s owner and top cartoonist Joseph Keppler, who was on hand with his sketch pad: only reporters recognized him. Rumors spread that Edmunds supporters had arranged for the printing. Still, delegates had to admit the magazine's impact with the mass of people wearied by political treatises. If the party ran Blaine, he would find himself racing, to the end, against his own cartoon image.[32]

That ugly reputation got an unwelcome addition for every unsavory politician that Blaine's side picked up, and early in June it picked up one of the

The Passing of Arthur

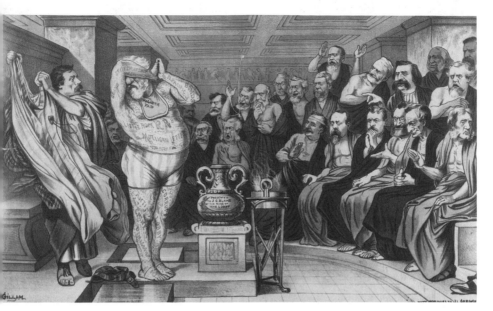

"Phryne before the Chicago tribunal. Ardent Advocate: 'Now Gentlemen, don't make any mistake in your decision! Here's Purity and Magnetism for you—can't be beat'"
(Bernhard Gillam, Puck, June 4, 1884). Playing off a famous picture by Gerome, Puck showed Blaine tattooed with his misdeeds. Whitelaw Reid of the New York Tribune unveils him. In the back row, Walter Edmunds strokes his beard, disturbed; William Boyd Allison of Iowa watches somberly; Benjamin Harrison throws up his arms in derisive amazement; John Sherman smirks; Black Jack Logan laughs out loud; muttonchopped senator Elbridge Lapham grins; Collector of the Port Robertson shrinks back in horror; and in the far right-hand corner, Don Cameron broods. In the front row, New York senator Warner Miller laughs; former secretary of the Treasury Benjamin Bristow gasps; Carl Schurz is not a bit surprised; William Evarts (soon-to-be senator) observes, mildly amused; young Theodore Roosevelt gazes, troubled; and George William Curtis turns away with disgust.

worst. Until the Arkansas state convention met, everyone had taken Powell Clayton's loyalty to the administration for granted. Certainly it had given him spoils enough. But by May, the former senator let it be known that his price for eighteen delegates from Arkansas and Texas was a job for himself as postmaster general in the next administration. The reply from the White House came back instantly: "Not for forty nominations." With that, Clayton went over to Blaine.

By the time the convention opened, the former senator's perfidy (and his price) were common knowledge. So on June 2, when Blaine's allies on the Republican National Committee helped slate Clayton for permanent chairman of the convention, it set off a political storm. Apparently, they meant it as a sweetener to Arthur's Southern supporters and a gesture to reassure other equally late converts that it was not too late to claim the rewards, if Blaine won the presidency. Instead, it enraged Arthur's friends. "This blank Clayton ought to have his head blown off!" one of them shouted. In reformers' minds, the selection gave clinching proof that Blaine was a man who would stop at nothing. (The choice was not, in fact, Blaine's idea, nor intended as a payoff.) Clayton stood for the worst aspects of Reconstruction: high-handedness, boss rule, and corruption. The convention would have to ratify the committee's selection, but could Blaine's friends pull it off? When Henry Cabot Lodge heard of the deal, he rushed to his friend Theodore Roosevelt in a rage. "I will move to put someone in over Clayton if I have to do it and vote for it alone!" he cried.[33]

There was no danger of that. By evening, Roosevelt and some of Arthur's New York supporters had come together. Until the early morning hours, the debate centered on who to put up. Regardless of their loyalty to Arthur, many Southern delegates would vote for Clayton; they could expect nothing more than a symbolic post from Republicans this year. The bloody shirt had been put away for the protected wool shirt. Using the tariff issue, Blaine would appeal to white Southerners outside of Republican ranks. Only a Southerner could beat Clayton, but which one?[34]

Former senator Blanche K. Bruce of Mississippi was invited to take the honor, and he refused it. (They could not know that Blaine's supporters on the committee had offered it to him first and only consented to Clayton at the insistence of Southern committeemen, many of them allied to Arthur.) Then someone suggested John Lynch's name. Lynch was a black Mississippi congressman of marked ability, as much the symbol of Reconstruction at its best as Clayton was at its worst. Lynch hesitated and then consented to run.

Word of the challenge had spread everywhere by the time the convention opened. There was no surprise when Lodge moved Lynch's name as a substitute for Clayton's. From the New York delegation Roosevelt rose, trembling, with an appeal to a finer tradition, the party's sacrifice for equal rights, without which no black would have the right "to sit within these walls." Delegates applauded, and while the galleries lunched on sandwiches and beer and politicians sent errand boys out for liquid "consolation," the roll call began. When the last votes were counted, Lynch had won by forty votes.[35] To veterans of the 1880 convention, this first clash must have brought back memories. Then, too, there had been a front-runner, backed by delegates who would hear of no other name, and only defeated at last when the opposition united to fill the chair with a man of their choosing and then to deadlock the nomination until a winning alternative appeared.

The Passing of Arthur

That sense of familiarity grew stronger on the following day, June 4, when S. W. Hawkins of Tennessee offered a resolution, pledging all the delegates to support the winner. There had been "whispers" that some of those present would bolt if "a particular candidate" won, he asserted. Traitors should have no voice in this convention. The sooner they were kicked out of the party, the better, a California delegate echoed, "whether they are the editors of news-papers or conductors of great periodical journals." Grant's friends had tried those strong-arm tactics in 1880, and the opposition had beaten them, the first sign that rival candidates could stop the third-term steamroller. George William Curtis, eyes flashing, his white hat crushed in one hand, mounted on his chair to speak against the motion. "A Republican and a free man I came into this convention," he cried. "By the grace of God, a Republican and a free man I will go out of this convention." Cheers erupted. Curtis saved his sharpest sting for the last: four years before, when such a resolution had been offered, it had been Garfield, now lying in a martyr's grave, who led the fight against it. Just as in 1880, the motion was withdrawn without a vote.

The Blaine bandwagon seemed to be stalling. When Arthur's forces helped make former senator John B. Henderson, an Edmunds man, the permanent chairman, the outlook for Blaine's nomination looked more un-certain than ever. Reporters eager for a headline therefore had some grounds for seeing in the early skirmishes the rough shape of a coalition being formed, one with the votes to stop Blaine. They were wrong, but Arthur delegates drew the fatal conclusion from their chance victory that the presi-dent could still win, if he stayed in the race.[36]

So did everyone else. Blaine faced a field in disarray. Some of his antago-nists were unsure whom to fight, and others were unwilling to fight at all. "The elements were in the convention to have beaten Blaine," Postmaster General Walter Q. Gresham wrote, looking back a week later, "and men of strong sense and of positive force could, and would have secured his defeat." Sensible managers would have withdrawn the president's name before the balloting, Gresham assumed, and set his delegates free to make a winning arrangement. Others blamed the Independent Republicans for not with-drawing their man instead in Arthur's favor.[37]

The charges held true, in spots. The nominating speeches offered the most obvious contrast between 1880 and 1884. Four years before, both sides had drawn forth eloquent, powerful voices. Roscoe Conkling, his curl tossing over an imperious brow, had given the greatest speech of his life for General Grant. But those who spoke for the candidates ranged against Blaine now were littler men. Their words barely rose above the buzz and hum of the convention floor. One country lawyer grumbled that he had heard better speeches in a cow case. Every candidate, it seemed from the speeches, was a knight, or wore the white plume of Henry of Navarre; even Abraham Lincoln, rough and plain, came decked in the language of medieval chivalry, and if the crowd could have heard a word, they would have grown mightily sick of the clichés.

The big story was not in what the orators said but in what the crowds did. The moment Chairman Henderson mentioned Blaine's name in his keynote address, he set off a demonstration. "Fire-Alarm" Joe Foraker's speech on John Sherman's behalf made the rafters ring, but not in what he said about Sherman; he had let slip a reference to Blaine, and the convention went wild. The enthusiasm was so contagious that Foraker almost joined it himself. And when the roll call reached Maine, and the presentation of its favorite son's name, there was a roar so loud that it drowned out the thirty-piece brass band. The walls shook. The gaslights guttered. Demonstrators snatched the flags off the wall to wave over their heads. Pure political boilerplate in the next Blaine speech set off the loudest, longest demonstration of all. Unaffected delegates shook their heads. The display turned an official gathering into "a mass meeting of maniacs." But they could not have matched it for their choice.

Victory did not depend so much on strong leaders as it did on trusty followers. That was where any chance of stopping Blaine really fell apart. Beyond Arthur, nobody had strength enough. Outside of New England, Edmunds had no substantial support. Logan had spotty support in the South and a firm grip on Illinois, but reformers would prefer Blaine to him. Searching for some dark-horse candidate, the Edmunds forces invited the friends of lesser candidates to a conference. Nothing came of it. Each candidate agreed on harmony—on himself; each invited all the others to step aside. And it was noted that Logan's spokesmen did not attend. Already, everyone knew that if Logan did drop out, it would be in Blaine's favor, which would put him barely a dozen votes away from victory.

Realism kept the minor candidates from making a deal. They could withdraw; they simply could not transfer their forces. Too many of their supporters either had Blaine or Arthur as a second choice. When, two nights later, the Edmunds men tried to work out some arrangement with Arthur, they ran into the same problem. Neither would accept the other, and neither could suggest a possibility to whom their combined forces could be delivered. "I could only rage impotently," Henry Cabot Lodge wrote later of that week of intriguing. "There was no possible way to beat Blaine."[38]

The one hope of a stop-Blaine movement was of some dark-horse candidate too popular to resist. On the evening of June 3, the Edmunds men

The Passing of Arthur

consulted and hit on General Sherman. Some Ohioans who favored Sherman's brother John nursed dreams of the general's name sweeping the convention floor—and then, at the last minute, with a little neat handling from the chair, all that support being transferred to their side of the family. The band even started practicing "Marching through Georgia," just in case. The general's response to the convention chairman's overtures provided the one memorable quotation to come out of the convention. "I would not accept the nomination if tendered me," Sherman announced. "I would not serve if I was elected." Blaine's opponents were so desperate that they tried to read this answer as only tentative.[39]

By June 6, when the balloting began, the stop-Blaine movement had run out of ideas. It could only play for time. Blaine could not get a majority on the first few ballots. His opponents must adjourn the convention before momentum built. It was an old trick, the same ploy that stopped the Blaine bandwagon eight years before. Not now. Blaine started in the lead, with 334½ votes to Arthur's 278, 75 short of a majority. But the second brought him fifteen more delegates. On the third, the pace quickened. The critical moment had come. Ohio moved an adjournment, but the Blaine men leaped to their feet, cursing, whistling, and shouting points of order. The motion lost. Blaine needed 36 votes to win, and they came from Logan's friends. As the secretary announced the results, the crowd shouted. Handkerchiefs, umbrellas, and hats flew in the air. George William Curtis did not join the cheering. "I was at the birth of the Republican party," he commented glumly, "and I fear I am to witness its death."

The Independent Republicans felt all the worse because they blamed themselves. Right after the second ballot, if the Massachusetts delegation had swung from Edmunds to Arthur, the momentum might have gone to the president. Arthur's friends actually thought they had just such an understanding with the Edmunds contingent, based on little more than fancy. The reformers were too hard on themselves. The Bay State delegation would never have swung to Arthur. In any case, Blaine's managers had Sherman's Ohioans in reserve for such an emergency.[40]

Logan's nomination for vice president seemed an almost natural afterthought. It was not so much a payoff for a deal consummated as an insurance policy. Together, the Plumed Knight and the Black Eagle seemed a perfect match. Blaine would speak to newer issues like the tariff; Logan would represent those of the party's heroic past. Given a place on the ticket, Stalwarts would swallow a Half-Breed nominee more easily.

In those first hours, as the wires carried the news, Republicans deluded themselves that the election was nearly won. Hucksters sold Blaine songs, badges, canes, and photographs in Chicago. Partisans fired cannons in celebration and rallied in front of newspaper offices to cheer. They were just loud enough to drown out more discordant sounds. One Republican businessman in New York hailed the nomination as "money in my pocket." With Blaine on the ticket, he explained, he would not give the GOP a cent that year. "Well, it is a great comfort to think that the wicked politicians were not allowed to pick the candidate and that the nomination was made by the people," Thomas Brackett Reed commented wryly. "The politicians would have been guided only by a base desire to win."[41]

The Passing of Arthur

We Love Him for the Enemies He Has Made

Sometimes it seemed as if the Democrats had more presidential candidates than constituents, and each pointed the party one particular way. If the party wanted to honor its traditions, it could always nominate Tilden's courtly vice presidential candidate, former Senator Thomas Hendricks of Indiana. If it wanted to honor its fresh recruits, Governor Hoadly of Ohio was angling for promotion. Nominating Randall would commit Democrats to a high tariff; choosing Morrison, Carlisle, or Abram S. Hewitt of New York would commit them to tariff reform. If they wanted stern ideas about the limits of government power, no man suited better than Supreme Court justice Stephen J. Field.

Except, perhaps, that last Jacksonian, former Senator Allen G. Thurman of Ohio. Having retired after two terms, Thurman was upright and forthright, flexible and folksy. "When I speak of the law, I turn to the senator as the Mussulman turns towards Mecca," Roscoe Conkling once remarked in a rare moment of humility. "I look to him only as I would look to the common law of England, the world's most copious volume of human jurisprudence." Acquaintances jested about his drinking, his fondness for French novels, and his pinches of snuff, but little vices shone like virtues, or a testimonial to a vanished age when small farms and crossroads stores dominated Ohio and political probity was a given. The red bandanna handkerchief into which the Old Roman blew his Roman nose became his symbol.[1]

A party with Field and Thurman in it was almost unmanageably big.

Where Field was known as an apologist for railroads' vested rights, Thurman fought any partnership between government and the corporations. Transcontinental railroads feared no senator more. "A fine, juicy roast of land grants is what sends Thurman's tongue a-wagging," one reporter commented. It was not mere play-acting. The Thurman Act of 1878 set terms for the Union Pacific's repayment of its debt to the government that were, if anything, too strict for the company to meet. Those who hoped for a Democratic appeal to minor Labor and Anti-Monopoly parties in the Old Northwest, saw real possibilities in the old man.[2] Those who wanted a rapprochement with business, on the other hand, could stay in Ohio and choose Senator Henry B. Payne, of the "Coal-Oil Democrats."

Talk of different candidates as they might, Democrats faced inescapable facts. Twenty-three years in the wilderness had taken away their keenness to lose gallantly for principle. The demand of the hour, as the *St. Louis Post-Dispatch* put it, was not tariff for revenue only but "campaign for victory only."[3] That narrowed choices considerably. If, instead of holding a convention, the party had advertised for eligible nominees, the notice would have read:

> TO LET. On four-year lease, with option for renewal, spacious Washington residence. Tenant must be white male, clean character, from pivotal state; favorite sons unable to carry own delegation in convention or state in election must not expect serious consideration; candidates from states sure to support the ticket anyhow will get consideration under special circumstances. Union war record useful, but not essential. Good credentials on issues of monopoly and administrative reform a plus. Under extremely unusual circumstances, advanced position on the tariff issue may be overlooked. Governor or elder statesman preferred. Please include references from reputable sources.

Nobody put Democratic requirements quite so crudely. Still, everyone knew what they were. Blaine's nomination simply might have induced the party to put the words "administrative reform" in italics.

There was nothing new in the requirements. Not since 1860 had the Democracy chosen anyone from the Congress for president, and then they had lost badly. Only three northern states—Ohio, Indiana, and New York—had the electoral vote and the competitive two-party system to make them worth winning, and to win the presidency, Democrats had to carry at least one of them. With one exception, front-runners for the nomination had come from these states for the last sixteen years, and New York provided the nominee every time, ever since 1864.

Taken together, then, the advertisement all but ruled out candidates from

We Love Him for the Enemies He Has Made

Republican states like Pennsylvania (Randall) and kept those from Indiana and Ohio (Hendricks, former Senator Joseph McDonald, Thurman, Hoadly, and Payne) only conditionally in the running: they had to have rock-solid support at home. Any man suspected of stooging for the corporations or Wall Street bankers (Payne or Field) would wreck party prospects. So would noted low-tariff spokesmen (Carlisle, Hewitt, or Morrison) or protectionists (Payne and Randall). Others less openly connected to the battle over the "horizontal bill" would be damaged in proportion to how well their views were known (Bayard, say, and McDonald). A Southern nominee with a war record to explain away (Bayard or Carlisle) would be extremely unlikely. In fact, when all was said and done, the party practically had to choose someone from New York or Indiana for first place. Among the four serious prospects there— Tilden, Hendricks, McDonald, and Cleveland—only the last was young and healthy enough to give Democrats more than a fighting chance.

The curious candidacy of Joseph McDonald illustrates the driving force behind Democratic nominations. A reporter, catching sight of him in Chicago just before the national convention, marked him for "a jolly old fellow, who wears his whiskers 'way round the corner,' under his chin, and who would see that everybody had everything they wanted if he got to be President." Honest, and conspicuously of the common clay—his nickname "Old Saddlebags" came from his youthful apprentice to a saddle maker—Mc-Donald was one of the few Indiana Democrats whose war record not even Republicans could fault. In a state where the party ran willy-nilly into greenback-issuing enthusiasms, McDonald spoke out bluntly for a currency backed in gold, and no other.[4]

Yet it would have been hard to imagine a candidate less fitted for the job. Everyone knew about the messy divorce case that McDonald represented in court, and how, soon after that, he married the plaintiff—too soon, said gossips. He had served one term in the House, ten years before the Civil War, and in 1875 won his only term in the Senate. In each position he had merely warmed a chair. Nobody could connect his name with any measure, nor so much as a glimmering catchphrase. Even Indiana could produce more obvious presidential material than that. There, his candidacy was merely a return of courtesies. In 1880, he had supported Hendricks for the nomination. Now Hendricks was expected to help him—but, instead, let friends suggest his own availability. From South Bend to New Albany, Democratic newspapers spoke of "the old ticket" of 1876, not so much, perhaps, because they wanted Tilden as because they expected him to refuse a nomination, and leave it to Hendricks, the tail of the ticket, to carry on alone.[5] Yet all the way up to the convention itself, from all the newspaper stir, it might have sounded as though the contest had narrowed to Senator Joseph McDonald against the field. McDonald's views had little to do with it; his location had everything.

Other candidates had an air of plausibility, especially Thomas F. Bayard. The Democratic Party "angels," with their open checkbooks, liked the Delaware senator above all other candidates. If August Belmont, the wealthy agent of the Rothschilds and former national party chairman personally could have chosen a president, he would have picked Bayard. So would the patrician senators from the New South.[6]

Bayard had run a strong race for the nomination in 1876, run a stronger one still in 1880. Civil service reformers knew how he disdained the patronage-hounds and everyday partisanship. For some, like his onetime Senate colleague Carl Schurz, that was record enough. Most Southerners would have preferred one of their own to a Northerner; a Delaware man almost qualified. His high-tariff colleagues like Henry G. Davis of West Virginia and Arthur Pue Gorman were willing to overlook Bayard's free-trade views, especially if they could write a protectionist platform. Anywhere in the East where Tilden and his allies had made enemies, Bayard was the natural rallying point. With the senator's known sympathy for "personal liberty," there was no reformer that Tammany Hall liked more, no low-tariff man that former senator William A. Wallace's Pennsylvania followers would prefer to Bayard. "*If the South are true to themselves, you will be nominated,*" Wallace assured him.[7]

But if the South were "true to themselves," the Democrats would lose in November. Bayard had not rallied round the flag at the start of the Civil War. He had rallied round the Constitution, narrowly interpreted, where states' rights were sacrosanct and where the federal government lacked the power to deal with secession. That might not be treason, but Republicans were sure to make the most of it. The more seriously the press took Bayard's candidacy, the more his past perspective dominated his future prospects. Finally, Delaware *was* Delaware, a vest-pocket state that the congressional gadfly of Jefferson's day, John Randolph of Roanoke, had described as "three counties at low tide and one at high."[8] It had precisely three electoral votes.

So always the speculation turned back toward New York and, improbably, Tilden. His appeal as a martyr had been worn threadbare. The Pendleton Act made his notions of administrative reform look outmoded. On the tariff issue, he played the artful dodger. Four years had turned the semi-invalid into a complete invalid. He swore off coffee and tea, without advantage, and even tried shock treatments from a galvanic electric battery, and sensed some improvement. But "improvement" was a comparative term. Callers came out shaken or shaking their heads. From either paralysis or palsy, his left hand

We Love Him for the Enemies He Has Made

was bunched into a loose fist, and his right arm trembled as it was outstretched to shake hands. When he sat and spoke, visitors could not hear him. Early in 1884, he suffered another stroke. He could not walk without help and could barely talk above a whisper. It was all very well for one Democrat to suggest keeping him on ice until inauguration, if the shock of winning the presidency killed him: "I do not think that he would look much worse if he were dead. We might stand him up and inaugurate him." But who would stand him up to run for the office in the first place?[9]

Yet it would seem as though the party could not do without him. No candidate had a "barrel" of such legendary size; no issue was so sure a draw among Democrats as the "fraud" of 1876. The Tilden "machine" was more like a memory than a reality, a scattering across New York of his old lieutenants with none of the central coordination and vote-getting ability that once had made it formidable. The old man's ability to carry his state rested on hope, not recent experience, but a party so long out of the White House fed on hopes and outdated premises. Tilden's friends nursed the boom. Some wrote fabulous descriptions of the old man's vigor. To believe the editor Henry Watterson in 1883, the former governor had recovered his old robustness. Eyes bright, cheeks rosy, wit incisive, he greeted his guest and insisted on an exhausting tour of the Gramercy Park mansion. It was "a favorite and malevolent way he has of punishing his friends," Watterson informed readers, "— climbing long stairs, meandering through labyrinths of decorative arts, and threading the tapestried and frescoed mazes of corridor and chamber."[10]

It was all a charade carried on by men who knew better. Aware that Tilden's health would not permit a nomination, Randall continued to urge him to accept a draft and kept pressing him as the indispensable man. The reason, very likely, was the presumption that Tilden's boom could be transferred to some other candidate of his choice: his friend Henry Payne, say, or Abram S. Hewitt, or just possibly his staunch friend Samuel J. Randall. Other aspirants may have reasoned that the more Tilden's fortunes were touted, the less chance any other New Yorker would have. So much the better for Joe McDonald, when the inevitable declination came. Some Democrats may even have reflected that the Tilden boom would encourage Republicans to nominate Blaine. Arthur's reputed hold on New York was his strongest asset, but it was common wisdom that Tilden's machine could beat the president's any day.[11]

Tilden no longer fooled himself. When one admirer came to wish his candidacy well, Tilden smiled. "My boy," he protested, "don't you see it is impossible?" Hendricks might want the "old ticket," the sage of Gramercy Park joked, "—and I do not wonder, considering my weakness!" Still he made no official statement. He was waiting for one last accolade, nomination by the state convention. Then he would issue a letter of declination, long prepared.[12]

Among the most interested parties watching him was Daniel Manning, Democratic state chairman. Raising himself from poverty to power by hard work, Manning had begun as messenger and copy boy for the *Albany Argus*, the official upstate party organ. As he worked his way up to editor and, thanks to Tilden, to the state chairmanship, he made contacts all across New York. No one knew the "hayloft and cheese-press" Democracy so well, or managed affairs with such a light hand. He kept his followers honest, never tried to boss the party, and stayed out of fights. For now, Manning would do the old man's will, but as an intimate friend, he knew that if New York was to carry off the nomination, it would have to groom someone else.

If not Tilden, then whom? Money and energy had closed off some of the more reasonable choices. As a master of legislative intricacies and the one Tildenite that Tammany Hall got along with, Abram S. Hewitt at least would have had the ability for serious consideration. But his candidacy and all other minor ones had been edged out of consideration by the most preposterous candidate anywhere, former congressman Roswell G. Flower, "a genial, fat-brained fellow with a barrel of money," as one observer described him with cruel accuracy. With no training in literature, law, or practical governance, and with plenty of Wall Street bankers and speculators for friends, he had beaten out another moneybags for the House seat in the silk-stocking district of Manhattan, served a single unimpressive term, and tried to parley it into a nomination for governor in 1882. Now he set his sights higher. His Park Avenue acquaintances gave him some following, and Tammany Hall offered him encouraging words, if only to fend off another favorite son it liked still less. Gradually, reformers took alarm. "There is probably not a jobber, nor a corruptionist, nor an office-broker, nor a dealer in votes, who is not counted as being for Flower," the *Nation* charged. Perhaps—if Flower did the counting. The "Flower-barrel" picked up delegates here and there, but that was all.[13] At worst, he could fracture New York's delegation and force the national convention to look elsewhere for a nominee.

Manning found a better alternative in the most natural place, in the Executive Mansion at Albany. With New York's electoral votes indispensable, any governor would have vaulted to the front rank of prospective candidates. But Grover Cleveland had special merits.

Later, Mugwumps would credit themselves for Grover Cleveland's nomination. Pointing to the reaction against Blaine, they ascribed Democrats' choice above all other causes to the determination to put public honesty

We Love Him for the Enemies He Has Made

ahead of all other issues, in their hope of luring Independent Republicans. The facts were rather different. Cleveland's draw as a symbol of reform was real. Democrats never lost sight of it. Still, that advantage needs to be seen in proportion. In a practical political sense, his feud with Tammany Hall hobbled him as a candidate as much as it helped him. His nomination might win Independent Republicans, but it risked working-class Democrats, Irish Catholics, and other groups to which Tammany appealed, and not just where Tammany held sway; the machine's disaffection really underscored a problem the governor would have all across the Northeast.

Cleveland's appeal rested on his ability to win. That had much to do with reform, but not everything. As much to his credit was his location and the fact that on the dangerous issues he remained a perfect blank. He had no ideas on the tariff that anyone knew about, no record of paltering with traitors in wartime, and no embarrassing states' rights statements from Reconstruction.

The managers, not the Mugwumps, would decide Cleveland's fate. Concerned more about regularity than reform, Manning felt misgivings about the governor. Still, he wanted to back a winner. It was to his interest to build support for Cleveland in New York once Tilden withdrew, and to time Tilden's withdrawal soon enough to get the "boom" started before the state convention in mid-June. Beyond New York's borders, Manning found friends among the bankers in politics like himself and the railroad magnates of the Midwest, notably James J. Hill and Alexander Mitchell. The governor had made no guarantees, but he had given New York a good business administration, and on national issues, he seemed quite safe. Quiet work on delegations pledged to favorite sons could bring them round to Cleveland as a second choice. Closer to home, other Tilden followers joined the effort: shrewd little Dan Lamont and the County Democracy machine's genteel speculator, William C. Whitney, after hopes dimmed for his own father-in-law, Senator Payne. In northeastern New York, Tilden's right-hand man, Smith M. Weed, handled matters. Lieutenant Governor David B. Hill, influential in the "southern tier" counties (those along the Pennsylvania border), was glad to do anything that would open a vacancy in the governorship. In western New York, Cleveland's personal friends had Buffalo covered. None of these men cared much for reform, civil service or otherwise.[14]

The real problem, possibly a fatal one, came in New York City's dueling machines, and especially with the uncertainty of what "Honest John" Kelly of Tammany Hall would do.

Those who paid Kelly a social call often were surprised. Instead of the disreputable Irish bully that cartoonists drew, they met a gentleman, grizzle-bearded and soft-voiced, a reasonably well educated conversationalist, as well-mannered as any of his neighbors in the fashionable Murray Hill district. Venture onto religious subjects, and callers would discover that Kelly was a devout Catholic, married to the niece of the first American cardinal. Though he would not mention it himself, he was a generous giver to religious charities. Was this the boss of Tammany Hall, the master of New York politics that his enemies described?[15]

It was, and it wasn't. Born in 1822 in New York's working-class neighborhood, Kelly had hustled as a newspaper office boy, apprenticed himself to a soapstone cutter, and set up in business in a small way. He worked, saved his money, and stayed away from liquor. It was his boast that he never went into a brothel in his life and entered a gambling house but once, and then only on business matters. Kelly became known as one whose word could be relied on, and a growing circle of acquaintances within Tammany Hall had the chance to put his reputation to the test. By 1854, he was sitting on the board of aldermen. Over the twenty years that followed, he went from congressman to county sheriff, and finally made a comeback in politics as the rebuilder of the Tammany machine after Tweed's downfall.[16]

Legend to the contrary, Kelly was neither king of the Hall nor tyrant over the town. New York City was not worse-run than ever, but better, and, as far as mob violence was concerned, much more orderly than when Kelly was born. When Kelly became city comptroller in 1876, he did not loot the city. He kept the books honestly, scrimped on public works spending, and kept taxes down. Even reformers acknowledged him "a very respectable financial officer." Kelly was ill famed for treachery. That, too, was more myth than reality. Keeping his word gave him much of his power; a boss that could not be relied on could not rely on his lieutenants for long. Kelly's real failing was not betrayal but vindictiveness to those who crossed him. At every national convention where Tilden's name came up, Kelly was there to warn that the old man could not carry New York and to hint that Tammany would see to it that the prediction came true. So he might, if he had had the power. But New York had gone for Tilden in 1876 despite him.[17]

The truth was that Kelly did not control the Democratic Party in the state, or in the city. There was no dictatorship and no dictator. Kelly tried to centralize Tammany's machinery. He made only limited headway. When the local organizations recovered from Tweed's overthrow, small-fry leaders regained a sense of their own prerogatives. They had bossed their wards, delivered the votes, and were not so easily directed. Some had visions of succeeding Kelly as boss and imagined that they could do so. Others could not wait. They walked out to build political machines of their own, bolstered

We Love Him for the Enemies He Has Made

the rebels in Apollo Hall, set up the Irving Hall organization, and backed the Swallowtail alternatives to Tammany candidates.

Kelly's Tammany could elect aldermen in some places. Citywide offices were always more dodgy. A winning nominee had to be respectable, preferably taken from New York's business elite, and possibly someone from among the clubmen, merchants, and high-toned lawyers that ran the Swallowtail wing of the party. The mayor in 1875 came as close to a pliant tool as any that Kelly's machine ever got, and even he was a Swallowtail diamond merchant. Men like those usually were not just balky doing Tammany's bidding. They did as they pleased, and, more often than not, it was to wage war on Kelly.

Occasionally, New York was governed by men not beholden to Tammany at all but put in by "reform" movements and coalitions determined to finish off the boss. Behind them was the money of Fifth Avenue and Wall Street, the elite journals, and, worst of all, most of the big dailies of New York. What use were the *Star* and the *Leader*, pitiful little Tammany organs both, against the *Herald* or the *Tribune*? Even the leading Democratic newspapers of the city, the *Sun* and the *World*, gave Kelly more raps than boosts. "No King, no Clown to Run this Town!" the *Sun* once called.

Kelly's "rule" therefore was more often tenuous than secure. His enemies often won, even when they were personally more disreputable than he. In 1878, the mayoralty went to Edward Cooper, Hewitt's well-heeled brother-in-law. Irving Hall claimed the credit; Swallowtails got the benefits. In 1880, Kelly elected William R. Grace mayor. Within months, Grace had joined hands with Kelly's enemies to wrest the Democratic Party in the city away from him. When Grace's term expired, Kelly had a say in his successor, but not the controlling voice. Another awkward two years followed of trying to deal with Franklin Edson, a Swallowtail mayor of fitful loyalty.[18]

Always Tammany had to fight other machines for mastery of the local Democratic Party. As of early 1884, the most important one was County Democracy, founded late in 1880 when the party nationwide blamed Kelly for losing the presidency by running Grace, a Catholic, for mayor. Remnants of other opposition machines coalesced with Tilden loyalists like Hewitt, Cooper, and former corporation counsel William C. Whitney to form an organization too strong to ignore. Upstate friends guaranteed them a respectful hearing at state conventions, but respectability did not carry reform principles with it. By 1883, the machine was run by Hubert O. Thompson, New York City's portly commissioner of public works. Thompson had more polish than Kelly, but he played politics in the same raw way and used the spoils as ruthlessly. The big scandals in New York over the next four years would involve his bribe-taking underlings far more than Tammany's.

Far from dominating the state party, Kelly found it a hard sell. Tilden's allies were strongest upstate, and Hugh McLaughlin's Brooklyn organization jostled Tammany for first place in line when a governor handed out the spoils. In 1881, the Democratic state convention had recognized County Democracy as the true representative of the downstate rank and file. A year later, the best that Kelly could work out was a share of the New York City delegation.[19]

It was a beleaguered Kelly, then, who had thrown Tammany Cleveland's way in the 1882 convention. At least then County Democracy would not get all the credit and the Brooklyn machine's nominee would be prevented from carrying the day. Kelly did not expect to dictate to the new administration but saw nothing wrong with gratitude. From his point of view, the governor had turned his back on those who made his rise possible.

Tammany's resentment of Cleveland had to do with more than spoils. Tammany had lined up with the antimonopoly movement. Cleveland's selections for the state railroad commission were far more to the railroads' liking than the radicals'. On labor legislation, Tammany had been at the forefront of Assembly measures. State senator Tom Grady's anger went beyond disappointed ambition. He had been a chief sponsor of the five-cent-fare bill; he pushed legislation to protect tenement work and end convict labor and had looked out for Catholic interests. Cleveland had used backstairs influence to prevent the last of those bills from coming to a vote. Even if Kelly could ignore old grievances, he had to think about his own hold on power. Cleveland's record would make trouble among the constituencies that Tammany relied on most.[20]

The boss, therefore, could make a strong case against nominating the governor on grounds that went to the whole issue of what exactly "reform" meant for Democrats. What he lacked was a position of strength. Open war on the nominee must be avoided. Most of his pronouncements that spring were reminders that other candidates might suit better. Bayard would suit him best because he would suit Tilden's old backers least; they still had not forgotten the sellout of 1877, and Bayard's connection with it. But Tammany made clear that it would take just about anyone.

Did that eliminate Cleveland? Not necessarily. Tammany had talked tough before and never delivered. Delegates outside New York City were so sick of the feuding on Manhattan Island that they were more likely to vote to spite Tammany than to oblige it, especially if they disbelieved its threats to bolt. Kelly's standing in the state party was so tentative that he could not afford anything worse than muted threats, unless he wanted County Democracy to win greater recognition as *the* Democratic organization for New York City. As

We Love Him for the Enemies He Has Made

"He courts the mother and means the daughter"
(Joseph Keppler, Puck, June 4, 1884). As Grover Cleveland works turning out reform
bills, the Democratic Party woos him while sweetening up Tilden to get at the
key to his "barrel."

Manning considered the possibilities, he may have reckoned Kelly's opposition as a manageable problem, if handled deftly.[21]

In any case, the first problem that took deft handling was Tilden. Far from inspiring a search for a true reformer, Blaine's nomination actually strengthened the clamor for "the old ticket." The Plumed Knight was so popular that someone who could rouse Democratic spirit in the North would be essential—that failing, someone likeliest to carry New York. When Alabama Democrats held their convention, Tilden's name set off deafening cheers. Louisiana's political managers pledged their state's delegation, too. Now, if ever, Tilden must withdraw. On June 9, Manning went to Greystone to hustle on the letter of declination and carry the governor's promise that Tilden would have a say in choosing the cabinet and could write his own ticket for New York's member. Tilden obliged, and with that the Cleveland boom was under way.[22] It was just in time. The state convention met in Saratoga just ten days away, and the national ticket would be selected three weeks later.

A sultry day greeted the delegates there. "Birds sing in the dusty-leaved trees, and the peacocks in Judge Hilton's park are crying for rain," one onlooker reported. Delegates in their white hats and Prince Albert coats expected an even hotter time on the convention floor. From downstate, the warring machines arrived in battle array and in County Democracy's case, with a regimental band. As the champion of civil service reform, it seemed only natural that Cleveland should have a good showing from the civil service, especially from those officials with patronage to grant: the state treasurer, the superintendent of public works, the commissioner of the Court of Claims, and, of course, the state civil service commissioner. On the other side, Flower showed up in person, sleek and sanguine, with a crowd of prominent friends. From the "southern tier" Lieutenant Governor Hill had rounded up firm Cleveland delegations. Elsewhere upstate, the picture was more mixed, and some of the delegates were mixed themselves, feeling friendly to the governor but not willing to turn the convention into a dogfight on his behalf.[23]

Manning knew what he wanted. At all cost, New York must not show a divided front. That would kill Cleveland's chances right away and would defeat Manning's own ability to act as a power broker for any other candidate at the national convention. He must get the unit rule, assuring that all seventy-two delegates to Chicago would vote as one. Ideally, the Democrats could instruct in the governor's favor and elect the four at-large delegates. But did Manning have the votes?

The answer to that seemed to hinge on who represented New York City, and here Manning miscalculated almost catastrophically. When the state committee met, he saw to it that his allies in the County Democracy were awarded the lion's share of the city delegation. Tammany threatened a floor fight and, if that failed, a walkout. They would carry their quarrel to Chicago, if need be. Only then did the Cleveland forces discover that they had tumbled into a scrap they might well lose. They had counted on support from the second most powerful delegation in the state, Boss McLaughlin's forces in Kings County. But McLaughlin took Tammany's side. If the convention unseated the County Democracy, the whole country would read that Cleveland's forces had been beaten in his own state. With Tammany sharing the New York delegation, there could be no chance of instructing for Cleveland, but with the McLaughlin machine resisting, there would be no chance of even getting through the unit rule.

The Cleveland forces bowed to McLaughlin's terms. His friends were given one of the delegates-at-large, and the County Democracy was nudged to propose an even split of the New York City delegation. Any effort to pledge New York to Cleveland was dropped, and the convention was allowed to vote through a rather perfunctory endorsement of his administration. Even that took some quiet arm-twisting. Tammany won more recognition than at any

We Love Him for the Enemies He Has Made

time since 1880. Under such circumstances, Kelly could afford to accept the unit rule and his followers could take off their little moss-rose Flower badges: nobody really thought they wanted Flower for his own sake anyway. If the slate of delegates seemed weighted in Cleveland's favor, a lot could happen in the three weeks before the national convention, and most of the ablest delegates, Kelly included, were his enemies. Their word would carry real weight with Democrats from other states. Some Cleveland men were shaky, others could be persuaded, and McLaughlin's Brooklynites were as likely to go one way as the other. Even if Cleveland had thirty-eight delegates sure, they would have a terrible time forcing the other thirty-eight to abide by the unit rule. Manning's machine had only barely escaped a complete wreck. Against any candidate stronger than Flower, the governor might have lost outright. The real winner was McLaughlin, who now held the balance of power at the national convention.[24]

Cleveland's nomination, then, depended on shifting contingencies. It depended on what other states did and how well they responded to the uncertain note sounded from New York.

Events after the Saratoga convention simplified the process considerably. With "Mossback" and "Coal-Oil" factions still settling scores from the winter's senatorial contest, Ohio Democrats brawled too bitterly to field a favorite son. Bayard's Civil War views kept getting a bad Northern press, and most of the other leading contenders found themselves out of control of their own states. In Illinois, Morrison suffered a humiliating defeat at the hands of his enemy, Chicago mayor Carter Harrison, who won the gubernatorial nomination. Since "our Carter" stood with Randall's protectionists, his victory suggested that Morrison could not even deliver the Democrats in his home state. California Democrats gathered in Stockton less to pick a candidate than to pick apart "the miserable poodles who trot after RR favors," as the convention's president would later call them. Antimonopolists read their enemies out of the party and put through fire-breathing resolutions against the railroad kings. They pledged themselves for Tilden first, Thurman next, "and for Field never."[25]

So the Democrats came to Chicago, still apprehensive, still nourishing themselves on fantasies of the "old ticket." One nose count put Tilden's strength at 274, with Cleveland 27 votes behind him, and Randall a distant third at 60. Louisiana's delegation needed extra assurances that Tilden really was out of it, and even then they took the news badly, feeling, as one of them put it, like "poor orphans."

Newspapers played up every uncertainty and boomed every prospective nominee. They published faithfully arguments for dark horses like Hoadly of

Ohio ("the only Democratic governor who has ever given any chance to the 'coons,'" one defender pleaded). But that was their business. Clearheaded observers knew that the odds strongly favored Cleveland or Bayard. There was nowhere else to go. Let the *San Francisco Alta California* reveal to its readers that Field remained a serious prospect; if forced to choose a railroad tool, the state's delegation would have endorsed a Chinese tracklayer first. As for Californians' own preference, Thurman of Ohio, his appeal was founded on the faith that he could carry his state in October—which would have to be pretty blind faith, with the Ohio delegation snapping at each other and the Democratic state central committee sharpening its knives for the old man. Choosing Randall or Carlisle would have been suicide, and when Indiana delegates talked up McDonald, their hearts belonged to Hendricks, who insisted that he was not running. Nobody thought Tammany Hall claqueurs were serious in proposing Ben Butler, but the very suggestion was enough to anger Southerners. "We have eaten crow, sir, in the past," one of them stormed. "We can eat it again, but by God, when it comes to forcing turkey buzzard like Butler down our throat we will revolt."

Thurman's weakness pointed out Cleveland's peril. United, New York could drive the convention, if not to the candidate of its choice, at least toward him. As long as any state's delegation was like Ohio's—"three . . . here for harmony and forty-three for hell"—the initiative would have to come from elsewhere. That was what made the unfinished business of the New York delegation so critical. Repeal the unit rule, or, worse still, keep it and fail to agree on a favorite son, and Grover Cleveland's candidacy would be done for. A man who could not carry his own delegation could not win his state in November, and if not, what good was he? Already, days before the gavel came down, Kelly and his friends were in town, insisting that Catholics and work-ingmen would give New York to the Republicans rather than give the presidency to Cleveland. And what of Tammany itself, reporters asked. "I will not lift my hand to elect him," Kelly said.[26]

Kelly's campaign faced its crucial test the day before the convention assembled. On July 7, the New York delegation met to decide whom to endorse. Nobody was surprised to discover Cleveland leading Flower, but the margin showed how little support Tammany Hall had: forty-six to twenty-three. At the last minute, Brooklyn's boss had swung behind the reform governor. A year of Cleveland favoring the McLaughlin machine had paid off. So had many years of rivalry across the East River, and apparently, some last-minute guarantees by Manning that the McLaughlin machine would have a free hand with Brooklyn's patronage. All was not yet lost for Kelly, if he could break the unit rule, and he and Tom Grady argued vehemently that nobody

We Love Him for the Enemies He Has Made

should be compelled to cast a vote against his conscience. Only ten delegates agreed with him.

With that decision, the momentum in the convention shifted Cleveland's way. Kelly could bustle to a stop-Cleveland caucus in the rooms of West Virginia's former senator Henry G. Davis, but he came into it empty-handed, unable even to promise his own vote. As Davis, Butler, Kelly, Wade Hampton, and others discussed Bayard's prospects deep into the night, Cleveland's lieutenants tallied up 450 delegates sure on the first ballot, just 97 less than the two-thirds needed. Quiet negotiations were under way for Pennsylvania's sixty. Randall was ready to give way to Tilden's heir, and all the more ready because, of all serious possibilities, Cleveland seemed the least committed to the tariff reformers—or, for that matter, their opponents. "To hell with the tariff!" one of his supporters roared. "Tariff be d—d. We want to win this fight and we want a man to win it with."[27]

A historical novelist could make much of the atmosphere of the convention that followed: the oppressive heat thickened with heavy rains, the hired claqueurs for Mayor Carter Harrison ushered past the guards to cheer his welcoming speech, the roar of applause in the California delegation when it spotted the stooped, large-framed man leading Ohio into the hall. "We have come two thousand five hundred miles to this Convention, and have now our first glimpse of 'Paradise' in the person of Allen G. Thurman of Ohio," a Californian yelled. Journalists drew the convention as theater, sketching the cast in loving detail, notably the spokesmen for New York City's rival machines. Then there was Kelly himself and his protégé, Tom Grady, young and impudent.

There were moments to remember, such as the one during the nominating speeches when General Edward S. Bragg of Wisconsin seconded Cleveland's nomination. The onetime hero of the famous "Iron Brigade" never feared an enemy and, as his colleagues in Congress knew, had a positive genius for making them. The word "old" flew from his tongue in deprecation of the great possibilities of the party, "the chivalric Bayard," "that sturdy old Democrat from Indiana," "that glorious old Senator from Ohio." The Democratic back numbers would troop after them to glorious defeat. What they needed was somebody to lead them to victory. Fresh recruits demanded a fresh leader, not "our old war-horses," fit to be put to pasture with honor. That leader was Cleveland, loved not only for himself and his judgment "and iron will." They "love him most for the enemies he has made." The crowds roared at that. They knew who Bragg meant, and so did Grady: "Mr. Chairman, on behalf of his enemies, I reciprocate that sentiment, and we are proud of it." Bragg turned on him. "Riddleberger of Virginia, who defeated the Democratic party in that State, would not be permitted to speak here," he shouted. His finger shot toward the New York delegation. "Behold the Riddleberger of New York!" The galleries yelled with delight; Grady just yelled.

All this drama made good newspaper copy. It probably affected no votes at all. What really mattered was Grady's motion to do away with unit rule on opening day. Tammany had a case, even if nobody could hear it; a nest of swallows in the hall's rafters drowned out Kelly's argument, and the murmur of the crowds made Grady inaudible. There was something preposterous about nominating a "reform" candidate by machine methods. But principle had nothing to do with the result. Ending unit rule would deflate the Cleveland boom. Cleveland's managers prevailed by 463 to 332.

After that, the only way to stop Manning's bandwagon was to unite the opposition around some other candidate. The search for an alternative went on without rest, but it never got very far. None of the candidates would give way. Some, like Randall, positively refused to join a stop-Cleveland movement. Negotiations within the opposition remained fitful until the balloting began, by which time it was too late. There were improvisations, all of which showed desperation more than deep-laid plans. A Thurman boom was launched on the second day of the convention. Delegates wrapped red bandanas around their hats and canes, looking to one reporter "like a band of army-hospital invalids." But Thurman never had a chance, as long as Ohio's delegation gave him no support. Outside of Indiana, no one seemed interested in McDonald, and even the Pennsylvania delegates did not take Randall's canvass seriously.[28]

More important still, the party managers worked to define the terms of the canvass in a manner that ruled out every candidate who had had anything to do with the tariff. Even as speeches hailed Thurman, inexplicably, as "the Bismarck of America" (his facial hair and principles both in the wrong place) or a giant fit to wear Tilden's mantle, the select few on the platform committee fashioned a tariff plank fit to win on. Editor Henry Watterson, Morrison, and Congressman Frank Hurd of Ohio pressed for an unequivocal low-tariff stand. Ben Butler spoke for the high-tariff end. Hewitt held the center with a compromise. It went no further than the straddle of 1876, and nowhere near the tariff-for-revenue plank of 1880. The Democrats pledged to lower duties, wherever it could be done without hurting industry or wages. They had no problem with incidental protection. It had Tilden's blessing, and Randall's, too; plainly, it was part of the arrangement by which the Cleveland forces meant to bring Pennsylvania's votes to their side when the time came.[29]

The convention was not ready to make free-trade advocate Frank Hurd's fight for him. On the evening of the tenth, Butler took the stand to argue for a

We Love Him for the Enemies He Has Made

minority plank, more explicitly protectionist and with specific promises of action on labor's behalf. A diamond glistening at his breast, a pansy in his lapel, he gave one of his most entertaining performances, urging action to protect union organizers from intimidation and members from dismissal and pleading for government-supported arbitration and federal funding for public education. Already having been tendered the People's Party nomination by Labor and Greenbacker activists, Butler's ideas of reform were anathema to the liberals who had narrowed the word's definition to honest administration, tariff reduction, and a professional civil service. (And to others than liberals. When he brought up his arbitration plan, one Southerner on the platform committee demanded: "Will this apply to my niggers?" "Your niggers," Butler retorted. "Have you any niggers? I thought I marched down there with my soldiers and settled that. If not, we will march down there again.") The delegates stomped and shouted him down and put through the majority report by eight to one.[30]

By the time the presidential balloting began, the hour was late, too late for more than a foreshadowing of things to come, but that sign was unmistakable. Cleveland began with 392 of the 547 votes he needed. Bayard's 170 put him a distant second, and Thurman's "boom" brought him only 88 delegates. Slightly under half of Ohio's delegation went for Cleveland.

Any chance of forestalling New York's favorite son depended on immediate action. Upon adjournment, the stop-Cleveland managers gathered in Butler's rooms to pick a common nominee. Hendricks seemed the obvious choice, the best way of tapping into that lingering sentiment for the "old ticket," but the former senator resisted. He wanted to do right by McDonald, still Indiana's favorite son. If he consented, it is conceivable that the argument used was one that Tammany was peddling and that the press corps had known of for months and never reported: that the New York governor had fathered an illegitimate child and was sure to be exposed before November. But Hendricks may not have consented at all, or, if he did, only very conditionally. Still, when the conference broke up at dawn, the organizers were confident. "We've licked this coon and sent Cleveland's chickens into their coop with their tails between their legs," a Tammany regular boasted.

They had done no such thing. Cleveland workers had put in a night's work themselves. Already, Manning had enlisted the support of John O'Day, Missouri state chairman and attorney for the St. Louis & San Francisco. O'Day was a notorious "railroad Democrat." His influence ran wherever the corporation ran track, including Arkansas, Kansas, and the Southwestern territories. The attorneys for railroad interests in Wisconsin, Iowa, and Kansas also lined up as Manning wanted them. Virginia, Illinois, and Wisconsin's delegations had all but agreed to help the front-runner when called upon. Southern states had promised to throw more votes Cleveland's way on the third ballot and were induced to break sooner, but Pennsylvania was the key. The sooner Randall withdrew, the sooner his withdrawal could make Cleveland unstoppable.[31]

When the convention assembled, Randall's name was withdrawn immediately. The second ballot began, and even in the first states on the roll, Cleveland gained slightly. When Illinois was called, the delegation's chairman got no further than mention of the one vote for Hendricks than a carefully staged demonstration broke loose. Indiana delegates climbed on chairs and kept the cheering going. Every time it subsided in one place, it rose somewhere else, louder than before, and noisiest of all among Butler's Massachusetts friends and Kelly's New York followers. Hendricks, deathly pale, tried to get up several times; very likely he wanted to withdraw his name, since Dan Voorhees pulled him down into his chair before he could speak. Finally, he fled the hall. As Voorhees came to the platform to announce Indiana's vote, a mighty shout went up. His appearance could only mean one thing: the withdrawal of McDonald's name and thirty Indiana delegates for Hendricks.

Then the Illinois delegation completed its poll of itself. The boom stopped dead. Hendricks, 1–Cleveland, 37. As other states gave their numbers, Cleveland kept gaining. Hendricks's supporters outside of the galleries amounted to little after all, one in each of the Carolinas, 13 in Michigan, 11 in New Jersey, 12½ in Massachusetts. If Pennsylvania had swung to Hendricks, the bandwagon might have started rolling. Instead, it gave Cleveland 42 votes.

With a shout, New York's delegates leaped to their feet. From all over the hall, members of various delegations rose, bellowing for recognition so that they could change their votes. As the governor's supporters bore an immense, hideously bad portrait of their candidate down the aisles (its "beefiness and prize-ox color" a "revolting sight," in one journalist's words), the galleries let loose a shower of cards, popcorn, wastepaper, and leftovers. The stop-Cleveland movement was over. Indiana switched from Hendricks to Cleveland. Every other state tried to do the same. The chair announced the result, but no one could hear him, perhaps not even himself. Cannons roared along the lake front, galleries shouted, and paper wads and tin cups rained on the sullen Tammany delegates.[32]

After that, there was nothing to do but adjourn while the party managers picked a vice president. The options narrowed to former Senator Henry G. Davis of West Virginia, whose money might float the party, or Hendricks, whose friendship with John Kelly and association with the "old ticket" might

We Love Him for the Enemies He Has Made

mend party disaffection. Davis had no desire to shed his fortune. Blaine was his personal friend, and Blaine's campaign manager, Steven Elkins, was a son-in-law. That left Hendricks. The delegates were delighted. Very likely he would have been their first choice anyway.[33]

Disaffected Republicans were too happy over Cleveland's nomination to care about his running mate. To their view, reform had triumphed at Chicago. Nothing could be further from the truth. Cleveland won because he came from New York, because delegates saw him draped in Tilden's mantle, and because he just might win the November election. "We are all satisfied," a Dayton newspaper asserted. "It is the old ticket, except that the old man sent his boy to take his place." But was the middle-aged "boy" up to the place? Could reform be defined by the phrase that a reporter put in Cleveland's mouth that summer, "Public office is a public trust"? John Kelly was not the only one who defined the term more broadly than the Mugwumps. Cleveland would make "a careful and good Executive," one of the anti-railroad Democrats in California wrote a friend, but he would be no active reformer, at least not in their terms. "Looking the thing squarely in the face and talking between ourselves there can be no genuine anti-monopoly victory won this year."[34]

10

The Public Be Crammed!

As delegates turned homeward, the cheering died and the worrying began. "It looks now as though we are soon to have a more bitter, personal, and disgusting campaign than we have ever seen and it will probably end . . . in the open purchase of votes," one Republican commented. Most insiders in both parties worried about something more practical: losing.[1]

Voters seemed restless, unpredictable. Boasts that one side or the other would carry the country "with a whangdoodle snort" came freely. Everybody conducted impromptu polls. "A very singular thing happened on a horse-car recently," one newspaper commented sardonically:

> A gentleman thought to canvass the occupants as to their presidential prefer-
> ences. He had taken the votes of two old ladies, and then inquired of the only
> male rider besides himself, "Whom are you going to vote for, my friend?"
> when the unsympathetic individual replied, "Go to thunder." It is clear from
> this incident that Mr. Blaine's majority in Massachusetts cannot be less than
> seventy thousand. A hard-workingman fell down on a banana skin last week,
> and has since been unable to do any labor; which proves conclusively that the
> votes of the workingmen will all be thrown for Blaine. An earnest Cleveland
> man, so his son informs us, will not vote in the coming election. He died last
> Wednesday. The Democratic candidate, it is believed, will lose many more
> votes in the same way. . . . "Blaine" is a word of one syllable, while "Cleveland"
> has two syllables. This will give the former an increased advantage among the
> younger class of voters.[2]

Behind the confident boasts, insiders complained of tepid rallies and clubs that organized, never to meet again. Why shouldn't this be a "dull campaign"? one New Yorker pointed out. "What issues are we to grow warm over?" "In 1880 the country was booming, business was booming," Congressman Joe Cannon of Illinois wrote one of his friends on the national committee. "Now we are not booming as much as heretofore; in fact from the business standpoint it's a 'demnition grind' & we will loose [sic] many votes. The voters are thinking a change can't hurt. In common with the rest of the animal creation our species shows its teeth when pressed or uncomfortable."[3]

If the financial panic and an economic slump were making voters show their teeth, as Cannon seemed to think, Republicans had a good chance of winning: now, more than ever, workers needed the tariff to keep out foreign competition. They might well buy the protectionist line that fears of Democratic tariff tinkering had shaken business confidence. But if Cannon was wrong, and the voters' uneasiness was moral, not economic, Blaine's record would become the inescapable issue.

Each candidate worked to shift the debate onto advantageous ground in his letter of acceptance. Cleveland retired into the Adirondacks to work past midnight on his. After painful effort, he sent his trusty secretary, Dan Lamont, a draft to read to Hendricks and Tilden. "I want the thing to suit those who are wiser than I," he wrote, "but I have given it a good deal of thought, and seriously hope that it will not be deemed necessary to change it." There was nothing disturbing enough to change. It planted the governor squarely in the Democratic reform tradition, where presidents left policy making to Congress, kept down spending, and hired officeholders strictly on their merits. Aside from endorsing the principle of civil service reform, Cleveland had no new ideas but took up a popular old one, a constitutional amendment holding every president to a single term. On the tariff, he said nothing at all, nor on just what he would do to advance the merit system.[4]

If Cleveland emphasized probity in office, Blaine concentrated on the blessings of the tariff and expanding trade with Latin America. To old-line Republicans' dismay, he disowned the bloody shirt. The South was changing for the better, Blaine insisted. The tariff would help bring the sections closer by benefiting all. Critics spotted a plagiarism from Washington's Farewell Address but overlooked the real surprise. Heeding the urgings of reform leader Andrew D. White, Blaine came out more strongly for the Pendleton Act than Cleveland had, and had specific suggestions for broadening its coverage to the consular service and ending the fixed four-year appointment for all appointees that gave every president the chance to purge the civil service for partisan ends.[5]

Blaine's first advance to reformers was his last, though not only from a lack of interest. Political etiquette required candidates to behave "presidentially": a conspicuous retirement, a visible disinterest in the outcome, and at most some choice words to visiting delegations. Anyone worthy of the highest office in the land must treat it as a duty rather than a prize, and for Blaine, whose ambition was one of the telling points made against him, discretion was doubly important.

In that sense, Grover Cleveland made a perfect candidate. As governor, he showed up for perfunctory appearances at National Guard rallies and county fairs. There was a great set piece on October 2, welcoming him back to Buffalo, with the city festooned in mottoes and Chinese lanterns. Two weeks later, Cleveland traveled to Manhattan, shook hands till his own ached, and watched a torchlight procession up Fifth Avenue, before showing himself to cheering crowds in Brooklyn. But nowhere did the governor go beyond generalities. His character, not his words, must sell his commitment to civil service reform or anything else.[6]

Blaine knew what the rituals were and did his best to follow them, at least in public. Journalists described him secluded in Maine, devoting his days to family affairs and work on the second volume of his memoirs. But behind the scenes, the candidate paced, fretted, and advised more than any candidate in previous history. Years of experience convinced him of how the election was best to be won, and as party newspapers went on the defensive explaining away his past, he watched the Republican campaign's momentum dwindle.[7]

Still, anyone wanting to glimpse the driving force of politics need go no farther than downtown New York City at Democratic headquarters on West Twenty-Fourth Street, in a onetime gaming house, or Republican offices at the Fifth Avenue Hotel. There, in rooms stuccoed and burnished, "gleaming with old gold," party managers set the tone and distributed the money for the campaign.[8]

Between presidential races, national committees hardly existed. The congressional committee handled fund-raising for House and Senate campaigns in off years; state committees tended to governor's races. Only a few weeks after the conventions did the national committee come into its own. In the few months remaining, it had to scrape together funds, sound the keynote, man the rallies, and see to it that all the state and local organizations worked in harmony.

Both parties looked to their moneyed men to run the machinery. Customarily, the top job went to a politician with business credentials. This year, choosing a businessman mattered more than ever because the Pendleton Act had cut off the money that the administration could shake out of government

The Public Be Crammed!

workers. Blaine suggested a Pittsburgh steelmaker, whose purse and organizing talents had helped overturn Don Cameron's Stalwart machine in 1882. Benjamin F. Jones of Jones & Laughlin had helped Blaine win the Pennsylvania delegation. He could pass the hat among his friends in the industry after putting a big contribution into it himself. When the national committee organized on June 26, Blaine had his way.[9]

A month later, Democrats made a like choice. All the leading contenders for the chairmanship were coal or railroad executives or bankers. Cleveland had hoped that Manning would take the job. Manning resisted. As editor, banker, and state chairman, he had more than enough work for one campaign. When the committee met, it laid the duties back on its current chairman, William Barnum, whose iron and railroad investments and talent for underhanded vote buying made him one of the savviest, if most unscrupulous, managers of Connecticut politics. "He is simply without a rival in that line of work," a Wisconsin partisan wrote. "He knows not only how to disburse money, but knows how to *raise* it. In the closing hours of the battle, when it is desirable to use '*party ammunition at short range*,' Barnum stands without a peer."[10]

Barnum and Jones were as much for show as for solvency. Both would reassure worried business interests that "safe" men ran the parties, and Barnum's reputation for winning at any cost heartened Democrats fearful of being outsmarted once again. Neither chairman really ran the machinery. Both gabbed too freely with reporters, and neither had the golden touch among their business associates. Jones even kicked at paying his $70,000 assessment, and Barnum never even showed up for committee meetings until late in the campaign. Other businessmen-politicians handled the day-to-day work. On the Republican side, everyone deferred to Stephen B. Elkins, Blaine's close friend and his choice for unofficial manager. Elkins had railroad and coal interests that put him on a first-name basis with other financiers, but he also knew the inner workings of politics. Democrats put their trust in a smaller advisory committee, chaired by Arthur P. Gorman, one of Elkins's associates in West Virginia investments.[11]

One reporter described Gorman as "the smooth-shaven and priest-like but not lamb-like . . . leader" of Maryland's Democrats. Far from it! Gorman's spelling left much to be desired, and his political ethics still more, but he was a superb political manager. He had been in the Senate quite a while—since 1850, as an eleven-year-old page boy. After a succession of patronage jobs around the Capitol, he went home in 1869 to overhaul Maryland's Democratic organization and man the machinery. Passing out the patronage of the Chesapeake & Ohio Canal and allying with the Baltimore city machine,

Gorman became the unmaker of governors. Abstaining from liquor and cigars, addicted to nothing but baseball and politics, the boss was too soft-spoken to admit he bossed and too shrewd to blurt any inconvenient asides to reporters. Attacks on himself he turned aside with smiling courtesy: "The matter is of no importance, I assure you."[12]

Gorman believed in discipline, organization, and quiet work. Early on, the national committee made itself a mailing list, with one Democratic contact in each of New York's two thousand election districts outside the metropolitan area and sent out circulars to all, for a fair measurement of disaffection among the rank and file. "Intelligent and able men," as the committee secretary described them, moved down the country roads, visiting every Democratic home for a reliable polling. The committee also hired a "stenographic trailer" to attend Blaine's public appearance and catch any gaffes.[13]

Beyond little innovations, the two committees were very much the match for one another in method and style. Both set up a special bureau to manage the appeal to German Americans and a branch organization to coordinate the Midwestern campaign; unlike the GOP, Democrats felt no need to set up a Southern branch as well, and saw little use in an outreach program for Protestant churchgoers. The greatest difference lay in the committees' connection to the candidates themselves. Gorman brooked no interference with his campaign. Others as pragmatic as he handled the money-raising and management. Manning took care of upstate New York, while William C. Whitney saw to funds among his downtown friends and quite possibly his in-laws at Standard Oil. Cleveland himself was kept informed through Manning and his old law partner, Wilson Bissell, but suited the committee best when he stayed out of the way. Improbable legend later told how, when Cleveland wrote up a long, labored defense of his private life, the manager simply tossed it into the fireplace. By contrast, Elkins served in the double capacity of surrogate for Blaine and go-between to Logan and the Stalwarts. Blaine wrote plenty of advice, much of it sound.[14]

Yet there were clear limits to what even talented managers could do. Political machinery took time to set in motion. All through August, complaints flowed against the managers of the two parties for their inaction or downright absence on vacation. Jones blamed "apathy, begotten of overconfidence," and the economic slump. Others blamed him. "You must not think this campaign is going to win by letting it alone," Senator Shelby Cullom warned Logan at the end of July.[15]

The real reason that the campaign started so slowly had nothing to do with Jones's energy and everything to do with a bare larder. Until the parties raised money, nothing could be done. National committee funds were not the only

The Public Be Crammed!

resource a party could draw on, of course. State and local committees raised money, too, sometimes from the same donors. And Gilded Age campaigns did not need money in such vast amounts as they did later. Far from asking for millions, most requests to the national committee ran in the hundreds: $200 a week to increase this newspaper's circulation, $265.50 to print off twenty thousand copies of a choice tariff speech. But it was also true that most contributors gave small amounts, and that included businesses with an interest in party success. From Des Moines' campaign clubs, James Clarkson raised $25,000 for the GOP—which was $5,000 more than all the state of Pennsylvania gave the Republican National Committee. Cincinnati business-men generally gave sums ranging from $100 to $500 each. In some congressional districts, candidates had to handle money matters on top of their other duties.[16]

National committees, therefore, were not the sole fund-raisers; they were not called on for massive amounts and had no way of raising them. All that admitted, Republican managers found themselves far short of the money they needed to wage the kind of campaign they had planned. From western Maryland, where Republicans had the best chance of keeping a House seat, their candidate pleaded that the state organization could afford no more than "several hundred dollars" in aid. Not a dollar could be raised locally, one Tennessee nominee lamented. "Always the expense of organization in his district has fallen on a few of us."[17]

The committee could give them little comfort and less money. Hard times dulled Republican contributors' will to pay. Blaine himself handed over $65,000, which, he complained, was $55,000 more than the only other GOP presidential nominee ever assessed for so much as a dollar. Elkins gave liberally. Chairman Jones lent the campaign $25,000. Other financial angels found themselves caught short or had excuses for not donating. The situation improved as election day neared but never enough to keep the committee from running on the edge of bankruptcy. "Money is coming in very slowly," Clarkson confided in mid-September. "There is actually no money to appropriate, or even to pay bills with." A month later, the committee had $60,000 less than nothing.[18]

Democrats did somewhat better. As their chances of winning improved, so did their array of potential contributors. To appeal to Independent voters, the national committee proposed a popular subscription. Sums of as little as a dollar or as much as sixty were useful in their own way; one Democratic newspaper credited this with raising four times as much as the entire campaign war chest of 1880. But mostly, the donations afforded publicity for Democratic pretenses that theirs was an uprising of the humble against the lords of capital and allowed them to print the letters accompanying the donations. Far less publicity went to the heavyweight givers, most of whom were Swallowtail Democrats from silk-stocking Manhattan or Democratic politicians with extensive business interests: Barnum ($27,500), Gorman ($15,000), Congressman William L. Scott of Pennsylvania, owner of coal mines and racehorses ($24,000), Abram S. Hewitt of Cooper & Hewitt's ironworks ($25,300), German-language editor Oswald Ottendorfer ($18,000), and others like William Whitney, Daniel Manning, and Cleveland himself, each of whom gave between $10,000 and $16,000.[19]

Democratic managers nonetheless shared the frustrations of their Republican counterparts. They could not fulfill all demands on the committee. When the campaign closed, the books put them $50,000 in the red. Chairman Barnum had to seek a new contribution from Wisconsin railroad tycoon Alexander Mitchell. Mitchell gave it, though he expected influence in return. Even then, Gorman found it impossible to pay back money he had borrowed for the campaign, with Manning's endorsement on it. Four years later, creditors were still hectoring him for money.[20]

Newspaper allegations set the overall sums spent at prodigious heights. Naturally it was always the other side that spent most lavishly, their resources without limit. From England, the free-trade Cobden Club allegedly collected $2.5 million with which to elect Cleveland, and it was common knowledge that English industrialists had been assessed on a systematic basis to pay for a low-tariff president. Anything crippling America's enterprises would be worth a fortune to foreign rivals. With less than 700,000 people, Maine's state election reportedly required a quarter of a million dollars from Republicans. At that rate, New York would take two million easily.[21]

The figures were dead wrong. Altogether, the Republican National Committee raised $431,000. Half of it came from the candidate himself, who passed on the profits from his recently published memoirs. Democrats did better. No one offered a reliable overall figure, but the bulk of their income came from some dozen major contributors, who gave $460,000 in all. Maine Democrats may have hoped for $100,000 from the national committee. More realistically, they sent an emissary to New York to ask one-fifth that sum. He came back empty-handed. Spending $20,000 to carry a state sure to go Republican was, as Chairman Barnum declared, "preposterous."[22]

Where the party controlled state government, it could provide workers and contributions. Most presidential years, Republicans held that advantage, but not in 1884. Democratic administrations in New York, New Jersey, Pennsylvania, Ohio, Indiana, and Michigan controlled the spoils there. Democrats in Indiana assessed state employees, all the way down to janitors in the deaf and

The Public Be Crammed!

dumb asylum. In Philadelphia, the Republican city machine shook the plum tree thoroughly, but it found uses at home for the whole $30,000 it raised. That left the federal administration for the national committee to tap. The law kept them from squeezing assessments out of department clerks, but laws had never stopped the collectors before. The administration's coolness to Blaine did. Party faithful printed up circulars asking postal employees for money, but Postmaster General Walter Q. Gresham kept the collectors out of his buildings. For every four dollars that assessments brought Republicans in 1880, they got one now. Frustrated party organizers ended up sending their "stand and deliver" order to Washington's nonofficeholding loyalists instead. The one exception was Colonel W. W. Dudley, head of the Pension Bureau. Later investigation showed that the field expenses of special pension examiners had risen by about 50 percent in the two months before the election and by twice that in Dudley's own Indiana.[23]

Dudley's willingness to work was a marked contrast to the sullenness of other Arthur appointees. The administration's friends had taken defeat personally. Early in the year, so the story went, the president heard that Blaine had declared his one ambition, "to live long enough to beat Chester A. Arthur." Arthur took it ominously. Still sore over losing the nomination twice in the past, Blaine no doubt thought that Arthur might feel the sting as bitterly now. But supposing that Blaine had his way with the delegates, the president added smoothly, perhaps he could "round off his career with an additional experience which I shall escape." Blaine caught Arthur's meaning instantly: "It means that in case I am nominated I shall have not only the Democracy, but the Administration to fight."[24]

Not the whole administration, as it turned out. Secretary of the Navy Chandler made his greatest contribution to Blaine's cause in fostering Ben Butler's third-party candidacy, and he did what he could to keep the campaign away from personal issues, involving himself deeply in the behind-the-scenes management. In October, he came back to stump New Hampshire for the campaign's final weeks, making fifteen speeches in all. Postmaster General Walter Gresham gave a more gingerly help. Part of his reticence was personal; he had detested Blaine for years and may well have been the insider who had leaked the railroad scandal to the press during the 1876 prenomination campaign. But Gresham also eyed a seat on the federal bench. Making political addresses would mar his prospects. During the campaign, too, he replaced Charles J. Folger at the head of the Treasury, albeit briefly. Learning the new routine took all his time. Late in the campaign, he put in a cameo performance, with a speech before a businessmen's rally in New York.[25]

Beyond that, the administration stayed aloof. The president declined to meet with the national committee, much less help it out. While Chandler opened the navy yard to Republican organizers to make sure of "a good showing," the post office machinery, which, as a former assistant postmaster general contended, was second in importance only to the Republican National Committee in its impact, lay "useless under Gresham and silently malicious under Hatton." Later, Chairman Jones would claim that he knew of only one speech given on behalf of the national ticket by any member of the cabinet—which said more for his lack of knowledge than for the administration's lack of interest.[26]

Secretary of the Treasury Folger gave the Blaine campaign its worst embarrassment. A sad, weary man since his gubernatorial defeat in 1882, he had turned recluse and was ailing badly. His department's influence and the spreading reports of how Blaine had worked against him two years before made some well-publicized reconciliation especially desirable—say, an exchange of notes between the two men, suited for release to the press. When Folger died early in September, Blaine's task became hopeless. The press erupted with a clatter of letters from party insiders as to whether Folger's 1882 betrayal and defeat had broken his heart and led to his death. One of those published was Blaine's own, from two years before, urging his friends to knife Folger's candidacy—the letter that he had assured the secretary had never existed.[27]

In contrast to administration Stalwarts, Logan and his followers threw all their energies into the campaign. Most years, vice presidential candidates were geographical counterweights, nothing more. Not just to a latter generation but to their own, names like William Wheeler and Chet Arthur had been less than household words. But everybody had heard of these two running mates. Many took them seriously as presidential material.

Once all the partisan rant was cleared away, careful readers would have discovered that the two men acquitted themselves surprisingly well on the stump. Something of a political hack though he seemed, Hendricks used his speeches to distance himself from the worst abuses of the spoils system. Notorious as a one-note blowhard on bloody-shirt issues, Logan abandoned sectional issues almost entirely. Instead, he lauded the accomplishments of five Republican administrations. "You're the mon wot will murther the King's English, and for that rayson alone Oi intend to vote for ye," an Irish Democrat supposedly told "Black Jack." Actually, Logan only bruised it a little. When Logan declared "free trade, State banks, a rotten and depreciated currency, state rights, and slavery" the monuments of Democracy, some listeners may have snickered that Logan, an antebellum Democrat and apol-

The Public Be Crammed!

ogist for slavery, ought to know. More ribald laughter came in response to Logan's insistence that the country's 60 percent growth in population under the Republicans "could not have been brought about under Democratic rule." Still, Logan and Hendricks found their services in constant demand. "If he can make such a good speech on what he knows nothing about," the *Chicago Tribune* pleaded after one Logan performance, "what kind of speech can he make on a subject that he does know something about?"[28]

Neither man discredited the ticket among party faithful, but their usefulness differed. Neither ticket yoked close friends together. After years in the Senate, Logan and Blaine felt only a wary respect for each other. "We never speak as we pass by, / Me to Jim Blaine nor him to I," one couplet ran. Through the campaign that followed, Logan served dutifully, but he always stood a little on the outside. He grumbled at a lack of press attention, complained at the want of an aggressive keynote for the campaign. Logan had a representative on the national committee but shared little of the power and no part of the broader decision making. When he showed up at Cincinnati that autumn, there was nobody there to greet him: no crowds, no brass bands, no reception committee, and no reporter to take down his words at the rally later in the day. (There was a reporter to take down his tantrum over such poor treatment, including some sensational remarks about the "tattooed man"; Logan's wife persuaded him not to print them.) All this was pure inadvertence, but it made Logan no happier. "If Ohio is carried, it will carry itself," he growled. "The present style of management won't carry it."[29]

Between Hendricks and Cleveland lay a different kind of distance, that of two strangers, politically and personally. Hendricks must have reflected that his age and experience had made him worthier of the presidency than the tyro topping the ticket. Yet he took well to second place. Rumors of resentment were scotched instantly. Within a few weeks, the candidates shook hands in Albany, and Hendricks came back glowing with praise. A month later, when reports circulated that Cleveland would be asked to step aside, Hendricks wrote a "private" letter, clearly meant for publication, dismissing the idea. Lest scandalmongers miss the point, Hendricks made it plain in his first major address. Departing from his text, adjusting his glasses to give the audience an admonitory glare, he dared slanderers to do their worst. "I would be willing to submit the ticket to the vote of the people to-morrow," he asserted. "I feel perfectly safe about Indiana." There was one anxious moment in Illinois, when the train Hendricks was riding struck a broken rail and pitched off the track. Cars were smashed and some twenty passengers injured, but Hendricks was able to pick his way out of the wreckage bruised but unshaken. Within a day, he had begun speechmaking again, complaining only that being so "bunged up" kept him from giving his speeches the extra polish they needed.[30]

While Logan defended, Hendricks attacked. His rank as a half-elder statesman allowed him to do what Logan's infamy as a political roughneck restrained him from doing. A respectable gentleman had the sheen to take the offensive. For Democrats, he defined "reform" in ways much more comfortable than the Mugwumps' civil service notions. A change of administration would throw thieves out: tens of thousands of them. In German American communities, he tied the Republicans to Prohibition, in credit-poor farm areas, he showed how the $400 million locked into the Treasury by excessive taxation had cut in half the circulation of paper money.[31]

Hendricks also brought the Democrats advantages that Logan could not match. Republicans had hoped that the vice president could bring the Stalwarts around. But Logan had never played the dominating role that Conkling had, and his pull with the Stalwarts in the administration was nil. Bloody-shirt oratory was his forte, precisely the topic that the national committee wanted to downplay. His strength lay among Western Republicans, the very ones most attracted to Blaine anyhow; and while he could deliver Illinois to the ticket, so could any candidate. He was the last man to appeal to liberal reformers and ideal for making them overlook Hendricks's defects. On issues of paper money or spoils politics, what difference was there between them, except that no one thought Hendricks personally corrupt? Which one was more the gentleman, more "presidential"? Long before the campaign closed, it was plain that Logan added no new strength to the ticket.[32]

Hendricks, on the other hand, made a real difference. The "old ticket" still had resonance. Party loyalists restive with so new and chancy a candidate as Cleveland found confidence in Hendricks, whose name had been mentioned as a presidential possibility for sixteen years. Certainly Tammany Hall's regulars were readier to give the vice presidential nominee a serious hearing. Apparently the Democratic National Committee used the Indianan as its go-between in its overtures to John Kelly. But Hendricks mattered still more in his home state. His appeal there was strong and his leadership generally acknowledged. As Logan stumped the West, Hendricks concentrated on Indiana. Without him on the ticket, the state would certainly have been lost, and the election with it.[33]

Hendricks had another appeal, as well. He could attack the tariff safely. Unlike Cleveland, he had widely published views on the issue. Three years before, in an article for the *North American Review*, he pronounced free trade impossible and incidental protection indispensable. Endorsing a tariff

The Public Be Crammed!

commission as the fairest means for adjusting rates, Hendricks distanced himself from Morrison's bill long before it was devised.[34]

That distancing mattered because tariff protection did. "Workingman, you cast your ballot for either Bread and water or buckwheat cakes and sausages," a Trenton paper challenged readers. "Which do you prefer?" Talking about free trade gave Republicans their best chance of raising a big war chest, though they also tried to terrify the holders of national bank charters and railroads with government land grants into sharing their wealth. But months passed before the issue really took hold. After the Morrison bill fiasco, selling the Democrats as free-trade fanatics was tough work, especially with a platform that, as one reformer sighed, "emitted no more than a squawk." Cleveland's silence and widely touted ignorance on the subject helped. As long as Gorman, Barnum, and Tilden's old associates could run the canvass, there was no chance of the party defining revenue reform in astringent ways, or, in fact, talking much about the topic at all. Gorman had protected Maryland's coal in the Senate, while Barnum lobbied the House against tariff reduction the spring before. Protectionist Democrats had to make sure that if Cleveland won, free-traders would not take the credit. Samuel J. Randall became an essential figure on the campaign trail in Ohio and West Virginia, with convincing explanations for the tariff plank as a guarantee for protection. Late in the campaign, the national committee assigned him to New York, New Jersey, and Connecticut, all in danger of going Republican, all thick with protectionist Democrats looking for reassurance.[35]

Democrats meant to keep the emphasis on Blaine's record. They were not, in fact, trying to dodge the real issues of the canvass. As they argued it, corruption *was* the real issue. Republicans were trying to make people believe that they should discuss a tariff for revenue only, Carl Schurz warned, when the country risked electing "a politician for revenue only." Blaine's conduct was just one symptom of the moral decay that ran through Republican government, from too many years in office. Everyone knew that the new steel navy was being built by the old stealing contractors. That there were no other recent scandals only showed how corrupt Republicans were, Senator Dan Voorhees of Indiana told one audience. "Expert thieves make very little noise." It was time for a change of parties, to go over the books and find the rascals who had not yet been detected. If sixteen thousand silver dollars weighed a thousand pounds, Governor Tom Waller of Connecticut calculated, and if a mule could carry that much, Republican thefts would take a mule-train twenty-eight miles long.[36]

There was more to it than professions of shocked virtue, though that

"He can't beat his record"

*(Joseph Keppler, Puck, July 30, 1884). As Stephen B. Elkins (with crumpled hat),
carpetbag former governor William Pitt Kellogg (with handkerchief), naval contractor
John Roach, and freebooting former secretary of the Navy George Robeson (in spectacles)
cheer him on, Blaine finds his reputation—all tattoos—pelting ahead. Note the wreaths
from well-wishing monopolists Cyrus Field, Russell Sage, and Jay Gould. Poking his head
from the trainers' tent is William Walter Phelps, offering a word to Whitelaw Reid.*

appeal promised great returns among discontented Republicans. Democrats
also used Blaine's corruption to drive home the point about the sinister
relationship between "monopolists" and Republicans. For Greenbackers or
working-class radicals, the secret deals to hand over the public lands to
railroad companies in return for fat commissions to prominent statesmen
said as much about Blaine's party as Blaine himself. All they needed to
clinch the argument was to point to Blaine's involvement in a projected
landowning syndicate in Ohio's Hocking Valley, where wage cuts had led to a
coal miners' strike, ugly and violent. Blaine's protests that he owned no stock
and that he had never owned an acre of coal lands were technically correct;
he had made a contract, with an option to invest in those lands, and had
agreed to enter the company as a director. Twenty-five thousand dollars'
worth of stock was held for him under another promoter's name, and Blaine
exchanged it for bonds. The fact that the speculation ended in nothing, and
that Blaine's only holdings in coal lands were in West Virginia, far from the
labor violence, was easy to overlook, just as it was easy to tie Blaine to the

The Public Be Crammed!

union-busting activities of his editorial mouthpiece, Whitelaw Reid, whose *New York Tribune* fought the Typographical Union. In fact, Blaine desperately wanted the dispute settled in the union's favor and held out the possibility of a Senate seat to Reid if he cooperated. Reid would not budge. "The thing is of far less consequence than you imagine," he wrote the candidate. "The men are mostly against us anyway, and are a thoroughly treacherous and unscrupulous gang, who think they see a chance for political blackmail." But Blaine's guess that the publicity would cost him five thousand votes may have come closer to the mark. New York printers formed an anti-Blaine club, and trade unions marched with banners calling for boycotting the *Tribune*. On Blaine's head orators put a system that bayoneted working men in the Hocking Valley "for asking bread when they can't get work" and jailing them for it in Pennsylvania. "One Hundred Million Surplus," one set of headlines warned. "This is What Blaine Wants. Jay Gould and His Ring Want It. They Mean to Get It."[37]

Democratic language rang with the language of antimonopoly, the kind that Southern and Western Democrats had been using for so long. In particular, it tied Blaine to the bad boys of Wall Street, Gould and Cyrus Field. This was by no means an attack on respectable business. On the contrary, Democratic targets were the ones notorious as union-crushers and speculators, not builders, and the ones whose wealth had depended on pliable friends in government. Attacking wicked predators had the added convenience of saving Democrats from offering any actual program for undoing the advantages that "monopolists" already had. Let Americans turn the rascals out, and justice enough would be done. One might describe it as rocking-chair radicalism, a sense of constant motion without any advance, except that Democratic solutions were not so much nonexistent as unsaid.[38]

If neither side could define the terms of the campaign, that was not because Americans were paying no attention. By mid-September, insiders no longer talked about public apathy. Underfunded though the parties' efforts might be, they were putting on quite a show. The outward panoply of politics amused, excited, and appalled observers, as well it might. "Campaign eloquence burdens the air," the *St. Paul Dispatch* summed up, "the public be crammed." Marchers, placards, speeches, torchlights flaring from coal oil receptacles, all seemed at their peak. Old-timers compared it to the two greatest razzle-dazzlers of the past, the "Wide-Awake" campaign of 1860 and the "Log Cabin" campaign of 1840.[39]

What did the spectacle mean, in the end? Genteel editors proclaimed it the triumph of showmanship over substance. Because war issues no longer appealed to the Northern mind as strongly, Republicans put on parades to gird voters' spirits. Because Blaine's character was so shabby, his backers had to drown reasoned argument out with a campaign of raucous cheers. Crowds that shouted, "Burn, burn, burn this letter!" very likely never read the letter itself to see if Blaine had written anything to be ashamed of. The last thing politicians wanted was a "campaign of education."[40]

Critics had evidence to back up their case, but the parades proved them more wrong than right. None of the slogans marchers bore was as good as a treatise, to be sure, and many were wild simplifications. Good taste alone should have ruled out such banners as "I am a sick man—Blaine," especially if marchers really believed him fatally ill, and even some bystanders must have scratched their head over the transparency, "Baseball and Governmental Reform."[41]

Yet what is most striking is how far the banners stuck to the large issues beyond candidates' personalities, and how enduring the sectional issue remained, in spite of the Republican National Committee's efforts to downplay it: "Free Ballot, but not Free Trade," "Free Homes," "Free Schools," "We know but one flag," "The South is satisfied with Hendricks's war record," "England is against Ireland. The Irish are against England. They are for Blaine," "Vote against the British free trade dudes," "Free labor against slave labor." As Republicans paraded, with potteries and coal dealers showing their products, or with floats on which smiths forged horseshoes and ironmongers turned out miniature steel rails, they made a statement about what the tariff meant for wage-earners that no pamphlet could have improved upon.[42]

The very way the parades were organized sent a clear message itself. Union veterans still marched in their faded coats. So did torchlight soldiers in costume uniforms. But often audiences saw processions of workers, divided by craft. Defining themselves as veterans, marchers spoke of a vision of the electorate as Americans together, bound by a common concern for a republic in peril. Distinguishing themselves by the work they did, the parade spoke for a very different kind of politics, where parties deserved to win because they appealed to individual pocketbook interests, all of which, combined, served the greater national good. Americans were both good citizens and breadwinners, of course, but the tariff shifted the emphasis from the first to the second.

No doubt Americans were "educated" in countless despicable ways. The partisan press stirred emotions and traditional loyalties rather than inspiring reflection. It did more than slant information in 1884; it credited outright frauds. Newspapers invented rallies and listed the personnel in countless nonexistent Ben Butler clubs. Joseph Medill, chief editor at the *Chicago*

The Public Be Crammed!

Tribune, was astonished to read that he had declared Illinois leaning Democrats' way, but was no more offended than Carl Schurz, who found it reported that, far from paying his own expenses, he demanded $250 for every speech he made for the Democratic ticket. These misstatements had purposes behind them. If Medill gave up on Republicans' chances in Illinois, contributors would decide to hold back funding. If Schurz was a reform speaker for pay, his arguments against Blaine's ethics held no weight.[43]

All the same, anyone who wanted detailed argument could get it. Newspapers described the spectacular parades, but they printed public speeches verbatim, and most orators gave closely reasoned arguments for and against Republican policies. They were like all speeches, selective in their proofs and full of sophistry, but there was material enough for those who wanted it in order to make a judgment and, in most of the North, alternative sources for those wanting the whole story.

Hoopla did not replace issues, then. It complemented them by stirring up the passions while newspapers and speakers drove home political convictions. But did it do the job it was meant to do? Undeniably, parades were widely attended. But were they unleashing real enthusiasm or trying to create it synthetically? Many insiders thought it the latter, not the former. Observers on the spot counted many fewer people attending a gathering than the newspapers reported; the "hundreds" of women from New York's high society who turned out for Blaine dwindled to fifty at most, and the forty thousand Buffalo residents who turned out to welcome Grover Cleveland home amounted to just a fourth that many. Indeed, many who showed up "spontaneously" were carted in from Pennsylvania and Canada, all expenses paid and no questions about political affiliation asked.[44]

For those who wanted a campaign more strictly of "education," the lesson seemed plain. But there *had* been such a campaign—there was *always* such a campaign, running alongside the spectacular one—and that did not seem to be working very well, either. Both parties set up "literary bureaus," though Gorman's work was easier. All he had to do was revive the one that Tilden had set up and hire its old head, former assemblyman William S. Andrews, to run it. Much of the real work was done by *Brooklyn Eagle* correspondent William C. Hudson, who supervised the publication of documents and did confidential missions. Circulars, squibs, and articles from his "Press Department," as it called itself, poured out of special offices on Broadway, for insertion in country newspapers. In Washington, the congressional committees no longer could do their old work of assessing officeholders, but they still could send out franked speeches by the bale. (Barely solvent and forced to sell documents at a dollar per hundred, the Republican body tapped the national committee for expenses and got a fraction of what it wanted, and then only when it became clear that the documents could not be spread any other way.) The national committees carried on their own pamphleteering operations. The more the parties sent, the more outlanders called for.[45]

It was never enough to suit the armchair critics. Complaints arose that Democratic managers were "too blind and stupid" to send out speeches by their members. At the end of August, states that should have been blanketed in franked documents against the tariff were being let strictly alone. The committee left one big mailing to the employees in the Capitol folding room, who, as good Republicans, sent out their own party's high-protection booklet in place of the speech that Democrats meant to send.[46]

But the managers may have understood realities better than the would-be educators. Perhaps it was true that by the end of September the Republican National Committee had shipped off three million documents. Nobody could guess how many of them went straight from the voter's hands into the trash baskets. Voters read newspapers, not speeches, an Illinois sheriff warned Democratic leaders. Wisconsin party manager E. C. Wall snorted that he "would not give 'a dollar a million' for documents sent out [in August]," and an Independent paper suggested that the way to do the circulation of documents best "would be practically not to do it at all."[47]

The truth was that the real educators in this campaign were not leaflets and stale arguments at all. They were events. Through their literature, parties could define the basic issues of the canvass as they chose, but from late July onward, circumstances, surprises, and the managing talents of state organizations would be the real forces defining how those issues played. In all those respects, indeed, the campaign would be one full of constant—and invariably unpleasant—uncertainties; for the fate of Blaine and Cleveland lay on the periphery of American political life: with the disaffected members of both parties and the nearly one-party South.

11

Love's Libels Lost

On July 21, 1884, the *Buffalo Evening Telegraph* turned itself, for a time, from a struggling afternoon scandal sheet into the most-read paper in the city. Responding to what its editors insisted was a crowd of inquiries about Democratic presidential nominee Grover Cleveland's personal reputation, the newspaper could hold its peace no longer. In three bold columns, it revealed to readers: "A Terrible Tale."[1]

What followed has become political legend, the anecdotal centerpiece of the 1884 campaign. Back when he had practiced law in Buffalo, Cleveland had had a liaison with a young widow, Maria Halpin, who in time had brought a child into the world, Oscar Folsom Cleveland. All at once, the clean divisions of the campaign that Mugwumps had hoped for, on the character issue, were put in jeopardy. Gloomily, New York's Independent leaders gathered around the table at the University Club, wondering whether they should withdraw their support for this rake in reformer's clothing. Then some bright Mugwump proposed the solution. Blaine's private life was as admirable as his public career was dishonest; with Cleveland, matters seemed just the other way round. The moral was obvious: put Cleveland in the office he was so fitted to hold "and remand Mr. Blaine to the private life which he is so eminently qualified to adorn." And then, as histories tell it, came the fitting climax. Grover Cleveland could have rushed into print with excuses. Instead, Democratic managers were ordered to "tell the truth." As the full story came out, the clouds of scandal melted away beneath the beams of political honesty.[2]

What serves for later onlookers as the defining moment in a sensational drama, or proof positive that Gilded Age politics was bereft of meaning, needs another look. The incident was no sudden eruption, nor, contrary to most accounts, a matter laid to rest early enough to lose its force by election day. The Maria Halpin scandal was one of three; it was orchestrated by the Republican Party and kept alive to the end of the campaign; it throve because of certain larger political realities unique to this presidential campaign and because of its connection to "real" issues; indeed, it spoke indirectly to those issues; and, lastly, it was closely bound to the gaffe that cost Blaine New York. Indeed, the whole tone of 1884 scandalmongering demands an explanation. Why did it happen, and why only this year?

What made the *Telegraph*'s "Terrible Tale" so dangerous was its scope and the peculiar qualities of its target. Not since Abraham Lincoln's nomination had any major party selected a candidate so briefly in public life. About him, any wild story seemed plausible and likelier to stick. The *Telegraph* was not telling one story but dozens, all of which together depicted a moral monster. No behavior, it seemed, was too vile for Cleveland. For years, he had caroused with Buffalo's lowlife. Beastly drunk, he careened through the streets. Whores were his regular companions. Once two reputable citizens chanced on a row in a saloon. They spotted Cleveland brawling over a prostitute with a fellow lawyer, "till they were both nearly naked and covered with blood." His debaucheries as mayor were a public scandal, and, even as governor, he revisited Buffalo's vice dens on a regular basis or debauched himself through a full weekend on willing wantons.[3]

Those who knew the *Telegraph* best would have read the article skeptically; the newspaper throve on personal scandals, and, apparently, on libel suits for defamation. But the *Boston Journal* was another matter. Staid, conservative, it remained one of New England's leading journals. Yet on July 22, it published the findings of a special correspondent sent to Buffalo, and they were as damning as the *Telegraph*'s. What made them especially credible was the testimony of ministers, one of whom, Rev. George H. Ball of the Hudson Street Free Baptist Church, apparently spoke from personal knowledge. No respectable family ever let Cleveland into their circle, he told the journalist. The governor was a whoremonger, a barroom roisterer who went on sprees at the Beaver Island Club, "a resort of lust and drunkenness." After one such a drunken frolic, he and his partner, Oscar Folsom, went out joyriding and lost control of the horses. Too intoxicated to save himself, Folsom was thrown to his death.[4]

Love's Libels Lost

Dr. Ball had been glad to talk. Indeed, he kept on talking through the campaign, and every few weeks came up with new details. He could cite many another Maria Halpin, the minister asserted. There was that German woman who was no better than she should be, and her two willing daughters, down by the railroad tracks, and Cleveland's visits there. A witness downtown had seen the portly governor, too drunk to walk, lugged downstairs. "Well-authenticated facts" all, and any individuals wanting to hear the names, meet the victims, or talk to Dr. Ball's sources need only come to Buffalo themselves and scan the proofs.[5]

The wider context to the Halpin affair needs emphasis. Without it, Cleveland's illicit liaison lost much of its force; with it, the incident became the most lurid illustration of a shameless life. Yet all by itself, the Halpin scandal could do damage. Chastity might matter to women, but women did not vote; men did. For the more devout among them, the governor's misdeed was damning by itself. But even more worldly folk, for whom the issue was whether Cleveland had acted honorably, would take offense, if the tale ran as the *Journal* and *Telegraph* told it.

Victorian morals deplored sexual relations outside of marriage but put a different stigma on men than on women, and still more on men who sought out the affair than those tempted and, in effect, seduced by womanly wiles. That was what made the *Telegraph*'s account so poisonous. Fathering an illegitimate child was, if anything, a side issue. Cleveland had not fallen. He had seduced a frail woman. When she depended on him, he had played the cad and then the coward. Having promised marriage, he broke the promise. The child was abandoned to an unfeeling world. When Mrs. Halpin became troublesome, Cleveland had a powerful friend abduct her and lock her up in a madhouse. Only the timely intervention of hospital officials saved the poor woman from being committed, and even then, they could not keep her from being bullied into a financial settlement with Cleveland that spared him any future expense. He was, in the language of the time, "unmanly."

If the larger context of Cleveland's transgression was what made it lethal and the obscurity of his background what made it plausible, those same two qualities were in the end what saved him. Sponge away the brightly colored background that the *Telegraph* and *Journal* had painted and Cleveland's affair would dwindle into an embarrassing incident, and, perhaps, not so damning after all. But Cleveland's defenders could do better. They could draw a different setting: the young man who worked to support his widowed mother and younger sisters, the sheriff whose sense of duty brought him to the gallows itself, to pull the trap that sent two criminals to their death, the tireless executive, poring over bills and petitions until two in the morning, the candidate whose every public action proclaimed his respect for the duty and dignity of his office.[6]

Because the Halpin case itself mattered less than the way in which it fit that larger landscape, Cleveland's courage made smart politics. "Tell the truth:" those three words, when published, did him far more good than any longer defense. No coward or libertine would have replied so.

From then on, reformers managed to strip the Halpin case of its whole damning context. Within a week, they had taken up Dr. Ball's invitation. Far from being universally believed, the fact-finding committee learned, the minister was telling whoppers that even the foremost Republican paper in town refused to believe. Instead of assembling the city's rakes, the Beaver Island Club had included Buffalo's finest citizens on its rolls. Their wives and children attended its social events. Oscar Folsom died sober. He had not been returning from the club nor in his law partner's company when killed.[7]

As for the many women in Grover Cleveland's life, another investigator, a lawyer sent by the reformers on the Boston Committee of One Hundred, uncovered the truth. Dr. Ball's "proofs" were worthless hearsay, too vague to confirm or disprove. The harder other committees looked, the less they found. Two clergymen had backed up Dr. Ball's accusations. Now they produced nothing beyond rumor. They referred to other Buffalo residents as authority for some of the tales. Every one of the people interviewed denied ever having said any such thing. Having boasted that his evidence was available to all, the editor of the *Telegraph* admitted that he had none, except about the Maria Halpin affair. The *Independent* sent Rev. Kingsley Twining to find out the truth. From those who knew Cleveland personally, he heard nothing but praise. Intimates, without dissent, pronounced the charges of drinking and whoring not just false but impossible. Cleveland may not have passed across the thresholds of the best families in Buffalo often, but not for lack of invitations. Hosts simply could not pull him away from his desk.[8]

Cut loose from the larger context of licentiousness, the Halpin affair would have dwindled, even if it had been exactly as the *Telegraph* described it. Indeed, it would have been more baffling than damning. How could Cleveland, who otherwise seemed to behave within the bounds of proper manly conduct, be a seducer? The answer that investigators brought back was reassuring. There had been no seduction, no breach of promise, no abduction, and no adultery. There had been an affair between consenting single adults, and Grover Cleveland was by no means the only one to whom Maria Halpin consented. Far from the delicate innocent, the investigators depicted her as that other stereotype that Gilded Age America had built up as one exception to the general picture of women as undefiled by sexual pas-

Love's Libels Lost

"Those dogs won't fight—they are dying of starvation"
(F. Graetz, Puck, August 20, 1884). But Republican manager Stephen Elkins and editor
Charles Dana of the Sun keep pushing the clerical slanderers on.

sion: the willing widow, who knew her way around. On September 14, 1874, Maria Halpin had indeed had a child, which she insisted was Cleveland's. Cleveland, it was reported, had had his doubts. Other men had shared her intimacies at the same time that he did. The problem was, they were already married. Some of them were Cleveland's close friends. As much for their protection as from his own sense of duty, he claimed paternity and provided money for support of the widow and child.

That was not enough for Maria Halpin. Lonely, disgraced, and caring for the child, she drank heavily, so much so that Cleveland grew alarmed for the boy's safety. He turned for help to his friend Judge Roswell Burrows, trustee of the Protestant Orphan Asylum. Burrows arranged the paperwork to commit the child to the orphanage, and in March 1876, Maria Halpin signed the consent forms. Cleveland paid the board bills and even gave her money to set up shop in Niagara Falls, some miles away. If Mrs. Halpin had been lonely before, she was utterly bereft now. At once she started trying to regain

Love's Libels Lost

custody. When the legal remedies failed, she abducted the boy. The trustees were reluctant to press charges. But the drinking continued and word came back to Judge Burrows that the boy was worse than neglected. He was in danger of being killed. It was Burrows, not Cleveland, who remanded the boy to the asylum, and when the mother resisted, the arresting officer on his own legal authority had her taken to an institution run by the Sisters of Charity. It was not, strictly speaking, a madhouse. Recovering alcoholics found treatment there, and no one tried to have her committed. It was a temporary holding tank until the child could be put into safe custody. That ended the affair between Cleveland and Mrs. Halpin.

By the standards of his day, Cleveland had done more than what was expected of single men. "After the primary offense," Rev. Twining summed up, Cleveland's conduct "was singularly honorable, showing no attempt to evade responsibility, and doing all he could to meet the duties involved, of which marriage was certainly not one."[9]

As far as Cleveland's supporters were concerned, that was the end of the story. Yet something deeply unsettling remains, once all the explanations are set down. The investigators felt free to pronounce Halpin a loose woman and to charge her with a number of other lovers. But they never bothered to interview her in person. Nor, apparently, did that part of the story come from Cleveland. It may well not be true. But, equally disturbing, few people shared the indignation of William Dean Howells at the moral convolution that it took to clear Cleveland at the same time that it reproved Mrs. Halpin. As "an enemy of that contemptible, hypocritical, lop-sided morality which says that a woman shall suffer all the shame of unchastity and a man none," he wrote Mark Twain, "I want to see [Cleveland] destroyed by his past."[10]

It was revealing, too, that Republicans, in asserting the importance of the scandal, could not settle for the limited wrong that the investigating committees admitted to. They had to restore the entire, discredited context in which the Halpin case stood, a plain confession that the male dereliction of which Cleveland stood guilty was simply not dynamite enough to sway voters. Harlots would flock to Washington at his summons, they warned, and find lodgings conveniently near the White House. "I'd not vote for Grover C.," one ditty ran, "Glutton, coward, dastard.— / Not Father of his Country— / Father of a Bastard!"[11]

But the Halpin scandal did not stand alone. By September, it had a rival. Even before *Telegraph* broke silence, Democratic newspapers had warned that they had tidbits quite as interesting as any beguiling widow could provide. The muttered threats got louder and more specific as the "Terrible Tale" spread. At first, the charges were couched as questions. A journal in

Love's Libels Lost

Louisville, the *Chicago Times* had heard, was asserting that as a young man, Blaine was forced to leave Kentucky to escape being lynched. What curious incident could that be referring to? (The *Times* knew perfectly well. It had spread the whole story on page one back in 1876 when Blaine was front-runner for the Republican nomination, and its appearance in a Kentucky newspaper had added to the strain on Blaine's constitution that brought on his physical collapse the Sunday before the Republican convention.) Other newspapers brought up the charges elliptically, as an example of just the kind of dirty slanders they abhorred, the kind that would become far more common if Republicans did not lay off Cleveland's private life at once.[12]

Then the story broke into the open. Indiana's capital had always been a city for journalistic bruisers; the standards of professional journalism and independence were weaker than in New York, Boston, or Chicago. On August 8, after two weeks of deploring the introduction of candidates' private lives into the campaign, editor and publisher John C. Shoemaker of the *Sentinel* threw out the clinching argument for leaving Cleveland's past alone. "There is hardly an intelligent man in this country who has not heard that James G. Blaine betrayed the girl whom he married, and then only married her at the muzzle of a shotgun," the *Sentinel* charged. If the story was true, his private character had a blot fouler, "if possible," than his public career.[13]

With other newspapers sure to pick up the story, Blaine acted at once. In a statement to the press, he pronounced the allegation as "utterly and abominably false in every statement and in every implication." Not only that. He wired Senator Benjamin Harrison of Indiana to start libel proceedings for $50,000 in damages. The case was purely for political effect in a closely contested state. A state court would have brought matters to trial quickly, but Blaine chose the federal court, and not, perhaps, only because the judge presiding and the federal marshal choosing the jury were both appointees who owed their position to Harrison's recommendation. Far from hurrying the case toward judgment, he had his attorneys put up delay after delay to assure that there would be no verdict until after election day. Once the votes were in, enemies charged, he would drop the suit, as indeed he did. But there is reason to suspect that Blaine had a more substantial goal than making a plausible show of righteous indignation. He may have been taking a calculated risk. Knowing that the *Sentinel* could not prove its charges, Blaine conceivably was counting on the lawsuit to force a complete retraction.[14]

If that were the case, he miscalculated. Beyond question, the *Sentinel* was caught dead to rights, and its lawyers knew it, if their arguments were any guide. There had been no seduction, no forced wedding, and more than thirty years of what everyone agreed was a singularly close companionable marriage.[15] Nobody could prove that the bride's father, six years after his own death, had forced Blaine to marry. Still, the newspaper's owners were not prepared to give up so easily. Just as Blaine may have meant to bluff them into settling, they raised the stakes to induce him to drop the suit by bringing out evidence surrounding a curious circumstance about Blaine's marriage. According to his campaign biography, published that August, he had married Harriet Stanwood in Pittsburgh on March 29, 1851. Their first child arrived on June 18th.

What were the facts? Of the basic story, there can be no doubt at all. As a young man visiting Kentucky in 1848, Blaine had taken a position teaching at a military academy in Georgetown. Not far away, in an old-fashioned brick house at the heart of town, there was a women's school, where the three Stanwood sisters taught. Harriet Stanwood struck those who knew her as the smartest of them all. What followed was a happy, an almost natural match. She and Blaine had become intimate, far more intimate than any of their friends knew. By late 1850, several people were beginning to notice changes in Miss Stanwood's figure. A few began to suspect that she might be in the family way. That winter, she left the Bluegrass, never to return, and around that time, Blaine departed, too.

A few gossips had hinted at some connection between the two events and surmised that Blaine might be father to the child—if child there was. But when Blaine returned to Kentucky to continue teaching, he came alone and there was no talk of any wife or child, no hint given by himself that he had indeed married. Yet, from the facts that his official campaign biography gave, that was exactly what had happened. There had been a marriage in Pittsburgh, after which Harriet had then gone home to her mother's house in Maine to await the arrival of the child, while Blaine himself went elsewhere; when a son was born, Blaine was a thousand miles away. Not until February 1852 did he see his wife again.[16]

Republican editors scurried for a way around the fatal arithmetic of a child born three months into a marriage. Witnesses came forward to announce that, to their personal knowledge, the Blaines had wed in a big public ceremony in Millersburg, that they had married quietly in Maine, that some other Blaine held that marriage in Pittsburgh, that everyone knew that they were husband and wife and no one wondered about the pregnancy, that there had been no marriage to know about, and that no one remotely imagined that Harriet Stanwood had been pregnant. All of these stories rang with conviction; each of them made nonsense of all the others; and every single one of them was bosh.[17]

That became embarrassingly clear when one last witness offered his own

Love's Libels Lost

"He *instituted the ordeal. Can he stand it himself?*"
(*Bernhard Gillam,* Puck, *August 13, 1884*). Puck *was not alone in spotting Blaine behind the Halpin scandal. In fact, Blaine very much wanted Republican papers to let it alone; rightly, he suspected that there was nothing there and that it would be one more distraction from an "aggressive campaign" focusing on the tariff.*

version of events. On September 19, as the *Sentinel*'s lawyers filed an increasingly damning set of queries about the Blaines' dalliance, and two days after the paper went to court for an order forcing the candidate to give the relevant information under oath, Blaine's friend William Walter Phelps released a "private" letter from Blaine himself (written apparently while Phelps was Blaine's houseguest and approachable in easier ways). There had, he explained, been two marriages, not one. After nearly two years' engagement, he and Harriet had married secretly on June 30, 1850, in Millersburg. There were two witnesses, both dead, no minister, no public notice, and no license; under the law of his native state, Pennsylvania, none was needed. It was only the following winter that Blaine began to feel doubts about the marriage's validity. Under Kentucky law, it seemed, it took a license certified by the clerk of the county court to make a marriage legal. A second marriage in Georgetown was out of the question. People would talk, and Blaine would forfeit his job. So in March 1851, James and Harriet went to Pittsburgh and held a quiet wedding. A child had been born the following June and died in his grandmother's arms three years later. His ashes lay beneath a stone in a Maine cemetery, though sacrilegious hands had recently defaced it by erasing the last number in the birth date—*an act that*, as any reader might infer, had been part of some obscure Democratic plot to confuse people about when he was born.

It was a very touching letter, throbbing with what sounded like a quite genuine indignation, and for evidence of the Pittsburgh marriage, Blaine could summon witnesses, including an old classmate, Congressman John V. LeMoyne. And yet, Blaine's indignation was more sincere than his explanation.[18]

For, as Democrats began to scan the letter, they came up with quite a few discrepancies. Except for Mr. and Mrs. Blaine, nobody alive had been at that first marriage, and nobody else alive had been let in on the secret afterward, not even LeMoyne. At the time, as if by chance, Blaine had come up to him on the street to explain that he was about to marry "a young lady, who was then passing through Pittsburgh with her friends; that her friends were opposed to the marriage, and that he could manage to get her out of the hotel for a short time if it could be arranged to have the ceremony performed." LeMoyne, completely taken in by this fairy tale, located a preacher and arranged a secret ceremony.[19]

Blaine's protest that in wedding without a license he mistakenly assumed that Kentucky law was just like Pennsylvania's had two problems. First, Pennsylvania statutes *did* require a license; second, Kentucky's had *not*. The requirement that Blaine had referred to was written into law in July 1852,

Love's Libels Lost

more than a year after the second marriage! A marriage without documentation or living witnesses certainly could have occurred, but there were other problems. June 30, 1850, fell on a Sunday. Among Protestants, as one journal pointed out, Sunday marriages were uncommon, indeed, almost unknown. Of one date, Blaine must have been sure, his own birth date. He was twenty, no more, and would not attain his majority until next January. "Who will pretend that Mr. Blaine thought that marriage by a minor, in secret, without license or minister, and on Sunday, was legal?"[20]

There was one last marriage scandal, and because it appeared at the tail end of the campaign, most accounts have made even less note of it than Blaine's. Late in October, Republican newspapers exposed the brutal facts about Prohibition nominee John P. St. John's first marriage. Wed at nineteen, St. John had regretted his decision almost at once. Within two months, husband and wife had separated. Seven years later, the wife asked for a divorce and remarried soon after that. So did St. John. There had been a child by the first marriage. St. John provided for the boy's education and when the young man was reading law took him into his own home. Later he landed him a government job. It was an unexceptional story, until the campaign smear artists got hold of it. They produced affidavits from people who had known the first wife many years after the marriage, ready to swear that St. John had starved her, deprived her of suitable clothing, and abandoned her. Finding someone who could take an oath "that St. John had wrecked her life" was easy. In the heat of a campaign, ardent believers were willing to swear to anything. With some creative writing, newspaper readers could infer that St. John's first wife had died of a broken heart twenty-one years after the marriage ended.[21]

Taken altogether, the three domestic scandals gave the 1884 election a distinct flavor. "The average editor and politician seem now to think that the Ship of State is a mud-scow," complained one paper. Then and later contemporaries recalled the campaign with a sort of disgusted wonder as a spectacle they had never seen before and hoped never to see again. Republicans accused the "male Magdalen" not just of bastardy but adultery. "Think of [New York attorney William M.] Evarts accepting the position of hangman, and sending the Black Maria to the jail and the white Maria to the lunatic asylum!" one deacon told a crowd. When Belva Lockwood, the Woman's Rights candidate, proposed a joint conference of the presidential nominees to arrange an official truce to the campaign of abuse, she not only found no takers, she was also warned by Republicans not to go into the same room with Cleveland; she *was* a widow, after all, "and Cleveland—well, he is Cleveland."[22]

In response, the most irresponsible Democratic newspapers played up "the Schoolmaster in Love" for all it was worth. The two worst offenders, as usual, were the *Indianapolis Sentinel* and the *Chicago Times*. With a libel suit already pending anyway, the *Sentinel* had nothing worse to fear and a perfect excuse for making the Blaine marriage editorial fodder just about every day. Special eight-page supplements by the thousands carried the whole history of the affair, including affidavits from Kentuckians, Blaine's letter and all. Late in the campaign, the *Sentinel* even hinted at new sexual enormities when it accused Blaine of promiscuous kissing during his campaign tour:

> Now, if ladies were voters, and it were ladies he practiced his osculatory art upon, we should not object—i.e., if the ladies did not. But this thing of his kissing men—of pressing his bearded lips upon bearded lips—is too aggressive. It is an oppression not authorized by the Federal Constitution, which must and shall be stopped, or in behalf of the honor of the Nation, the Sentinel will bring a $50,000 libel suit against this man-kisser. Last week, over in Ohio, Mr. Blaine kissed a man who boarded his train. No longer ago than last night he kissed two men in this city, and one of these two was a Democrat. It is thus seen that the habit is growing on him. So long as he confined this method to the Republicans the Sentinel did not complain, but he shall not play it on Democrats with our consent.

What if the man-kissing habit should spread among other Republicans, the *Sentinel* wondered. "If you are not sighing for the nectar of plumed knight lips, keep out of the path of the Republican candidate. We will wager he would kiss any man, even the dirtiest in the United States for his vote."[23]

The "terrible tales" of 1884 did mark the campaign as special. Still, it is necessary to draw some distinctions. Defamation was nothing new. It was as American as a mud pie. Add all the worst accusations together, and it was plain that in thirty years, the only presidents who had not stolen money or usurped power were those too stupid to figure out how to do so. Treason, corruption, incompetence, selfishness, greed, megalomania, and just plain mania were the common coin of political cant. It was perfectly in order for newspapers sixteen years before to list the relatives of Horatio Seymour who had died in lunatic asylums. After that, reporters had a duty, not just a right, to describe those first telltale symptoms of a man two months away from the madhouse. Caricaturing Ulysses S. Grant, a would-be Caesar, sodden on his imperial throne, was done so often that it became cliché.[24]

Even the revelations about the sexual life of candidates had some precedent. For years, Republicans had done their best to pin the badge of sexual deviance on Democrats. In 1856, a whispering campaign had imputed homosexuality to James Buchanan; in 1872, Horace Greeley was accused of endorsing "free love and free farms and all that." The attacks on Tilden in 1876 were better veiled; only in private letters could one afford to write, as one newspaperman did, that the candidate was "the most utter old spinster that was ever bent on Presidential masturbation." Still, orators made much of his perpetual bachelorhood, just as Republican papers four years later would wonder how real men could vote for General Hancock, who, they fantasized, wore a corset. Democrats preferred their opponents oversexed. Who had not heard about General Grant's *other* wife, a Western Indian, and his three half-breed sons?[25]

Clearly, discretion, good taste, or Victorian moralism never entirely dominated political discourse in Gilded Age America. Yet taken in context, the accusations prove less than they seem. Attacks on a candidate's public character were far more common than discussions of his private life. The one exception was a public figure's drinking capacity, and that, like his table manners, was acceptable because it was so unexceptional. Even there, reporters exercised an off-again, on-again discretion. They knew perfectly well that the Speaker of the House went on binges. But, unlike Edmunds and Thurman, his drinking actually interfered with his talents. So even in newspapers that accused him of being a British tool, in the pay of the free-trade Cobden Club, John G. Carlisle's sprees went unreported.[26]

With all the exceptions noted, that sense of discretion applied even more emphatically to a politician's sexual life, and not because public figures held themselves to such impeccable standards that no reporter could find them out. James A. Garfield had had an adulterous affair, which was not unknown to journalists.[27] They seemed to know more about President Chester A. Arthur's intimacies than they admitted outright. In both cases, that knowledge went no further. In presidential races, exposures of family secrets were made guardedly: a verbal nudge and a wink, the spoken word freighted with much more left unsaid.

Why, then, did all bounds break loose in 1884? Because far from being sideshow attractions, the sex scandals were central to the larger campaign. The revolt against Blaine's nomination had been based almost exclusively on the character issue, specifically his honesty as a public official; but that, from the first, had not just involved how he made money but what he had done in return, and for whom. Mugwumps and Democrats were not just trying to prove that he was a rascal; behind him they saw the railroad monopolists, the privileged special interests to whom Republican policy had given free access to the public treasury.[28]

Character issues *were* the larger issues of government policy, and for

Republicans no less than for Democrats. The "party of moral ideas" had been forced to cope with many in their own ranks clamoring for Prohibition. If enough of them deserted, Blaine would lose his electoral majority. They could be converted back again by election day, if only the issues they cared about most, the moral issues, were given fullest play.[29]

Republicans could hardly move closer to the Prohibitionists on the liquor question. Doing so would cost as many votes as it gained. But there were other ways to bring the church vote round, and one was to find an issue upon which Dries and Wets could agree. The importance of family was just such an issue. And in a year when many Irish Catholics seemed restive in Democratic ranks, a sex scandal seemed heaven-sent for drawing all creeds together. It might efface those suspicions so deeply held between Protestant Republicans and Catholic Democrats. It could provoke equal indignation in evangelicals, with their distrust of Catholicism and secular Americans for whom the very name "the party of moral ideas" sounded an alarm, like a fire bell in the night. (That appeal to temperance-minded Republicans, too, explains why Republicans had to stick with the whole story, even when it had been discredited. Cleveland as libertine was useful; Cleveland as saloon-going rowdy doubly so).[30]

Finally, the Maria Halpin scandal was meant to discredit the Mugwumps as moral guides. However little *they* might be convinced, Republicans still in the ranks could be persuaded that the Maria Halpin scandal was nothing worse than a repayment in kind. After all, the charges against Blaine rested on the exposure of private letters, his business correspondence. Even if the scandal failed to take with voters, it might elicit a popular demand to draw the boundaries of legitimate debate anew, with topics like Blaine's railroad speculations on the outside of it; it might even deter the Democrats from releasing more of those damaging letters later in the campaign.[31]

The "terrible tales" did not just help the two parties to overcome extraordinary circumstances and to take advantage of onetime opportunities to raid each other's preserve. They also were used in ways that reaffirmed the larger message of the campaign. Protection of the home fit nicely with Republicans' promise of protection for American workers. It suited their language of all Americans as a family in harmony, so unlike the Democratic emphasis on a country of warring and irreconcilable interests. That need to fit the sex scandals into the broader party message also explains the curious way in which Blaine's marriage played in the Democratic press. For with the exception of a few scandalmongering papers, most editors put their emphasis not on Blaine's depravity so much as his dishonesty. In pulling apart the lies in his letter, their main aim was not to prove him a wanton; it was just one more

Love's Libels Lost

proof that the man could not tell the truth to save his life—and it was a single incident among many. Coming clean with the public was not a private matter. It spoke directly to his fitness for the presidency.[32]

One question remains: Why did the presidential campaign of 1884 not set the pattern for campaigns to come? It would not be enough to say that Cleveland's four years as president belied all the allegations against his character and brought forth, even among his opponents, a grudging admiration for his solid virtues; nor did his marriage in the White House to Frances Folsom, the daughter of his old law partner, inoculate him against the slanderers. His accusers simply could have shifted ground, as, indeed, some of them did in 1888. The charge became wife-beating and physical cruelty. But, significantly, such accusations had to spread through a whispering campaign. They never reached the public platform nor, until the campaign ended, the Republican press.[33] Apparently, the Republican and Democratic managers, before the campaign got under way, made a tacit agreement on the boundaries of legitimate debate and had enough control over the national press to hold those boundaries tight. But why did both sides see fit to make it and keep it? Any answer depends on conjecture, but a close study of the 1884 campaign offers some pretty good grounds.

Scandalmongering, however pervasive it may have been, never dominated debate, and one reason for that was that the old attitudes toward the bounds of proper political discourse had such staying power. Editorial columns found Maria Halpin an irresistible topic, but their audiences, apparently, did not. With some effort, a historian can find the kind of war chants in campaign parades that every standard account of the campaign gives a privileged place: "Pa! Pa! I want my pa!" or, a sarcastic quotation from Cleveland's letter of self-defense to the wife of Rev. Henry Ward Beecher: "Of course—of course—of course—I go to church!" But it does take effort. With only the rarest exception, crowds gave voice to more traditional issues: "No, no, no free trade!"

Even then, the most common suggestive reference "We Go for Brains, not Beef" could have had several meanings. Cleveland, after all, weighed well over two hundred pounds. As for Blaine's marriage, there was never a single reference to it, either in campaign speeches or in the popular display of any public gathering.[34]

For that last lack, the credit belongs not just to the rank and file of the Democratic Party but to its leaders. Far from purveying the scandal of James and Harriet Blaine, the national committee steered clear of it. The Indiana committee renounced any connection with the *Sentinel*'s campaign or faith in its charges. Late in July, a well-wisher showed up at the Governor's Mansion ready to sell "evidence" on Blaine's private life. Cleveland was willing to buy, and when the packet of damaging proof was handed to him, he paid for it without a word. "Are all the papers here?" he asked. Assured that they were, he stuffed some other documents of a like character into the envelope, and then, without reading any of them, tore them to pieces over the waste-basket. The contents were then burned in the open fireplace. "The other side can have a monopoly of all the dirt in this campaign," he told his private secretary. Some time after that, when word came that new allegations had come into party managers' hands, the governor threatened to quit the ticket if they were used against Blaine. Late in the campaign, Democratic restraint weakened momentarily. The *Chicago Times* hinted at evidence tying Blaine to loose ladies in Washington, but then the "mud-batteries" fell silent almost at once.[35]

And that, really, should not be too surprising. Far from appreciating the stories, many editors, including many Republican ones, felt as uncomfortable with "Polecat Politics" as their readers did. They argued, truthfully, that the scandal had first appeared in Democratic newspapers and, not so truthfully, that they were forced by inquisitive readers to deal with a scandal that they found utterly distasteful. (One Democratic newspaper likened it to a girl who told her suitor that as long as her hands were free, she would keep him from kissing her, "and there is rope in the barn.") Not until Cleveland's defenders published their explanations around August 11 did most leading Republican newspapers go beyond some vague innuendo about the Maria Halpin scandal; only with Blaine's letter in mid-September did many Democratic newspapers think the issue one fit for their discussion, and most of those that did tried to put as much distance between themselves and the *Indianapolis Sentinel* as possible.[36]

It was not just the problem of inconsistency—that denouncing Republican mudslingers went badly side by side with articles slinging mud at the Republican candidate's personal life. Where coverage of a candidate's personal life was concerned, the tradition of past campaigns still held, and changes in newspaper readership had made those reservations even stronger. Only the most sensational newspapers published articles on such indelicate topics; more than in the antebellum era, they had advanced beyond the strict confines of serving as party organs. They spoke the party line, directed at their male readers, to be sure, but wider news coverage and a wider readership had made them adapt to fit a family audience. With the shift from partisan journalism, a certain coarseness had been refined from a press no longer so exclusively directed at men. The *New Orleans Picayune* spoke for Southern papers in general when it dismissed the topic as unfit for decent readers.

Love's Libels Lost

Editors with any respect "for American homes" would leave such topics strictly alone. To a lesser extent, the same rule applied to campaign meetings. One Republican congressman complained at the disadvantage his party faced, compared to Democrats. They could go into luxurious detail about Blaine's career, without fear of offense, but Republicans had to guard their tongues about Cleveland's past, "because in republican audiences we have ladies in attendance."[37]

Others in both parties did more than refrain from discussing the allegations. They denounced "the scandal fiend" in unmistakable terms. "It's a nasty business, and the principal issues in the campaign will be fornication and adultery," Robert G. Ingersoll, the great infidel lecturer commented disgustedly, "—great country!" From the pulpits, Republican ones included, came the same note of reproof, and it struck a chord in the congregation. At one performance of *Othello*, there was a stir when one actress uttered the lines,

> Some eternal villain,
> Some busy and insinuating rogue,
> Some cogging, cozening slave, *to get some office*
> Devised this slander.

And when she went on,

> Put in every honest hand a whip
> To lash such rascals naked through the world!

the crowd broke into applause.[38]

There was another reason that 1884 was an end as well as a beginning to "terrible tales," and it may have been the strongest. The low road simply did not work. No doubt the Maria Halpin affair affected some votes. Contrary to the impression generally given, Cleveland's defenders had not neutralized the issue, and the emphasis on the scandal did not dim once the "truth" had been told. On the contrary, many newspapers lunged onto the attack only after the Democrats had issued their explanations, and a noisy minority kept on pressing the charges until the election. Every new exposure of Blaine's public record brought the Halpin scandal before the public, with new specifics that needed refuting. Democrats claimed that the Republican National Committee had a secret slander bureau working full time, spreading tall tales. To all the women attending a Buffalo dinner for Grover Cleveland, partisan organizers sent packets with no return address, with a pamphlet elaborating on the candidate's peccadillos, but there were plenty left to blanket the Midwest. Before the West Virginia election, copies of a damning pamphlet addressed to the Methodist clergy of Ohio were distributed far and wide. Scornfully, Roscoe Conkling described how "those white pages, black with the soot and slime of scandal, fell upon the hills and dales . . . like the flakes of a wintry snowstorm."[39]

But did it work? "Fools! fools!" the chairman of the Philadelphia Republican committee exclaimed, as he waved around a copy of the *Buffalo Telegraph*, sent to him for use by party managers. "The idea of running a campaign on a thing like that!" Certainly as a way of clouding Mugwumps' sense of a moral choice between the two leading candidates, the Halpin scandal had been a flat failure. As one editor put it, "He was a good husband, a kind father, and an estimable pirate." Instead, it made Democrats all the more dependent on the Schurzes and Godkins as character witnesses, and all the readier to define the issues their way. (And it may not have done Mugwumps' reputation as hermaphrodites much harm to associate with so virile a candidate. They gave Cleveland class, and he gave them sex.)[40]

What the Halpin scandal had done, in fact, was cost the Republicans time, desperately needed, to make the case for tariff protection. To win the kind of victory Republicans needed, one big enough to win back the House as well as to retain the presidency, free trade must not be a leading issue among many. It must be the all-consuming issue, spoken forcefully enough to make workingmen crowd to the polls for their families' sake. By mid-September, the time for rousing that fervor again was running out.

Love's Libels Lost

12

Windypendents' Day

Girding for war, the two parties found themselves threatened from within. For later onlookers, one of those revolts, the Mugwump rebellion against Blaine, mattered most. In that fight on corruption and spoils politics, they insisted, lay the real meaning of the presidential contest. Republicans put equal weight on the Irish American defection as the first great step toward a realignment in the North. Add them to the converts in the Upper South that the tariff issue would make, and Democrats would be shut out of national power for a generation.

Converts there were, certainly. Their potential strength tugged and shaped the major parties' appeal to the voters and in the North very nearly defined the Democratic message. In one state, they made all the difference between defeat and victory. But a less-noticed story of 1884 may be how firmly, how often, party lines held. The "windypendents," as one Republican editor christened them,[1] could not muster all like-minded reformers to their side, and the Irish revolt in most places amounted to less than the revolution Republicans expected. Yet in each case, the disaffected had good reason for breaking free. How had the two major parties stanched their losses?

Blaine's nomination set off a chorus of protests. "That he represents all that is Philistine, pretty much all that is objectionable in the Republican party, if not in American politics, ought to go without saying," one disgusted partisan wrote. "And to yoke him with Logan! It is all horrible." Postconvention collywobbles were nothing new. Backers of other hopefuls took time reconciling to Tilden and Hayes, even to Garfield. This time, unhappiness ran deeper. Arthur's newspaper apologists like the *Chicago Daily News* and the *New York Herald* repudiated the nomination. So did some of the most prominent big-city papers in the East, the *New York Evening Post*, the *Springfield Republican*, the *Boston Herald*, the *Boston Daily Advertiser*, and the *Brooklyn Union*.[2]

Characteristically, the actual bolt began in Boston, where the culture of reform had bred institutions able to mobilize an uprising effectively. On June 7, the Massachusetts Reform Club met at the Parker House. Among the rebels signing the protest were the first families of Boston society. The list of names read like a reunion of the *Mayflower*'s descendants. "All was excitement, and everybody was on fire," one participant noted in his personal journal. "Not a man in the room wished to support Blaine." Charles Francis Adams, son and grandson of presidents, sent his blessing. Within forty-eight hours, the more ardent spirits had gathered in Josiah Quincy's law office. A rally brought out so many followers that the meeting place could not hold them all and it had to be moved.[3]

New York insurgents followed Boston's lead, though they were impeded by the lack of any such framework as the Reform Club on which to build. Carl Schurz appeared in the front ranks immediately. So did E. L. Godkin of the *Nation*, R. R. Bowker, and Everett Wheeler. "Put me down against Blaine one hundred times in letters two feet long," the Reverend Henry Ward Beecher exclaimed. On July 22, the Independent National Conference met in New York City to announce itself implacably against Blaine.[4]

"The Blaine movement is really a conspiracy of jobbers to seize on the Treasury, under the lead of a most unprincipled adventurer," Godkin wrote an English acquaintance.[5] Righteousness, especially so stridently expressed, often makes a poor impression, and Republicans would call their renegades "Pharisees," thinking of the pious Jews who gave thanks to God that they were not as other men were. But the Pharisees had not been run out of the ancient church for holding to its original spirit. As Mugwumps aptly suggested, the real parallel for the Pharisees might be found among the regulars, loyal to "the forms and ceremonies" of their religion and putting them ahead of conscience itself.[6]

The truth of it was that for many of the Mugwumps, rebellion came hard and with much soul-searching. They did not want to leave Republican ranks, and many of them would make their peace with the party after the election. For George William Curtis, the anger cooled and then rekindled. Leaving the Republican convention, he knew that he could not support Blaine. Nor could *Harper's Weekly*. Taking no sides in the campaign had no attraction for him.

The writing on the wall.

(Joseph Keppler, Puck, *June 18, 1884). As the handwriting of Republican revolt appears on the wall, Blaine cowers, protected by* New York Tribunes, *and Logan, dressed in Indian garb, quails. So do the monopolists around the table: in front of a tureen of monopoly stew, Gould, Vanderbilt, Field, and John Roach cringe or hide. Whitelaw Reid rises in confusion; Robert Ingersoll, who christened Blaine the "Plumed Knight," flees, bone in hand. On the far end of the table are New York Assembly Speaker Husted and Chauncey Depew, willing servitors of railroad interests. Joseph Medill of the* Chicago Tribune *throws up his hands in horror. To the right of him, Dorsey and little Tom Platt are too disturbed to have seconds on Star Route shortcake. The similarities to McDougall's cartoon (see Chapter 17) are obvious; between the artistic abilities, there was no comparison.*

As he had once put it, "A neutral in politics is like a neutral in sex." But accepting the Democrats came hard. He paused for reflection and tried to delay any commitment from the heads of the firm. Cartoonist Thomas Nast bristled at that. "Speaking for myself," he snapped, "I positively decline to support Blaine, either directly or indirectly, even if the Democrats should nominate the Devil himself." The Harpers agreed. They ordered a strong editorial in the very next issue—"as strong as you like, Mr. Curtis." "Make it stronger than you like, Mr. Curtis," Nast told him. Curtis did it, but not, we may imagine, without some misgivings.[7]

So might all the Mugwumps. They knew that their uprising would not be forgiven. The logic used against the Mugwumps was often as convoluted as one could have devised. That they chose *not* to knuckle under when the party spoke showed that they lacked all "manly" qualities. They were trying to stifle the independent thought of voters by offering an alternative to the mainstream parties. "A free land develops free men," the *Iowa State Register* assured its readers. "They will accept no dictation from men who claim superior virtue or superior wisdom." But of course what the *Register* objected to was not the Mugwumps' attempt to bully men over whom they had no control but their insistence on offering Republican voters an alternative to following party dictates blindly.[8]

The abuse was intense and personal. They were shown, as Curtis was, paltering with the killers of blacks. Republicans declared them unpatriotic, accused them of being bought with English gold or subverted by English ideas or acting as agents for German chancellor Otto von Bismarck, and charged them with making speeches only for pay or abandoning the party out of thwarted ambition. (The father of two Mugwumps, former attorney general Ebenezer Rockwood Hoar, had somewhat more perspective. He had no objection to Mugwumps leaving the party, he protested; he just wished they wouldn't slam the door on their way out). At Blaine's direction, Republican papers tried to prove that the Harper brothers opposed Blaine out of pique at not getting publishing rights to his memoirs. Education was persistently set against "manly" pursuits, physical labor, and service on the field, and each of these activities was associated with true Americanism. A Mugwump, Horace Porter quipped, was "a person educated beyond his intellect." They were professors, scholars, "gentle hermits." Having been out of politics, they had no business venturing in.[9]

> Extremes have met at last, I see,
> Extremes in our society;
> Dude, culture, and aesthetic dude,
> In cane and kids, on dainty food
> Puffed and swollen, vain and grand,
> Now with the Bourbons takes his stand.
>
> Restive, for long he murmured loud
> To see the workingmen that crowd
> Highways of the Nation go on
> In thick phalanx to Washington—
> Rail-splitter, tailor, tanner, they
> Claimed all the honors of their day.[10]

Gearing the attack in these ways served Republicans' immediate purposes precisely. By stressing the affinity between English habits and reformers'

"The mistake of a lifetime"
*(Judge, August 16, 1884). George William Curtis, in women's dress, is the seduced
and abandoned woman, carrying her Independent Party love child.*

politics, they could underline the campaign theme that Republicanism
meant Americanism, while Democracy would sell out the country's industrial interests to England. Using the language of class resentment, they could
appeal to workingmen—Irish Americans especially—without offering anything substantial. Striking a blow at the snobs would be easier to do than, say,
passing a law forbidding contract labor or mandating an eight-hour day.
"Vindicationist" politics never called for legislation; winning the election
paid the party's debt in full.

There was more to it than that, however. The emphasis on manliness and
"gentle" qualities was unusual, even in Gilded Age politics. The Independents were "the delicate, dainty few." Those associated with them were likely
to be seen as dressing "after the manner of the young Anglomaniac." The
term "dude" in 1884 meant more than a well-dressed gent. It implied a very

specific kind of attire then in vogue among the scions of the leisured rich, where frailty, languor, and an obsession with perfect apparel mattered in the extreme; it was the opposite of robust masculinity and, as far as most newspapers were concerned, a fit source for mockery:

> He's one of the beaux,
> With cardinal heaux,
> His bangs they repeaux
> Clear down to his neaux.
> He has quick-fitting cleaux
> And sharp-pointed teaux,
> And no adipeaux
> On his spindle-shanks greaux.

What observers were describing took on all the characteristics of sexual deviancy. Deriding "the curled and corseted, perfumed and padded specimens of effete masculinity," the *New Orleans Daily Picayune* saw a trend for society belles to wed the "brawny workingman," the "muscular and horny-handed sons of toil" instead of fashion's darlings.[11]

Now that same sneering language was applied to the Mugwumps. A Republican stump orator, claiming that he had met a "specimen Independent," described him: "His hair, of course, was parted in the middle. They generally draw the line of independence there. He had very peaked shoes, and trousers into which he appeared to have been hammered by a pile driver. In an exceedingly genteel lisp he informed me that he 'wefused to go with the wiff-waff for Blaine, and he wegwetted that the wepublican party had let the wowdy element pwevail.'"[12]

The step from the language of effeteness to effeminacy was an easy, swiftly taken one. The cartoonists showed George William Curtis as "Miss Nancy," the wronged widow or the delicate maid. The language of the attacks on the Mugwumps was that associated with women: "the political flirts," "Mother Hubbards," "wet nurses," or the "sewing society in Staten Island," their gatherings simply "quilting-bees." A home for orphans and old maids having opened in Meriden, Connecticut, the Indianapolis paper urged George William Curtis to apply. He was, it explained, "eligible for admission on both counts."[13]

The abuse had about as much grounding in reality as if it had been applied to Theodore Roosevelt and Henry Cabot Lodge—as indeed it was, until they announced for Blaine. But such charged language revealed much about the meaning of partisan faith. Regularly, candidates would be praised for "manliness." What that meant, in partisan terms, was not so much the courage to do right as the fortitude to play the game. "Manly" behavior entailed dropping objections once a decision had been made. Independence showed self-indulgence, immodesty, a lack of self-control. It followed that those who broke with the party over candidates were behaving in a childish way, or, in the capricious ways that society associated with women. True men believed in something strongly, but that belief could only be shown through their support for the political institutions that allowed those beliefs to be made into practical action. A real man, in other words, stood by his party, right or wrong, just as he would his country.[14]

The argument, from Mugwumps' point of view, was nonsense. They, too, used the term "manly," but for them the true test of manliness was the courage to follow conscience wherever it led. Fighting the bosses took moral and sometimes physical courage. How men parted their hair mattered less than with whom they parted company, and often parting company jeopardized their futures more than staying silent. "I could not get the office of fence-viewer today," a Dedham Republican wrote after Cleveland's election, "for the simple reason that I have tried to prevent the election to the presidency of a dishonest man." Party bolters were blackballed from respected clubs and read out of the party. They were not afraid to lose and keep on losing, so long as the cause was just. "In a country so constituted as ours," one of them would write later, "there are few deeds more admirable than that of a public man who, devoted to a principle, is willing unflinchingly to face a hostile majority."[15]

The reformers acted not because rebellion was easy but because many of them felt that they had no choice. Beyond Cleveland, a Democratic conversion to civil service reform was hard to see, and Hendricks stood for just about everything that they deplored. Even so, they could make a case that Blaine's ethics were more than doubtful, and that a man on the make set the worst possible example for those he carried into office with him. One only had to look at the Grant administration to see how far corruption could go when a man of easy conscience sat in the White House.

And, Mugwumps asserted, it had been an easy conscience not just on money matters but wherever principle and political advantage pointed opposite ways. Over the years, Blaine had been a moderate on Reconstruction measures and the great bloody-shirt orator, a protectionist who stacked the Ways and Means Committee in tariff reformers' direction when votes depended on it, the sponsor of anti-Catholic constitutional amendments, and a bidder for Irish Catholic votes. Now Blaine, the Speaker who once had put Ben Butler in charge of the committee on civil service, the equivalent of choosing a cat to tend an uncaged canary, claimed to be a convert to reform—

this, two years after mocking reformers and three years after having used the State Department to reward his friends and the Garfield administration to pick a fight over spoils with Roscoe Conkling. All politicians were opportunists to some extent, but Independents had some reason for wondering whether such a changeling and proven liar could be trusted in any promise he now made.[16]

Apparently at Blaine's urging, former senator John Henderson of Missouri came away from Augusta to try to win Carl Schurz back to the cause. Schurz's influence among reformers was high, though his impact among German Americans may have counted for more. Henderson appealed to his old friend to reconsider. Events showed that so good a man as Cleveland had no chance of winning the nomination, he wrote Schurz. Instead, it was "quite certain" that "that old political trickster, Tilden" would be chosen. Surely Schurz could not back such a man. High office would purge Blaine of his bad followers and partisan ways. "If he has been a Prince Hal in days gone by, when responsibility comes he will be a Henry V. The Falstaffs that have followed him . . . will not be recognized in shaping his policies." Schurz had other opinions about Cleveland's chances, and he knew his Shakespeare well enough to know a bad parallel when he saw it. "I cannot look upon Mr. Blaine as a mere jolly Prince Hal who has lived through his years of indiscretion and who the presidency will certainly make a new man," he wrote.[17]

Later historians would judge the Mugwumps harshly. By bolting the Republicans, supposedly, they split the civil service reform movement. It would never recover, and those who fought one another in 1884 could never work together again. "Realistic" reformers would have taken Blaine and hoped for the best rather than driving up the dead-end of Independent action. But to the Independents, their action was realistic and inescapable. Again and again, mainstream managers declared that change was useless outside the major parties. Let Ohio's Prohibitionists and the temperance laws of the early 1880s stand in answer! or the Michigan Democrats' coalition with Greenbackers! Clearly, change often came when members of the major parties used the only sanction in their power against those who held the machinery: the organized transfer of their votes to some outside agency. The Pendleton Act had changed conditions. Whoever won, Congress would leave fresh civil service legislation strictly alone. Only through presidential action could advances come. Between a known spoilsman and a governor who had signed a state civil service law into action and defied Tammany Hall, the choice was clear. Standing by Blaine, the Mugwumps would have split civil service reform anyhow. What Democratic ally would believe them sincere, if they bowed to party regularity, even when so reproachable a man headed the ticket? What sincere reformer would abandon reform because his allies had chosen conscience over expediency?[18]

The Independents themselves certainly had more than a symbolic importance. Indeed, to judge from the noise they made, theirs was no revolt, but a revolution, extending far into the Republican ranks. Thanks to Democratic cooperation, the Mugwumps were able to define one of the most compelling issues and to keep Republicans on the defensive. Time and again, Godkin's *Nation* and *New York Evening Post* made charges that Republican newspapers had to explain away. The rebels produced speakers for Democratic rallies and money to bring out fresh Democratic votes. Of all the active campaigners, Carl Schurz took front rank. Among German voters, he was in constant demand. His speeches were powerful indictments of Blaine, concentrating not on billingsgate but on a precise evaluation of the record. Democrats needed him and were glad for his services.[19]

Even more useful was the Mugwump concentration on Blaine's corrupt dealings. In September, it was they who induced Mulligan to release those letters he had kept back eight years before. The new material drove home the charges against Blaine, proving that he *had* lied, that he had tried to suborn false testimony from Warren Fisher to his transactions, and that the arrangement with Tom Scott had taken place within weeks of the House passage of the bill subsidizing Scott's Texas & Pacific Railroad. One small postscript gave Democratic crowds their marching cry for the rest of the campaign: "Burn, burn, burn this letter! Kind regards to Mrs. Fisher!" Editorial apologists echoed Blaine's claim that the letters had nothing in them to be ashamed of. On the contrary, the correspondence showed his honesty and fidelity to his friends—so much so that many Republican newspapers refused to publish them. Later in the month, it was the Mugwump press that nailed down another Blaine lie about his involvement in a coal and iron company in the Hocking Valley in Ohio. Republicans were still trying to explain Blaine's railroad holdings well into October.[20]

Perhaps the Independents who did the most to shape the campaign were those who put a symbolic face on it, the cartoonists of *Harper's Weekly* and *Puck*. In the months to come, *Puck* would make "the tattooed man" a household phrase. The image ranked as "one of the most terrible things of the kind ever published," one newspaper commented—high praise indeed. Reportedly, Blaine considered suing the artists for obscene libel and dropped the idea for fear of making the corruption issue even more prominent than it was.[21] Still, Republicans had never expected much comfort from *Puck*. Nast was different. He was one of their own to the bone and for years harried party renegades, Schurz especially. Indeed his anger at Blaine began in 1879 on very Republican grounds when the Maine senator called for closing the doors on Chinese immigration. Such a violation of treaties might offend a liberal reformer as kowtowing to the mob, but Nast's ire was an old radical's fury at racial bigotry. The middle-class households taking *Harper's Weekly* might be convinced by him where no treatise could change their minds. Nast's Blaine was a man on the make, a carpetbagger raking in whatever could come his way. To add injury to insult, he looked suspiciously like Boss Tweed! Most damaging of all, perhaps, Nast shoved Blaine's paltering with Irish Catholics before the magazine's heavily Protestant readership; and no one could draw Irish ruffians and jailbirds more nastily than Nast.[22]

Republicans knew how it hurt. They would insist that Blaine was really tattooed with his virtues, that Washington and Lincoln were tattooed men in their day, and that, really, the abuse offended readers rather than persuading them. They saved their fiercest language for Nast, who became a traitor, a sot, a has-been of so little influence that no cartoon of his should go un-challenged. Even as they pooh-poohed the cartoonists, Republicans scram-bled to corral some of their own. *The Judge*, New York's other leading political-cartoon weekly, became earnestly partisan for the first time, and Republican editors lauded its mediocre artwork far beyond its deserts. (Some of the ideas were good; some, indeed, were suggested by Gillam, who drew for *Puck* but voted for Blaine). Boston Republicans founded *Jingo*, and city papers experimented with daily cartoons, most of which were crude doodles. All of these, as one Republican later admitted, had "little or no value."[23]

Yet for all its achievements, the Independent revolt of 1884 amounted to less than the party had hoped or intended. The newly created National Committee of Independents handled the placing of speakers west of the Hudson, while the Boston organization tended New England's schedules. But that was more a reflection of organizational weakness than strength. Outside of the Northeast, where there were no active reform organizations to propel work onward, the revolt often went no further than a paper circulated for signatures. In Indianapolis, reformers chose a committee that, having met once, considered its main duty done for the next two months. Nationwide, the Independents provided some money ($23,836 of it going to the national committee), but mostly what they provided was pamphlets, articles, and manifestos, certified by committees chock full of professional reformers and reform-minded professors. Theirs was the true "campaign of education," and, though it was heartily welcome among Democrats who were never so pleased as by one set of Republicans' character reference against another, after a while, the practice had a wearying sameness. "It is about time, we would suggest, that a conference was held at Young's," the *Boston Traveller* suggested after one more Mugwump manifesto. "It will then be in order to rally at Quincy and Cambridge, and by that time the public would be delighted to have those excellent people write an open letter to themselves, and sign it twice over apiece, in accordance with the pleasing precedent set in that regard early in the campaign. [Blaine's carrying Maine] should be met by another vigorous address, to be followed rapidly by a conference at Young's, meetings at Quincy and Cambridge, and another very strong open letter to themselves. . . ." Outside of the Northeast and a few of the larger Midwestern cities, Mugwumps came in short supply, and only in New York could they take credit for swinging enough votes to decide the election.[24]

This was not because reform had no constituency. But if not every opponent of Blaine was a reformer, not every reformer came out against Blaine. Of Blaine's firmest opponents in the Massachusetts delegation, only one, young John F. Andrew, son of the great "war governor," fell out of the ranks. But George F. Hoar stood by the party. So did Congressman John D. Long and Governor Robinson.[25]

Theodore Roosevelt never reconciled himself to Blaine as a man, but he made his peace with the party right away. Packing himself off to the Dakotas, he let reporters know that he was not fleeing the campaign itself or the party nominee. By mid-October, he was back in New York, his face burned "a bright terra-cotta," boasting of bagging grizzlies ("three terrors," as he blithely described them) and readying his sights for some verbal shots at Cleveland. Henry Cabot Lodge had fought Blaine to the last ballot, and then, coming home from the convention, pondered the choices. "It was the bitterest thing I had to do in my life," he remembered a year later. "To bolt would have been the easiest thing in the world and the pleasantest, but in my eyes it was dishonorable." It was also politically inexpedient for the Republican state chairman, who had congressional ambitions.[26]

Even Edmunds came round, after a fashion. The Vermont senator confined his campaign appearances to a single speech, free of any mention of Blaine. That he thought Blaine a scoundrel and the tool of railroad interests was an open secret. It was widely reported that he had written a friend that whenever he and Thurman "joined hands against Jay Gould and fellows of that sort in the Senate, James G. Blaine has invariably started up from behind Gould's breastworks, musket in hand." Edmunds denied having written so, but his demurral was so damaging to the candidate that Republican papers could only print his letter after wholesale cropping. There were even rumors for a while that reformers, with Edmunds's tacit support, would put a third party into the field in Vermont. But nothing came of it, and the best that Mugwumps could claim for the senator was that, if he supported Blaine, he got no pleasure out of doing so.[27]

Why did the Lodges and Edmunds refuse to break up with their party? To judge from the recriminations, ambition and cowardice made the Mugwumps' former allies recreant to reform. As usual, Godkin was the most venomous: Hoar's defense of Blaine plunged him "knee-deep in perversion, tergiversation, and sophistry." Roosevelt and Lodge had turned opportunist and were sure to pay for it politically. "What is disappointing people now is . . . that [Roosevelt] has not more faith in honesty." In fact, the Mugwumps were not the only ones to wrestle with their consciences; nor were they the only ones whose consciences won. For many, conscience pointed toward party regularity and the chance to keep on doing good once the election was over. "Whatever the result . . . the parties will remain," Lodge explained. "By staying in the party I can be of some use. By going out I destroy all the influence and power for good I may possess."[28]

Even so pragmatic an explanation bears too harshly on those Republicans who stood by the candidate. No hard-and-fast rule explains why some decided one way, some the other, but a general trend can be seen. A commitment to civil service reform was not enough to turn its supporter against Blaine, any more than a lack of courage was. Other issues came into play, issues that came together to pose a larger question: What was the Republican Party's main responsibility? If one assumed, as so many Mugwumps then did, that tariff protection did America a positive injury and that bloody-shirt issues were irrelevant to the needs of the age, then Blaine's moral character mattered. It was not just that he would endanger reform. He was wrong on the other great issues of the day. On the other hand, high-tariff Republicans had a good cause beyond the candidate for sticking with the party. Reformers like Hoar and Lodge disliked the low tone of politics. But they could not close their eyes to the wrongs done to blacks in the South. This was not a one-issue contest, and on all issues but ethics, Republicans stood in the right. Even on that one, there was room for argument. Cleveland must advance reform in the teeth of a spoils-hungry party; the many reformers in Republican ranks would nudge Blaine forward, whether he liked it or no. Thomas Brackett Reed had a point when he suggested that in joining the Democratic Party, Harvard's president "was evidently thinking more of the courage of his convictions than the sense of them."[29]

It is, then, too simple an explanation to say that the partial containment of the Independent revolt showed the power of partisanship in Gilded Age America, much less the seducing force of political ambition. That begs the question: Why did partisanship wield such a power? The Mugwumps-that-weren't provide an answer. Partisanship was not simply a habit, too hard for ordinary mortals to break. It rooted itself in issues and a clear sense that either party's principles, put into action, would affect working families and the relationship between white and black Southerners. At the same time, the loyalty of the Hoars and Lodges showed not just how right Blaine's strategy was, but how wrong. The tariff tugged at the loyalty of the "best men," but so did the problem of political justice down south. The Republican campaign could abandon the bloody shirt; it could not drive the wrongs that had given rise to that tactic from Republicans' minds.

13

Ireland Sold for Gold!

Even as Democrats counted on reformers, Republicans banked on an Irish American revolt. At first, the hope seemed wholly improbable. A month before the Republican National Convention, the leading Irish American newspaper of the Northeast, Patrick Ford's *Irish World and American Industrial Laborer*, lamented the irrelevance of his compatriots in party managers' calculations. Any pundit knew that "the Irish vote is fixed and unchangeable." So neither party tried to bid for their support.[1]

Like most editorials, Ford's had their share of blarney. The Irish vote was more than myth but less than monolith. For lots of reasons, Irish American men generally voted Democratic, when they voted at all. Settling largely in the urban centers of the North, where Democratic habits were less outlandish and caused less trouble to an immigrant hoping to fit into American society, they had special need for help that the big-city machines were only too happy to provide. Even if they had trouble knowing who their friends were, the great mass of Catholics among them knew who their enemies were, in the nativist legions that rallied within the Republican Party and the casual middle-class shopkeepers who put "NINA" (No Irish Need Apply) in their windows. But it was not true, as one Irish Democrat wrote, that "an Irishman in the Republican ranks . . . is as much out of place as a game chicken in a cage of buzzards."[2]

One might look no further than the central figures in the Republican effort in 1884: John Devoy, Patrick Ford, and Dr. William Carroll. All were names for Irish nationalists to conjure with. Each of them expressed a different strain of militance. Since the 1870s, Ford had spoken for the Greenback-Labor movement, assailing the monopolists and spotting Jewish conspiracies against the Republic. Carroll and Devoy were among the originators of the Clan na Gael, the strongest Irish revolutionary society in America. It was an impressive roster; but it was also nothing new. The GOP had made arrangements with Carroll, Ford, and Devoy in 1880, too, through the agency of Philadelphia businessman Wharton Barker.[3]

What had changed was the potential number of followers that the Republicans' bellwethers could lead. For many of the Irish, Democratic loyalty no longer seemed enough. Nor, indeed, had it ever been. With so many of the unskilled workers Irish-born, the labor movement often took on a markedly Irish flavor. Stirring up the coal fields of Pennsylvania in the 1870s, the Mollie Maguires, a secret society that used threats and violence against management, ended their career behind bars and on the gallows. From the sandlots of San Francisco, the Workingmen's Party found its most articulate voice in Dennis Kearney, an Irish drayman whose attacks on railroad monopolists and Chinese immigration momentarily shattered the two-party system in California and refashioned the state's constitution. By 1884, the country was coming to know Scranton's mayor, Terence V. Powderly, as leader of the Knights of Labor. As Patrick Ford's full newspaper title made clear, these Irish Americans had not exchanged a cultural for a class identity. The two were merged. "The enemies of the Irish movement are found in every case to be the enemies of the American labor movement," the paper summed up.[4]

That mixed identity pushed some Irish Americans away from mainstream party politics. They were willing to consider labor party alternatives, or, indeed, settle their grievances without recourse to parties at all. It also gave many of them particular grounds for disliking Grover Cleveland, "as brutal an anti-labor tyrant," in one Brooklyn Irishman's words, "as any of the blood-sucking landlords of Ireland." "I impeach Grover Cleveland in the name of the great army of workers who have built our mills and factories, our docks and railways," Rev. George W. Pepper, the foremost Protestant Irish American figure, told one crowd. "I impeach Grover Cleveland in the name of 15,000 car-drivers and conductors in New York City. . . . I impeach Grover Cleveland for his inhumanity in vetoing the wise measure abolishing child labor in the mills." (That there was no such bill and no such veto did not concern the audience.)[5]

Even more visible to political planners in 1884 was the spreading appeal of Irish nationalism that changes in Britain had brought about. In the 1860s, the Irish Republicans of the Fenian Brotherhood had been radicalism incarnate, invading armies without a country. As they went into decline, the main force for Irish nationalism shifted to John Devoy's Clan na Gael, but it never commanded the whole movement. There were also the Fenian remnants under Jeremiah O'Donovan Rossa, whose "Skirmishing Fund" gathered some $50,000 to use in murdering English officials and devising poison gas for use in the House of Commons. Patrick Ford's *Irish World* spoke for a very different insurgency, blending labor radicalism with Irish patriotism.[6] Conservative Irish Americans kept their distance from all of these alternatives.

Then in 1879, everything began to change. Famine and crop failure brought Ireland near revolution. Eviction, emigration, shooting, and repression: these events of the next four years gave Irish American nationalists a common cause and, with Charles Parnell's battle for Home Rule in Parliament, a common leader. Parnell was no radical, and the Home Rule movement in America was mainstream enough that even non-Irish Americans could support it, many Republicans included. Breaching party lines, attracting a wider support in the Irish community than any movement hitherto, the new nationalism seemed ready-made to shake voters out of their Democratic regularity.[7]

If it could be done, Blaine's supporters meant to give it a try. Perhaps sensibly, they concentrated on two elements, the working-class Irish that followed Patrick Ford and the "National" element, those most active in the Irish patriotic movements and least involved in Democratic Party politics. "They are the active force in Irish politics, the only class who have shown independence of the politicians," John Devoy assured GOP leaders. Any other ground but "national sentiment, or of the position and standing of the Irish race in America" would gain Republicans nothing.[8]

The nationalists had certain strengths. Among them, they directed the great national organization the Irish National League, of which Alexander Sullivan had been the first president. They had friends among the leading Irish newspapers, including Patrick Ford's *Irish World* and General Michael Kerwin's *New York Tablet*. Sullivan stepped down as president in August and stepped onto the public platform as one of Blaine's advocates. The league was supposedly nonpartisan, and when the convention met in Boston, delegates were assured that it would take no stand on the contest. But by September the new president, Patrick Egan, three years in America and former treasurer for the Irish Land League, was a Blaine spokesman. Repudiating Cleveland early in September, he declared the governor an "enemy of every just right of the toiling millions," "the pet candidate of . . . the entire English press."[9]

The evidence of an Irish American defection from the Democrats was

"The Blainiac programme. The lion's share of the campaign procession"
(F. Graetz, Puck, *July 23, 1884).*

plain from the start. The only questions were, how big was the revolt? and, would the converts stay that way till election day? One manager estimated that they had taken in over half the Irish Catholic voters in New Jersey's Hudson and Essex Counties. Priests attended every party rally there and elsewhere were said to be forcing their parishioners into line, against the decrees of the local Democratic machines. Still, GOP estimates were often such stuff as daydreams were made of. When the Republican National Committee estimated that two-thirds of the Irish vote in New York City leaned to Blaine and the other third to Ben Butler's People's Party, that left no Irish Democrats at all.[10]

Anyone who assumed that party habits had dissolved lived on fantasies. On the contrary, the whole Irish uprising was contingent on *not* appearing to be what Republicans wanted it to be: the permanent transfer of Democrats' most trusty supporters to the other side. Alarmed at news that a convention of Republican Irish Americans would be called, John Devoy wrote the *Chicago Tribune*'s publisher a warning. The moment Irish Americans heard Republicans sounding the call, they would hold onto their Democratic allegiance more strongly than ever. Instead, potential converts must be reassured that they could desert for this election only. No effort must be made to turn them into permanent Republicans. That could come later. For now, prominent Irish Democrats must take a very visible lead.

That sense of contingency, of unease, in such as Devoy showed how difficult any long-term break in Irish political customs would be. It also revealed one of the reasons that the Irish "revolt" amounted to somewhat more in July than it would in November—though, it must be cautioned, quite enough to have saved the election for Blaine, had there not been other revolts among trusty Republicans. As Devoy acknowledged, only a few "very intelligent" countrymen embraced Republican principles or Blaine himself. They were affected mostly by the "objectionable character of the Democratic candidate."[11]

It followed, then, that the appeal to the Irish strengthened the Republican commitment to make Grover Cleveland's character a leading issue in the campaign. That, and not attacks on the Democratic Party, were the surest way of winning Irish votes; the latter would only harden Irish Americans' dislike of the Republican Party. Alleging that England wanted Cleveland, "the standard-bearer of British Free Trade," was just a run-of-the-mill campaign lie; most Republicans talked that way. It was something special when Patrick Ford announced that Cleveland's nomination came about "because the Know Nothings demanded him" and that "the Irish were told to 'go,'" even if one assumed, as Ford did, that the Mugwumps were Know-Nothings. Blaine's aggressiveness, crowds were assured, would work to freedom's advantage, and might even lead to war with England; and England's war was Ireland's opportunity. "Bedad!" one Irishman exclaimed, "if Blaine's elected, Ireland will be free in thirty days!"[12]

The Mugwump revolt served Republican purposes well, too. Among the Independents were some of the bitterest abusers of the urban Irish. Nast's cartoons drew the Irish as dirty Calibans and Romish apes, images that like much of his other work he seems to have learned from Sir John Tenniel, England's most influential cartoonist. Godkin used words in the *Nation* to draw almost as unflattering a portrait. Founded originally as a German American humor magazine, *Puck* had transformed over the years into one read by the native-born middle class. As it did so, its broad attacks on all ministers shifted into a special derision of Catholics and Jews.[13]

Most of all, Republicans relied on the tariff to bring working-class and nationalist Irish voters into the ranks. Protection struck a blow at England; English gold rode on Democratic victory. Supposedly, English newspapers feared Blaine above all others. English manufacturers had raised a slush

Ireland Sold for Gold!

"The spread of American ideas"

(Thomas Nast, Harper's Weekly, August 9, 1884). Nast was referring not just to the nationalist cast that Blaine gave his tariff and foreign policy stance but to the Know-Nothing "American" Party. The carpetbag label plays on the candidate's recently published memoir, Twenty Years in Congress.

fund to elect a free-trade president. The quickest way to Home Rule was to protect America's home markets.[14]

Yet, when all was said and done, many, and probably most, Irish Americans simply never joined the revolt. As with the Independents, the Blaine converts were a phantom army, long on display, shorter in actual array. Republicans reported a vast movement into Blaine and Butler's camp in Newark. A reporter for the *New York Evening Post* paid a call on the Irish Blaine Club, and found that its address was a building of offices and courtrooms. The hall where it had held a monster rally was fifteen feet by twenty-four, and nobody in the building was aware of any meeting there with more than a dozen people. Republican managers paid all the bills. When a supposed Irish Blaine Club published its list of members in Auburn, Illinois, even Democrats were surprised at the names—especially some of those Democrats who found themselves recorded among the organizers of a society they had never heard of.[15]

The existence of Blaine Irish American clubs may have revealed how awkwardly Republicans fit Irish Americans into the ranks. Democrats needed no special Irish clubs. In many neighborhoods, the party caucus looked like one already. For years, Democratic politics had given Irish recruits an instant welcome and a swift promotion. "The Democratic politicians understand the Irish vote better than the Republican managers," Patrick Ford admitted late in the campaign. Organizers like Elkins may have done their best, "but they lack the experience that our opponents possess in this direction. To Republicans the Irish vote is a new field." It was also a field that they came to cultivate only late in the campaign, and with skimpy supplies of money.[16] Until then, organizing the Irish American vote was left to Irish American leaders themselves.

Those, as it happened, were the ones least bound to the party system, and their ability to organize a political movement within the two-party system was limited. It had failed in the past. O'Donovan Rossa may have hit near the truth when, in wry self-deprecation, he urged Ben Butler to send campaign advertising to Rossa's *United Irishman*. "'Tis on the straight ticket," he assured Butler, "and it controls the Irish vote—of the writers."[17]

Anyone who imagined a united Irish American vote for the Republicans, then, was deluding himself, and far more than any sensible Republican manager ever did. Republicans were not willing to make the sacrifices necessary to bring out that vote, and they lacked the machinery to bring about a wholesale conversion. Blaine could not erase memories of the long anti-Catholic tradition of his party, any more than adopting the tariff as an issue could banish memories of Reconstruction among white Southern conservatives. Republicans certainly could find chance phrases that showed Democratic contempt for the Irish. But for every remark they found, Democrats could find a dozen from the newspaper that Blaine had edited in the 1850s and from the Catholic-baiting political campaigns of the 1870s. When the *Indianapolis Journal* within memory had raged against the "unterrified hordes of bog-trotting repeaters," "the imported cattle, mostly Irish," its editor had a tremendous challenge persuading yesterday's "brute creation" of his discovery that Republicans were the only friend that the Irish could trust.[18]

Ireland Sold for Gold!

A united Irish American vote for the Republicans was also dangerous. Blaine's appeal to Irish Catholics may actually have cost him votes, as well as gaining them. In the countryside, many Republicans took badly to the party's flirtation with a church they had always distrusted. Stories circulated quietly that Blaine was himself a Catholic, that he wore a rosary under his shirt, or a chain with a cross on it.[19]

Even as it opened cracks in the Democratic Party, Irish nationalism pulled itself apart by entering mainstream politics. One reason was that, beneath the surface, the Irish American movement remained deeply divided: Irish Americans had so little in common beyond a sympathy for their former homeland. Where they came from in Ireland and when made a difference in how militant a nationalism they held. Those from Munster, the generation that had come with the Great Famine, might be found among the revolutionaries, less nationalist than leftist; those from Cork a generation later were likelier to arrive in America with strong faith in the possibilities of an Irish nation. And these were counties where English customs and institutions held fullest sway. For those from the Gaelic outland, where Irish was the spoken tongue, the ancestral land was not so large in scope as Ireland; it extended no further than Connemara. Founded in the same neighborhoods, the militance of the Mollie Maguires was worlds distant from the religious emphasis of the Catholic Workingmen's Society.[20]

With all these differences, economic and cultural, the Irish nationalist movement never took one coherent, consistent shape. Even at the height of Parnell's power, it was not so much reborn as momentarily congealed. Already by 1883 there were fissures visible. The most obvious was between those who had embraced the conservative economics of Parnell and those who favored a more radical land reform, on the basis that single-tax reformer Henry George had spoken of. By 1884, the radical land reformers under Michael Davitt were sharply at odds with Parnell. Patrick Ford's *Irish World* had been under attack for some time; its call for a rent strike had fit into the mainstream of Irish opinion in 1880, but not so as times got better. The president of the American Land League, General Patrick Collins of Boston, numbered himself among Ford's enemies, and so did John Boyle O'Reilly, whose nationalist credentials were as strong as Ford's own. John Devoy of the *Irish Nation* and his followers were separate from Ford's, and growing more so by early 1881, and the split remained unhealed.[21]

The mix in Irish nationalism had changed, in other words, but many Irish nationalists had not. And the one fact that had always been constant remained so. The Fords and Devoys were fighting for a politically militant minority of the Irish American vote. Far from the dynamite and "Molly

Maguire" stereotypes that middle-class readers often conjured up, Irish folkways left many of them intensely conservative. Emigrants longed for the old country all the more ardently because they found discomfort in an America of machines and change. The more propertied they were, the less they appreciated the violent end of Irish nationalism. In many ways, the Irish Americans had much to conserve. By the 1880s, two out of every three were American-born. They were rising, and leaving both the worst of their poverty and neglect behind. Those who moved into the middle class showed it in part by distancing themselves from their Irish roots. In the first generation, the letters flowed back to the old country, lamenting the green Arcady that they had left. Not so many came in the second generation.[22]

The exiles had become Americans with an Irish flavor, but not enough to upset a system that was working for them, and well. For those who wanted to fit in, it was often best to mute their ethnic character, to assert their Americanness. Irish American nationalists would honor Ireland but stress also the Irish contributions to America, their countrymen's service to the Union army in wartime, and the parallels between the American ideals of the Revolution and those of Ireland. Far from resisting the public school systems, Irish Americans became teachers there and hailed public education as a blessing. New England's politicians, for their own part, wanted as little assertion of Irish values as possible, if only to keep the native-born Americans from being too provoked. By 1880, three priests in four were American-born, and in many communities they led the way for temperance movements and for reconciliation with the Yankees of New England. This muted sense of Irishness might well change, but in the 1880s it had more influence than ever before.[23]

Instead of embracing Patrick Ford's radical notions, most Irish Americans were fearful of reform of any kind, and wary of its consequences. They knew what it meant; they had seen it in action, usually at the hands of meddling Protestants and Republican officials. Reform meant cheap, uncaring government, with lower taxes for the affluent and fewer services for the poor end of town. Reform meant closing the saloons on Sunday, and, if possible, all the time, and shifting the patronage from city hands to state ones through metropolitan boards. Reform meant a war on gambling, prostitution, and even on museums, parks, and Sunday concerts that violated the Protestant Sabbath. All of these impulses made Irish American politics strikingly conservative, and, as far as the issues that mattered to their communities, strongly Democratic.

Egan, Sullivan, Ford, and O'Donovan Rossa could lead their followers, but mainstream politics bred a host of Irish American leaders, too, and most of

Ireland Sold for Gold!

them, like the Roosevelts and Lodges, had no intention of sacrificing their careers over one man in one election or, for that matter, for the distant goal of an independent Ireland. In a society where religious prejudice could stymie an ambitious Irish person's advance, politics afforded one of the great exceptions. Politics *did* pay off. By the 1880s, it was paying off better than ever. In 1884, Boston elected Hugh O'Brien, its first Irish mayor; another nine years, and John P. Hopkins would be elected in Chicago. More than even in Tweed's day, the leadership of Tammany Hall was Irish and Catholic.[24]

Yet this sense of arriving encouraged Irish American leaders not to stray down radical paths or join working-class movements that they could not control. They went from workers to politicians, and their constituency was different: more based on Catholicism than class, more eager for some notion of respectability. Politics tamed Irish leadership, and the leaders helped tame the voters.

Thomas Kinsella shows how the requirements of politics silenced revolt. Until his death in early 1884, Kinsella gave an authoritative tone to the *Brooklyn Eagle*, one of the best newspapers in the metropolitan area. Kinsella was born in Ireland, and his editorials stood with Ireland against its oppressors. Some of America's fullest, most insightful coverage of Ireland came from the *Eagle*'s Dublin correspondent. Kinsella was president of the St. Patrick's Society in Brooklyn and a close friend of Henry George, whose ideas on land reform found a privileged place in the *Eagle*. Irish Americans listened when Kinsella spoke. Those in Brooklyn read his paper and no other.

But Kinsella owed his rise to Democratic politics, and he never shook free of the party. He had begun as an apprentice in a printing office. Political connections made him postmaster, water-board commissioner, and congressman. Kinsella might let his independence carry him into war on Hugh McLaughlin's machine; but there was never a chance that he would let it take him into some other party's ranks.[25]

Blaine, in short, could not win the whole Irish vote because there *was* no Irish vote, no ethnic bloc so tightly woven together that it could be delivered in one piece to a candidate. There was not even an Irish nationalist vote. There were many groups, sometimes working together, sometimes fighting for influence. Their purposes were different; so were their definitions of Irish American interests. Far from splintering the Democrats, the Republican overture pulled apart the Irish nationalist movement, just as Blaine's nomination pulled apart the liberal reformers. It could not have escaped Democrats that a very special kind of Irish American supported Blaine. The *Detroit Free Press* hit close to the mark when it described the stump speakers as the "professional savers of Ireland," whose only converts were "those Irishmen who believe that Irish independence can be gained by living in New York and advocating wholesale murder in London."[26]

Democrats were not going to let that support go entirely unattended. At Bull-baiting, Democrats had spokesmen equal to any Republican ones. They could depend, for example, on William E. "Richelieu" Robinson, a militant Anglophobe who as Brooklyn congressman offered resolutions to demand that England surrender Ireland to American authority. Listeners hoping for reference to blood, bayonets, and dynamite had their fill. They were reminded that knights were an English custom; what did it say of Republicans that their marching clubs called themselves Plumed Knights? At the centennial celebration at Yorktown in 1881, every Irishman in the world had been insulted by Americans firing a salute to an English ship—and this, with Blaine manning the State Department! Democrats even found help from the dynamiter wing of the nationalist movement, in the form of O'Donovan Rossa himself. In October, his paper, the *New York United Irishman*, brought forth a blast against Blaine, characteristically intemperate. "A Vice Conspiracy!" headlines trumpeted. "Ireland Sold for Gold!"[27]

But Democrats were not playing for the dynamiters. On the contrary, they exploited the uneasiness with the "professional Irishman" and the hunger of middle-class Irish Americans to fit into American society. They went for the respectable center of Irish nationalism. Devoy, Ford, Dr. Carroll, and O'Donovan Rossa put together could not match the appeal of Charles Stewart Parnell, Ireland's own champion of Home Rule. Republicans knew it. Their emissaries tried to persuade Parnell to endorse Blaine, according to published reports, and got nowhere. Parnell's mother was available, but not for Republicans. She held an honored place on the Democratic platform.[28]

So in dividing the Democrats, the Irish American movement also divided itself. If Blaine could depend on the *Irish Nation*, the *Tablet*, and the *St. Louis American Celt*, then the *Buffalo Catholic Union* and the *Milwaukee Catholic Citizen*, the *Boston Pilot* and the *Irish-American* made peace with Cleveland almost at once. By October, the *Catholic Citizen* had come round, so far that it was peddling charges that Blaine was a Know-Nothing and refusing to print proof to the contrary. Even John Devoy of Chicago felt the pressure. A joint-stock company owned his *Irish Nation*. Devoy favored the Republicans, but most of the stockholders were Democrats. As long as the *Nation* stayed out of partisan politics, that was of no concern. But Devoy had put the paper against Grover Cleveland, and almost at once he had to fend off challenges to his editorship. Many of the paper's big financial backers withdrew, carrying

Ireland Sold for Gold!

the paper close to ruin. Only promises of aid from the shipbuilder John Roach tided Devoy's journal through.[29]

When Egan broke his promise to stay out of politics, a storm of wrath broke in the Irish Land League. His and Sullivan's advocacy of Blaine added to the forces, already present, that pulled the membership in separate ways. Conservatives, led by Father Thomas J. Conaty, resisted the revolutionary side of the league, and had distrusted Sullivan from the first. Now Democratic regulars pitched in and continued to assail Egan and Sullivan long after the campaign ended. By 1886, John Devoy and his allies were also at open war with Egan and Sullivan, and in alliance with the Democrats. The Irish National League had become a shambles, so discredited by Patrick Egan's leadership that it no longer could raise money for the Irish cause, and so controversial that Parnell himself refused to give it his endorsement.[30]

The internecine warfare between Irish Americans offers just one example of how disruptive partisan involvement could be for those outside the party system. When the Women's Christian Temperance Union met in St. Louis just two weeks before the election, it hoped to show the strength of a cause 150,000 women strong. Gathering at the United Presbyterian church, banners before them proclaiming them "For God, home, and native land," the delegates heard President Frances Willard list the year's accomplishments. Even "to the most casual observer [she] seems to be radiant with the 'beauty of holiness,'" the recording secretary wrote. "Her sweet womanliness, unruffled amid the greatest excitement in conventions; her silvery eloquence, . . . and the exquisite simplicity of her character has carried her unspoiled through that wonderful adulation which has been showered on her the world over." She would need that poise; when her silvery eloquence endorsed St. John, not all the delegates cheered. Among the stronger critics was Mrs. J. Ellen Foster, who had written public letters endorsing Blaine. She tried unsuccessfully to keep the convention from endorsing St. John. Resentments long outlived the session. Republicans tried to set up a separate WCTU under Foster, and for years separate WCTU organizations would vie throughout the Midwest.[31]

With close connections between Prohibition and woman's suffrage movements, the 1884 campaign also pulled woman's rights advocates one way and the other. St. John's party favored giving women the vote. With some exceptions, Republicans refused to go that far and even used the Prohibitionists' commitment to pull temperance voters away from them. Yet many suffragists knew that Republicans offered the only real hope for advances in the future; and on other issues, such as laws against polygamy and the wide-open saloon, Republicans looked like the truest defender of the family. Some of them all but admitted that even a Democratic commitment to equal rights would never make them change parties. Republican success must come first, even if that put suffrage last. Wherever WCTU leaders led the battle for the ballot, their commitment to St. John was sure to disrupt the suffragist cause. The Kansas Equal Suffrage Association splintered for years; the movement in Washington Territory divided permanently. Helen Gougar, head of Indiana's Equal Suffrage Association, practically read Republican women out of conventions by keeping the meeting date secret from them; they, in turn, boycotted meetings that she called. By 1900, Indiana's movement had quarreled itself out of existence.[32]

Together, the temperance split, the Mugwump half-revolt, and the frustrated quest after the "Irish vote" tell much about the resilience of the two-party system and the perils of partisan action. Reinforced by a national chorus of editorial voices, sustained by money and tradition, the Democratic and Republican organizations could break any outside movement that stepped directly into their path. So the Farmers' Alliance would discover, half a dozen years hence, when it tried to transform itself from an agency for change into a separate political party. The Populist Party died from many causes: cheated, bullied, out-reasoned, outspent, it was doomed to seduction and destruction from the moment it began. But two generations of partisan tradition certainly made its task as nearly impossible as that which Patrick Ford attempted in trying to weld the Irish vote into a Republican weapon.

Ireland Sold for Gold!

14

Sideshows

The scandals the public knew about were not the whole story by any means. While Republicans roared and Democrats chanted, their managers fought a secret war against the "sideshow" parties.

By 1884, the once-worrisome Greenback Party had sputtered out most places. It still fielded candidates in Midwestern states and elected one to Congress from Iowa in 1882. But scattered islands of support could not give it national prominence, and most of the votes its candidates got were lent them by one of the two major parties. Outside of New York and off the Great Plains, there was no Anti-Monopoly party to speak of, and many of its leaders there had gone Democratic since 1882. In some Midwestern cities, independent labor parties were just beginning to form.

Apart, none of them could do anything. Together, their sponsors hoped for something better. The three groups would make an imperfect fit, putting different issues foremost and with varying interest in broadening the political nation to include wives, mothers, and working women. What all the groups shared was the conviction that money and monopoly made the laws to serve themselves, and that government must be used to right the balance. Some wanted thorough railroad regulation, some government ownership. But all believed that the economic system, left to itself, made a society of millionaires and paupers and put democracy at risk. When they came together in a convention in May, they had chosen the one man who could bridge the gap between Greenbackers and Labor, Ben Butler himself.[1]

Nobody mistook Butler for one of the downtrodden. He had plenty of money. For an impoverished party, that made him twice as attractive. Someone must foot the bill for a campaign. But delegates also knew that Butler thought right on the big issues. "I am a woolen manufacturer at home," he joked with one crowd, "and when I see a man with seven patches on his pants, I make up my mind that he is not consuming enough of my goods." A system that gave a Nebraska farmer fifteen cents a bushel for corn that dealers sold for seventy-five cents in the East was badly askew. Miners in Ohio's Hocking Valley earned seventy cents a ton for the coal they mined and had to pay for their own lights and explosives, until management fired them to take on Hungarian immigrants willing to take sixty cents. Tenant farmers toiled the cotton fields of Iowa and the South, while "whole principalities, whole kingdoms" of public lands went for free to the railroad kings.[2]

The Prohibitionist indictment of the two major parties came from a different direction, but it shared Butler's conviction that the system worked only for those willing to pay for it. When WCTU president Frances Willard appeared before the Republican platform committee, she got fifteen minutes to make her case; brewers got an hour and a half. Committee members shrugged off the twenty thousand signatures on the temperance petition. "Kick it under the table," someone on the platform committee said, and that was where the janitor found it on adjournment, smeared with tobacco juice. On July 23, the Prohibition Party gathered in Pittsburgh and nominated John P. St. John.[3]

Based on absolute number of votes, the People's and Prohibition Parties hardly seemed worth the trouble. Many Southerners still had the chamber pots made just after the war, with Butler's face painted in an appropriate spot inside them; some may still have been in use. Most laymen treated the Prohibitionists as psalm-singing cranks, Americans who really could use a few drinks. "No wonder St. John is hopeful," a Mugwump paper remarked. "He cannot allow his spirits to go down."[4] In his wildest dreams, Butler himself only expected to carry a state or two, which, if the breaks were right, would throw the election into the House, where he could force the two major parties to bid for his support.

Most people shrugged off the sideshow parties. Not party managers. Victory would depend on a few Northern states. There, every vote counted. Butler's appeal to Irish Americans and to workers would make him dangerous in the normally Democratic downtown wards of the Northeast. The Prohibition vote had its strongholds in country towns of the North and radiated out from the local church on the green. Every Protestant pastor was a potential party organizer, every church a potential meeting hall. Too many

Sideshows

votes up the Hudson for St. John, or even in Massachusetts, or Kansas, and Republicans were done for. For Republicans, then, the trick was to make sure that Butler stayed in the race and that St. John got out. For Democrats, winning depended on a big Prohibition vote and a People's Party without any people in it.

All through the campaigns, the sideshow parties found themselves cosseted and buffeted by Republican and Democratic managers. Indeed, without that encouragement, at least one of the two would not have fielded a candidate at all.

Butler's sympathy for the People's Party cause had not gone so far as to induce him to accept the organization's nomination. He delayed through June, hoping to use the threat of a separate candidacy to get better terms for workers from the Democratic platform and a better candidate. Incensed after Chicago, he still hesitated. Without big concessions, he could never support any Democrat, but an independent run would be an expensive luxury. Standing alone, the People's Party would have to pay for meeting halls, ballots, and literature. It had no congressmen to frank documents, as Republican and Democratic committees did. Not even Butler's bank account could stand the costs of a serious race. Republican managers must come through with funding.[5]

Republicans were tempted but wary. Blaine could see the pitfalls from the first. "One course would hurt in some states and help in others, and *viceversa*," he wrote Elkins. "The whole problem is this, *viz*: If Butler runs he will get 250,000 votes, more or less—less probably. If he does not run who will get the majority of these votes? I think I would, and hence would gain by his staying out." The general certainly had tremendous possibilities. The most widely read Democratic newspaper in New York, Charles Dana's *Sun*, backed him. It might do wonders, and if Tammany Hall put its muscle behind Butler, as seemed possible at midsummer, he could put New York, Connecticut, and New Jersey into Republican hands. But the general would draw best among the very Irish Americans and factory hands that the Republican tariff campaign hoped to draw from the Democrats. On the other hand, leaving Butler unsustained would be unthinkably risky. He might not run, leaving dissatisfied Democrats to drift back to their own nominee. Even worse, he might stay in the race, in which case his only hope lay in deals, state by state: fusing with Republicans here and Democrats there, with the People's Party's ally providing most of the money and calling the shots to suit itself. Fusion with the Democrats in Pennsylvania or New Jersey—even Illinois—offered terrifying potential. An ideal candidate would keep up a separate ticket just where Republicans stood to gain the most.[6]

*"Helping the rascals in—a burglarious scheme that may be suddenly spoiled"
(Joseph Keppler,* Puck, *October 22, 1884). Ben Butler, on editor Charles A. Dana's
shoulders, helps Blaine break into the White House, or will, if the Independent vote
doesn't stop him.*

Within a fortnight of the Chicago convention, Butler was being wooed by both sides. Democrats descended on him, beseeching him to turn down the Greenback nomination. Quite without authority, they assured him of the governor's high regard and hinted at "recognition": New England's patronage, or even the attorney generalship. Butler listened, uninterested. Arguing as one high-tariff Democrat to another and as a personal friend, Sam Randall came visiting. But nobody could pledge Cleveland to Butler's policies, and negotiations ended. Republican overtures fared better. When Secretary of the Navy Chandler arrived at the Portsmouth Navy Yard late in the month on the *Tallapoosa* to honor survivors of an Arctic expedition, Butler came on board. Soon Democrats were talking of the "Tallapoosa treaty"; actually, the general probably came to an understanding days before. The last place he would have ratified it would have been at an event honoring one of his old constituents, and with Samuel Randall at his elbow. Wherever the deal was made, Republicans made one, promising the People's Party $5,000 a week throughout the campaign.[7]

One week into August, Butler accepted the presidential nomination and set out campaigning by train. Crowds turned out everywhere for what was sure to be the best show of the season. Labor organizations threw him a parade in Detroit. The audience in the park was so large that Butler had to struggle to push his way up to the platform. Hosts of "blushing young beauties" met the general's train in Owego. Most of them had just come from a Prohibition parade and were wearing big white St. John badges, but at every other stop, farm women, some in bonnets and everyday calico dresses, rode in the wagons to hear him. The candidate appeared everywhere in black broadcloth, usually with a crimson flower at his lapel, and he minced no words. Crowds in upstate New York burst into applause when Butler told them that as president he would "either go into my seat or into my coffin, and . . . stop these murders North and South or I'll have a lot of first-class funerals to keep me busy." Democrats mocked the plush palace car that the worker's candidate rented for his travels and described in lascivious detail its embossed leather ceilings, Spanish mahogany writing desk, stained-glass decorations, and "nickel-plated toilet apparatus." Roughs threw tin and wooden spoons at the platform. Butler supporters, unaffected, donned spoons as badges and predicted victory.[8]

A good show in October was not enough to give Butler a good showing in November. He was presiding over a coalition and not a coherent party. The Nationalists, as Greenbackers called themselves in some places, overlapped with the Labor Party men and with the Anti-Monopoly organization, but not entirely, and their outlook was different. The workingmen's contingent was high tariff; the Greenbackers, when they gave the issue any thought, inclined toward a low tariff; city laborers objected to sumptuary legislation, while Greenbackers inclined to the Prohibition side. Going west, Butler found that he could not have driven his supporters into Republican ranks if he would. There, where the Greenbacker portion of the organization was the strongest, members were used to an alliance with the Democrats and meant to stick by it. In Iowa, for example, General James Baird Weaver had been the Greenbacker presidential candidate in 1880. As a congressman, his name became nationally recognized. Out of the House for four years, he meant to get back in, and with Democratic help.[9]

As Eastern Democrats railed at the Butler movement as a Republican front, Republican managers fumed that it was putting them more at risk out west than the whole venture was worth. Butler put a stop to negotiations for a joint electoral ticket in Ohio, Illinois, and Pennsylvania but went along with fusion in Michigan, Iowa, and Nebraska. In retrospect, it looked Machiavellian: fuse with Democrats where they had no chance, and keep it from happening in states like Connecticut or Maine where they did, but the November outcome did not look so inevitable in early September. With the right breaks, Republicans could see Blaine losing every Republican state between Wichita and Youngstown. If the "old devil fish" really had a working arrangement with Blaine's friends, why was he "slashing around Pennsylvania . . . with his swashbuckling speeches"? "It looks to me very like Butler has agreed to help the Republicans in the East for half of his campaign expenses, & the Democrats in the West for the other half," James Clarkson grumbled.[10]

In fact, the Butler movement was a series of mirages, each melting into vapor on close inspection. A working-people's party without help from Terence V. Powderly's Knights of Labor was not going anywhere, and Powderly steered clear of any commitment. (Powderly apparently was thinking more as a protectionist and as an Irish American—neither of them inconsistent with his role as defender of American workers; quietly, he was working with Philadelphia merchant Wharton Barker to tug Irish votes over to Blaine, and apparently with considerable success.)[11] Many local labor organizations were readier to fall in line, but the Butler campaign, perhaps taking them for granted, never sounded the call to bring them into ranks. In California, there were strong hopes that the Workingmen's Party movement could be revived and could deliver the state to Butler. It had been a formidable power in the late 1870s; why not again? But the movement quickly dissolved under the pressure from both major parties and the self-serving quality of third-party leaders, many of whom found themselves the only cause worth fighting for. Each faction accused the other of incompetence or crookedness. Neither had any money and suspected that their leaders were swimming in cash given by one of the two major parties for selling out.[12]

Divided or whole, Butler's forces could not make a good showing without money, and here, Republican promises notwithstanding, his movement ran on a shoestring. Most of his publicity would have to come for free; a personal campaign, making speeches, and winning newspaper coverage would have to do the service that parades and brass bands usually did for major parties. For that reason, too, he could not afford to mount any challenge out west without letting state parties make the best arrangements they could with the Democrats.

Promises made were not the same as promises kept, and by late September Butler found his party in desperate shape. The Republican National Committee had not even given "the pittance which they promised in aid," he protested to Chandler. Everything had been spent just keeping his New York campaign going; nothing remained for the rest of the country. "Now before the first day of October we should have at least $25,000 beyond what was understood, i.e. $5,000 a week. This is imperative to success. I have done all that I can do and more than you thought I ought to do. Will you see that this is done?"[13]

It was not done, at least not to the People's Party's satisfaction. Unluckily for Butler, he sent representatives to discuss increased funds with Republicans just as they were scraping the last possible pennies available, for the Ohio campaign. By October 7, matters had reached a crisis. His campaign manager wired Butler from New York: "People here will do nothing I think unable." Only after several days of equally discouraging news did another emissary assure the candidate even that existing agreements would be kept. In all, the People's Party campaign received $70,000 from Republican coffers. It was nowhere close to enough.[14]

Butler's money troubles may have been made worse by the Republicans' commitments elsewhere. Irish American organizations would not work for free. Local Republican managers did not care what kind of arrangements anyone else had made; they would go after every potential Butler voter they could get. Plenty of supplicants claimed that they could deliver the Greenback and Labor votes to the Republican slate with a little labor and a lot of greenbacks. Finally, the GOP struggled with the question of how to handle the other sideshow party, and where to get the funds to make it secure.

The Prohibition Party caused the Republicans difficulties in various directions. Edging closer to the Dries on temperance issues might lessen the desertions to a third party, but it would excite the worst fears of German voters in the Midwest, and Germans already were rated as rather dodgy. No group was more open to the conviction that Blaine was a thief, especially when Carl Schurz, their most celebrated countryman, assembled the evidence. Unfriendly remarks about the "Continental Sunday" might drive them into Democratic ranks for good. Damaging though it might be in closely contested states in November, the Prohibitionists' separate ticket might actually improve Republicans' chances in Ohio by emphasizing for the large, fickle Wet electorate how unacceptable to the real Dries the GOP was.[15]

Republicans had gazed uneasily on the Prohibition movement from the start. When the minor party held its convention in Pittsburgh, Republican agents attended, too, hoping to nudge the convention in the right direction, either into preventing any nomination or arranging for a nominee ready to drop out "at the proper time, if need be." At all costs, editor and Republican manager James S. Clarkson wrote Blaine, the Republican ticket must be kept from endorsement by the delegates—remote though the prospect was. When the delegates did nominate, the party press held its fire. A few gibes at St. John's eccentricity satisfied most editors, along with an occasional appeal to Prohibitionists to consider the practical benefits of holding to Republicans. At the same time, everything must be done to appeal to St. John's churchgoing constituency on other grounds. For that purpose, stressing the moral issue was indispensable. At the very least, it rallied clergymen into Republican politicking without offending either side in the saloon controversy.[16]

And it was not wholly clear that St. John would accept his nomination. For two months after the convention, he issued no letter of acceptance. The Prohibition Party was based on a cause, not an ambition for offices. It ran to claim attention; conceivably, St. John simply meant to publicize temperance. Then, rather than damage the Republican Party, he might refuse the nomination or withdraw some time in October. Official withdrawal—after Ohio had voted on October 15—would serve best, but just dropping an active campaign would slim the Prohibition Party turnout. Quietly, Republican leaders tried to feel out the best means for arranging that withdrawal.[17]

But doing so seemed less likely as time passed. St. John did accept. This was quite a sacrifice for a man of such modest means. Or was it? Republican managers had their suspicions. It was common belief that Democratic cash underwrote the whole Prohibition campaign. To keep the party headquarters running and food on the table for John P. St. John would be the best possible investment for drawing legions of natural Republicans away from Blaine in November. Such a scenario made sense; after all, it was what the GOP was doing with Butler. And it could hardly come from anywhere else; Republicans had hunted up the biggest potential donor, John D. Rockefeller of

Sideshows

"Prohibition's pet. St. John: 'It's cold, and lonesome, and not exhilarating—
but I like it, oh, I like it'"
(F. Graetz, Puck, October 15, 1884).

Standard Oil, to "see if we could shut off supplies," and found him "heartily with us."[18]

Then, on October 5, 1884, when the Ohio state campaign was in full swing, one James F. Legate paid a call on Republican Party headquarters in Cincinnati. It was not by chance; he was hunting out Clarkson, one of the insiders that the Republican National Committee had sent from New York to tend to details. For a generation, Legate had ranked among that legion of forgotten operators behind the scenes who "fixed" politics by secret deals. In Kansas, he had spent years making himself useful for politicians needing a clever agent without much scruple. Back during Andrew Johnson's impeachment trial in 1868, it had been Legate who carried an offer from Senator Samuel "Subsidy Pom" Pomeroy to the White House. With the president needing a few Republican votes for his acquittal, the senior senator from Kansas was in the market; if popular reputation served as any guide, he never was anywhere else. Nothing came of the intrigue except an ugly exposure of the Kansans. Legate later bragged that he had collected $10,000 for his own services during the trial and $50,000 more to give a senator in return for his voting acquittal—which never made it that far. He also shook down Pomeroy, and then, finding how well it worked, blackmailed him again.[19]

With Pomeroy's downfall five years later, after he tried to bribe a legislator to reelect him, Legate found new associates, Senator Preston J. Plumb and Governor St. John in the struggle against the saloons. Now he had come to stump Ohio for the Republican ticket but kept his friendship with the Prohibition nominee. That made him an ideal go-between, if one were needed. The managers may have wondered, too, about the chance circumstance that summer: Briefly, there had been two Prohibition candidates for president; the other had been none other than "Subsidy Pom." For reasons not made clear, Pomeroy had withdrawn in St. John's favor. It would have been natural to suspect that the hand behind the scenes had been Legate's.

All these dealings gave Legate very plausible credentials. More than that, he brought Clarkson a letter of introduction from Senator Plumb, freshly dated from the day before and pronouncing the bearer as "able to treat for St. John." It seemed that the former governor of Kansas hoped to make a deal. Aware that his candidacy was hopeless, he thought that there could be no harm in selling out. With Legate to handle negotiations, they could both become rich men. St. John considered asking a quarter of a million dollars for doing so. Legate took credit for making him settle for $25,000.

What would the Republican high command say to Legate shaping the campaign in ways best suiting Blaine's purposes? By timing where St. John would speak, and where not, the Republicans could concentrate the Prohibition uprising to "safe" states and leave it with a token impact in closely contested ones. Better still, Legate's "friend in Ohio" would give a speech declaring that the only practical choice this year lay between whiskey and loyalty and whiskey and disloyalty and that, as a Union veteran, he preferred the first. Then he would withdraw from the race. Did Clarkson think his associates on the national committee would be interested in a Prohibition sellout?

As a well-posted Iowa newspaperman, Clarkson must have known of Legate's shabby reputation. In Kansas, as one resident put it, "you could not convict a dog of barking on his sworn testimony, unless it was well corroborated." Still, he leaped at the offer. He had been expecting it for quite some time. Since temperance could never prosper without Republicans in power, St. John could not be running in earnest. Selfish reasons must explain his candidacy. Clarkson never doubted that Legate spoke for St. John: the emissary waved around a telegram from the former governor, inviting him to visit. If that was not proof that St. John had summoned him to discuss a sellout, what was?

Nor did Clarkson feel any compunction about getting his side to bribe a candidate to drop out of the race. If St. John *was* on the take, why should he collect it from his natural enemies, the saloon's defenders? If doing something was right and proper, paying a person to get out of the way so that it could be done was right and proper, too. And beating the Democrats was right. Clarkson knew that. Against them, it was entirely "right to use false and treacherous means."

The only real question in Clarkson's mind was a practical one: would his superiors raise the money Legate was asking for? On the one hand, the opportunity seemed too good to pass up, but, on the other, money was very tight. The national committee was moving heaven, earth, and Jay Gould's railroads just to meet the bare needs of the party for Ohio. To raise $25,000 more would be nearly impossible without stinting other requirements just as pressing. Not wanting to promise anything without higher authority, Clarkson wired to New York for advice.[20]

The national committee members there were even more uncertain than Clarkson, for a very good reason. With Butler's campaign manager and personal secretary haunting the committee headquarters, the timing couldn't have been worse. To lock up New York in November, Republicans would have to pay St. John to get out and Butler to stay in, and they had no way of getting the funds to do either, right away.

With money so precious, party managers were not going to commit it without knowing exactly what they were buying. They decided to send out one of the biggest financial wheeler-dealers running the campaign, the St. Louis railroad promoter R. C. Kerens, to scan the situation. He, Clarkson, and the committee's majordomo for the Midwestern campaigns, Colonel William Dudley, could make the final decision.

As soon as Kerens got to town, the serious negotiations began. If fresh proof of the candidate's good intentions were needed, Legate provided a convincing one. For a down payment of $10,000, which could be handed over later on, St. John would catch a "sore throat," cancel all his speaking engagements in Ohio for the rest of the campaign, and leave the state that very night. And sure enough, the next day St. John *had* left Ohio, never to return.[21]

For ten days the deals went on, never consummated, always one step away from being consummated, with secret meetings and telegrams in code flying between the managers and Legate. Perhaps the managers were delayed by the scramble to find some kind of money to pay Legate in—and just possibly, they tapped $10,000 in funds from the Justice Department, supposedly paid to special deputies in Cincinnati on the state's election day. The record remains misty. What was clear was that by October 15, when the polls opened in Ohio, Legate had gone to New York to seal the bargain with the Republican National Committee himself and that by that time, there *was* a bargain, worked out back in Ohio.[22]

But Legate never got his money. It may have been, as he explained it afterward, that the committee had never meant to pay him and were out to get St. John's cooperation as long as they could, for free—with promises as their only down payment. It may have been that the Ohio returns told Republican managers that St. John didn't need buying. They had done so well there, and Prohibitionists so poorly, that the national election in November was in the bag. That money now could go where it really might make a difference, to Ben Butler's sideshow instead.[23] But there is another possibility, and the evidence for it was pretty nearly conclusive. For the first time in a week, committee members had started thinking.

St. John certainly had given Republican managers something to think about. On October 10, the New York State Temperance Alliance, a Republican front created for campaign purposes, held a meeting to request St. John to retire from the contest. The timing may have been coincidental. More likely it was the national committee's way of giving the Prohibition candidate the opening he needed to withdraw. After all, if things worked the way as promised, that retirement would have to be sometime within the week.[24]

St. John could have used the invitation as his excuse to hint at quitting. Or he could have said nothing at all. That would have turned up the pressure under the Republican managers to seal the deal and fork over the cash. Instead, the candidate did something that, in light of what Legate had been promising, made no sense at all. He fired back an instant, devastating reply. Point by point, he showed why, from his view, no true temperance man could support the Republican Party. And lest anyone misunderstand him, the candidate made quite clear that he was in this race to the finish.[25] What could St. John have been thinking, to make a reply like that?

All at once, committee members may have wondered whether Legate was trying to sell a commodity to which he had no title. Or was it they who were being sold?

Looked at anew, the truth seemed embarrassingly obvious. All the evidence of St. John's intentions, no matter from whom it seemed to come, led back to Legate. Not one scrap of paper, not a single independent witness, had shown that St. John even knew about the dealings, much less approved them. Since the Prohibition committee had scheduled his departure from Ohio weeks in advance, and sent him into Michigan to speak—"sore throat" and all—to ten thousand listeners, Legate's down payment on a deal delivered precisely nothing.[26]

The committee may have figured out all of this, some of it, or none of it. Whatever the reasoning, Republican managers pried themselves out of Legate's clutches without passing over a penny. Legate went back to Kansas, his palms still itching for the $10,000 he claimed to have earned.

If Republicans could not buy St. John, at least they could martyr him. Until negotiations broke down, the party press had dealt gently with him. No longer. Moral parties were especially vulnerable to an assault on their candidate's own morals. Now St. John was painted as a hypocrite, a spouse abuser, a sunshine patriot, and the handiest tool of the saloon keeper next to the corkscrew.[27]

The strategy may rank as the worst mistake of the campaign. According to one account, St. John had continued to run his symbolic race, playing no favorites, until word of the attacks on his personal life reached him. Furious and stirred to greater fury by the reports from national headquarters at how strongly the stories were taking in upstate New York, St. John had a score to settle with his slanderers. He canceled his Western appointments. Hereafter, he would devote his attentions to the one state that Blaine had to carry to win. A fortnight remained before the election, and St. John put it all to stumping upstate New York.[28]

"The movement was sustained almost entirely on Democratic money," one national committeeman wrote Logan, "& the St. John Committee were in constant communication with the Democratic committee." Insiders estimated that Democrats spent $38,000 on St. John after the October elections and groused that Republicans could have secured him for $3,000 less.[29] If by that they meant that the candidate had been bribed to run and could have been bribed to quit, they were certainly mistaken. St. John had not been willing to sell out for money because he had never been in the race for the money. He was the one being that baffled party managers: a true believer.

Other speakers, who believed in the cause, took pay for speaking in that campaign. Anybody with an active professional life lost money every day away from the office, and party committees were perfectly willing to pay expenses plus something on the side. St. John was relatively poor. Very nearly all his income came from lecturing for temperance at $50 a night. But the cause meant so much to him that when he won the presidential nomination, he canceled all his speaking engagements and went into the campaign at his own expense. The ministers handling the party's finances felt bad about such sacrifices from a man of so modest means. They offered him compensation. "Not one cent," St. John snapped. Every penny that went to him would have to come out of the funds for printing up campaign literature and ballots for the election. "Let us at least pay your railroad expenses," the party chairman, Rev. John B. Finch, begged. The candidate relented that far, at least, but only if there was money left after the party had paid for ballots and campaign documents. Unpaid he left them, and unpaid he remained.[30]

Wrong though they were about the Prohibitionist candidate's motives, Republicans guessed right about the source of his party's funds. Democrats had no more compunction than Clarkson did. As one $2,000 contributor put it, the third party was "a 'Providential Ally' that could be honestly utilized to our benefit. . . . It had no cohesive quality about it, was liable up to the last moment, to collapse at any time. Money was required to perfect the organization and hold it intact." Democratic investments that fall created a body "in good working order" that served well in future state campaigns, at least until Finch's death threw the machinery into less reliable hands. By October, Finch had made arrangements with two of Tilden's master spirits on the Democratic National Committee, William C. Whitney and Smith M. Weed. When they provided less money than he asked for, Finch demanded more and got Whitney's promise "that everything should be made right if the work was done and results followed."[31] Indeed, by acting as the GOP's go-between in the Legate intrigue, Clarkson may well have made "everything" righter still without knowing it. According to one plausible story told four years later, word of Legate's negotiations had reached Prohibition Party headquarters in New York. Sensing an opportunity, Finch had rushed to Nebraska's Democratic National Committeeman George Miller to break the news and take bids for not selling out. Word quickly came back from the party's impresario, Arthur Pue Gorman, himself. The Prohibition campaign could draw $25,000, but the money and St. John's campaigning must be used exclusively in New York, where it counted.[32]

All these intrigues were *not* all that unusual. Part of any campaign, inescapably, was the buying off of political trouble. In one case the trouble was made deliberately so that it *could* be bought off. Around August 1, dispatches from Boston reported that the National Council for the American Political Alliance had called on its state councils to select a presidential nominee. Two months later, the papers announced that the Alliance had settled on "Captain" William Ellsworth of Philadelphia, and that Ellsworth had accepted and drawn up a platform. Everything about the organization was mysterious. Ellsworth had no listing in the city directory. His group's mailing address was a box in the main post office, and nobody else admitted membership in it, though the "Captain" flourished signed letters from famous men with whom he was on intimate terms, including two former governors of New York. Detailed press accounts explained to readers that the organization was anti-Catholic, antiforeign, and perilously large. It had 600,000 members, and expected to draw 1.2 million votes come November.

Everything about it sounded plausible, except the numbers. Back in 1876, the American Alliance had endorsed Rutherford B. Hayes and caused him a few sticky moments with foreign-born voters when his secretary's letter of acknowledgment became public. Even a nativist organization of more modest proportions would pull away Republican voters and hem in Blaine's room for maneuver. Every appeal to Catholics, naturally, might win the Alliance more converts. Putting Ellsworth out of the race would be money well spent.

But Blaine's campaign never had to spend it. Reporters, sent to interview Ellsworth's vice presidential candidate never found him. No such person existed. The Alliance did not exist, either, and never had. The 1876 letter was as much of a hoax as the 1884 press release. The newly hired secretary for the Alliance had met Ellsworth just once, heard rapturous tales of vast sums, readily available for setting up a party organ, and suspected that something was wrong when asked for a two-dollar loan, which Ellsworth never repaid. A month before election day the sheriff of Philadelphia impounded all of the Alliance property to pay for a gravestone that Ellsworth had bought on credit.[33]

There was one more example. This time the victims were found among Ben Butler's friends in the People's Party. With or without Republican subsidies, it lived a pinched existence; and as election day approached, the problem worsened. Seven thousand dollars might pay for poll watchers at New York City's 712 polling places, but who had $7,000?

Then an offer came from an unexpected source. Tammany Hall had cash enough, but with close municipal races pending, it could use some spare votes. What about a swap? If the People's Party would vote for Tammany's city and county tickets, Tammany would vote for the People's Party legislative ticket; and just possibly, they might do Ben Butler a good turn, too. Best of all, Tammany would pick up the tab for printing the ballots and manning the polls. It was an offer too good to refuse, especially when Tammany boss Kelly and his mayoral candidate, Hugh Grant, made the deals. Grant even promised to write a check for the cause himself.

With all arrangements made a few days before the election, there was not time for much—except a little double cross. When the ballots were delivered in bundles to the local organizers for the People's Party, the Butler electoral ticket was there, all right, but the rest of the names were Tammany men, for legislature as well as the city. The Tammany machine figured that voters intending to cast their ballots for the People's Party might know the name of their presidential candidate but not be quite so familiar with those running for Assembly. They figured right in some neighborhoods. Ballot distributors there only caught on after the votes were counted. Elsewhere, party organizers spotted the trick too late to rearrange and print up the right ballots for their own people. When the polls opened in many neighborhoods, those ballot boxes and poll watchers that Tammany had promised were nowhere to be seen; nor were some of the poll watchers that the People's Party itself had paid for. Other People's Party poll watchers got paid in rubber checks. If any of Butler's vote in New York City came from Tammany, it seems to have come and gone before the votes got counted. Worse yet, those swindling tickets had come to the local workers straight from People's Party headquarters. Nobody had raised the alarm. Could the men at the top have been so blind? Or had liberal donations closed their eyes for them?

Many party workers were morally certain of the answer. Some quit at once. Others stuck around, just so they could accuse each other when the votes were all in. When People's Party leaders got together, the questions began: what had happened to the party funds? what had happened to the ballots? Some members were accused of making deals with the Republicans and running Blaine presidential tickets at Butler's expense. One meeting broke up in a row, with each side calling the members of the other liars. "I have seen so much treachery in that district," one local pro shouted, "that I do not wish to have anything to do with that gang again."[34]

The 1884 election was not the first time that minor parties had been played with, like gloves on a major party's hand, nor that organizations outside the mainstream broke up in allegations of insiders selling out. Nor would it be the last. Historians who admire the idealists on the edge of mainstream politics may have underestimated the flaw built into any challenge: the understanding that winning was impossible. Always there was the temptation to sell out for the best deal the minor party could get, always the difference between those who favored the third party as a statement of principles and those on vacation from Republican or Democratic faith who saw the outsiders' movement as a way of bringing their old party back to the right principles. Just as with suffragists, Mugwumps, and Irish nationalists, the two great parties were strong enough to warp or fracture every other group they touched, even when that touch was a caress. Yet it was also true that the third parties, like Butler's and St. John's, may have thriven because the Whitneys and Clarksons had an interest in letting them live. It was the competitiveness of Democrat and Republican that made possible the influence, as well as the irritation, of minor party challenges, and in the process compelled the two major parties to bend their own programs to accommodate them.

15

Carrying the War into Africa

Most historical accounts of the 1884 campaign never venture south of the Ohio. Why should they? The North provided most of the hoopla and nearly all the suspense. Smart money could bet on Connecticut going one way or the other. Only a born fool would gamble on Republicans carrying Georgia.

But this is precisely why the unwritten story may have been so important. From the start, Democrats had a near lock on the former slave states. That advantage of 153 electoral votes allowed them to clinch victory by concentrating their money and time on a few Northern states. To overcome the Solid South, on the other hand, Republicans had to assemble a virtually solid North. Some states they could take for granted. No Democrat had ever carried Vermont. Winning Pennsylvania, Minnesota, or Kansas would take wonders. Still, that left plenty of states from the upper Mississippi to Boston Harbor to fight for, and fight hard.[1]

Republicans had an alternative. They could try to break the Solid South and force Democrats to take nothing for granted. "Carrying the war into Africa,"[2] as the strategy was known, was less an invasion than a raiding party. Steering clear of the Democratic strongholds, Republicans would concentrate on the *weak*-holds, where disaffection and a sturdy opposition party had won before. Just two or three Southern states, no more, and Republicans would build up margin enough to withstand reasonable Northern losses.

The GOP needed wins down south in more than the presidential race. Regaining the House depended on carrying at least half a dozen Southern districts. So Republicans could not afford to write off the black vote even where statewide victory lay out of reach. Without the "Black Districts" in North and South Carolina and the "Shoestring" along Mississippi's riverfront, the House would stay Democratic.

Could it be done? As Republican strategists looked south, they must have seen what was apparent: there were many Souths, not one. Each would require a different sort of campaign. Across the cotton states, a meager white leadership directed a vast black rank and file with conspicuously less success every year. Victory depended on getting out a full black vote. Reminders of the party's equal rights tradition might stir that, though beleaguered loyalists were likelier to respond to promises for help renewed: if not protection at the polls, then federal money to sustain the public schools. North of the Gulf states, another kind of constituency would take a different appeal. White Republicans in eastern Tennessee and western North Carolina numbered in the thousands. Men respected in business and public life were open to persuasion. In Nashville and Chattanooga, the commercial classes had lived under Republican city governments and found themselves none the worse for it. Race-baiting had no such sway in Memphis, as in the Mississippi countryside, a day's ride south. By appealing directly to the disaffected white voters and believers in a New South, Republicans could make prosperity, not race, the leading issue. As Virginia congressman John S. Wise put it, the parties could draw the lines between "the nigger-killers and free-traders" and the protectionists.[3] Farther north still, in the Border South, Republicans could even find areas where wartime memories worked in their favor. A Confederate record did no good in large parts of West Virginia, Maryland, and Kentucky. Missouri had contributed more Union army recruits than half a dozen Northern states put together.

An emphasis on economic issues might work to Republicans' advantage in the industrializing Border South, but it had real uses across the Deep South, too. By itself, in any fair election, black turnout would carry South Carolina, Louisiana, and Mississippi. But mobilizing the black vote would be impossible without rousing the whites. They had the guns, the courts, the election officials, the money, and the power on their side. Without substantial support from the "respectable" classes in the white community and forbearance by leading politicians on the Democratic side, any effort must fail.

Yet there did seem to be ways of making white Southern leaders relatively indifferent to a Republican win in the presidential race. Louisiana sugar planters wanted tariff protection. Landowners up the Mississippi River wanted levee building and channel dredging. Parsimonious state authorities were starving the school system, and many white Southerners looked to

Washington to make up the deficiency. A Democratic president and House would impede any such use of public money and by cutting the tariff would bring less revenue in. Republicans would spare the surplus, the better to build up the South.[4]

The stigma of drawing the color line also explains why Republicans went out of their way to make alliance with any white dissenters they could find. Without breaking the color barrier themselves, without associating themselves with homegrown rebellions against the Democratic leadership of the South, the GOP must lose. But an alliance with independents would give the regular Republicans protective cover.

Ever since the end of Reconstruction, the South had grown an ample supply of disaffected Democrats. In appearance, the independent movement looked more promising than it actually was. In many places, momentary disgruntlements had given rise to a party bolt. In some areas, the uprising was no greater than personal resentments, the thwarted ambitions of Democratic politicians. Even if real issues played, the role of personality often gave them force and meaning they might not otherwise have. Once Democrats shared the offices with the leaders of the disaffected group, the faction's principles—its grievances, as far as they were given to the public—melted away, too. Lasting victories could not rest on candidates like Georgia's Henry Parsons, who two years before he went independent had told the Democratic convention, "Josephus was not a better Jew than I am a democrat; nor was Ruth more true to Naomi than I am to the party."[5]

Yet there were places in which real issues had created an independent movement, and where those issues remained unresolved, and, indeed, irresoluble by the party in power. In Missouri, West Virginia, Virginia, North Carolina, and Tennessee, Republicans had a substantial cadre of white leaders and, better still, of white followers, enough of the latter to elect congressmen with some outside help, and in all of those states, there were white dissidents ready to support any major party challenge to the Democratic leadership.[6]

Their grievances were varied and, in many cases, justified. Even defenders of the so-called Redeemers faulted them for lack of imagination, if not integrity. "Slipshod and weak," one Alabama editor labeled the governments he had done so much to elect, "conducted without order, system, plan, design, or purpose."[7] He could have said the same of Texas, Mississippi, or Missouri.

Louisiana did not even have the excuse of integrity. The state's flamboyance made it unique, even among Southern romanticizers. Gothic romance pervaded its reputation, and Visigothic barbarity permeated its poli-

Carrying the War into Africa

tics. "Redemption" came in an epic of mutual cheating and bullying after three years of virtual civil war. Once in control, Democrats announced election returns to suit themselves. A system of rotten boroughs, vote fraud, and treachery propped up rottenness at the top. Behind the governors, the notorious Louisiana Lottery shared power with reactionaries and a New Orleans city machine that could have given Tammany Hall lessons in rascality. Around Governor Samuel McEnery stood men who made office a paying proposition. Within Democratic ranks, opposition grew. To win renomination in 1884, "McLottery's" chums had to pack delegations and manipulate the rules. An uprising of reformers and protectionists that could win the state that fall seemed at least imaginable.[8]

North Carolina had no such scandals, but its restiveness had gone further. Democrats never won more than 54 percent of the vote in any governor's race. "This negro question is the one lion in his path towards Republicanism," a Raleigh party worker wrote North. "Remove that and this state breaks from the solid South forever." Even without it, an independent movement had made great advances over the past three years. The county government system that took local power out of the hands of black voters in the eastern part of the state made no friends among whites in the western mountains. They wanted "home rule." They also shared blacks' enthusiasm for the Blair education bill.[9] Republican Party chairman J. J. Mott and President Arthur welcomed a coalition on those grounds in 1884. At Mott's behest, the party held its convention at the same time that Liberals had theirs and endorsed their nominee, Congressman Tyre York.

Born in the mountains and raised behind the plow, York represented the western insurgents at their most democratic. No tenants plowed his fields. York split his own rails, studied medicine on his own, and became a country doctor with a wide practice. Four terms in the legislature never changed him. Always he returned home, dressed in plain clothes, ready to tell the political news in the upcountry dialect and arrive every Sunday at his country church on muleback. As a longtime Democrat from an overwhelmingly white constituency, he was the epitome of Southernness, and of the broader appeal that Republicans were looking for. If anyone could win, he could; if any state in the Upper South could be won, North Carolina could be.[10]

It did not take a rich fantasy life, then, for Republicans in New York or Washington to persuade themselves that Blaine, the tariff, and the Blair bill, would crack the Solid South around the edges, if not break it entirely. Those in the know calculated a fighting chance not just in North Carolina but Florida, and a likely win in Louisiana and the two Virginias. Blaine himself took black former congressman John Lynch's breath away by assuring him that there would be no trouble in Mississippi. As a gentleman of honor, his friend Senator Lucius Q. C. Lamar would "see that I get a fair count." Some Republicans continued believing in victory to the last, or claiming they did. "Nothing but the most outrageous fraud and violence could defeat me," one Florida nominee promised two weeks before the election.[11]

Still, if "carrying the war into Africa" held promise, it came at a price, a price all the higher since President Hayes made his peace terms with the white South. Campaign thunder could not exist anywhere without certain essential ingredients: a strong active Republican press to drive home the party message, organizers on the local level able to distribute ballots and prepare the voters with campaign appearances and rallies, and a coordinated effort from the top.

Eight years of Redemption had left Republican organization local at best and nonexistent at worst. Tennessee's was in better condition than the average. Party machinery ran efficiently in the mountain counties. Wartime memories and local favors assured a good GOP turnout there. Republicanism was unbeatable around Knoxville and formidable in Chattanooga. Much the same could be said for other Appalachian states, and for the black counties shoved into the North Carolina second congressional district. But there was no state organization able to make a serious canvass beyond the party's enclaves. Even where the party was least handicapped by issues like race and Reconstruction, such as Delaware, Republicanism lacked a statewide reach, much less a grasp. Customhouse patronage made Louisiana's machinery seem well-heeled and gave party managers more favors with which to keep dissidents in line. But outside New Orleans, the organization was "a thing of shreds and patches," as a federal marshal complained. Black leaders had no followers they could count on come election day, making them, in one observer's analogy, like a frontispiece "when the body of the book has flown with the winds."[12]

Time, common purpose, and a lavish supply of money could help set these defects right. But the start-up costs required lay far beyond Southern Republicans' means, just as that sense of harmony lay beyond the power of the party's rank and file. As one Yankee reporter commented about North Carolina, "Nearly all the tall hats and 'biled shirts' in North Carolina are Democratic."[13] Enormous sums would need to be diverted from the national campaign. Federal officials who had worked heart and soul for Arthur's nomination would need to redouble their efforts, knowing that Blaine's friends would insist on sharing their jobs. Finally, Republicans would need to frame the issues of the canvass not just primarily but exclusively around the tariff question. The breeze from waving the bloody shirt up North, however small

Carrying the War into Africa

by comparison with past campaigns, would blow strong enough to set Southern Democratic banners waving. And with all these conditions met, there was still no certainty of winning a single Southern state.

The price would have been hard to pay in any election year. It was far out of reach in 1884. A sullen administration did nothing for Southern harmony, and money came not at all. In each of four counties with black majorities, a Florida congressional candidate protested, registrars had struck upward of a thousand Republican votes from the roster. Restoring the names would take money, to make appeals and bring in witnesses. So must all the Republican organizations, every one of them a charity case. Nowhere was outside aid so needed, so urgently requested, or so unavailable. From Alabama, William Stevens expressed bewilderment. The Black Belt in the state had a twenty-five thousand Republican majority, and still the party "can scarcely raise funds enough to have our tickets printed. Canvassers must put their feet into the road and walk from point to point to uphold the party that has made rich and kept fat miscreants who are recipients of its life-blood."[14]

Virginia fared little better. Having stood by Arthur, General Mahone found adjustment to the Blaine candidacy a difficult experience. He had taken his Readjusters into the Republican ranks earlier in the year, not to serve the state party so much as to rule it. Naturally the old-time Republicans complained, and as Blaine's original supporters, they won a sympathetic hearing from the national committee. With the little general dictating who should run county committees and monopolizing the presidential electors, rallies turned into feuds, with one faction walking out as soon as the other took control of proceedings. It was a common report (probably more common than true) that Mahone had told national committee members that he "wanted nothing of the committee but money, and he wanted that d—d quick." Fifty thousand, he thought, would carry Virginia and elect six congressmen.

These disputes threatened the party's chances. A divided organization was doomed to lose, and the national committee determined to put its scanty funds elsewhere. As late as the end of August, not a penny had gone from the high command into the Virginia campaign, and warnings circulated that until Blaine's friends got square treatment, nothing would be forthcoming. By mid-September, the national committee had written off Virginia as unwinnable.[15]

Mahone's struggles revealed the other problem with Republican coalition-building. The marriage of parties often barely outlasted a honeymoon period. Even in North Carolina, many of the party faithful trooped after their candidate with misgivings. York might win, but his Republicanism hardly went to the bone. His four terms as state legislator had shown him as deep-dyed a Bourbon as any Democrat could claim and only a belated critic of county government and funding for the public school system. While he could defend the protective tariff, he had nothing good to say about the rest of the Republican platform, and his past pronouncements spoke loud and clear against all of it, from the Blair bill to tax reform.[16]

In the Deep South, the flirtation with independents only added stress to a party already torn within by disagreements about how far Republicans ought to distance themselves from black aspirations. By 1884, Alabama's old factions had melted into two, each led by whites but worlds apart on how to cope with a white-run South. George Turner and Paul Strobach led the true believers, convinced that the party must keep its commitment to equal rights. Former senator Willard Warner and former governor William H. Smith spoke for the old Whigs, who put economic development first in the Republican program and felt that the less said about equal rights the better. In Georgia, General James Longstreet worked to build a lily-white Republican Party. His supporters held their own state convention in 1884. A proposal was made to invite black Republicans to hold a separate convention and at least make the semblance of cooperating with Longstreet's followers. Even so mild a step toward racial accommodation was voted down. The defeated delegates walked out. This made headlines, not political history: all told, the convention had fourteen people. That summer, Longstreet lost his place as U.S. Marshal, and his faction perished as an organized force.[17]

Coalition brought resentments into the open, if only because the one issue on which independents could not take a Republican position was the one that black voters cared most about. York was quoted as having once growled, "The more you do for the d—d negroes, the less grateful they are." Republicans in Alabama's Eighth District shook their heads over their nominee for Congress as he tried to explain how his belief in a free ballot and fair count squared with his past opposition to blacks' voting at all. Everywhere, Republicans splintered between coalitionists and straight-out party men, dividing, as one regular put it, "like an open pair of compasses held together at its head only, on national issues."[18]

More than issues were involved. To many of those who cared most about the party, a surrender of its name and character would cost more than victory would be worth. Parties that put themselves out of business temporarily would find it harder to be taken seriously in the future. They would be nothing more than a tagalong, hitched to whatever bandwagon could carry them within reach of the fat offices. "Straight-outs" scorned the "sell-out crowd" that held federal offices as partisans purely for pelf. "If you go to a

Carrying the War into Africa

convention and ask for a State ticket, they will yell you down like a kennel of wolves on the verge of starvation and mark you at once for political extermination," one Alabaman wrote sourly. True Republicans looked forward to the day "when they can hang the scalps of certain Federal office-holders [from their belts]."[19] So wherever coalition triumphed, the "straight-outs" resisted. In North Carolina, they mustered strength enough to call a convention of their own and issue a separate state ticket.

In the cotton South, where Republicans had no hope for their state ticket, these feuds made the most difference in congressional races. When blacks in the Mississippi Delta insisted on having one of their own for Congress, white Republicans bolted, declaring it useless to brave Democratic shotguns for a "muttonhead." In Alabama's Fourth District, the party's conservatives nominated circuit judge George Craig, a former Confederate soldier descended from one of the first families in the state. Within days, his defeated black competitor, Jere Haralson, had taken the field as an independent. He may have been "the deadest negro politically in Alabama," as one newspaper charged; "the women laugh at him, and the little boys even call him a Democrat." But his candidacy, subsidized and orchestrated by the Democrats, doomed Craig's already doubtful campaign.[20]

This was no isolated instance. Southern Democrats made it their custom to foster splinter candidacies or to publicize possible revolts in Republican ranks, the better to justify their own rigged returns and improbable black votes. Blacks bolted against Horatio Bisbee in Florida's Gainesville congressional district, and some went over to Josiah Walls, whom Democrats praised as "an intelligent colored man, full of fire, eloquence and enthusiasm." Each side held its own convention and ruled out the other as fraudulent. When the two nominees held a joint appearance, Bisbee's followers saw to it that two brass bands struck up the moment Walls opened his mouth and kept drowning him out until the players tired. Then they and all of Bisbee's supporters marched away from the rally, carrying all the torches that lit the stage with them. Some of this was the indignation of principle, some the expression of long-standing rivalries and battles for power inside the party organization, but much of it, we may surmise, was inspired, funded, and sustained by Democrats, who made the simple calculation that the sum of one Republican and another vying for an office was zero Republicans elected.[21]

Alabama Republicans hesitated to make a party campaign at all. The state convention that met in Montgomery in April chose to leave selection of a state ticket to the party's executive committee, which did nothing. Those partisans dreaming of some "People's Anti-Bourbon Ticket" that Republicans could support unofficially were disappointed. A convention of independents did meet in June and chose a full slate. Then it collapsed. Half the candidates refused their nominations. The whole ticket was withdrawn. What followed was virtually no campaign at all. Some places where Republicans held a clear majority hosted intense local contests, but most counties put up no Republican nominee.

Republican leaders were not so much selling out as facing a reality. For all the hopes of the national managers, Democrats were not letting the race issue drop and were using their control of government to keep power in their hands alone. A vigorous Republican campaign would kill and injure Alabama's party organizers and voters to no good purpose. The bigger the turnout Republicans brought to the polls, the bigger the Democratic ballot box frauds would grow to count them out. It had happened before. It would happen again. Participating in a process so badly vitiated would only give the Redeemers moral cover: the *appearance* of a legitimate, competitive race.[22]

The skeptics could make a good case; the proofs that fall were overwhelming. Democrats had the money to put on aggressive campaigns, to buy black speakers and voters, and to finance black independent candidacies. Republicans admitted what was perfectly obvious, that some of the black vote took up "the tempting baits of glittering gold and silver," all the more so because in so many places if a Republican ballot could not be sold, it had no value at all. It simply was an invitation to harassment, intimidation, and violence, and if cast, a piece of wastepaper, counted for the wrong side if counted at all.[23]

Democrats paid not just to make blacks vote right but to keep them from having any ballot at all. Voting in the Carolinas required a ticket certifying that one had registered. It would be asked for at the polls. But Democrats turned the extricating of those certificates into an art form by making them pass for legal tender. Saloons would take them in place of cash; so would country stores, circuses, and minstrel shows. So the news that John Robinson's circus was headed for South Carolina in mid-October 1884 threw one knowledgeable Republican into alarm. "I need not expatiate in the *delight* colored folks take in circuses," he reminded the national committee.[24]

Other methods took legal muscle rather than money, and Democrats possessed that, too, in overwhelming preponderance. Most important was control over the local registration boards. Since county governments usually were a Democratic stronghold, the Republicans had every chance of seeing the registration lists purged on one technicality or another. Democratic newspapers called on party managers to scrutinize on election day every name and challenge every colored voter against which some case could be made.[25]

Not that all blacks were kept from voting. In Louisiana, the Democrats used their authority to make sure of a good turnout, at least after the count-

Carrying the War into Africa

ing had begun. Every insider knew the saying, "A dead darkey always makes a good Democrat and never ceases to vote." Black registration actually grew with Redemption, and faster than the eligible population. They all were counted for Democrats. Maryland permitted the same privilege to its white dead that Louisiana did to black ones, where Democratic county officials controlled the registration rolls.[26]

Usually, whites needed no resurrection. Whatever the North chose to do, Southern Democrats played as rough a game of sectional politics as ever. "Did any of you ever on the field of battle see your flag totter and fall almost on the gory ground, and see man after man seize the beloved colors and bear them aloft?" one Georgia orator appealed. "I see from the glistening eye that there are those here who have seen, and who in times past that have tried men's souls, have seen the standard raised from the dust and planted on the enemies' batteries. Let us rally round the flag, boys! rally once again." (Since it was a Confederate audience, he discreetly omitted the words that followed; the last thing listeners were inclined to do was to shout the battle cry of freedom.)[27]

That spirit, Tyre York found to his cost, was enough to rouse white North Carolinians against their own interests. The old war issues always came up. They could hardly help doing so when Democrats put two generals, one colonel, and a major on their state ticket. York was a doctor, but General Alfred Scales could pull rank on him; when he arrived at a rally, horsemen, 150 strong, were there to welcome the general and escort him through the crowds. Scales spared no opportunity to remind voters of the wounds suffered in the Confederate cause, and when York responded that they were in the back of Scales's leg, the Democratic crowd shouted and waved pistols at him.[28]

The problem of a nation of local presses, nationally circulated, made Republican difficulties acute. The party could mute its bloody-shirt orators, but it could never muzzle several thousand editors. As long as there were articles in Northern papers criticizing the South, some Southern "exchange" would read, clip, and reprint them to remind readers of who their enemies were. Those Democrats determined to stress sectional differences always had the chance and always could assemble the rhetorical proof that the Republican heart remained unchanged, that the tariff was an irrelevant issue, a ploy to deceive Southerners into voting against their sectional interests.[29]

Democrats could always find statements fit to inflame the Southern heart. Republicans, especially those in the northernmost states, never quite reconciled themselves to Blaine's soothing syrup. They warned that Cleveland's victory would allow Texas to split into five new Democratic states, enough to give the party a lock on the Senate, especially once Arizona and Utah were

admitted. Then free trade would bring the North to revolution, even secession. "Democratic Free Trade will give to the South what the Rebellion was
designed to secure—allegiance with England," one partisan wrote. Others
brandished "positive proof" that Democrats meant to pension 300,000 Rebel veterans, pay compensation for liberated slaves, and elect Cleveland, in
one Bourbon's words, "if we have to shoot every d—d nigger in the South." Of
course Cleveland would give the South all it asked, one newspaper insisted.
A forty year old unable to resist "a single, average widow" could never hold
out against Southern bullies.[30]

Republicans underestimated how quickly, how naturally, the Democrats
would find reasons for erecting the color line anew. When Edward McPherson of the GOP congressional committee announced plans to mount a serious campaign down south, he used language that would have been unexceptional in any Northern journal. Southern Democrats treated it as an
impudence and the threat of an invasion by some foreign power. "I guess you
will send down some of your negro brethren," one partisan wrote McPherson. "Well, my advice is this Mack if you have any friends that you want to
dispose of send them down but you had better let the undertaker measure
them first and if you want them buried at home get rates for transportation of
the corpse over the different express lines."[31]

From Democrats' perspective, the race issue made perfect ethical sense
even when the other side went out of its way not to raise it. No matter what
the opponents' principles, there was never a question of where they expected
to draw the bulk of their votes. "If the negroes were not allowed to vote we
would hear nothing of his independent candidacy," one Georgia newspaper
growled, as a Democratic bolter challenged the regular nominee. It took too
much faith in the good nature of men of proven ambition to assume that, in
power, the independent would work to satisfy his supporters' needs or join
the Republican Party openly for a reelection. "I tell you, fellow-citizens, that
independence of democracy means dependence upon republicanism," Congressman Thomas W. Grimes of Georgia warned. Conversion to Republicanism was the only way that "independentism" led. "Look at Chalmers! Look at
Emory Speer! Look at Mahone! Where are they today?"[32]

But if Democrats saw the black behind every independent movement,
they saw the independent movement behind every black aspirant to office.
The inspiration that hope of victory gave them, the example that bolting
against Democratic leadership provided, encouraged blacks to seek more
offices than white party managers would have granted otherwise. "In Troup
[County], they met and passed resolutions, threatening that if the white men
attempted to protect the sanctity of their homes by administering summary

Carrying the War into Africa

punishment to negro fiends, they would resort to violence to protect these brutes," a Democratic orator thundered. "Why, in your own county, I am told that one of them in addressing a negro meeting the other night said: 'This is our first chance in years. The democrats are dissatisfied with their men. Your duty is to support . . . any one who will disorganize the democratic party. Win this, and when you go to see a white man on business, you will neither be forced to stop at the front gate or go to the back door.' "[33]

Blacks voting for black candidates proved how dangerous universal suffrage was. Blacks voting for white ones proved the same thing; when they spurned their own race for another, black voters showed that they voted on mercenary grounds. "He can be bought with rewards, as he is now bought with promises and threats," one Democratic correspondent reminded readers. As the rich grew richer, their power to buy the black vote would increase. There was only one way out: disfranchisement.[34]

The race issue had a thousand possible means of expression from ridicule to reviling. No white candidate could escape being tarred with his backers' color, not even one like Horatio Bisbee, who ran for Congress in Florida against a black independent challenge. On the one hand, he was accused of hating blacks. "In a room at Jacksonville, he [complained] that he slept with a colored woman two years ago and he hadn't got the smell off him yet," the black challenger charged. On the other hand, black convicts were said to favor him overwhelmingly:

> Another black feller kem in view,
> An' boasted of what he useter do.
> Said he: "I'm a thief from boyhood up,
> An' I've never airned a sip or sup.
> Many a time I've tried ter 'scape,
> My latest crime was childhood's rape.
> I wanter vote for Bisbee.[35]

"He would ravish this State with fire and sword, if he could," an unnamed Democrat put in, "and nothing would suit him better than a war of races."[36]

Of course there would be no war. The peace of the mid-1880s was based on more than legal jerry-rigging. It was based on the memory of violence past, and the constant hint of force held in reserve. "There has never been but one serious conflict in this state between the white man and the nigger," a Democratic presidential elector told blacks in his Florida audience in 1884. ". . . Then we had barbecued nigger. . . . Don't you forget that we are not going to see this government go into the hands of anybody who promises you half the offices." Few public figures put matters so bluntly, at least when there was any chance of Northern newspapers reporting them, and the speaker found himself dropped from the presidential ticket forthwith. But the message came through clearly all the same. Reporters coming south to report on race relations in a later campaign were warned out of town and threatened with mob violence, especially if they were spotted "talking with niggers." The one admitted white Republican in town guessed that some two hundred other whites there felt as he did; saying so would only open them to abuse, turn them into social outcasts, and hurt their businesses, and all without the slightest hope of a real majority of the votes being declared an official one. If blacks ever turned out in full force, as he put it, "there would be hell in two hours."[37]

In time, there was not even much need for creative counting. Aware of the odds against them, many blacks quit trying to vote. Those like W. S. Ferris, a former slave and postwar planter in Noxubee County, Mississippi, made no apologies for it. "I tell you, I've been through hell-fire, and so have all the rest of the colored people," he would tell one Northerner in 1888. "We've got to make our living, and we've made up our minds to let politics alone till the time comes—if it ever does—when we can vote just as we please without risking our lives every time we go to the ballot box." Did his people mean to vote, the reporter asked a black barber. "Well, I don't reckon many of 'em will," the barber responded. "There ain't any use in our voting, because it has to go one way here, and it always does. You see, the white people do all the counting, and they make high, low, jack, and the game every time."[38]

Things worked out much the same in the Upper South, where blacks were fewer, as they had in the cotton states. Virginia Democrats talked tariff some, Internal Revenue taxes more, and Negro rule most of all. Let party faithful remember the black who boasted the year before, "I have already picked out a white girl for my wife, and as soon as the election is over I am going to pay my addresses to her—Miss Mollie—over there," or the Negro who vowed that where sending his children to a white school was concerned, he "would have his rights or have blood." Blacks wanted "mixed schools and mixed marriages" and shouted that they would have them. (There was no contemporary evidence of any blacks saying any such things.)[39]

Bourbon though he was, even York could not inoculate himself against a campaign of open race-baiting used to drive his white support from him. In joint appearances with Alfred M. Scales, he was on the defensive from the first. Scales let the tariff take care of itself. "Do you endorse civil rights in the meaning as interpreted by Fred Douglass, Bob Ingersoll and others?" he demanded. A bill was pending to end segregation; would York vote for it? ("Thunderation," York exclaimed, "you know there is no civil rights bill, and you know that the school bill separates the whites and blacks.") If York was still a Democrat, opponents charged, then he ran with bad company; if he was a Republican, that made him a race-mixer. "What makes you keep howling nigger?" York pleaded. "Don't you know there are four nigger papers bought by Democrats to advocate General Scales?" In the Upper South, a race-baiting campaign could not kill the GOP; it could not silence the issues of tariff and prosperity, not as long as there were Republican newspapers here and there to carry the message. Hill counties with no blacks were not about to panic over mixed schools. Still, white-lining did serious damage, and the worst in areas where whites held the power amidst a substantial black population. Anxious Republicans begged the national committee for ammunition to show that Northern Democratic leaders had put through state civil rights laws and that "scions of the old ruling families" now commanded "negro Regiments."[40]

Race panic built to a crescendo in the week before the elections. Louisiana newspapers invented Republican plots to hire black deputy marshals to count in illegal black votes and discovered nonexistent shipments of repeating rifles bound for New Orleans, for use in the coming race war. In Florida, Democrats exposed plots to bring two or three thousand Georgia blacks into the state for election purposes. The proof was conclusive: advertisements on the northern side of the border inviting them to attend a torchlight procession in Jacksonville and offering to pay their round-trip fare. Of course the guests would not go home again, until voting was completed. Senator Chaffee of Colorado was on his way to Florida, doubtless lugging "the bag," cash-stuffed, from the Republican National Committee.[41]

If Chaffee was, in fact, on his way to Florida, he never made it there. By October, most Southern Republicans had been written off, and they knew it. Even with inside help, Florida Republicans could not get the funds they wanted, and their candidates had to do their best on their own resources. "We have been so severely let alone, and discounted by all Republicans outside of the state that we begin to feel ashamed of our audacity in claiming any chance against the wisdom of the managers," a North Carolinian wrote headquarters bitterly.[42]

Louisiana blacks were not let alone. Just at the start of November, white Democrats attending a Republican rally in Iberia parish got into a fight. They had come prepared. When shooting broke out, the largely black audience fled. Many fugitives were shot in the back. "Stray shots" left half a dozen lying dead along the roadside toward town. Others disappeared into the bayous forever. Perhaps fifty were wounded, probably more, and the coroner certified to at least eighteen blacks killed. The level of casualties suggests an "incident" planned in advance, in the customary Louisiana fashion, to send a hint to Republican blacks not to show up when the polls opened. It worked. The cry of Northern black papers that their Southern brethren must make a white man "bite the dust" for every black shot down, and burn down the assassins' houses were not the voices of militance but of desperation. The editors knew well that neither the local courts nor the federal government would ever call the terrorists to a reckoning.[43]

Blaine's bid for the South had failed. All it had done was mute much of the Northern press on issues that many Republicans still cared about. Only in mid-October did the candidate face the truth. Then on his way through Indiana and Illinois he unfurled the bloody shirt anew. Cleveland's election would weaken "the bond of union," Blaine warned audiences, because "the men who organized the Rebellion" led the Democratic Party. "It would be as if the dead Stuarts were recalled to the throne of England, as if the Bourbons should be invited to administer the government of the French Republic, as though the Florentine Dukes should be called back and empowered to govern the great Kingdom of Italy." Blaine made a poor prophet. The real consequences would come on election day, not after it: an administration put into power by the denial of those equal rights that a refurbished Republican Party no longer had the heart to defend.[44]

Carrying the War into Africa

16

Local All Over

Federalism made every national campaign a patchwork. Less subject to the will of candidates than their twentieth-century counterparts, the national committees found themselves more affected by the vagaries of campaigns in thirty-eight states. Bustle as they might, the managers on Broadway were very small drivers managing a very large team of horses.

And this should not be any surprise. Most of the power, patronage, and legislation in nineteenth-century America lay beyond the federal government's control. Even in presidential years, local politicians fretted about lesser offices and plotted their campaigns accordingly. Except in the few key states of the industrial North, state committees handled matters as they pleased without much outside meddling or money. National managers had to draw up their rosters of speaking engagements with a state's special needs in mind. Often they found it impossible to get the speakers they wanted at the times they wished: the state committees had scheduled the star performers to suit themselves.

Issues varied in intensity from place to place. Local conditions forced an adjustment in the mix. Moving west across an electoral map, the tariff worked differently in various places. Cross the New York harbor from Manhattan and the free-trade advocates fell away. Industry, not importing interests, had made Paterson and Trenton. Protectionism had the edge in every argument in New Jersey and Pennsylvania. Democrats dodged the topic or concentrated on the inequities in existing schedules. Ohio was slightly more uncertain. There was room to talk free trade in Toledo, as Congressman Frank Hurd did, and to defend wool duties in Mansfield. Democrats in Indiana inclined more to agrarianism and silver coinage than those in surrounding states.

So, too, the German vote mattered far more in Ohio than in Indiana, much more in Chicago and Wisconsin than downstate Illinois. That affected how the temperance issue played. Irish Americans were nowhere near as important a factor in Western cities as Eastern ones. Fitly, when Blaine finally did raise the bloody shirt aloft in October, he did so in South Bend. War sentiments had marked the two parties more deeply in Indiana than in any other Midwestern state. Here alone, Democrats could get by in politics with a copperhead past. By contrast, the least hint of tepid loyalty damned a candidate in northern Indiana or Iowa. "Republicanism in [the Dubuque area] is not a logical conviction," one journalist wrote; "it is a baleful fanaticism. . . . The war is still in progress in this region, especially among members of the farming community. . . . The women are worse than the men; they are intolerant, ferocious, implacable."[1]

Patchwork politics gave the parties a needed flexibility, but it raised a host of anomalies. In Iowa and Nebraska, Democrats allied themselves with the Greenbackers, while in Missouri, Republicans did so. As Iowa Republicans roared over the bargain and sale of Greenbackers and published mock advertisements ("WEAVER & GILLETTE, wholesale dealers in GREENBACK VOTERS! Contracts made with any responsible persons for the delivery of stock on any side of any question, on terms to suit"), their fellow partisans hailed a similar alliance in West Virginia. "There are fusions and fusions," the *Minneapolis Tribune* explained. Some were "immoral," and most were "unfortunate."[2] Others, evidently, were Republican.

Every fusion carried with it a particular baggage that affected the way campaigns dealt with national issues. Even as Iowa Democrats encouraged Prohibitionists to set up their own state organization and drain off Blaine voters, Missouri partisans conflated the Dries' cold-water army with the Blainiacs. The reason was obvious. Since Greenbackers inclined toward Prohibitionism, that meant an Iowa Democracy shy about exploiting the liquor laws as a campaign issue and eager to assure their coalition partners that on one more issue Republicans stood in the wrong, whereas Missouri Greenbackers' alliance with the GOP left Democrats with nothing to lose. They stood to gain more by a campaign loud in appeals for "personal freedom."[3]

Still, what happened in one state could affect the results in others. The success of Prohibition in Kansas had immediate effects on crusaders in nearby Iowa, just as Iowa's efforts toward railroad regulation served to inspire Minnesota, next door. With Republicans committed to placing a Prohibition amendment on the ballot in 1884, Missouri Democrats were advised to turn their eyes west and north, where temperance reigned. "In each one of those states you fooled about," the *St. Joseph Gazette* lectured German voters; "and . . . you cried good Lord to-day and good Devil tomorrow; and you stood by the Republicans year out and year in, . . . and what has been the result? Proscription as intolerable in some instances as Russia's despotism, and confiscation absolutely of millions upon millions of dollars' worth of valuable property."[4]

Maine provided an even more salient example. A constitutional amendment banning the sale of alcohol would have made for a hot campaign anywhere else. But Maine was no Ohio. Prohibition made the statute books in 1851. From every platform, party speakers spoke its praise, and five thousand women in the WCTU were ready to help voters turn out on election day. Democrats left the liquor question strictly alone. There were no votes to be gained and quite a lot of small-town Democratic votes to be lost. The one real advantage of Maine's proposed Prohibition amendment lay outside New England: German voters out west would watch how Blaine himself voted. If he supported the amendment, they might stick by Democrats. If he voted against it, Prohibition-minded Republicans might vote for St. John. (Anything so plain to Democrats was clear to Blaine. Arguing that local issues like Prohibition should not muddy a national campaign, he cast no vote on the amendment.)[5]

State idiosyncrasies loomed large in a national campaign because Americans had so many election days. Thanks to the federal system, states still chose governors and congressmen when they pleased. The number of exceptions had dwindled; over the past twenty years, New Hampshire, Connecticut, and Rhode Island had moved their early spring elections, and Nebraska, Pennsylvania, and Indiana had given up their October polling dates. But that still left Alabama and Kentucky voters to troop to the polls in August, while Maine, Vermont, and Arkansas made their choices in September. West Virginia and Ohio still carried on as "October states."

Maine, Ohio, and West Virginia thus stood in for opinion polls in Gilded Age politics. Winning early, winning big, had a bandwagon effect. It could inspire party workers and tap the wallets of doubtful contributors for the general election. A big loss would tear the heart out of a campaign. The October states had done that to Democrats in 1868 and 1880. Money and speakers must go where they would make the difference the soonest. If the

"A magnetic statesman"

(Zimmermann, Puck, September 3, 1884). Democrats got it wrong. Blaine did not
face both ways on the liquor question that fall; he faced neither way.

efforts of the national committees had an ad hoc feel to them, then, the string
of immediate deadlines, stretching from late summer into mid-October, were
one reason.

This year, the early states proved decisively indecisive. Maine and Vermont sent mixed messages. Democrats never had a chance in Vermont. They
lost in a landslide. Yet to their surprise, Republican margins were down.
Sharing Senator Edmunds's distaste for Blaine, many of the party faithful
had stayed home.

Recent history gave Maine Democrats only the illusion of hope. Helped by
a Greenback insurgency, they had carried the governorship in 1880, their
first win in twenty-five years. But four years had changed the odds. Republicans had won the state back. The Greenback movement had dwindled to
nothing, its old leaders converted or bought into allegiance to the mainstream parties, its membership lists obsolete. Maine voters swore by the tariff

Local All Over

and by their Plumed Knight's stainless purity. The real question was not whether Republicans would carry the day, but by how much.

Blaine would need an unusually big win at home to impress voters elsewhere. So Republicans threw in all their ready cash. Senators and congressmen packed the podiums. There were torchlight processions, picnics, excursions, and endless oratorical fireworks. Potential stay-at-homes were warned that Democrats meant to wage a "still hunt." An enemy better organized than anyone dreamed lay hidden, pockets full of British gold to buy Maine's purchasable voters. The Republican state committee scared themselves into a panic on fantasies like those. The real reason nobody could spot the Democratic campaign was that there was none. Learning from 1880, the national managers had written off the Pine Tree State. Last time around, they had starved Ohio and Indiana to carry Maine and lost both as a result. This time, the money and speakers would go where they counted.[6]

With so one-sided a contest, the Cleveland campaign braced for a bad defeat and got one. The Republican state ticket won by nearly twenty thousand, a broad margin even for a presidential year. "Where is the independent mud throwers," one party regular gloated. From the size of the turnout, it would seem, they had shown up—and voted as Blaine did.[7]

If the ethics issue had not swept all before it, what about the inroads that temperance had made? That would be for Ohio to answer. Republicans had a less marked advantage. They usually carried the Buckeye State in presidential years, though not comfortably, and often because an Ohioan headed the ticket. Boosting Republican confidence would take more than a narrow lead: ten thousand votes, at least. A Democratic win would finish Blaine's chances for good.

The fight for Ohio revealed how jerry-built the Republican campaign was and with what miserable resources, managerial and financial, it had to work. By mid-June the state committee had organized. On paper, its personnel, with connections to the Ohio business community, looked impressive: Foster, Foraker, Cleveland industrialist Marcus A. Hanna, and for chairman, the experienced John F. Oglevee. Yet for a month, nothing happened. Frustrated regulars bombarded the national headquarters with complaints. Foster was sick, Foraker sea-bathing, and Hanna on a Western trip, a journalist wrote in late July. Nobody was "taking any interest except Oglevee, and . . . he is saddled with a debt of $3,000 left over from the last campaign." A month later James S. Clarkson had come west as the national committee's eyes and ears. What he found alarmed him. The committee had sound plans—all sound, but no action.[8]

Most counties had their campaign committees by August, with active workers for each ward and voting precinct. Blaine and Logan clubs sprang up everywhere. But state leadership was essential if a coherent "hurrah campaign" was to be put together. Speakers had to be sent out. Their routes and schedules needed central coordination. Many areas had more will than wallet. There had to be a statewide war chest for partisans there to draw upon, and an agency able to make the hard choices between needy areas clamoring for funds. Yet as far as candidates for Congress could tell, the state managers were wholly unaware of their existence. Nominees had to invite speakers on their own, beat the bushes for money to pay their travel expenses, and write to Washington for documents to spread among the voters. The state committee was asked; it never sent a one (and when the congressional committee did send one candidate sixteen thousand franked speeches, it billed him for them). Committee members pleaded that nothing needed doing until September.[9]

Party managers were only making excuses. What really held them back was poverty. Democratic reports had Ohio awash in money from the protected interests. New York City produced $150,000 by itself, Chicago another $300,000. These fabulous expense accounts for vote buying were simply fables. Clarkson arrived at the headquarters in Columbus to find that the state committee had spent a bare $2,000, $500 more than it had collected. Cursing provincial incompetence, Clarkson tried his own hand at fundraising. He printed up a subscription form and got ready to round up contributors. His journey ended instantly when the first prospect he picked, loud against the committee's slackers and good for a $5,000 pledge, offered a measly $200, which, he added, was "more than any one else in Columbus would give." Clarkson gave up.[10]

"I am not really pleased with the situation," one insider wrote Senator Sherman late in August. "No one knows what the liquor men will do ultimately. And the temperance men are sensitive. Up to the present time our people have seemed a little faint of heart, and the Democrats correspondingly jubilant. . . . My judgment is the Germans in the state are pretty solidly against us." Clarkson's letters did not allay Blaine's worry. "It is plain that the Democrats are going to stake the whole fight on Ohio," he wrote. They, at least, had "plenty of money," brewers' and distillers' mostly. Every Republican organizer he talked to agreed that winning was possible, but no more than that. "It is of no use to disguise the fact," Clarkson warned Blaine. "Ohio is in bad shape—very bad shape. Our people there are down & the Democrats up. We must change the positions."[11]

Ohio was not the only problem that had sent Clarkson west. Indiana

Local All Over

seemed just as doubtful. Republicans had to win it in November, but no major Northern state would take more work. Accustomed to close races in which every ballot counted, Indianans had fostered a notorious class of marketable electors, and the miniscule group of undecideds wielded unusual influence. Together, the two classes of doubtfuls may have amounted to twenty-four thousand votes; that, at any rate, was the Democratic state committee's reckoning. Other guesses were higher. The *Indianapolis News* calculated the vote sellers at eight hundred in just one county, and twenty-eight thousand across the whole state, and, one political insider told its reporter, former national party secretary Stephen Dorsey's notebooks listed every one of them.[12]

Republicans did their best, but they were hampered by John C. New, state chairman. "Very wise, sphynx-like and chilly," one Democratic newspaper reported of him, with "great intellectual heft." The heft didn't show. New stood with the Stalwarts, if anyone, and while he radiated confidence, pronouncing Indiana "sure" two months before the election, others did not share his confidence. He got along well enough with Senator Benjamin Harrison, less well with gubernatorial nominee William Calkins, and terribly with Postmaster General Gresham's followers. As an Indiana politician with extensive inside connections himself, Pension Commissioner Dudley sent word that New had no talent for organization and was drunk "most of the time." New's pockets bulged with statistics and figures, mostly wrong, about how many voters would turn out and where. "The State committee was as inefficient as could have been desired by the Democratic managers," a Blaine editor grumbled afterward.[13]

Someone full of "steam & enthusiasm" would be needed to rescue matters in both states, preferably a man with more experience than scruples. The national managers must set up a branch office rather than trusting local talent. Clarkson picked out Colonel Dudley of the Pension Bureau for the job. Dudley had a wide reputation as a "practical politician," one whose first principle was winning. As commissioner, he had come into disrepute for an "unscrupulous disregard of all the rules of official morality." Dudley was willing to quit his present job, "if he could do it in self-respecting shape" (that is, if Blaine would promise him some decent office like commissioner of patents when he won) and without making an enemy of New; the commissioner had his eyes on Indiana's other Senate seat, and could not afford to rile the publisher of the *Indianapolis Journal,* a shrill if formidable Republican organ. Any Western headquarters must bring the Indiana state chairman in as a titular member, with the real authority elsewhere. Dudley would act as an all-purpose troubleshooter, especially to handle the money. By early September, the arrangements were complete. Dudley sent in his resignation, effective after the election.[14]

How effective he was *before* the election was an open question, though it was not his fault alone. The Midwestern states were strapped for cash. Five thousand dollars from the national committee in late summer "set things in motion" in Ohio, but with the election less than a month away, the committee was still scrambling for pennies. A. L. Conger carried the tin cup around. His connections with New York businessmen and his fellow ironmongers won his appeals a respectful hearing. This year, though, he won little more than that. Business firms did not usually contribute, and executives felt hard-pressed by the recession. The head of a steam-forge works gave ten dollars and allowed that he might give fifteen more, but only if it was absolutely necessary. Conger's own business partner in Syracuse was so alarmed at the danger of Democrats winning Ohio that he offered to send "say 25 or 50 dollars." Many other businessmen would not give at all. Friends put their explanations in apologetic terms, but either they had given to the national committee already—as Pittsburgh steel magnates had—or they had no spare change to give. Loyal Republicans paid assessments of $25 apiece, and some as much as $100. By September 22, with three weeks till election day, total funds, national and state, amounted to $12,500.[15]

Indiana fared worse. The state relied especially on "torch light and bass drum," as they put it, and that meant heavy infusions of cash. In past campaigns, Indiana had been one of the October states. Neither side could afford to neglect it. Transformation into a November state after 1880 had given it lower priority, at least until Ohio, Maine, and West Virginia had been satisfied—assuming the national headquarters cupboard wasn't bare by then. So until late October, the Republican National Committee could only spare $5,000 for Indiana, and the state committee, once it was spent, found itself still at least that far into hock. With less than two weeks until election day, Senator Benjamin Harrison was forced to turn to his own private stock of contributors, notably Wharton Barker of Philadelphia, for support. Barker showed a "generous interest," which, combined with some $600 raised from his other Pennsylvania friends, amounted to just $1,150. The usual contributors were already so tapped out that they thought themselves prodigals for giving anything at all.[16]

Still, the Republican campaign managed to function. As September ended, doubts lightened in Indiana and vanished in Ohio. There were several reasons for this. For one thing, Ohio's Democratic Goliath was a giant only in its enemies' imagination. Within, the same old feuds continued. Instead of opening up his checkbook, Oliver Payne tried to make as small a contribu-

Local All Over

tion as possible. He had to give—Democrats had just elected his father senator, after all—but there was no reason to bury a low-tariff party in money. Protectionists and tariff reformers turned their back on each others' candidacies, and the "Coal-Oil gang" harried Senator Payne's enemies from the winter before. John R. McLean's *Cincinnati Enquirer* favored Cleveland only technically. It was one of the first major newspapers to print the whole Maria Halpin scandal, and its most popular correspondent, "Gath," barely hid his Republican sympathies. Even at the height of the campaign, Democratic readers could expect a column or two from him on page one, vindicating Blaine's good name. For a time, Republican managers flirted with McLean and the Paynes, hoping to work out some arrangement to neutralize them completely. The Democratic organization itself stumbled along in near disarray. Cast out of the chairmanship, John G. Thompson created a new power base, centered on campaign clubs coordinated through a branch assembly in Columbus. Potentially, the clubs worked in tandem with the state committee. In practice, they behaved like a rival with its own schedule of speakers and rallies.[17]

Estimated at fifty thousand votes, the German communities had swung the state twice in the past two years. But a lot had happened since 1883. Democrats had left the liquor laws pretty much alone, and Republicans were not about to enlist in any new crusade. Brewers in Cincinnati kept their wallets shut when Democratic fund-raisers came begging, and a few returned to their Republican habits. Perhaps they appreciated the warnings that Senator Sherman is said to have given them: the likeliest way to hand the Republican Party over to the Prohibitionists would be for liquor manufacturers to let go of it. Republicans would do best, however, if national issues blotted out state ones. Partisan habits among the Germans did not vanish in one year or even two. As Sherman noted, that love for personal liberty fit too well the party that showed its love of liberty by ending slavery. Democrats had to win German Americans over; Republicans had to simply win them back.[18]

In a campaign so short on funds and on time, there was only one way of doing that, and that involved attention from national candidates. "Black Jack" Logan was canvassing the state already. At Mansfield, more than three thousand listeners stood in a drizzling rain to hear him speak at the depot. In Bellaire, marching clubs and torchlights met him at the station. The general might talk tariff at every industrial center, and he hardly missed a one from Toledo to Youngstown, but the Union soldiers in their old uniforms and the telling banners spoke of other national issues. Sneering at the manners that prompted him to spit in one ill-wisher's face, Democrats had to admit that he made a bully stump speaker.[19]

Then in August, John Sherman offered an unorthodox suggestion. Blaine must abandon the customary retired life of a presidential nominee and step out onto the campaign trail. If he wanted Ohio in November, he must bid for its votes in October. Elkins was so impressed with the advice that he passed Sherman's letter on to Blaine.[20]

The strategy carried serious risks. Custom curtailed how far presidential candidates could advance their own fortunes. Taking one's cause on the road had failed badly for Andrew Johnson in 1866. For Horace Greeley's presidential bid in 1872 it had been catastrophic. As long as a politician didn't say anything, he would not have to explain or retract it, but campaigners were talking all the time. Asking for people's votes would put a nominee "in the attitude of a supplicant," one Republican warned, with no certainty of changing a vote. "To suppose that any intelligent men who have made up their minds are going to change them after gazing at Mr. Blaine a few minutes seems to me absurd."

Still, the appeal was made because nothing else seemed to work. There was apathy even in the Republican stronghold, the Western Reserve. Only a magnetic presence could stir the faithful. It was a risk, undoubtedly. But it was less so than going into the homestretch with Ohio already lost—and lost it could be, unless desperate innovations were tried.[21]

Blaine had been considering some such tour ever since his nomination. His friends had promised that he would take to the hustings, as part of the "aggressive campaign." What may have decided him was more than Ohio. It was, as he explained later, the only way to get the campaign back on track. Personal issues had dominated. He alone could shift attention where it should have been all along, to the tariff.[22]

So on September 17, with Maine safely Republican, Blaine left Augusta, making stops through New England and New York. During a stop at the Fifth Avenue Hotel, a stout, heavy-set man, leaning on a pair of crutches paid him an unexpected call. As Blaine's friends caught sight of him, they rose to their feet: it was General Grant, come to make a public show of friendship and support. At Fremont, Ohio, former president Hayes introduced him to the crowd and the two exchanged compliments.[23]

Blaine did excellent work. He never misspoke. Avoiding personalities, he devoted his energies to the tariff. He was clear, forceful, and apparently persuasive. The crowds loved it. Twenty-five hundred listeners came to hear Blaine in Dunkirk, along Lake Erie—and Dunkirk was a Democratic town. One place tendered him bouquets, another displayed a portrait of Garfield, a third arched the track with an evergreen bower labeled "Protection." In the big cities of Ohio, Cleveland, Cincinnati, and the like, the ovations just got bigger. Plumed Knights, drill corps, social clubs, and rolling-mill hands marched and cheered, and sometimes they got a look at Blaine and Logan both, campaigning as a joint concern. Democrats sneered at the "hippo-drome," a candidate "exhibiting himself like a dime-museum." A few of them remembered that Greeley's trip had killed him and cheerfully pre-dicted like effects for Blaine. His eyes had "a peculiarly singular appear-ance," the *Cleveland Plain Dealer* thought, hinting at insanity. But it was Ohio that went crazy. "The whole state is a blazing camp-fire," Congressman John D. Long wrote Henry Cabot Lodge. Novelist and one-time presidential secretary John Hay thought that Blaine's visit had been worth ten thousand votes to the ticket.[24]

Blaine's presence not only inspired Republicans. It shoved discussion back onto the tariff issue, and there votes were waiting to be gained. Hard times took the edge off the tariff's reputation as a guarantee of high wages, but it sharpened its outline in other ways. "Protection has nothing to do with the dullness," a Youngstown Republican told one reporter. "On the contrary, we are not protected enough." Coal miners in southeastern Ohio went on short hours and reduced pay. High-tariff spokesmen found them a scape-goat. Every steelmaker who bought used British steel rails, entered at a low duty as scrap iron, could cut back on how much coal he bought for the furnaces. One Cincinnati ironworks closed down a week before the election and promised to reopen only if Republicans carried Ohio and to suspend indefinitely if Grover Cleveland won the presidency.[25]

"We think you can do us the *most good* by giving us *something strong* on 'High Tariff,' " a linseed-oil maker wrote Sherman. "*Our* L.S. oil business would be more . . . *utterly ruined* by free trade than any other perhaps." Every other protected interest would have challenged that last statement, Ohio's wool growers especially. And the tariff's appeal was not confined to Ohio. Ironmongers and railroad employees in Terre Haute and South Bend looked particularly susceptible to conviction, and a thousand votes might swing round in "the great shops & foundries" of Fort Wayne. "By this sign we can conquer in this fight," one partisan predicted. To "down Democrats our American Policy is in every fight the argument."[26]

As the national issues imposed themselves on the canvass, Ohio drifted out of the doubtful states, and Indiana became less certainly Democratic. "They *say* they will carry Ohio in October," a national committeeman admit-ted after listening to local Democrats' forecasts. But they were "always carry-ing the State before, but rarely on election day." Even those assertions pe-tered out a fortnight before the polls opened. Party insiders had made a careful count and knew "we shall not succeed . . . unless by accident."[27]

Excitement intensified as the election approached. Party workers handed out leaflets to churchgoers the Sunday before polling. Two black churches in Columbus dropped evening services to hold political education workshops. Shops there and in Cincinnati sent their workers home for a long weekend, reopening once the returns were in. In Indianapolis, crowds filled the streets in front of newspaper offices at dusk on election night, waiting for the latest bulletins.

By midnight, the Republicans among them were racing through the downtown celebrating. "A Triumph of Corruption!" the *Cincinnati Enquirer* screamed, as crestfallen Democratic leaders tried to explain why they had never really expected to carry the state. Pension agents had done four weeks of buttonholing needy veterans and promising them quick action on their claims, two thousand deputy marshals had bulldozed Cincinnati's voters, and "wealthy stock-jobbers and monopolists" had swamped Ohio in one million dollars of vote-buying cash and filled the polls with "the scum of the country, thieves, ex-detectives, repeaters, and governmental officials." (In fact, the Republican National Committee had been able to send a little over $40,000 six days before; Jay Gould finally came through with five thousand after seven other contributors had pledged equal amounts. Even then, the money came from Republican politicians like former congressman Levi Morton and editor Whitelaw Reid, not from the tariff-fattened industrialists that Blaine had been counting on.) Under those circumstances, Democrats pleaded, not losing in a landslide was as good as winning, which, one news-paper suggested, was like the old man who explained his glee at having rheumatism: "I'm so glad I haven't got the gout, too."[28]

Even though no more than 11,244 votes separated the major parties (about 1.5 percent), Ohio had proven decisively that the liquor issue could not translate into Democratic gains in a presidential year. There, as in every other state contest except West Virginia, traditional party lines had held. Cuyahoga, Lucas, and Erie Counties, where the temperance revolt had brought the biggest shift into the Democratic ranks, now made the most emphatic shifts back again. If Ohio Republicans were disaffected in secret, as Mugwumps had asserted, their voting performance kept that secret safe. There was no chance of Democrats' recovering lost ground in the next three weeks. Traditionally, October's winners added to their lead in November (as indeed Blaine did, winning 50.9 percent, for a one-point gain; Democrats slumped from 48.51 percent to 46.9 percent). Talk about a Mugwump upris-ing in the Buckeye State dwindled to a murmur of excuses. If not there, where? Maine had given a better than usual Republican majority, Vermont's had dwindled to a mere two Republican votes to each Democratic one, and in

West Virginia the big defection came among Democrats, where their usual margin was cut by two-thirds. Potential independents elsewhere lost heart after Ohio. What part of the floating vote that chose to go with the winners drifted Republican. Some party leaders calculated the Ohio victory as worth six thousand more Republican votes in Indiana. Everywhere it gave Blaine's friends a boost in morale. "The Blackeye Ohio" placards boasted in one Iowa parade. "Sweet Maria, ain't Ohio Halpin the cause?"[29]

Blaine had saved the day. Democrats agreed, grudgingly. What he said, however, mattered more than who he was. Because Blaine forced the focus back to national issues, the temperance question faded out of public debate. Democrats' tariff straddle cost them votes among wool growers and in working-class neighborhoods. A protectionist like Martin Foran could run a thousand votes ahead of the Democratic state ticket and win reelection, but in Toledo free-trader Frank Hurd ran hundreds of votes behind it and lost his seat. Republicans gained most in the cities, manufacturing towns particularly. One paper-mill town registered its first Republican majority since 1865.[30]

And yet, the October states also showed the limits of the tariff issue's appeal. No Southern state seemed so promising or had so many active Union veterans. "West Virginia is not West 'Virginia,'" a reporter assured readers. Loyal in wartime, it was more "a Southern Pennsylvania." In its northern panhandle, the glassworks and ironmakers swore by protection. State issues cut sharper elsewhere. Counting on farmers' anger over a Democratic governor who had raised their tax rates and filled a deficit by filching $300,000 from the school fund, business-minded Republicans nominated the Greenbackers' candidate. "A black and tan conglomeration," snarled the Democratic candidate for governor, "—something that is worse than Bourbons." That would have been hard to imagine. Democrats disagreed among themselves, but between the "Kanawha Ring," which had no program beyond keeping the state patronage to itself and the combination of coal mine owners, and railroad promoters bent on carving up West Virginia, the state was one of the least governed, indeed misgoverned, in the nation.[31]

Agrarian radicalism and business promotionalism may have made an unlikely combination for Republicans, but it might just work. The national committee held out fond hopes. This was, after all, campaign manager Stephen B. Elkins's own state. Taken now, it would lead to Republican gains farther south and assure a Republican House for years to come. "Everybody you meet is talking politics," one correspondent enthused a week before the election. "West Virginia, like Ohio, is ablaze with Republican enthusiasm."[32]

Wheeling may have been. Beyond its limits, the coalition sputtered, underfunded, its members restive in each other's company. No less than in Ohio, political victory came down to money. Influential Democrats needed buying in every precinct, and struggling independent newspapers languished for proper support. Even with Elkins on the national committee, the commonwealth got no sum remotely like the $50,000 operatives thought vital. The national managers did buy subscriptions to leading newspapers and scattered them where they would do the most good; to the state committee's indignation, however, they sent it the bill (the committee refused to pay). One congressional nominee jotted down his own disbursement of local funds, county by county: $200 for Jefferson, $200 for Hampshire, $50 for Morgan, $10 for Prester, and $1,585 in all, leaving him with a surplus after the election of just $15. Greenbackers had been promised funds to distribute their own literature and sustain Greenback speakers on the hustings. The funds never put in an appearance, and neither did most of the speakers. Democrats had fatter cats to draw on: the retinue at every county courthouse and state agency and Henry Gassaway Davis, the once and future U.S. senator. In his own interest, if not Cleveland's, Democratic legislators and editors could expect help, if only a few hundred dollars' worth.[33]

Republicans also underestimated West Virginia's Southern exposure. The duty on imported coal counted for less than the lockouts in West Virginia mines, where white employees were dismissed and black ones hired at fifty cents a day. From Washington, Congressman Eustace Gibson exposed alleged plots to import blacks by the thousands into the state to vote Republican in November. If deputy marshals backed the intruders, Gibson warned, they should expect "a great deal of killing."[34]

Democrats also showed an unusual flexibility. They nominated the one candidate likeliest to appeal to farmers and workers, E. Willis "Windy" Wilson, a severe critic of the Democratic administration just ending and no friend of business-minded Bourbons. Elect such a man, the *Wheeling Intelligencer* stormed, and corporations would shun West Virginia, "and we will be left in the woods, with the thunder of civilization all around us." In fact, the very threats uttered before Wilson's nomination—that the Baltimore & Ohio and the Chesapeake & Ohio Railroads would fight him to the death—strengthened his appeal with antimonopolists poised on the edge of the Greenbackers' ranks. The threats were not carried out, any more than Wilson's promises of railroad regulation could be. Democrats were not fools enough to talk low tariff where it would cost them votes, and their two high-tariff senators were as good a guarantee as any capitalist could ask. West Virginia did not go as decisively Democratic as Ohio had Republican, but Wilson won comfortably.[35]

Local All Over

Flexibility to suit local conditions, then, gave Democrats a fighting chance even in states with active industrial interests and a powerful third-party movement against them. That meant hope in Indiana, as well as West Virginia. No factional jealousies cut Democratic ranks, no disorder troubled the state committee's counsels. Reporters could call at the official headquarters in the *Indianapolis Sentinel* building and quiz the chairman and party secretary. The real work went on at a secret rendezvous in a hotel nearby, where daily three-hour meetings looked into every aspect of the campaign, probing for weaknesses.[36]

Those weaknesses would not include the candidate for governor. Democrats nominated Isaac P. Gray, a Union cavalryman. "D—n it," another delegate protested, "what do you want to go for Gray for? Why, when [Senator Daniel] Voorhees was dodging up the alleys to keep from getting shot [in the war] the other fellow was looking for him." That, of course, was the point. "Colonel" Gray's wartime services gave Democrats protection against the bloody-shirt oratory that Indiana Republicans specialized in. Other possibilities included General Mahlon D. Manson, with *his* Union war record. But Manson had always been a straight-out Democrat, and Gray had been a Republican until a dozen years before. Visitors to Manson's headquarters wheezed at the first potent draw of the cigars they were given. "You can get a mild article across the way," Manson's manager told them. "We keep our democracy and our tobacco of the strongest kind." But Democrats needed a "mild article." They found it in Gray.[37]

With experience as interim governor and twenty years of stump speaking to his credit, Gray was made for the campaign trail and made a worthy opponent to the Union veteran and former prisoner of war that Republicans chose, Congressman William H. Calkins. Both men went before the voters tarred as the swindlers of widows and schoolchildren, mulcters of the state education funds, wreckers, and pirates. Appealing to the Irish vote, Gray was accused of having joined the nativist Know-Nothing movement in the 1850s, and among Prohibition-minded Republicans, Calkins's fondness for the bottle, or several dozen, became common remark. Liars swore out affidavits implicating and clearing the candidates. Understandably by mid-September, Calkins was heartily sick of the contest. "If it were not too late, I would remedy it by getting off the ticket," he wrote.[38]

Unlike in Ohio, Democrats pinned their hopes on Prohibition's friends rather than its foes. With Republicans having taken a less advanced position to begin with, they stood no real danger of losing German votes. Ardent Dries were another matter. Some of them insisted on a third party. Others had demanded guarantees from the Republican convention that a Prohibition amendment would be put before the voters. Spurned, they threatened a revolt. Democrats helped the disaffected keep out of temper; even a few inflexibles could cost Republicans the state.[39]

Ohio helped Republicans in Indiana by injecting spirit into the cause and by freeing the national committee's attention and cash for an effort there, but there were no guarantees. The party's fortunes were mending, a Republican insider wrote Treasury Secretary Gresham, "but *it needs to*—for a month ago or even two weeks ago . . . we should have been badly beaten." Blaine devoted time to Indiana, but much depended on Dudley's quiet work, much more than in Ohio. Just what he had in mind remains obscure, if suggestive. In the campaign's last days, coded telegrams flew to New York from "Creep," as Dudley signed himself, warning that Democrats had sent "two Beecher beggars." Unless the national committee could scrape up "onyx ovids" [three— possibly five—thousand], the outlook would be uncertain. But the money lagged behind. Only late on November 1 did the funds arrive, "scarcely better than no help at all," Clarkson wrote later. How they were used is unclear. Dudley's coded message implied a payoff, possibly to Indianapolis ward bosses, for mustering potential voters.[40]

Still, Indiana needed far more money than it got, and the national committee would be blamed for starving Dudley's committee. Poor funding meant fewer "floaters" to buy. Journalists spotted many fewer strangers in town than had been present in 1880, notably blacks carried into the southern counties from Kentucky. Colonization generally took time to set up and a corruption fund assembled early; the late application of money didn't give Republicans time to do much. Both sides admitted afterward that there was just about no visible vote fraud that year. "The state is quiet as a nunnery," one reporter put it.[41]

From all these contrary indications, what could a close observer deduce in mid-October? The early returns were decisive in every respect except picking the next president. For all the scandalmongering about Blaine's public indiscretions and Cleveland's private one, the traditional party lines held. In no state had the Mugwumps or the Irish defection made more than a particle of difference. If Maine and Ohio were any guide, the temperance issue would cut a very small figure—but just enough of one to mean trouble in an extremely close race. Where local conditions applied, the minority party could make gains, but the two great national issues, the tariff and the bloody shirt, worked to keep partisans steady. Mute the latter though Northern politicians might, the unspoken issue of the bloody shirt, Southern-style, was practically unbeatable in the former Confederacy. South of the Ohio River, the tariff would not make Democratic states into Republican ones; north of it, protec-

Local All Over

tionism sold much better, especially with Blaine as the salesman. With a charismatic candidate and an appealing issue, the Republicans had the advantage all across the North.

The vital question was, how decided an advantage? enough to carry New York? The Empire State always had mattered in both parties' calculations, but not as much as it did, now that the evidence was in. Back in summer, each side had been able to devise scenarios for winning without New York's electoral vote: the unusually strong prospects of a Greenbacker-Democratic coalition in Michigan and Iowa, with twenty-four Republican electoral votes theirs for the taking, and the Greenbacker-Republican coalition wresting the Democratic Border South from its longtime possessors.[42] Now those hopes were gone. There would be no breakthrough, south or west. As New York went, so went the presidency.

Clerical Errors

Depending on New York's thirty-six electors, Republican managers knew, was just asking for trouble. Prohibitionists, Irish nationalists, Greenbackers, Labor Party men, Anti-Monopolists, Stalwart Republicans upstate, and "machinists" downstate each had clout enough to swing the election. Bringing all these groups together on Blaine's side would take tremendous effort, not to mention money and promises. The moment New York looked like a must-win state, the price for cooperation would soar. If Blaine won, Stalwarts would be first in line, demanding offices. Handing out the spoils would reopen all the old feuds. For leading national committeemen, the best outcome would give Blaine so big an electoral majority that he would owe New York's factions nothing.[1] By autumn, cold reality had replaced this fine midsummer night's dream.

Winning would take two things: the usual big Republican turnout upstate, and a slender Democratic margin downstate. North of the Harlem Bridge, the Prohibitionists were a worrisome presence, but they were easier to calculate. They had their societies and speakers. At every rally they held, undoubtedly, some Republican was there counting noses and taking names. The Stalwarts were harder to predict. Hardly any of them were likely to cast a Cleveland ticket; they were Stalwarts, after all. But they might stay home or support St. John. Just how many would, nobody knew. Many of Conkling's old lieutenants had rallied to Blaine. Former governor Cornell had special incentives to keep his friends in line: he wanted to be elected senator that winter.[2]

For quite a while, Blaine and his friends even had visions of bringing Conkling round. The former senator's disgust with Arthur and the "man-milliners" of politics, knew no bounds. Later, there were stories that he sent a messenger to the national convention to bless any candidate able to beat the president. Rumor had it that Blaine and Conkling had reconciled. A cottage industry in unofficial interviews and choice quotes, good enough to have been genuine, sprang up, all proofs of the sweetest good nature on both sides. In Augusta, Blaine's heart leaped at the prospect that his old rival might make a campaign speech. "It would be an immense thing for us," he wrote Elkins. "How can he be induced to do it?"[3]

Republicans took three months to discover that he couldn't. The six speeches that Conkling had supposedly agreed to dwindled to three, and then to one. Well into October, a few partisans still waited expectantly. Back from the law offices at the corner of Broadway and Wall Street came a thunderous silence. Litigation agreed with Conkling. Juries loved to watch him, immaculate in his stiff, glistening shirt and unanswerable in logic, and Conkling loved having an audience. He could be "Hyperion and Adonis in one," and, what was more, collect big fees for it. Swapping that for his old occupation, where his successes were met with abuse, seemed a poor bargain. Reporters found the former senator surprisingly cordial. But he would say nothing about Blaine, not even against him. To everyone his answer was the same: "I am out of politics."[4]

He meant it, though neither side believed him. Later, stories circulated of Conkling toiling with quiet malevolence: abusive letters to the *New York World*, signed "Stalwart Republican," too brilliant to be any hack's work, prodigious efforts to convince friends that all great rulers, like Cleveland, "had been strong in their animalism." In time, historians would turn a bit of newspaper apocrypha into a full-blown exchange that "Lord Roscoe" would have given years off his life to have delivered. As the story went, a Republican committee called at Conkling's law office to ask his services in the campaign: let him name his price! The chance made perfect theater. Conkling smiled. "Gentlemen," he is reported to have said, "you have been misinformed. I have given up criminal practice."[5]

In fact, Conkling most likely stayed right in character all through the campaign, nursing a Homeric sulk, like Achilles in his tent—or, more aptly, the Conkling of 1876 and 1880. "Well, there will be a funeral," he told a friend sourly, "and you and I will at least have the consolation that neither of us will ride in a front carriage." Privately, his feelings were scorching, especially after Treasury secretary Folger's death. Folger alone kept Conkling's regard. As he followed the judge to the grave, his mind surely ran, where other Stalwarts' had, to the way in which an unfeeling president and perfidious Half-Breeds had set Folger up in the governor's race two years before. Long afterward, Conkling explained his conduct in 1884 with restraint. He had "withheld his support," he told a friend. There was nothing personal in it. But as he spoke, Folger came back into his mind, and the fury in Conkling's heart poured forth: "foul treachery," "one of the blackest pages in American political history." The man from Maine was "as directly responsible for the death of Mr. Folger as though he had run him through with a knife."[6]

When the election was over, Conkling served as counsel to the Democrats during the dispute about the returns. Beyond that, he left both parties guessing to the very end. On October 24, over one hundred old Stalwarts in Oneida issued a press release, giving seven reasons why they would not vote for Blaine. The movement started in Conkling's old hometown in the office of his former law partner. Friends of his signed the manifesto. They had reasons for acting on their own. Half-Breeds had been boasting that every Stalwart head would roll in the basket once Blaine got hold of the offices. Naturally that stirred ill feeling. Even the national committee heard murmurs on that score. It almost sent a special envoy upstate with reassurances, and years later, James Clarkson was still kicking himself for not having done so. Still, it was hard not to wonder whether Conkling spoke through the signers. His own signature was conspicuously absent. One bitter Republican later summed up Conkling's role as "not worth a rotten egg to one side or the other," but that missed the point. By doing nothing, the former senator freed his friends to do their worst, even as he showed how desperately the party still needed him.[7]

But did it need him so desperately? By late October, the Stalwarts' growling outside of Oneida County had become a dim background mutter. Some insiders estimated that no more than a few dozen votes would be lost to the party. Even so, if the Stalwarts seemed less disgruntled, they were far from being gruntled. A heavy turnout depended on inspiring a fighting faith, but the Stalwart-run Republican state committee was not up to the job. Its members got along badly with the Blaine loyalists on the national committee from the first. Each suspected the other of neglect or mismanagement. "Certainly there is no such organization as I have seen in some former campaigns," Reid told Blaine. As a result, cheering reports upstate meant nothing: nobody had done the careful canvass on which to base them. "Inef-

Clerical Errors

ficiency all admit & some charge treachery," one insider on the national committee raged. State committeemen complained that Blaine's special friend Stephen Elkins had swiped their lists of contributors, drained them dry, and never passed over the funds they promised. Ohio had been won by starving New York of speakers and spending. When the state chairman sent the national committee a protest, nobody bothered to reply.[8]

If matters upstate gave Republican managers unease, they could take comfort from their opponents' troubles in New York City. Not in a dozen years had so many Democrats gone so sullenly into a presidential contest. Some were sure to stay home or vote another ticket. The only question was how many. Democratic leaders looked to Tammany Hall for the answer. No other organization could salvage so many Irish Americans and lower-class voters, now already as good as lost. John Kelly must give Tammany its cue.

But Kelly didn't. As July and August passed, national committeemen fidgeted. Mugwumps suspected the worst. If Tammany had come out for Butler or Blaine, it would not have surprised them a bit. There was really no chance of that. Cleveland and reform would be a bitter draught for the boss to take, but take it he must. Tammany Hall had paid dearly for bolting the ticket in 1879 and putting its local interests first in the presidential race the following year. Restoring its dominance even over metropolitan Democrats had taken four years of exertion and humiliations. One more "betrayal" would make the County Democracy uprising of 1880–81 look like a tiff at a church social. If Cleveland lost New York, Kelly would simply have put him back in the Governor's Mansion for another year, with every reason for wanting to do Tammany Hall a lasting injury; if he won New York without Kelly's help, it would be even worse. That could happen. The boss could not count on delivering the "boys" to anyone but a Democratic candidate—quite the reverse. Every ward leader would make his own arrangements. An unknown number of Tammany voters would vote for Cleveland regardless. The greater the defection, the weaker a machine looked. After all, Tammany's influence was based on delivering the vote. It dared not risk the vote delivering itself.[9]

The road out of the Democratic Party ran nowhere. Republicans could offer nothing really worth having. Momentary cooperation would open the way for Irish Catholics to vote Republican, and habits, once set, became hard to break. Assembly districts only barely Democratic would be lost for good, and with all the patronage a Blaine administration could disburse, the next boss of New York would most likely be "Johnny" O'Brien.

Kelly held back, hoping for miracles. Perhaps the Halpin scandal would force Cleveland off the ticket. Then the national committee could pick a new

"Ready for business. To go to the highest bidder"
(Bernhard Gillam, Puck, *July 23, 1884). John Kelly auctions off a decidedly*
Irish-looking Tammany vote.

nominee more sympathetic to practical politics and antimonopoly, and Ben
Butler would drop his own candidacy. Even without a fresh ticket, Tammany
could wait to be wooed. Cleveland would make no promises. "I had rather be
beaten . . . than to truckle to Butler or Kelly," he wrote. But party managers
kept their lines open. Certainly not by chance, Hendricks chose to share his
vacation at Saratoga Springs with his old friend, and the boss headed home
in a better frame of mind. Early in the fall, David Bennett Hill paid a visit to
Hendricks. Very likely he did more than exchange pleasantries about the
weather. Not a scrap of evidence shows that the vice-president-to-be promised to act as Tammany's advocate in the next administration; none shows

that New York's lieutenant governor reminded Kelly that a Cleveland presidency meant a Hill governorship and that friends in need would not be forgotten. But some understanding would have been natural. So, too, would have been very strong hints from the party managers that Kelly could write his own ticket in return for his support—his own municipal ticket.[10]

Such a concession would matter more to Tammany than just about anything else. Blame the reformers for that. Under the statutes passed that spring, the Tammany-run board of aldermen had lost its hold over mayoral appointments. The machine now had just one way to keep its friends in big offices and its enemies out. A strong mayor's office required a strong Tammany man to fill it. With faint prospects of rewards from Washington over the next four years if Cleveland won, city offices had to go into safe hands.

By late August, Kelly's decision had been made. On September 5, he called the district leaders together and rallied them behind the Cleveland ticket. A mass meeting of Tammany's general committee ratified the decision a week later. From then on, the organization stood loyal, at least officially. A fortnight before, state senator Tom Grady had read the omens and quit the state committee. He would campaign for Butler, braving Democratic egg-hurlers. None of Tammany Hall's high command sided with him.[11]

Yet mistrust persisted. There had been talk of some compromise to bring the rival Democratic organizations together on a municipal ticket. County Democracy was willing to accept a compromise choice for mayor. But when Tammany Hall met, the members did a shocking thing. They chose to go it alone. None but straight Tammany men were nominated, and to head the ticket, they chose Hugh Grant, already one of Kelly's most trusted lieutenants.[12]

Grant was a young, wealthy realtor, with genteel manners and a fondness for driving fast horses and playing baseball. American-born, but of Irish parents and Catholic faith, he would draw well just where Blaine hoped to make inroads. Not a word could be said against the integrity, experience, or talent of any of Tammany's city ticket. A month before, the board of aldermen had pushed through a swindling streetcar franchise scheme. Members had been bought openly. Later, some would go to jail and others to Canada. Grant had stood virtually alone against the bill, which gave him the patina of honesty. Even so, reformers and Democrats outside Tammany were appalled. Whatever favors Grant had to give would go as Kelly directed, and the Public Works Department, with its fat contracts, would slide out of County Democracy's control.[13]

Within hours of Tammany's decision, reformers were looking for some respectable alternative. It did not take them long to hit on William R. Grace.

First elected mayor by Tammany four years before, Grace had proven his courage and independence of machine politics almost at once. Protestant voters had lost their fear of him, and Irish Catholics might still flock after one of their own. County Democracy wanted someone more easily pushed around, tried to get guarantees from Grace before committing itself, and when it failed on both counts, enlisted with the reformers. Genuinely unwilling, Grace spent ten days trying to escape the nomination before giving his consent.[14]

When that happened, all bets were off. No selection would offend Tammany managers more. His ingratitude to the machine had made him Kelly's enemy for life. Grace's candidacy assured two Democratic tickets in the race to the very end and a sullen mayor, denied the renomination he thought his due. By launching a self-denominated "Citizens'" ticket, the reformers and County Democracy put Cleveland's election at risk. Both sides now would devote themselves to winning the local offices, whatever the cost. Both would have a vested interest in trading off votes with the one party willing to spare them. By selling out their mayoral nominee, Republicans could win Democratic votes for Blaine. "Kelly says to the Republicans, if you will vote for Grant, I will have my influence brought to bear for Blaine," one Republican summed up, "and by the time we make an addition of 20,000 by 'purchase,' Blaine will not fail to become the victor."[15]

That was hope speaking, but fears still spoke nearly as loudly. Division, disaffection, and diffidence: these three qualities made New York utterly unpredictable, and party managers hated unpredictability. With October half-gone, efforts on all sides intensified, and almost inevitably the cry went west for Blaine to work one last wonder.

His Ohio swing had been all too successful. As soon as it ended, Republicans elsewhere demanded encore performances. Michigan insisted on seeing him. So did St. Louis. But the loudest requests came from New York. For all their brave talk, the national committee worried more every day. Blaine's presence would rouse ardor in Republican hearts and raise money for the coffers. Nothing else could.

Blaine hesitated. He was tired and wanted to go home to Augusta to recover his strength. New York friends were talking of having him speak to a businessmen's fund-raiser on October 29, but Elkins disliked the idea and Blaine thought it "the height of absurdity." Rushing to New York to rattle a tin cup would "leave a panic in the West & make one in the East." Couldn't someone already on hand do the job, someone discreet and on a first-name basis with the magnates like Levi P. Morton? Still, there was no denying that Blaine's personal appeal had saved Ohio, when nothing else could. It had

Clerical Errors

shifted public debate to the tariff issue, opening the "aggressive campaign" at last. In all his speeches, the Plumed Knight had been statesmanship itself and living proof that the papers lied in making him out as debased or dying. Then, too, those ovations he received at every stop must have been a tonic to his soul. They gave steady reminders of how deeply he was loved in a campaign of stinging abuse—a constant refutation of the news stories of hosts of Republicans sulking or readying Democratic ballots. If there must be a banquet, and if sending Logan would not serve (though Logan was eager to do it), Blaine's best course would be to downplay the occasion as far as possible by making it one stop on a larger, longer campaign swing through New York.

Still uncertain, Blaine contacted scores of Republican insiders to see if New York really needed him. Replies poured into his suite in Detroit. All agreed that the state could be won. Most thought it would be, especially with so many downstate Democrats sulky, but nothing could be known for sure. *Tribune* owner Whitelaw Reid's letter may have carried decisive weight. A masterpiece of gingerly optimism, it set out the perils and prospects. Things went better than expected in some ways, worse than others. Feeling was "good" among Republicans generally, but Ohio's enthusiasm was lacking. "In a word I suspect that the condition of the interior is still what that of Ohio was before you went into that State. If your state and county committees can be backed with money enough to put the proper machinery in motion . . . I believe this State will give an unusually large Republican vote."[16]

If. But as Reid noted, that money was in short supply. Democrats had a massive slush fund. Stock market speculators and gamblers were giving generously. The enemy was confident, more so even than in Ohio.

So Blaine turned east. On the twenty-sixth he opened one last tour, speaking across upstate New York. At Elmira, former Stalwart Thomas C. Platt shared the stand with him. Crowds in Binghamton, Deposit, Port Jervis, and Middletown gathered to cheer and hear. Forty thousand supporters welcomed the candidate at Paterson, New Jersey, with a parade, cannon, and fireworks. Then on October 28, Blaine reached New York City, where his wife and daughter waited to welcome him at the Fifth Avenue Hotel. Everything had been fixed for an uplifting finish.[17]

The idea of a mammoth rally of ministers on Blaine's behalf came from one of the undercover agencies set up by the Republican National Committee, the so-called Religious Bureau. Managed by Rev. R. W. McMurdy, the bureau kept shy of press coverage, and rightly. The less its labors were noticed, the more effectively it could work. McMurdy had no money for clerks. He wrote letters, clipped out articles, and did mailings by himself. Every so often he arranged a speech before religious gatherings. Quakers,

Mennonites, Seventh-Day Baptists, and other minor denominations received pamphlets specially framed with their concerns in mind. Much of McMurdy's labor, however, was aimed at religious papers not fully aware of Cleveland's private character. It may well have included anonymous mailings to keep the sex scandals alive. Sometime in October, McMurdy thought of the crowning touch and coaxed his superiors into letting him send out invitations to a thousand or more clergymen in the metropolitan area.[18]

For more than a month, Republicans had been recruiting ministers to do their dirty work for them, while politicians talked up the tariff. It was not just that revenue reform made poor fare for sermons; increasingly, party managers may have realized that politicians had the worst possible credentials for mouthing pieties about the family. Only a profession known for high-mindedness could handle certain kinds of filth without being soiled worse than the victim. So the Republican press printed warnings by ministers that the governor would bring "a loose woman . . . and an illegitimate son" to Washington with him, or that he was a "self-convicted, and self-confessed criminal." Along with the letters, the Republican committee staged audiences with Blaine. A crowd of Congregational ministers called on him in Boston, and ninety Methodist clergymen paid their respects in New York. Democrats and Republican priests vied with each other to present their favorite candidates with canes, voted as a tokens of "church people's" esteem.[19]

There was nothing spontaneous in the gathering this time, and nothing new except its size. Spilling from the carpeted hall into the reception rooms on the parlor floor of the Fifth Avenue Hotel, the crowd may have included five hundred ministers or two hundred, or fewer. Hostile newspapers accused many clerics of being ringers sent to swell the procession. Suspicious cases ducked out of the way when reporters tried to get their names. More revealing about the uneasy alliance of religion and Republican politics was the makeup of the crowd. Republicans wanted as broad a sampling as possible, to show that *all* churchgoers shared their concern with the family values that a moral leper in the White House put at risk. But only two Catholic priests, just one rabbi, and no Episcopalians attended. The usual Republican Methodists and Presbyterians made the bulk of the crowd. Most of the visitants came from small towns upstate, and even they made up a small fraction of the pastors invited. There was not a nationally recognized figure among them. However much they may have despised Cleveland (and some actually supported him), most ministers shunned the political role that McMurdy and his friends were tendering them.[20]

Blaine had risen and breakfasted late. He was mulling over the daily schedule when the shouts from the crowd down below brought him into the

Clerical Errors

hall, his wife at his side. As he descended the steps, onlookers agreed that he had never looked better, rested and pink-cheeked, a statesman at the height of his powers. From the foot of the staircase, a minister with a bald head and vermilion side whiskers called the gathering to order. Resolutions were presented. They had all the familiar phrases: "purity of the personal character of these standard bearers," the opponents' "conceded personal impurity," "disloyalty" (meaning Hendricks), "this insult to Christian civilization" (meaning Cleveland). The election mattered "for virtue in the home, for protection, . . . for war against polygamy." (Polygamy was no side issue. For more than a month, Republicans had been hinting that the Mormon Church favored Cleveland because his views of sex and theirs were identical. There were even allegations that the Church of the Latter-Day Saints had gathered a slush fund for the governor.)[21] Then the long, tedious round of speeches began. At last it was time for the chairman of the meeting to make a few remarks.

It is important to emphasize what historians have not: the occasion was carefully planned, the culmination in a campaign long honed to perfection, and inextricably linked to the Maria Halpin scandal. On the same day that the ministerial pep rally was staged, Republicans unleashed their last great contribution to the character issue with sworn statements detailing the circumstances of St. John's unhappy first marriage. Long hinted at, they also produced an affidavit, signed by Maria Halpin herself. If it could be believed, there had indeed been no affair. Cleveland had raped her. Having had his way, she claimed in her statement, he had boasted "that he was determined to secure my ruin, if it cost him $10,000, or if he was hanged by the neck for it." When she came to him with news of her pregnancy, the father-to-be snarled, "What the devil are you blubbering about? You act like a baby without teeth." She never saw him again.[22]

Nothing could have set off the ministers' benediction on Blaine better than proofs that his rivals were a rapist and a wife-beater respectively. It was a most wonderful coincidence, and would have had a striking effect, but for one stray remark that deflected public attention away from family values to quite a different set of cultural issues.

That was the chairman's doing. The intended master of ceremonies had bowed out a few days before the meeting. A new one had been chosen; he had even written out some remarks, but that very morning, ministers from rival denominations had objected. Each wanted his own faith to do the honors. Eventually, the clerics compromised by picking the oldest minister present to be presiding officer, one Dr. Samuel D. Burchard.[23]

Nobody at headquarters had heard of him before. After the luckless minister had finished, some Republicans were sure that he had been a Democratic agent provocateur. When they found that a leading upstate Democrat had forgiven him a $4,000 debt right after the election, they took that as the purchase price.[24] In fact, "the man who opened his mouth and swallowed a Presidency" was no rascal, and he was much more than the "Silurian or early Paleozoic bigot" that the *Sun* pronounced him. Reporters described him as a tall, awkwardly built man of two hundred pounds, something over seventy, benign, urbane, and fatherly.

Born in upstate New York, he tried school teaching, until asthma sent him south to Kentucky for a warmer climate. There he enrolled in courses at Centre College in Danville. When cholera swept through the state, all the teachers fled. So did the doctors; but Burchard stayed on to minister to the stricken. By the time he graduated, he had a reputation for conscientiousness—rather too much, by Kentucky standards, since it included a frank hatred for slavery. The Union Theological Seminary found him a pulpit in one of Manhattan's modest Presbyterian churches. His congregation prospered. A new, larger church had to be built to accommodate the parishioners. When fire destroyed it, congregants wrote up a subscription list by the light of the flames and raised every penny then and there. Burchard moved on in 1879, much beloved, to officiate at a red brick church in the fashionable Murray Hill district. He was a lifelong enemy of the saloons, a steadfast Union man who had assembled a regiment of volunteers in the church basement, but not noticeably anti-Catholic. Perhaps his own explanation later is the best, that like many preachers he could hardly resist a good alliteration, "a mere rhetorical flourish," and improvised on the spur of the moment.[25]

"We are Republicans," he told Blaine, "and don't propose to leave our party and identify ourselves with the party whose antecedents have been rum, Romanism, and rebellion. We are loyal to our flag. We are loyal to you."[26]

From the crowd came more than one hiss. Standing on one of the lower steps, Frank Mack, the local Associated Press (AP) reporter, stirred. "Did you get that?" he muttered to one of his stenographers. "Bet your life—the old fool," his subordinate replied. Some onlookers thought they saw Blaine start violently. Perhaps he did. Later, he told one friend that the remark had cut through him like a knife. But memory can play tricks: Blaine told other acquaintances that he had been mulling over his own remarks and failed to hear Burchard at all.

Which was it? The official report of his speech certainly suggested more engagement than Blaine made out. Journalists described the nominee, much moved, tears glistening in his eyes and voice trembling with emotion at the honor paid him. His words could be read as a thinly veiled assurance that the

Clerical Errors

causes that evangelical ministers held dear would find a warm friend in the White House, temperance included, as well as an apparent dig at Cleveland's character. Yet all of Blaine's apparently contradictory explanations could be squared with one more that he gave to a few confidants. He *hadn't* heard— not precisely. The buzz of the crowd, the indistinct voice of the old minister, the need to tailor his remarks to half a dozen speakers so far left him less than fully attentive. And when Burchard uttered those fatal words, a thrill may indeed have passed through Blaine, of fear mingled with doubt. What *were* those words? "Rum, Romanism, and rebellion"? or "rum, *Mormonism*, and rebellion?"[27] In view of the association of Mormonism and Cleveland's sex life, the latter was just possible. Taking issue with a eulogist's remarks was embarrassing at best, but even more so if Dr. Burchard had not slurred Catholics at all. It might even stir up those Republicans whose suspicion of the Catholic Church went deep and whose uneasiness with Blaine's Catholic relations might incline them to cast a Prohibition ticket. Besides, Burchard was just one speaker sandwiched between others. It would be far better for Blaine to give an address answering all the eulogists in general terms. Presumably, nobody would publish a full record of the ministers' remarks. What they said was not news. Blaine's response would be.[28]

The candidate may have weighed the risks so. But if he did, he made himself the hostage to events. If he could have vetted the AP stenographers' copy before it was sent off, he could have confirmed what those words had been and added a comment or two setting himself apart from them. Blaine tried. As the gathering broke up, he summoned Mack, only to find his stenographer gone already. A flicker of annoyance passed over the candidate's face. Then he shrugged the whole matter off. There was nothing he could do but wait to see how the newspapers played it.[29]

But they *didn't* play it, and that was what made the damage infinitely worse when the uproar began. Long after the event, everybody wanted credit for making the common a national catchphrase. Admirers told how a Democratic spy caught the words that every reporter had overlooked and rushed it to his boss, Colonel John Tracey, of the national committee's newspaper bureau. Excited, Tracey rushed it to Gorman, who sat gloomily pondering Blaine's almost certain election. Gorman read the transcript impassively until he reached the fatal words. Was this verbatim? Surely Blaine had answered it? As the truth dawned, Gorman leaped into action, ordering Tracey to see to it that every newspaper in the country ran the words the very next day. "If anything will elect Cleveland these words will do it," he told his friends. Blaine could not control the damage now. "The advantages are now with us."[30]

If the incident happened, Tracey failed badly at carrying out Gorman's directions. The words first appeared in the *Brooklyn Eagle* that very afternoon, and in many Democratic newspapers the following morning, but by no means all. For all many readers would have known, Blaine never even met with the clergy. Even papers including a full report treated the incident as the inconsequential faux pas it was. What interested them was the modest credentials of the clergy or the desperation of a rapscallion who had to call in two hundred character witnesses. "A regular Blaine dodge," sniffed the *Boston Herald*, which took only the gentlest swipe at Burchard, who, it suggested, surely must have offended the man from Maine with all those Catholics in his own family. Party orators inveighed every night in Brooklyn. It took two days before a single one of them even referred to the ministers' meeting. Gorman himself spoke to the press on Friday about the reasons he foresaw victory. Yet not a word relating to Burchard's gaffe two days before passed his lips.[31]

Worse still, Republicans took just as long to realize that the ministers' meeting was a liability. For two days, offending quotation and all, they had played up the event as a defining moment. "Democrats Denounced," a typical headline ran. "New York Clergymen Declare the Democratic Nominees Unfit for Office." A few editors sensed the risk they ran. Reid's *New York Tribune* left out the key sentence. The *Indianapolis Journal* cut out the single word "Romanism." Many others left out Burchard's remarks, though less from embarrassment than for lack of space; many Democratic papers made the same decision. As late as Sunday, editors continued to showcase the occasion as proof that morality lay on the Republican side and as a trusty election guide for churchgoers of all sects.[32]

Only late on Friday, October 31, did the storm start breaking. Suddenly party managers in Brooklyn and New York sensed trouble among the rank and file. Not till Saturday, seventy-two hours after Burchard's remarks, did Blaine try to make amends. By then it was too late. Denials so long delayed lost half their power to convince. The feckless McMurdy was hauled before his superiors and given a scorching half hour, and his bureau was shut down instantly. Beyond that, Republican managers could only spend their time cursing Burchard, which they did until, in one partisan's words, the very air around the Fifth Avenue Hotel went blue.[33]

Overnight, Burchard's address came to rank with the Know-Nothing almanacs of the mid-1850s, with their woodcuts of martyred Protestants. In not speaking, Blaine was scored for betraying his own kin to appease the bigots. His ambitions, the *Indianapolis Sentinel* suddenly discovered, cloaked "a sectarian revolver with which he will . . . shoot at one of the great religious

Clerical Errors

orders of the country." Republican editors tried to ignore the whole controversy. Blaine did not. "I am sure that I am the last man in the United States who would make a disrespectful allusion to another man's religion," he told an audience in New Haven. "I should esteem myself of all men the most degraded if . . . I could . . . make a disrespectful allusion to that ancient faith in which my revered mother lived and died." The following evening, press accounts told how a delegation of Catholics called on Blaine to congratulate him for his brave remarks. (There was no delegation in fact. The incident as well as his gracious reply were all a literary exercise, set down in Blaine's own handwriting on yellow foolscap and shoved into an AP reporter's hands for publication as real news.) Rebuking Burchard at the time would have been in "bad taste," Irish nationalist Alexander Sullivan explained, as bad as if Cleveland had rebuked a Mormon delegation come to laud his views on "another question." That Sunday, Republican workers stood at Catholic church doors, passing out handbills with clarifications and apologies for the whole affair.[34]

Explanations may have limited the damage. They could not repair it. Local organizers spread broadsides headed "R.R.R." Most of them attacked Blaine's silence. Some even put the slur into his mouth. As the campaign train pulled into New Haven, a snowstorm of leaflets blanketed the cars. Every door, step, and windowsill in Indiana seemed to have "R.R.R." chalked on it. All the old stories about the Blaine who dodged his mother's funeral to avoid Catholics' presence took on new plausibility. Irish Republicans talked bravely in public. In private, they found the pressure from friends and family hard to bear. Explaining Republican loyalties to one's neighbors always had been awkward. Now it became very nearly impossible. "The election was all safe . . . until that miserable, pusillanimous, canting, hypocritical, double-dyed traitor . . . made his speech," a party operative stormed. "That cleaned us out."[35]

It certainly helped clean out the fresh Halpin scandal. Democrats had just enough time to track down Mrs. Halpin and publish her story themselves. She pronounced the affidavit false from beginning to end. "I have no quarrel with Mr. Cleveland," she said, in what might stand as the definitive character reference. "He is a good, plain, honest-hearted man who was always friendly to me and used me kindly."[36] Democrats noted her response, but by then it hardly seemed to matter, thanks to Burchard.

By itself, the "three R's" would have made Blaine's Wednesday in New York a day to rue, but nearly as bad an evening followed at the fund-raising banquet at Delmonico's. With memories still fresh of the "soap" dinner four years before, any gathering would have provoked jeers and dark suspicions among Democrats. They had a pretty good idea of how the money would be spent, and of what Blaine would give the donors in return. Garfield had given Jay Gould a justice on the Supreme Court, editors warned; Blaine would give him four. The roster included judges, civic leaders, and clergymen, but the most noted names were millionaires like Gould and Cyrus Field, who made their money through speculation and special legislation on their behalf. In a bleak autumn of economic slump, the last place a presidential candidate should go was to a dining salon decorated in tropical palms and exquisite flowers, with meals lit by silver candelabras.[37]

Blaine spoke well enough. In cold type, his speech made a lucid defense of tariff protection and a conservative foreign policy. It made plain the risks magnates faced from Democratic control: threats to the national credit and the national banking system, or even repeal of the three Reconstruction amendments. All the same, in so uncertain a business climate before such a crowd, Blaine's words seemed ill judged and ill timed. The magnates were doing well, but many of their employees were not. Over *pommes a l'Anglaise* and kingfish *à la Richelieu*, prospects looked rosier to the diners than to newspaper readers, and every dish was lovingly listed in the official AP report.[38]

After the "filet de boeuf à la Clarendon" had been cleared away, Blaine would find it harder to appear labor's true champion, especially since the *World* greeted the event with a cartoon prepared by Walt McDougall and Valerian Gribayedoff, "The Royal Feast of Belshazzar Blaine and the Money Kings." Perhaps inspired by a *Brooklyn Eagle* editorial that coined the phrase, the cartoon had been in the works for days. It featured guests set down on the invitation list who missed the dinner, like Elkins and railroad titan William H. "public be d—d" Vanderbilt. The artwork was crude, but in its power it ranked with Thomas Nast at his best. There sat the smirking monopolists. Diamond breastpins glittered. "Lobby Pudding" and "Gould Pie" sat before them. Below the table, a poor family begged for crusts. Within an hour, the *World* had sold every copy and had to run off thousands of extras. Gorman's committee made a gigantic broadside of the cartoon and plastered it on walls across the city. Marchers carried enlarged versions of it as they paraded the streets. Republicans fumbled for an answer. The *Tribune* identified the begging man as Cleveland and urged readers to guess the identity of the woman and boy alongside him.[39]

The dinner even failed in its main purpose. Most of the prospective contributors kept their bankbooks shut. Others promised funds and, when the election went the other way, welshed. Amid hoots at Burchard and "Belshazzar's Feast," all hope of making an aggressive campaign drained out of Re-

Clerical Errors

"Belshazzar Blaine and the Money Kings"
(Walt McDougall, New York World, *October 30, 1884). Not all those pictured attended;*
clearly, the World *had worked up the faces from the projected guest list days ahead of time.*

publican managers. They spent that last weekend explaining, not accusing. "If Blaine had eaten a few more swell dinners, and had a few more ministers call on him, we should not have carried a northern state," Logan reflected sourly.[40]

Behind the sensational stories, there may have been another, quieter but far more significant for Cleveland's chances. As the election approached, Tammany Hall's perfunctory support for the presidential ticket took on body. Burchard's remarks helped, but the process had been under way for two weeks, as the party managers committed themselves to Tammany's city ticket. Just after the Ohio elections, the governor paid a call on the boss. It may have been no more than a courtesy call, though some of Kelly's friends were sure that the two men had come to some understanding. Later Tammany insisted that Cleveland had all but promised the second-best patronage plum in town. When Grant's backers held a rally, they had Thurman and Bayard for speechmaking and a friendly if noncommittal letter from Cleveland himself. Tammany speakers did their best to show that they were even more ardent Cleveland supporters than Grace's crowd.[41]

That was why money had been so needed at Delmonico's to begin with.

Dealing with Kelly, Republicans could promise offices. Dealing with local ward bosses took money. Later, insiders alleged that the $50,000 they collected from Jay Gould at the last minute were thrown away: the national committee gave them to local Republican boss "Johnny" O'Brien for distribution. Nobody ever saw a penny of that sum again, except O'Brien. But the troubling thing was how *immediate* and local the kind of deals being planned were. Apparently, not even the Tammany small fry could be counted on. O'Brien's main hope lay in "individual arrangements" between Republican voters and their "personal friends among Democrats."[42]

When the presidential candidate reviewed the Hall's paraders at the end of October, there was Kelly himself in the procession. As his carriage passed, he lifted his hat to Cleveland, and the crowds roared. At least one ward leader was summoned before the boss and warned against making votes for the local ticket by selling Cleveland out. "You know what the result will be if your district does not go right," Kelly told him. The ward leader knew. "John Kelly would discipline his own brother if he found him guilty of trading off Cleveland," he told a reporter later. Anxious about reports from New York later in the campaign, Hendricks sent a friend to learn the true situation from the boss. Kelly was frank. The machine could not overcome all the difficulties ahead. Still, the state would give Cleveland a majority "inside of 5,000." More troubled than before, the emissary hurried back to Indianapolis with the news. To his surprise, Hendricks's face cleared. Tammany's leader had given his word. "If Kelly said the state will be carried, it will be."[43]

Lord! But We Skirted the Edge!

It took more than a week to be sure of New York, but Democrats started celebrating early. Together with New Jersey, Connecticut, Indiana, and the Solid South, the Empire State gave Cleveland 219 electoral votes to Blaine's 182. Crowds stuck tin roosters in their caps and blew tin horns past midnight. "We've got 'em!" they shouted, "'Rah! 'Rah! Hooray for we, / We've hung Jim Blaine on a sour apple tree." Clubs in Hartford paraded an effigy of Blaine with an empty "soap" box at his feet. "We could not be bought by Gould or Silver," the banners read. "Organized Labor Has Succeeded." Partisans brawled in the Indianapolis streets, and elsewhere they gave rebel yells. One group even grabbed a black youth and sold him at a mock auction. New York bookmakers wrung their hands. They had bet on Blaine, with ten to eight odds.[1]

It almost paid off. Blaine had lost Connecticut and Indiana, both of which had gone for Garfield in 1880. Democrats' share of the vote increased sharply in Nebraska, Iowa, and Michigan, where they had made alliance with the Greenbackers. A little Mugwumpery and a lot of Ben Butler had taken thirty thousand votes off Republicans' margins in Massachusetts. Indeed, east of the Rockies, there were only two Northern states where Blaine bettered Garfield's percentages: his own Maine and protectionist Pennsylvania. But he carried eighteen of the twenty-two states outside the South, and southward, "Garfield's heir" improved on Garfield's performance, especially in Missouri, Mississippi, and West Virginia, where Republicans worked in tandem with the Greenback movement, and Virginia itself, where Mahone's

Readjusters had swollen the ranks. In a dozen Southern states, Blaine increased Republicans' share of the vote. Indeed, in eight he did better than his party would next time around. Garfield took less than forty percent of the vote in ten Southern states; Blaine did that badly only in five. Nationwide, Republicans' share of the presidential vote had fallen by less than one tenth of one percent since 1880, and Democrats' had risen by a bit over a quarter of a percent. Even with a far more efficient suppression of the black Republican vote down south, Cleveland fell far short of Tilden's quarter-million-vote national plurality in 1876 (Tables 5, 6, and 7).

Fears for the tariff cost Democrats the whole Pacific coast and slimmed Democrats' grip on the House by forty seats. Republicans picked up five of California's six House seats, gained two in Massachusetts, Missouri, Virginia, and Ohio, four in Wisconsin, New York, and Pennsylvania, and one in Connecticut. Democrats won Indiana's governorship again but lost Connecticut's. "We skirted the edge. Lord! but we skirted the edge," a Democratic editor wrote Sam Randall. "That Divine Providence, which is supposed to protect idiots and children, must have protected the Democratic party."[2]

New York decided the race, but Cleveland's was a niggling, close victory. He was beaten in his own ward, his own city, his own county, and his own

TABLE 5. REPUBLICAN SHARE OF THE VOTE, BY SECTION

	1880	1884	1888
North	52.5	51.12	51.03
New England	56.08	50.71	54.18
Northeast	50.39	49.66	50.28
Old Northwest	51.47	50.51	49.52
Plains	59.6	55.96	53.71
Pacific	49.5	52.43	51.84
South	38.44	41.61	40.24
Deep South	32.1	33.67	27.35
Upper (Confederate)	43.36	46.82	46.2
Border (Union)	40.77	44.44	46.0
Nation	48.3	48.2	47.8

Source: Congressional Quarterly's Guide to U.S. Elections, 440–42
Note: New England = Conn., R.I., Mass., N.H., Vt., Me.; Northeast = Pa., N.Y., N.J., Conn.; Old Northwest = Ohio, Ind., Ill., Mich., Wisc.; Plains = Minn., Iowa, Kans., Neb.; Pacific = Calif., Ore., Nev., Colo.; Deep South = S.C., Ga., Fla., Ala., Miss., La., Tex.; Upper South = Tenn., N.C., Ark., Va.; Border South = Md., Del., Mo., Ky., W. Va. Connecticut is included in two categories because of its double character.

Lord! But We Skirted the Edge!

TABLE 6. DEMOCRATIC SHARE OF THE VOTE, BY SECTION

	1880	1884	1888
North	44.21	44.99	45.12
New England	42.1	40.74	43.18
Northeast	47.89	46.77	47.17
Old Northwest	44.7	46.4	46.49
Plains	32.46	40.6	38.89
Pacific	46.62	44.74	44.88
South	57.66	56.64	57.0
Deep South	63.91	64.91	69.09
Upper (Confederate)	55.05	52.7	52.0
Border (Union)	53.51	52.39	51.09
Nation	48.3	48.5	48.6

Source: *Congressional Quarterly's Guide to U.S. Elections*, 440–42
Note: For states in each section, see Table 5.

TABLE 7. WHERE REPUBLICANS GAINED MOST AND LOST WORST IN THE 1884 PRESIDENTIAL ELECTION

State	Gain/Loss over 1880	Gain/Loss over 1876	Gain/Loss in 1888
Virginia	+9.4%[a]	+8.5%	+0.6%
Nevada	+8.6	+3.5	+1.3
Missouri	+7.3[a]	+4.6	−0.7[c]
Texas	+6.9[a]	−1.3	−3.4[c]
West Virginia	+6.7[a]	+5.6	+1.2
Mississippi	+5.9[a]	+3.8	−9.7[c]
Louisiana	+5.1	−9.3	−15.9[c]
Maine	+3.8	−1.3	+2.2
Minnesota	−3.5	0.0	−4.6
Wisconsin	−3.6	−3.6	−0.6
Rhode Island	−4.1	−4.1	−4.2
Iowa	−4.6[b]	−6.1	0.0
Michigan	−4.7[b]	−4.6	+1.9[c]
Delaware	−4.8	−4.8	+0.3[c]
Nebraska	−5.6[b]	−7.5	−3.8
Massachusetts	−10.1	−9.4	+5.0[c]
South Carolina	−10.6	−26.8	−6.2

Source: *Congressional Quarterly's Guide to U.S. Elections*, 439–42
[a]Figure includes Republican-Greenback alliance
[b]Figure includes Democratic-Greenback alliance
[c]Reversal of the 1880–84 trend

congressional district.[3] Normally, Democrats could expect a fourteen-thousand-vote plurality and in 1882 came near two hundred thousand. This year Cleveland's barely broke a thousand. His total vote was 28,658 more than Hancock's in 1880, and better by 27,851 than his own totals from 1882, but Republican stay-at-homes had turned out, and in New York City, some Democrats had gone with Blaine. Reformers pointed at Kelly's braves, but Tammany Hall could make a pretty good case that Cleveland lost the most where the County Democracy had the most clout. It would be only natural to assume that those who bartered off the presidential ticket the best would win the most Republican mercenaries for its city slate, and Grace had beaten Tammany's Hugh Grant. Republicans had no doubt on the matter. As the votes came in, party insiders differed about whether Kelly had double-crossed them or simply kept to his promises to the Democrats, but they all agreed that Tammany had delivered Cleveland the goods.[4]

At least, its master had done so as far as he was able. Even more reliable Democratic machines found themselves hard put to keep the Irish in line. In spite of Burchard, Blaine polled a bigger Irish vote in New York City, Chicago, and Boston than any Republican presidential candidate before him. Thus, in Brooklyn, Cleveland actually got fewer votes than Hancock had in four of the twenty-five wards: the top three Irish wards, and one that ranked seventh. Six of the seven most heavily Irish wards ranked among the seven in which Cleveland's percentage of the vote declined the most. By contrast, Blaine improved on Garfield's share of the vote in only five wards, all but one of them among the top five Irish wards. In Troy, the pattern was even more distinct: Cleveland's percentage decline from Hancock's was worst in four of the five most Irish wards (Table 8). This did not mean that the Irish joined the Republicans as a whole; in both cities, the most Irish wards were also the most Democratic ones, as usual. But the party's margin had been slimmed considerably, and of course every vote lost was one less to offset the usual Republican majorities upstate. If there was any of that vaunted defection by German voters in either city to make up for Irish losses, it showed itself everywhere but at the polls.[5] Gorman guessed that New York City defections amounted to 35,000, while another insider put it at 100,000 statewide.[6]

Just about anything could have defeated Blaine in New York, with so small a margin. Then and later, Republicans would claim that cheating stole their victory. Eventually, they narrowed the scene of the crime to Long Island City and Gravesend Bay, and fingered Patrick "Battle Ax" Gleason and John Y. McKane as the fixers. McKane had the know-how; election fraud charges eventually put him into Sing Sing. As Terence V. Powderly, head of the

TABLE 8. PARTY GAINS AND IRISH VOTES IN TROY, NEW YORK, 1884

Ward	Percent Irish-Born	Ranking	Cleveland's Gain on 1880	Blaine's Gain on 1880
10th	21.0	6	3.04	−6.82
2nd	12.6	12	0.25	−2.54
4th	11.23	13	0.16	−3.99
1st	20.40	7	−0.48	−2.54
7th	20.16	8	−2.192	−1.12
5th	13.89	10	−2.44	−7.72
13th	13.38	11	−2.69	−3.18
9th	27.80	4	−3.15	−3.14
3d	16.54	9	−3.19	−0.07
8th	30.32	2	−3.65	−1.73
6th	24.70	5	−7.56	0.13
11th	30.09	3	−7.75	2.54
12th	35.21	1	−15.2	8.45

Sources: Figures on Irish population are from the 1874 New York State Census; election returns are from *Tribune Almanac*, 1885
Note: The wards are listed in order of Cleveland's gain or loss over the 1880 Democratic share of the vote. "Ranking" refers to the comparative Irishness of the ward. The 12th ward, with the most Irish-born inhabitants ranks as no. 1, and the 4th ward, with the fewest, ranks as no. 13.

Knights of Labor, noted some years after, mainstream parties customarily "reinterpreted" votes for workingmen's tickets their own way. According to Blaine's later biographers, both he and Butler knew about the frauds. Butler's protests got him nowhere, and Blaine dropped the issue for the sake of the public peace.[7]

Proofs of fraud always glide just beyond the boundaries of demonstrable fact. Chairman Jones could assure one reporter that a thousand colonized voters in New Lots, just outside of Brooklyn, gave Cleveland the victory. "Over 700 more [votes] were cast than registered," he protested, and this less than a month after registration closed. Since New Lots cast only 2,899 votes, one might imagine that some longtime resident would have noticed for himself that one voter in every four was an outlander; nobody had. Election officials would have marveled at the surprising increase in the electorate; but none of them did. There was nothing to marvel at. Jones to the contrary, the turnout was less than in 1880 and two hundred less than the registered vote. Local Republican officials gaped at Jones's allegations. "Simply preposterous," a town supervisor exploded. "I do not believe half a dozen irregular votes were cast; in fact, I do not know of one."[8]

Republican committee members claimed to know for a fact that the returns in Kings and Queens County "had been tampered with since Tuesday night." Before the claim was hours old, it had been knocked on the head by Al Daggett, Brooklyn's leading Republican manager, a man who knew every trick in the book and had shared in the election supervisors' labors on election night to make sure that Democrats tried none of them. In Queens County, party managers knew nothing about alleged frauds. Nor did local leaders in New York City's Twenty-Sixth Assembly District, where Jones claimed to have found 426 illegal Democratic votes.[9]

In the immediate aftermath of the results, Blaine found plenty of reasons for his defeat, none of them fraud at New York's polls. Butler's correspondence that November bulged with letters lamenting the party's poor showing. There had been treachery, incompetence, broken promises. But not one letter complained that the official returns cheated Butler of a single vote. When Blaine's brother-in-law, Edward Stanwood, repeated the accusation of a stolen election in 1912, he was set right, pretty thoroughly by members of the committee chosen by Democrats to oversee returns in November 1884. They showed clearly how difficult any fraud would have been, with poll watchers of both parties present on election day, and with bipartisan returning boards in every precinct. "It was a lack of votes, not a theft of votes, that lost the State to Blaine," William Chandler acknowledged.[10]

New York City leaders placed the lack squarely on the silk stockings. "We made every concession possible to the brownstone men," Johnny O'Brien complained. "We gave them the judges and the Comptroller, and then, Shylock-like, they wanted the last pound of flesh—the Mayoralty. We pulled the rein there, . . . and they knifed him and Blaine, too." Sixty thousand Independent Republicans had dropped away from Blaine, "Clint" Wheeler told reporters. "If it hadn't been for the disaffected Irish, Blaine's defeat would have been a Waterloo." Other figures for the New York Mugwumps were lower: Jones put it at 40,000, the state chairman at 25,000.[11]

With equal justice, Blaine's friends could blame the Stalwarts, not so much Conkling's as Arthur's. They denounced the New York post office for not sending its employees to work the polls and even passed along reports that Arthur's own in-laws voted the Cleveland ticket. Undoubtedly a more generous administration would have raised more funds, and more funds might have saved New York.[12]

More important upstate, the Prohibitionist votes held pretty close to their

TABLE 9. UPSTATE AND DOWNSTATE MARGINS IN NEW YORK

1876 Downstate	77,151 D
1876 Upstate	44,409 R
Democratic margin	32,742
1880 Downstate	53,906 D
1880 Upstate	74,939 R
Republican margin	21,033
1884 Downstate	63,301 D
1884 Upstate	62,254 R
Democratic margin	1,047

Source: Tribune Almanac, 1881, 1885
Note: Downstate takes in New York, Kings, Queens, Richmond, and Suffolk
Counties. Grover Cleveland's margin in New York County itself was 43,127 votes;
Hancock's in 1880 had been 41,285. The real differences, though, came in suburban
Suffolk, where a Republican margin of 454 became a Democratic lead of 553, and in
Kings County (Brooklyn), where a margin of 9,311 votes rose to 15,729.

numbers from two years before. Compared to 1880, their impact was tremendous, a gain of 23,489 votes. Nobody questioned where most of them came
from: Garfield's upstate margin from four years before had been shaven by
ten thousand votes. Sixty percent of St. John's total came from twenty-seven
heavily Republican rural counties in western New York. Many of the Dries
may have been Stalwarts in disguise: the counties where Conkling's friends
had once dominated now cast Prohibition votes by the hundreds. Patterns at
the local level were messier to be explained by a simple calculation that for
every vote Blaine lost, Prohibitionists gained one; in many towns, Blaine
would still have run behind Garfield in absolute numbers, and sometimes in
his share of the vote. But statewide, whatever losses that slack local campaign
management and disgruntled Mugwumps and Stalwarts caused would have
been more than offset by the unhappy Democrats, especially the Irish American ones—if the Prohibition ticket had not remained in the field. Practical
Republicans hated themselves for missing a great opportunity. Congressman
Seth Milliken of Maine put it blunter than most when he told a reporter, "St.
John should have been purchased and John Kelly 'fixed.'"[13]
   Opportunities always look brighter when they are past, and Republicans'
promotion of Butler's candidacy proved to have been money wasted. The old
general's 1.7 percent of the vote compared badly with the Greenback Party's
3.3 percent four years before. James B. Weaver's presidential bid had done

best in Texas, Iowa, Kansas, and Missouri. But there was no Butler slate in Missouri this year; Kansas gave him less than one percent, Texas barely more, Iowa one vote in two dozen. Only in Maryland and Massachusetts (where the former governor could count on a loyal following) did the People's Party take more than one vote in ten. In New York it was closer to one vote in sixty-six. Slightly less than seventeen thousand voters cast their ballots for Butler there. In a two-way race, Republicans might have gotten some of those votes, certainly not all, and possibly not a majority.[14]

Burchard's gaffe hurt not so much by its driving the Irish vote back into Democratic ranks as in making last-minute conversions harder. For all the talk of desertions, not one Irish leader, national or ward heeler, not one Catholic priest, not a single Irish newspaper or organization announced a switch of sides because of the "three R's". The press never found a single Irish American voter ready to admit that this was what drove him from Blaine's cause. Those Irishmen most committed to the Republican cause grasped for reasons to stay, not to bolt. Among the undecided and those looking for an excuse to remain Democrats, "rum, Romanism, and rebellion" surely worked more powerfully. One reporter guessed a 50,000-vote loss to Republicans in New York. A national committeeman put it at 30,000, with 2,000 more lost in Connecticut's Naugatuck Valley and 6,000 more in two New Jersey counties. In each case, the Irish turned a Republican plurality into a Democratic one. "In Wayne we lost 200 Catholic votes & in Allen at least 500 from the alliteration business," Dudley mourned, and so it had been all across Indiana, wiping out the party's prospective 4,000-vote margin. "Until Burchard's speech we were beaten in New Jersey," a Democratic former senator told one reporter two years after. ". . . It was that speech which saved us, I have no doubt."[15]

In giving out the honors, no one thought to single out one particular Irish American: Hugh McLaughlin, the Brooklyn boss. Having swung the state delegation behind Cleveland at the national convention, his machine now delivered mammoth majorities. For every one vote that Blaine gained on the party's 1880 totals, Cleveland gained six. In raw numbers, that translated into a fifteen-thousand-vote Democratic margin. Let Mugwumps claim the credit for Brooklyn; McLaughlin meant to claim the spoils. Cleveland's managers in Chicago had promised him the patronage. The only way for them to deliver the offices would be for him to deliver the vote. (He did; they didn't, and in 1888 the boss spared himself the exertions—one reason why Cleveland lost the state and the presidency.)[16]

Outside Thomas Nast's home, a crowd gathered, with the most sensible postmortem of all:

Lord! But We Skirted the Edge!

THE WORLD SAYS THE INDEPENDENTS DID IT

THE TRIBUNE SAYS THE STALWARTS DID IT

THE SUN SAYS BURCHARD DID IT

BLAINE SAYS SAINT JOHN DID IT

THEODORE ROOSEVELT SAYS IT WAS THE SOFT SOAP DINNER

WE SAY BLAINE'S CHARACTER DID IT

BUT WE DON'T CARE WHAT DID IT

IT'S DONE.[17]

All of them applied—to New York. By the same token, the Democrats had lost in 1880 because Tammany Hall ran a Catholic for mayor. The real question was, why was it so close that New York made the difference? It certainly was not the character issue alone; there was no Mugwump revolt south of New York harbor.[18]

Blaine ran a better race than any other Republican could have run. The love his followers held for him may have allowed a bigger turnout than Republicans would have won otherwise. Arthur's handicaps were plain on examination: the contempt in which he was held, the natural suspicion against "accidental presidents" being allowed to use the office to ensure their own succession, and his all too visible lassitude. Knowledgeable observers agreed that he would have lost Ohio in October. Then Republicans would have faced hopeless odds in November, even if by some miracle he could have brought a sharply divided party behind him in New York.

Yet it is just possible that a few changes in Blaine's campaign strategy could have elected him. Instead of the simple message of tariff protection, what if Blaine had taken the line of the Republican platform, promising revision to remove injustices while keeping the essential structure intact? What if orators and newspapers had embraced modest reforms and laid their emphasis on the Democrats' inability to do the job? Tariff revision at the hands of the tariff's friends would have gained votes rather than losing them, especially if each state's press defined revision to include only those rates not protecting local products.

Another issue offered Blaine possibilities not taken. What if he had laid more stress on those few lines in his letter of acceptance, favoring an expansion of the merit system? There would be no converting the most distrustful Mugwumps, the Godkins and Schurzes. But for wavering Independent Republicans, a steadier appeal from the stump and from the press that civil service reform would be preserved and indeed would be strengthened might have been decisive. There was no reason that the Republican Party should have abdicated its position as the party of administrative reform, or why

"Out of a job once more!"

(F. Graetz, Puck, November 5, 1884). Republicans no longer need the bloody shirt, clerical slanders, and allegations that British gold would elect the Democrats.

it could not have made more of the Democratic Party's feeble commitment to change.

The one problem Blaine could not have done anything about was the campaign fund's bottom line. The Gilded Age system certainly spent less money. The political process was built on the legwork of volunteers rather than the extravagances of a sales campaign. Amounts spent, however, have nothing to do with needs. We can find plenty of reasons for Republicans losing in 1884. But the lack of money made difficulties impossibilities and added to the risks.

Imagine a Republican campaign given full administration backing and a lavish bank account. Within reach, Jones and Elkins would have found money for all the things they never had money enough to do: pay Irish American leaders and fund Patrick Ford's newspaper, put Butler's party on a sound footing and spend generously on Indiana as much as two weeks before the election, and tide over the consciences of more local leaders of Democratic machines—maybe give Legate a little something on account, just in

Lord! But We Skirted the Edge!

case. Free from financial worry, Blaine might not have closed the campaign at Delmonico's. No Burchard, no Belshazzar's Feast . . . all these things money could have done.

Blaine lost by a series of accidents, misjudgments, and shortfalls. Still, none of them would have made a difference in a fair political system. The race was close precisely because of the unfair advantage that an undemocratic South had given the Democrats; and a close race, by necessity, cost more to win. In any honest, fair contest, Republicans might well have carried Virginia, Louisiana, Mississippi, and South Carolina. Florida and North Carolina were not impossibilities. Yet only in the Upper South did they put on a formidable performance, and even there, Virginia was the only really close one (Table 10).[19]

Neglected at the last, gubernatorial nominee Tyre York lost, though by North Carolina standards he made a respectable race of it. Democrats won by over twenty thousand votes, and Grover Cleveland by nearly as much. Without "fraud and violent disregard of the Federal and State election laws," General Mahone thought, Republicans actually would have eked out a majority in Virginia. In counties with fifteen hundred more black than white voters, the Bourbons won by five hundred votes. That margin could have been reversed, with "measurable help," and the general laid the blame where it belonged, on the well-publicized neglect that the national committee showed. Word that they were being written off only discouraged Republicans, who took their livelihoods in their hands by turning out on election day. Farther south, returns were far more dismal. Twenty-two independents had won legislative seats in Alabama two years before. Now ten survived. In Texas, Democrats carried every legislative seat but six.[20]

Everywhere, there were allegations of stolen elections. In Noxubee, Mississippi, Democrats let Republicans put their ballot through a slit in the side of a building, where it was alleged a returning official could cast or discard the vote as he liked. Many Republicans supposedly had no ballots. The party had sent them by mail, and Democratic postmasters allegedly destroyed the packages before they could be delivered. In Florida, Republicans' nominee for governor accused Democrats of stuffing the ballot boxes in four black counties (Democrats denied it). Democratic canvassers did throw out boxes from some neighborhoods on technicalities. In Madison County, where Republicans usually polled a heavy vote, Democrats staged an election-day riot and foreclosed a full turnout in three precincts by terror and bloodletting. Ballot boxes were stolen, as Democrats admitted—although they protested that no harm came from it: the boxes were empty.[21]

How was it that Democrats had won the five Southern states where blacks

State	Percentage of Votes	Gain/Loss over 1880
Virginia	48.9	+9.4
West Virginia	47.8	+6.7
Tennessee	47.7	+3.4
Florida	46.7	−0.9
North Carolina	46.6	+0.2
Maryland	46.1	+2.1
Missouri	46.0	+4.6
Delaware	43.2	−1.4
Kentucky	42.9	+5.5
Louisiana	42.4	−9.3
Arkansas	40.7	+0.8
Alabama	38.7	−1.3
Mississippi	35.7	+3.8
Georgia	33.8	+5.8
Texas	28.4	−1.3
South Carolina	23.4	−26.8

Source: *Congressional Quarterly's Guide to U.S. Elections*, 440–42

had an outright majority or were strong enough in company of the white Republicans to swing an election? (Tables 10 and 11.) The answer, Democratic editors explained, was obvious. "The inferior Ethiopian race will as naturally follow the intelligence of the Caucasian as will a lesser body gravitate to a greater." With no white Republican leadership in the countryside, blacks voted Democratic by default. That begged the question, of course, as to why white Republican leaders dared not show themselves outside cities. It did nothing to explain Mississippi, where on the face of the returns 69 percent of the black vote failed to vote at all. (Even taking the official count at face value, Democrats took no more than one black vote in nine.) The other argument, that blacks stayed away from the polls because they felt that a Democratic presidency posed no threats to their interests was just as bogus. The ink was barely dry before that excuse was belied: all across the South, supposedly complacent blacks were thrown into a panic by the expectation that Cleveland's election would mean the restoration of slavery.[22]

The palpable unfairness of the Southern returns and the closeness of the contest were two reasons why Republicans took defeat so bitterly. They had been counted out, cheated of a government that was their due simply be-

Lord! But We Skirted the Edge!

	Republican	Democratic
Alabama	5	15
Georgia	9	44
Florida	7	2
Louisiana	16	21
Mississippi	8	31
South Carolina	3	23
Texas	12	2

Sources: U.S. Census, 1880; *Tribune Almanac*, 1885

cause in so much of the country an open election with all the trimmings had been made impossible. Had there been bold enough spirits at the top to launch a coup d'état and hold onto the government at all hazards, Republicans in the ranks were ready to sustain them. "Are the people of the North going to permit the votes of the *Southern states* to be used in deciding the present contest," one officeholder pleaded. ". . . Are you going to submit to have yourselves counted out by the rebels and their northern allies (the fools)." One Democratic insider claimed to know for a fact that Republicans had seriously considered declaring the election invalid, if Virginia's electoral votes had made the difference; there, at least, they could prove themselves cheated of a majority. Just after the results became final, a Jerseyman approached Senator Thomas F. Bayard with a plan to make him president in Cleveland's place. Democratic governors only needed order their states' electors to switch. Bayard gave him a stern lecture and sent him on his way.[23]

Abuse rained down on Burchard from both parties. Old friends fell away. Acquaintances shunned him. Thousands of insulting letters landed on his desk and kept on coming until his death in 1891. His congregation dwindled, until finally the church trustees forced him to retire. Comic actors threw his name into their routines for an easy laugh. Burchard took it meekly, though the blows hurt, and in time he took consolation that he had been "a humble instrument in the hands of a greater Power." When he visited the White House in 1887, the president and his wife gave him a gracious welcome if not an affectionate one. He even came to admire Cleveland himself, supporting him for reelection in 1888.[24]

Others faced loud recrimination, St. John included. Clarkson could not hold his peace about the failed deal. He also met an absolute denial on the Prohibition candidate's part. "Either St. John is a consummate liar or Leggate [*sic*] is a consummate fraud," one of the Republicans in on the transaction wrote, perplexed. "Which is it?" Clarkson quickly discovered how difficult it would be to make the charges stick without tarring Republicans worse than St. John. The moment he fingered Legate as the go-between, knowledgeable observers grasped everything. The GOP had been played for suckers.[25]

Feverishly, Republican insiders tried to track down the proofs they needed. Many people beside himself could testify that St. John had made overtures, Clarkson asserted. So they could—and each one of them had been informed of the overtures by Legate. Legate denied everything. Anyone imagining that he asked for that money for St. John had misunderstood him; rather, he wanted $20,000 for the Republican campaign in Kansas. From the *Chicago Tribune*, the *St. Louis Globe-Democrat*, and the leading Republican organ in Kansas a shower of revelations about the whole deal scattered rhetorical brimstone around Legate and St. John. Desperately they scoured St. John's public statements for prevarications. When he pronounced the charge against him "an infamous and malicious lie," the *Globe-Democrat* headed the statement, "St. John Attempts Another Evasion."

Republicans may have been convinced by the interchange of letters and interviews that went through much of the winter, but nobody else was. As they had so successfully shown that they had tried to buy St. John and failed, the Prohibition Party chairman suggested, Republicans might turn their attention to the related topic of which leading Prohibitionists they *had* managed to buy and at what price: the national committee most likely still had the contracts and the receipts, and it had already shown its inclination for that line of work. "It is about time for the sober men in the Republican party to take the 'bedlamites' in charge, conduct them to the hospital, and put them under such treatment as their malady demands," the *New York Evening Post* chided. Far more cynically, a Democratic newspaper made the failure to buy St. John one more reason that the Republicans deserved to lose. "As the Republicans did not put up then they had better shut up now."[26]

Mugwumps paid for their recusancy for years. Although Democrats had benefited, they heartily wished that their new allies would go away and had panic attacks that one of them might worm his way into the cabinet. "I'd take 'em out and drown 'em, as I would a litter of blind pups," one congressman advised Republicans. The Independents had no intention of claiming a reward. Indeed, those in Boston issued a public renunciation, partly as a warning to those in their ranks who might be tempted to cash in, which, one Mugwump grumbled, was as insulting a reflection as posting the sign "Beware of Pickpockets" at a prayer meeting. Republican clubs started expulsion

Lord! But We Skirted the Edge!

proceedings against suspected reformers. Rev. Beecher came near being driven out of his Brooklyn pulpit by Republican vestry.[27]

In the Blaine household, there was bitterness, beyond any doubt, though most of it that observers saw came from Harriet, not from James. Friends found it hard to be around "the 'Queen of Sheba'" for months thereafter. Others in the family remained convinced that Burchard had been a Democratic plant, bought and paid for. Blaine, for his own part, professed not to care much—certainly not as much as his friends might imagine. "You know— perhaps better than any one—how *much I didn't want* the nomination," he wrote his friend Murat Halstead. It was no personal repudiation; only fate, luck, and "an ass in the shape of a preacher" had kept him out, in a year when no other candidate had a chance. Later he added the Solid South to the list. Asked how he felt, Logan remembered the story that Abraham Lincoln had told about the man who stubbed his toe: "The worst of it is I'm too big to cry, and it hurts too bad for me to laugh."[28]

Behind his placid front, Blaine nursed lasting resentments. He may have forgiven Conkling, but not the president. When a few Stalwarts mounted a campaign to elect Arthur senator, Blaine rushed into print to put a stop to it. With his chivvying, the *Tribune* exposed the halfheartedness and treachery of the administration during the campaign. Blaine's anonymous letters and insertions were needless. The last thing the president wanted was another public office. Gresham's coolness would be long remembered, too. In 1888, Blaine and his friends would see to it that the former postmaster general came nowhere within striking distance of a presidential nomination. And Blaine didn't forgive George Edmunds for such lukewarm support, either. Two years later when they met at President Arthur's funeral, the Vermont senator offered his hand to his old colleague. Blaine refused it.[29]

Cleveland, too, bore lasting scars from the campaign. He never entirely forgave Buffalo for the slurs on his name, and when he came to the presidency, acted to vindicate his integrity by action. The "you-be-damned" quality, admittedly, dated at least to the days when as mayor he had plunged into the mortar and mud of a sewer ditch to spot the contractors' swindles for himself. Still, his doggedness in strengthening the presidency and wrenching it from close congressional control had connections to that search for vindication.[30]

19

Justice at Last!

Having groaned through a quarter century of Republican rule, Philadelphia's former mayor Richard Vaux could only scribble in literary gasps as the returns came in. "Whew!!" the old Democrat wrote a Southern friend. "Oh!! Ah! Bless my soul!! . . . Oh ye gods! Justice at last! The light has broke, bursted out!!! . . . Thank God. Have faith. Take courage."[1]

Republicans would need that courage more, especially those dreading the return to power of a Solid South. Just after the election, prognosticators spotted the lawsuits that, once they worked their way through the courts, might open the way to "reimburse" Rebels for wartime losses. A Democratic president would recast the Court of Claims into "the swiftest mill for most of the grist. The same President of Southern murders and Northern frauds will, as fast as vacancies occur in the Supreme Court . . . make it a mill for the same purpose."[2]

None of these awful events occurred. The president-elect moved at once to scotch widely believed rumors that the new administration would re-enslave black Americans. Cleveland neither packed the bench nor removed what paltry civil rights enforcement there was. The administration appointed blacks to minor civil service positions, and in the North the Democratic Party advanced further toward guaranteeing basic civil rights regardless of race.[3]

Cleveland's administration meant reform, just as the Mugwumps had hoped. The classified list expanded, and with it the federal workers safe from a partisan purge. Sometimes Cleveland kept on Republican officeholders,

"Men may come, and men may go; but the work of reform shall go on forever"
(Joseph Keppler, Puck, November 5, 1884). *Puck and Keppler's virile symbol for the
Independents shows Columbia the foundations for a monument to reform. Mugwumps
George Jones (New York Times), George William Curtis, and Rev. Henry Ward Beecher
carry on the work below, with Schurz managing matters above.*

though less often as time went on. In states where civil service reformers could swing votes, they won recognition, and the White House doors were always open to Mugwump leaders. The president listened politely to their lectures, though he sighed privately that many, like Schurz, made themselves hard masters. But again, the changes did not go as far as they hoped. Cleveland had no new thoughts on advancing the merit system, certainly not of making the four-year terms that most officeholders had into lifetime occupancy. Only offensive partisans got the sack before their terms ended, but offensiveness was interpreted liberally, and when Republican civil servants' terms closed, trusty Democrats replaced them.[4]

Democratic rule neither rewrote the country's political economy nor undid the "war tariff." The president applied his energies to scrutinizing pork barrel bills and private pension measures. He opposed an inflated money supply and accepted the Interstate Commerce Act, which established a national railroad regulatory commission. Cabinet officers worked to put Western federal lands into homesteaders' hands and to take back the land grants given to railroads for work not completed on time, but none of these threatened "monopoly." Only in late 1887 did the president come round to tariff reform. What he had in mind was far from free trade. In any case, as long as Republicans commanded the Senate, no Democratic program could pass, just as Democratic control of the House blocked Republican pressure for the Blair bill and a comprehensive veterans' pension act.

Nor did Cleveland and reform drive the bosses from politics. "Mr. Kelly has done so much for politics, and politics has done so little for him, that I think he ought to dissolve the partnership," Ben Butler commented. A broken man, worn out by his hard work on Tammany's behalf, Kelly relinquished command before the end of the year. In June 1886, he died, just a few weeks before Tilden's passing and Hubert Thompson's demise. Attending the funeral were reform Democratic mayors, cabinet members, and congressmen, all of whom owed their careers at the start, if not in the end, to Kelly.[5]

Tammany Hall survived Cleveland's years. For all the tough talk, it won a share of administration patronage. By the time Cleveland left office in 1889, New York City had a Tammany mayor and, where policy was concerned, a Tammany governor. County Democracy dwindled and shut up shop. When the former president won renomination three years later over the machine's bitter opposition, it said much about the difference in bosses that Richard Croker pledged his support immediately. It said even more about Tammany's power that his word was all Cleveland needed.[6]

For ten years after the Mugwump revolt, New York City's reform move-

Justice at Last!

ment battered at Tammany in vain. It was not, as one ward boss sneered, that they were mere morning glories, quick to blossom and to fade. The Godkins never faded or tired. But as St. John and Butler could have told them, movements outside the two-party system were more dependent on the old organizations than the organizations were on them. Without the all-out support of the Republican machine, without a robust County Democracy to line up votes, reformers would lose every time. The might-have-been Mugwumps from 1884 could have told Godkin how readily reform-minded New Yorkers could find grounds for voting regular, just by giving the issues a different comparative weight: clean streets and tax cuts counting for more than the gin joints standing wide open on Sundays. And when the reform crusade of 1890 turned the Protestant pulpits into political grandstands, and murmurs about rum and Romanism stirred the air, perhaps Dr. Burchard could have suggested how perilous a thing that was in a city of immigrants. For like reasons, Hugh McLaughlin ran Brooklyn's machine into the 1890s, and the Republican organization in Philadelphia tightened its grip beyond anything dreamed of in Mugwump days.[7]

The election did not even end Blaine's prospects. By 1888, Republicans wanted him more than ever. It took two separate refusals of a nomination before the party turned elsewhere. Even then, his supporters played so crucial a role in nominating Benjamin Harrison of Indiana that Harrison had little choice but to make Blaine secretary of state. When he quit the cabinet in 1892 a disheartened, dying man all at once grown old—the tales of Bright's disease true at last—three days remained before the national convention. All the same, his friends still were able to mount an embarrassing challenge to the president's renomination.[8] By then, the tariff, that issue that he had helped bring into public attention, had become the unfailing stock-in-trade of mainstream party politicians.

Had nothing changed, then? Had the fights been for nothing? On the contrary, Cleveland's election marked a significant moment in Gilded Age politics in several ways.

The old political system had never seemed stronger. Yet the Democratic victory was just one sign of the change. A politics of economic interests and moral imperatives was shaking partisan loyalties. The partisan system of financing elections was giving way to one more dependent on contributions from outside the organizations. As never before, the two major parties had found themselves dependent upon interest groups beyond their own ranks— in this case, organized on the outskirts of the political system into the two minor parties. But the appeal that Democrats and Republicans had to make were not to the bolters so much as to the members of their own ranks who *might* bolt, because the issues raised—Irish nationalism or labor reform or temperance—counted for more than party loyalty. To a great extent it worked, but the omens were there.

For the Prohibition Party did not fade away, and the problem of its sympathizers persisted. Across the North, Prohibition candidates for Congress would take votes enough to make a margin of difference between Republican victory and defeat in 1886. In 1888, with less fanfare, the Prohibition Party would increase its vote to near a quarter million. It would carry a bigger share of the total electorate. Four years later, both the total vote and the share were up again. The elimination of the Prohibition Party as a serious threat in the mid-1890s did not give Republicans control of the House again, but it certainly helped. If it remained a relatively minor irritation on election day, Republicans made it so by making concessions to their temperance supporters. Charles Foster's strategy in Ohio proved right in the end. As long as Republicans put Prohibition on the ballot, tightened laws relating to the sale of alcohol, raised the cost of saloon licenses, and continued to press for new changes, they could trade short-term losses at the polls for long-term gains. Just such a sacrifice hit may have saved New York for the Republican presidential ticket in 1888. Warner Miller, no longer senator but tied closely to the Dries, took the gubernatorial nomination and made the issue of a high-license law the centerpiece of his campaign. His bid, naturally, would bring out the largest possible Republican vote upstate, where temperance views were most strongly held. By campaigning as a stiff temperance man, he may have thrown away his margin and sent David Bennett Hill back for another term as governor. The national party was the gainer. In 1887, the Prohibition state ticket had taken 41,000 votes. Now it took only 30,231.[9]

In general, Republican gambles elsewhere paid off as well. Where temperance advocates were in control, the liquor question cost the party votes, but only at first. Within a few years the measures excited none of the same bitter protests, and in most states the party managed to hold onto power in spite of its actions. When cultural issues helped drive states into the Democratic column in 1890, it would not be meddling with the saloon that did it but meddling with the schoolhouse.

Freed from the temperance sideshow, the lines that the 1884 election had obscured slightly became clearer every year. By 1888, Republican commitment to protection had strengthened. The only real division lay between those who thought the "war tariff" sufficient and those who wanted duties made prohibitive, a "Chinese wall" around America's home markets. By then, the Democrats had shifted, too, but in the opposite direction. Randall's band of Northeasterners still could prevent tariff reform as late as 1886.

Justice at Last!

Morrison had written his last reform bill; steelmakers' money brought a full turnout of millhands to beat him for reelection that fall, and Speaker Carlisle nearly came in second in a one-man race when the Knights of Labor cast their votes for a protectionist Labor Party candidate. But the tariff reformers were closing in on Randall. Pennsylvania patronage that had gone all his way in Cleveland's first two years now shifted to William L. Scott, the low-tariff coal king. House Democrats clipped Randall's powers as Appropriations Committee chairman, while enemies at home stacked the state committee against him. By the time Congressman Roger Q. Mills reported a fresh tariff-cutting measure to the House in 1888, Randall was a beaten man. Dying slowly of cancer, he lived long enough to see Cleveland's administration turned out for its tariff tinkering and a Republican House beginning work on a revenue measure of its own; he did not live to see the McKinley bill passed, or its author, like Morrison and Cleveland, remanded to private life for the host of evils blamed on the changes in rates.[10]

Republicans had learned that by itself, the tariff would not be enough to crack the Solid South. Victory required a solid North, and the more North the better. So the party pressed harder than ever for the admission of Western states with trusty Republican majorities, and sounded the trumpets to rally all those who loved the Union. Even the tariff talk sounded different. By 1888 it was built, more solidly than ever, on those twin terrors, an English conspiracy to destroy American freedom and a Rebel plot to avenge their losses in wartime by bringing ruin to every milltown north of the Ohio. Every private pension veto the president sent in riled the old soldiers. Party papers never doubted that Cleveland spent till past midnight studying the bills: how else could he so often have been in the dark about their provisions? Veterans of the GAR refused to march under a banner welcoming the president when they held their national encampment in 1887, and Republicans made the most of Senator Benjamin Harrison's war record when they ran him for president in 1888. Tradition connected Cleveland's loss of Indiana in 1888 to vote buying in "blocks of five," but the veterans actually may have polished him off. Turning out more heavily than the electorate at large, they had a score to repay the "Jumbo" in the White House.[11]

Just because no new Confederacy arose did not mean that Cleveland's election changed nothing. With a Democrat executing the federal election laws, white Southerners hardly needed waste their time trying to repeal them. They could cheat and steal as much as they liked. Deprived of all hope of federal protection or patronage, Greenbacker and Independent movements were extinguished across the Deep South. They would not revive until Democratic national power faltered. The black vote declined further. Condi-

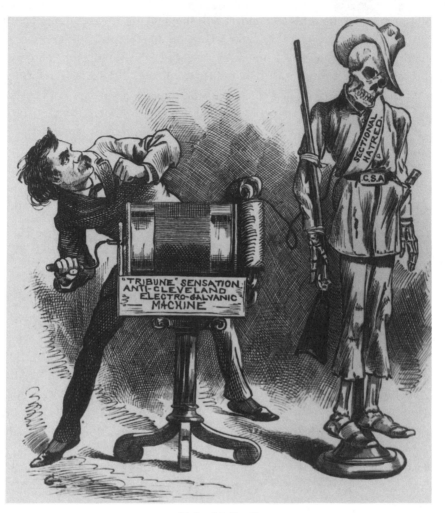

"A dead failure"
(Bernhard Gillam, Puck, *June 10, 1885).*

tions in 1888 were worse than in 1884, and the Republican Party in the cotton belt was ever more a fading memory. Mahone fought to the end for Virginia, but the odds grew greater every year. In that sense, Cleveland's four years made a real difference, a disastrous one.

One might suggest that Cleveland's administration did Democrats no less damage. Until 1885, the party had been an all-purpose opposition. Now it must choose one path, that of the Cleveland administration. One could still hold to the faith as Randall had and be a protectionist, still endorse currency inflation schemes even as the president issued letters favoring "sound money," and argue for labor legislation and railroad regulation on the state level while administration Democrats cast a cold eye on both in Washington. But the balancing act became harder. When a factory owner boasted that he was a Democrat and a protectionist in 1894, an editor could liken the statement to a plea, "I am a Christian and a robber."[12]

The appeal to Labor and Greenback Parties flew more plainly against what the party's chosen leader proclaimed as official Democratic doctrine. It also ran the risk of having the president take the patronage away and put it into friendlier hands. Democrats were more constrained than before, and as Cleveland officials rewarded the railroad managers with their share of the spoils, that sense of constraint grew. It would not be enough to tear the party apart yet. That would wait until Cleveland's second term, and the issue of reflating the money supply by stepping up the Treasury's coinage of silver would become lethal only when economic depression gave force to the argument for bold measures. Then the uprightness and courage of Cleveland showed its worse side. On a moral issue like monetary policy he could brook no compromise. As late as 1892, the party kept its balance. But the catastrophe that cost Democrats Congress and president well into the new century was already shaping itself. With Cleveland in charge, the commitment to conservatism had been made.[13]

So had the commitment to a new kind of campaigning. The "brass band, the red light, and the mass meeting seemed suddenly to have lost their power," James Clarkson commented years later. To the *New York Tribune*'s thinking, "too many bands and banners, too much coal-oil and excitement" had cost Blaine votes. Quiet work, the circulation of newspapers, and "missionary efforts in school districts" would have served the cause better.[14]

For those insiders that thought so, party salvation required a permanent campaign organization rather than a momentary jerry-built effort. Year-round clubs must replace the Plumed Knights of a season. There, Republicans could indoctrinate their cadres. Documents distributed just before the election converted few. A steady distribution over many months would build an informed Republican electorate. For nonmembers, campaigning must become more intimate, more family directed. Looking back on the miscalculations of 1884, Clarkson set the period down as the time that politics itself began to change, with discussion shifting "from the open field, as in Lincoln's day, to the private home," from "sentimental to economic issues — the evolution into education as the superior force in American politics."[15]

Clarkson's view was wrongheaded both prospectively and retrospectively. Republican turnout had been high in 1884. Thanks to Blaine's concentration on the tariff, economic issues had been given greater weight than "sentimental" ones — perhaps more than was good for the party. Clarkson also was wrong to think that the style of persuasion needed change to fit the changed issues. Clubs and indoctrination helped any party, admittedly. Republican faith made Republican voting sure. But there was nothing inconsistent with an old-fashioned campaign in all that. As for a shift out of public places and into the private home, a campaign of pamphlets and leaflets, "educational politics" worked only if families bothered to read what they were given, an extremely doubtful assumption.[16]

In fact, economic issues could be addressed as emotionally and effectively on the stump as "sentimental" ones. Very often the economic issues *were* sentimental. They appealed to emotions as much as to a sense of immediate interest, and they could be simplified into catchwords with ease: "British gold," "Cobden club," "open the books," "John Bull," "free trade." By adding to the tariff's sentimental edge, its appeal to patriotism and to family values, later campaigns would only make it a better sell. There was nothing unsentimental about the tariff reform "argument" Democrats used in the wake of the lockout at the Homestead steel mills in 1892. New York business-men marched the streets chanting, "Bill, Bill, McKinley Bill, / Paid to Pinkerton men to kill."[17] No real inconsistency existed between the issues and the methods of the campaign. Still, it was an outlook that took hold with an increasing number of Republican insiders.

Politics would change. The campaign of "education" would replace that of hoopla in presidential races, and the more it did so, the less enthusiastic voters would become. After 1896, managers would package the candidate, rather than the party. With tubs more money than before, they could afford a campaign of advertisement. All these transformations accompanied a shift from the old-fashioned partisan press and the wholesale federal spoils sys-tem. The main forces sustaining popular politics weakened, not the least of which was a vote that party managers could buy, sell, or manage with custom-made split tickets and five-dollar gold pieces. With the coming of the secret ballot—muddling to the uninitiated, incomprehensible to the illiterate, and carefully guarded to discourage certain kinds of political alternatives to the mainstream organizations—turnout fell and continued to drop in the new century. By the 1920s, party managers could not have put on a hurrah cam-paign if they had wanted to.[18]

Who would want to? By popular reputation, the 1884 election still stands alone as the meanest and most meaningless campaign of the Gilded Age. As this book suggests, that reputation fits some of the facts but leaves out many more. What lessons can historians draw from it?

First, real issues were at stake in 1884. Far from showing that Gilded Age

politics had lost its point, that the two parties were so similar that personalities were the only thing that they could disagree about, the election
showed a two-party system that was healthy because it expressed an ongoing
debate about issues, ones connecting an uncertain present with an inspiring
past. Even the concentration on the candidates' personality was more than
prurience; it tied in with the larger economic and social issues, of a moral
government and a responsible and responsive state. With two indistinguishable parties, quite conceivably there would have been far wider swings in
political allegiance. But most Republicans, most Democrats, rallied to the
good old cause.

Naturally, who won or lost made a difference. That the national outcome
in 1884 did not lead to sweeping political change had less to do with the
fakery of the major parties' promises as with a stalemated Congress. Blaine's
foreign policy was not Cleveland's, and the Republican commitment to the
tariff showed itself most plainly when the party did command majorities in
both houses. A Democratic Congress might well have brought repeal of the
election laws, as it did in 1894. As it was, it sped the movement toward a solid,
one-party South and a partisan professional civil service.

Second, the political system, for all its pageantry, showed how far politics
remained the mainstream politicians' game. Third parties had a life of their
own, but, except in the moments of crisis, they lived largely on the sufferance
of the first and second parties, both of which had an interest in keeping them
going, and in a culture in which much of their potential support came from
disaffected voters longing for a good reason to go back to the Republican or
Democratic ranks from which they had come. "Revolts" inside the party
needed outside encouragement and a voice. Without the right conditions,
they petered out, just as Mugwumpery did in Indiana or, to some extent, the
Irish revolt in Boss McLaughlin's Brooklyn. Republicans had no level playing field south of the Ohio River, nor, indeed anywhere where they lacked the
money and the newspaper support to make their case.

There is a third, powerful lesson from the story of 1884. Money did more
than pay for brass bands and barbecues. Needing it made paupers out of
parties unable to dun the officeholders. It added to the pressure on the
Democratic side to be conservative and "respectable," to mute attacks on the
national banks and the protective tariff, to speak about running government
like a business and administrative reform in terms that voters in all classes
could appreciate. It gave Republicans an added reason to emphasize the
tariff in 1888, when money was to be had by "frying the fat" from the
industrialists directly interested in where rates stood. Lack of money made

the Greenback Party look to millionaires for its presidential candidates and to Tammany Hall to help it print up its ballots.

Only by keeping the backroom needs and deeds in mind can we save ourselves from being seduced by the outward attractiveness of Gilded Age politics. There was much to attract, even in the Kellys and Butlers. Deep veins of principle ran through Stalwarts and Swallowtails, and even men eager for power turned their minds to how it could be used not just for its own sake but to make policy. The mainstream parties' dominance of the political system assured a more comprehensive outlook than that of the more focused outsiders, Mugwumps, Prohibitionists, and farmers' parties. By mediating between their demands, the politicians may have put through programs likelier to stand the test of time; Prohibitionists, for example, were far more successful at enacting the laws they wanted than in keeping them on the books for long. Even more than on matters of policy, recent historians have appreciated the display and the public involvement of the Gilded Age system. People sang; they marched; they *cared* about politics, and in our time, the contrast excites a wistful feeling that the reformers and destroyers of old-fashioned partisanship went wrong somewhere. Taking the politics out of politics, they took the life out of democracy. All that may make us forget the price: a politics propped up by managers' secret deals and a partisanship so strong that it could shatter any social movement that got too close to it; a political process in which manipulation of the right to vote and suppression of all news about the opposition were common, and indeed customary; and a party loyalty so intense that believers like James Clarkson could feel that any means of winning justified itself. To hear Democrats tell it, they won every presidential election from 1876 through 1892; they were just cheated out of it three times in five. Republicans declared, and believed, that on any fair count, they had been the victors every time but the last. Tissue ballots and shotgun intimidation robbed them of states rightfully theirs.

These liabilities were bad enough in themselves, but there was another cost to the political process. Real conspiracies against freedom only made imagined ones seem more plausible to those who were prepared to believe; made-to-order "outrages" only made the real ones easier to discredit, for those who wanted to. If Americans so often voted to save their liberties, it was because both parties tried to make them think that their liberties were in danger, not just from bulldozers but also from British gold. The paranoid style for which the Populists would be pilloried by later historians was the natural child of the mainstream parties.

Around Gilded Age politics clung not just the exhilarating smell of kerosene from the torches that the marching clubs carried and the acrid scent of

Justice at Last!

gunpowder from endless fireworks but the stench of corruption and suspicions of corruption. Amid the shouts and campaign songs, ever audible, are the charges of turpitude and treason. If we would look to a purer and better politics in our own time, we would be wise to see the Gilded Age system as it was. Otherwise, we may find ourselves as badly sold as the men who, up till the last minute, thought that they were buying St. John.

Notes

AtC	*Atlanta Constitution*
BaC	*Bangor Commercial*
BanM	Frederic Bancroft MSS, Columbia University, New York
BaW&C	*Bangor Whig & Courier*
BayM	Bayard Family MSS, Library of Congress, Washington, D.C.
BlaM	James G. Blaine MSS, Library of Congress, Washington, D.C.
BoH	*Boston Herald*
BoT	*Boston Evening Transcript*
BrE	*Brooklyn Eagle*
ButM	Benjamin F. Butler MSS, Library of Congress, Washington, D.C.
ChaM	William E. Chandler MSS, Library of Congress, Washington, D.C.
ChaM(NH)	William E. Chandler MSS, New Hampshire Historical Society, Concord, New Hampshire
ChDN	*Chicago Daily News*
CHS	Cincinnati Historical Society, Cincinnati, Ohio
ChTi	*Chicago Times*
ChTr	*Chicago Tribune*
CiC	*Cincinnati Commercial*
CiCG	*Cincinnati Commercial Gazette*
CiE	*Cincinnati Enquirer*
CiG	*Cincinnati Gazette*
ClaM	James S. Clarkson MSS, Library of Congress, Washington, D.C.
ClPD	*Cleveland Plain Dealer*
CoMo	*Concord Monitor*
ConM	Arthur L. Conger MSS, Rutherford B. Hayes Memorial Library, Fremont, Ohio
CR	*Congressional Record*
DawM	Henry L. Dawes MSS, Library of Congress, Washington, D.C.
DMISR	*Des Moines Iowa State Register*
DtEN	*Detroit Evening News*
DtFP	*Detroit Free Press*
ElkM	Stephen B. Elkins MSS, West Virginia Collection, West Virginia University Library, Morganton, West Virginia
HdC	*Hartford Courant*
HdTi	*Hartford Times*
HSP	The Historical Society of Pennsylvania, Philadelphia, Pennsylvania
InJ	*Indianapolis Journal*
InN	*Indianapolis News*
InS	*Indianapolis Daily Sentinel*
ISHS	Illinois State Historical Society, Springfield, Illinois
ISL	Indiana State Library, Indianapolis, Indiana

IW	*Irish World and American Industrial Laborer*
LC	Library of Congress, Washington, D.C.
LoC	*Louisville Commercial*
LoC-J	*Louisville Courier-Journal*
LogM	John A. Logan MSS, Library of Congress, Washington, D.C.
MacM	Wayne MacVeagh MSS, The Historical Society of Pennsylvania, Philadelphia, Pennsylvania
McPM	Edward McPherson MSS, Library of Congress, Washington, D.C.
MHS	Massachusetts Historical Society, Boston, Massachusetts
MnTr	*Minneapolis Tribune*
NOP	*New Orleans Picayune*
NOT-D	*New Orleans Times-Democrat*
NYEP	*New York Evening Post*
NYGr	*New York Graphic*
NYH	*New York Herald*
NYPL	New York Public Library, New York, New York
NYS	*New York Sun*
NYSL	New York State Library, Albany, New York
NYTi	*New York Times*
NYTr	*New York Tribune*
NYW	*New York World*
OHS	Ohio Historical Society, Columbus, Ohio
PhI	*Philadelphia Inquirer*
PhP	*Philadelphia Press*
PhR	*Philadelphia Record*
PoEA	*Portland Eastern Argus*
RanM	Samuel J. Randall MSS, Rare Book and Manuscript Library, University of Pennsylvania, Philadelphia, Pennsylvania
RBHML	Rutherford B. Hayes Memorial Library, Fremont, Ohio
ReiM	Whitelaw Reid MSS, Library of Congress, Washington, D.C.
RN&O	*Raleigh News and Observer*
SchM	Carl Schurz MSS, Library of Congress, Washington, D.C.
SFAC	*San Francisco Alta California*
ShrM	John Sherman MSS, Library of Congress, Washington, D.C.
SHSW	State Historical Society of Wisconsin, Madison
SpR	*Springfield Daily Republican*
StJG	*St. Joseph Gazette*
StLG-D	*St. Louis Globe-Democrat*
StLP-D	*St. Louis Post-Dispatch*
StPPP	*St. Paul Pioneer Press*
WhIn	*Wheeling Intelligencer*
WhtM	Stephen M. White MSS, Stanford University, Palo Alto, California
WVUL	West Virginia University Library, Morganton, West Virginia

INTRODUCTION

1. *ChDN*, November 8, 1884; *InN*, November 8, 1884; *NYW*, November 8, 1884.

2. Keller, *Affairs of State*, 544–46; Goodwyn, *Democratic Promise*, 22; Sproat, *Best Men*, 117–18; Morgan, *From Hayes to McKinley*; Blodgett, "Emergence of Grover Cleveland," 133–68. On the election's insignificance, see Norton et al., *People and a Nation*, 607; Merrill, *Bourbon Leader*, 64; Benson, *Toward the Scientific Study of History*, 38; Nevins, *Grover Cleveland*, 159; and Dobson, *Politics in the Gilded Age*, 149.

3. Keller, *Affairs of State*, 545–46.

PROLOGUE

1. *ChTi*, November 5, 6, 1884; *Mechanicville (N.Y.) Mercury*, November 7, 1884.

2. *InN*, November 4, 1884; *StPPP*, November 6, 1890.

3. "August," *Cazenovia Republican*, September 25, 1884; *InJ*, November 16, 21, 1884.

4. *InJ*, September 10, 1884.

5. West, *Lincoln's Scapegoat General*, 373–77, 401–7; *ChTr*, September 4, 1884; Benjamin F. Butler to John B. O'Reilly, July 27, 1884, ButM.

6. *Oneida Dispatch*, October 17, 1884.

7. *DtFP*, June 24, 1884; Juergens, *Pulitzer and the World*, 81–83; *NOP*, September 29, 1884; Whitelaw Reid to Henry Ward Beecher, October 7, 1884, ReiM.

8. *NYGr*, February 4, 1876; Halstead, "Defeat of Blaine," 170; *PhP*, April 20, 1884.

9. William White, *Masks in a Pageant*, 92; Foraker, *I Would Live It Again*, 132; Hudson, *Random Recollections*, 128; Mitchell, *Memoirs of an Editor*, 313–14; Peck, *Twenty Years of the Republic*, 290.

10. Nevins, *Grover Cleveland*; Merrill, *Bourbon Leader*.

11. *Cazenovia Republican*, August 28, 1884, October 11, 1888.

12. R. McMurdy to Major Bickham, November 5, 1884, LogM; *InN*, November 4, 1884.

13. *ChTi*, November 5, 1884; *InN*, November 3, 1884.

14. *NYS*, November 8, 1884.

15. Samuel Fessenden to John A. Logan, November 5, 1884, and George F. Dawson to Logan, November 5, 1884, LogM.

16. Thomas Sherman, *Twenty Years with Blaine*, 94–95.

17. Nevins, *Grover Cleveland*, 184–85.

18. Armitage, *Grover Cleveland*, 207–9; Hudson, *Random Recollections*, 218–19.

19. W. W. Dudley to A. L. Conger, ConM; Stephen B. Elkins to John A. Logan, November 5, 1884, George F. Dawson to Logan, November 5, 6, 1884, Samuel Fessenden to Logan, November 6, 1884, B. F. Jones and Dawson to Logan, November 6, 1884, and John C. New to Logan, November 7, 1884, LogM.

20. *Oneida Dispatch*, November 7, 1884; *InJ*, November 6, 1884.

21. Stephen B. Elkins to Whitelaw Reid, November 7, 1884, and Blaine to Reid, November 6, 18, 1884, ReiM; Samuel P. Fessenden to John A. Logan, November 8, 1884, and J. T. Torrence to Logan, November 6, 1884, LogM; *NYS*, November 7, 8, 1884; *ChDN*, November 8, 1884; *InJ*, November 9, 1884; *NYEP*, November 21, 1884.

22. Msgr. Fitzgerald to Grover Cleveland, November 7, 1884, Lamont MSS, LC; *InN*, November 7, 1884; *InJ*, November 7, 1884; Hudson, *Random Recollections*, 224–25.

23. *InN*, November 7, 8, 1884; Nevins, *Grover Cleveland*, 186; *NYW*, November 8, 1884.

24. Arthur P. Gorman to Henry G. Davis, November 9, 12, 1884, Davis MSS, WVUL; John Lambert, *Arthur Pue Gorman*, 110–12; Stealey, *Twenty Years*, 28; *InJ*, November 12, 1884.

25. *Poughkeepsie Daily Eagle*, November 18, 1884; Stephen B. Elkins to John A. Logan, November 14, 1884, LogM; Charles H. Gray to A. L. Conger, November 9, 1884 (quote), ConM; Frank B. Loomis to James S. Clarkson, November 17, 1884, ClaM.

26. Beale, ed., *Letters of Mrs. Blaine*, 2:120–21; James G. Blaine to Stephen B. Elkins, November 7, 1884, ElkM; Hudson, *Random Recollections*, 227.

CHAPTER ONE

1. Hair, *Bourbonism and Agrarian Protest*, 113–15; *NYH*, November 1, 1884.

2. Jensen, *Winning of the Midwest*, 2; *NYH*, November 1, 1882; Harlan, *Pennsylvania Constitutional Convention Debates* (1873), 1:676–80; *Elmira Daily Advertiser*, October 31, 1884; *ChTi*, November 4, 1884; Fram, "Purifying the Ballot?" 101–9.

3. *ChTi*, November 1, 1884; James E. Harvey to David Davis, October 31, 1883, Davis MSS, ISHS; James J. Faran to William Allen, September 17, 1876, Allen MSS, LC; *InN*, November 4, 1884.

4. House, *New York Election Frauds*, 40th Cong., 3d sess., H. Rept. 31, minority report, 106, 121.

5. *InN*, November 7, 1884; James J. Faran to William Allen, September 17, 1876, Allen MSS, LC; *PhI*, October 12, 1870; Richardson, *William E. Chandler*, 165; Reynolds, " 'The Silent Dollar,' " 191–211.

6. Reynolds and McCormick, "Outlawing 'Treachery,' " 838–48; *NYEP*, November 14, 1884.

7. *InN*, November 7, 1884.

8. *InJ*, November 8, 1884; *Poughkeepsie Daily Eagle*, November 2, 1880.

9. *Elmira Daily Advertiser*, November 1, 3, 1884, *RN&O*, November 2, 1880.

10. Altschuler and Blumin, "Limits of Political Engagement," 875–79; *ChTi*, November 4, 1884; *CiE*, November 7, 1884.

11. *MnTr*, August 6, 1884; *ChTi*, November 5, 1884; *Elmira Daily Advertiser*, November 5, 1884; *InN*, November 4, 1884.

12. Ryan, *Women in Public*, 42–51, 139–40; Rebecca Edwards, "Gender in American Politics," 78–91.

13. *NYH*, November 1, 1882, November 2, 1884; *BrE*, December 15, 1884.

14. Peck, *Twenty Years of the Republic*, 88.

15. McGerr, *Decline of Popular Politics*, 14–17, 107–13.

16. Summers, *Press Gang*, 45–58.

17. McGerr, *Decline of Popular Politics*, 17–22; *SFAC*, July 5, 1884; *HdTi*, November 1, 1884.

18. McGerr, *Decline of Popular Politics*, 22–23, 38–41; *NYH*, October 28, 1888; *Mechanicville Mercury*, October 3, 1884; *Saugerties Telegraph*, October 23, 1884.

19. *Meriden Daily Republican*, October 27, 30, 1884; *DMISR*, September 12, 1884.

20. McGerr, *Decline of Popular Politics*, 12–14; Jensen, *Winning of the Midwest*, 9–11; *Troy Daily Press*, October 25, 1890.

21. McGerr, *Decline of Popular Politics*, 23–33; Jensen, *Winning of the Midwest*, 11; *Meriden Daily Republican*, October 25, 1884; *Trenton Daily State Gazette*, October 16, 1884; *Watertown Daily Times*, October 6, 1888; *Cazenovia Republican*, October 16, 1884; Watson, "Humbug? Bah!" 889–90.

22. Altschuler and Blumin, "Limits of Political Engagement," 868–73; Baker, "Culture of Politics," 179–81; Henry Ward to Samuel J. Randall, July 31, 1884, RanM.

23. Leonard White, *Republican Era*, 291–97.

24. Altschuler and Blumin, "Limits of Political Engagement," 858–68; Brann, *Brann, the Iconoclast*, 7:54; *DtFP*, June 15, 1884.

25. Silbey, *American Political Nation*, 111–12; W. Davis to Thomas R. Bard, November 22, 1880, Bard MSS, Huntington Library, San Marino.

26. *Lewiston Evening Journal*, January 1, 28, 1880; *BaW&C*, November 12, December 26, 30, 1879; *PoEA*, September 7, 8, 9, 1880.

27. Silbey, *American Political Nation*, 218–24.

28. Dobson, *Politics in the Gilded Age*, 164–68, 188–90; Sproat, *Best Men*, 273–81; Blodgett, "Mugwump Reputation," 867–87; McFarland, *Mugwumps, Morals and Politics*, 18–54.

29. Henry Dawes to Electa Dawes, January 14, 1883, DawM; Garraty, *Henry Cabot Lodge*, 78.

30. McGerr, *Decline of Popular Politics*, 46–52.

31. Armstrong, "Godkin's *Nation*," 491–93; Villard, *Fighting Years*, 119–24.

32. Sproat, *Best Men*, 145–66, 172–84, 205–18.

33. *NYEP*, December 5, 1884; Mencken, *American Language*, 106–7.

34. Villard, *Fighting Years*, 122; Blodgett, *Gentle Reformers*, 30–40; Wayne MacVeagh to "my dear sir," February 20, 1884, MacM.

35. Hoogenboom, *Outlawing the Spoils*, 1–12; Summers, *Era of Good Stealings*, 89–95.

36. Summers, *Era of Good Stealings*, 50–54.

37. Silbey, *American Political Nation*, 192–95, 224–32.

38. Ibid., 199–213.

CHAPTER TWO

1. Summers, *Era of Good Stealings*, 131–34, 259–70.

2. Flick, *Samuel Jones Tilden*; Mushkat, *Reconstruction of New York Democracy*, 180–90, 197–200, 245–47; John Bigelow to Whitelaw Reid, May 7, 1875, Bigelow MSS, NYPL.

3. *BaW&C*, June 30, 1876; *Nation*, February 13, 1879; McGerr, *Decline of Popular Politics*, 71–75; *NYGr*, August 16, 1876.

4. *NYGr*, July 6, 1876; Mitchell, *Memoirs of an Editor*, 294.

5. Hirsch, *William C. Whitney*, 108.

6. *CiG*, July 31, 1876; Kelley, "Thought of Tilden," 176–205.

7. J. D. Waddell to Alexander Stephens, December 17, 1876, Stephens MSS, Duke University, Durham; William M. Browne to S. L. M. Barlow, December 13, 18, 1876, Barlow MSS, Huntington Library, San Marino.

8. Benedict, "Southern Democrats," 489–524.

9. Hoogenboom, *Rutherford B. Hayes*, 288–94, 304–6.

10. Ibid., 306–9; Grenville M. Dodge to Uriah H. Painter, March 27, 1877, Painter Family MSS, HSP.

11. George Lunt to Thomas F. Bayard, October 29, 1877, BayM.

12. William Gillette, *Retreat from Reconstruction*, 324–34, 346–50, 358–62; Hirshson, *Farewell to the Bloody Shirt*, 29–44; Welch, *George Frisbie Hoar*, 77–82; *NYH*, December 1, 1877.

13. Foner, *Reconstruction*, 588–95; *DtEN*, October 29, 1888.

14. Hair, *Bourbonism and Agrarian Protest*, 76–78; J. D. Kennedy to Charles S. McCall, August 23, 1878, McCall MSS, South Caroliniana Library, Columbia; *NYTi*, July 21, 1878; *NYTr*, October 28, November 11, 1878.

15. *NYTi*, July 10, August 11, 12, 13, 14, 1878; *NYTr*, August 20, September 4, 1878.

16. *NYTi*, July 25, 1878.

17. *DtEN*, October 27, 29, 1888; Wynne, *Continuity of Cotton*, 111–13; Anderson, *Race and Politics*, 3–6; Cooper, *Conservative Regime*, 103–5; *NOT-D*, September 6, 1882.

18. McKinney, *Southern Mountain Republicans*, 75–123; Rabinowitz, *Race Relations*, 282–323.

19. Rebecca Felton to John Sherman, October 15, 1881, and O. F. Kepler to Sherman, October 20, 1880, ShrM; George B. Cowlam to Elihu Washburne, December 11, 1879, Washburne MSS, LC.

20. *CR*, 50th Cong., 2d sess., app., 111–12; *AtC*, February 9, 1886.

21. *Norfolk Virginian*, July 12, 1883; *Frankfort Tri-Weekly Kentucky Yeoman*, June 8, 1880; Edward R. Sinker to William E. Chandler, June 4, 1884, ChaM; Peskin, *Garfield*, 466 (quote).

22. William Brindle to Samuel J. Randall, February 19, 1877 (quote), and W. T. Smithson to Randall, February 21, 1877 (quote), RanM.

23. P. Curran to Samuel J. Randall, February 26, 1877, Samuel C. Ingersoll to Randall, February 17, 1877, W. B. Richardson to Randall, February 28, 1877, and A. T. Beocus to Randall, February 26, 1877, RanM.

24. J. B. Brawley to Samuel J. Randall, March 9, 1877, RanM.

25. Peskin, *Garfield*, 503–5; Howe, *Chester A. Arthur*, 130–31; Edmund Smith to William E. Chandler, June 29, October 31, 1883, ChaM(NH).

26. Polakoff, *Politics of Inertia*, 112–18; S. L. M. Barlow to Manton Marble, August 16, 1886, Marble MSS, LC.

27. Flick, *Samuel Jones Tilden*, 429–38. *Nation*, February 13, 1879; William Dorsheimer to Francis Kernan, October 11, 1878, Kernan Family MSS, Cornell University, Ithaca; William Johnston to Rutherford B. Hayes, March 1, 1879, Hayes MSS, RBHML.

28. Flick, *Samuel Jones Tilden*, 417–18, 443–50; *CiE*, June 13, 1877; Genen, "John Kelly," 206–15; *Nation*, August 21, November 6, 13, 1879.

29. Flick, *Samuel Jones Tilden*, 423–24, 446–50.

30. J. S. Moore to William R. Morrison, January 12, 1880, Morrison MSS, ISHS; J. S. Moore to Thomas F. Bayard, December 20, 1879 (quote), BayM; Henry B. Payne to Alexander Long, April 27, 1880, Long MSS, CHS; William M. Springer to John M. Palmer, April 13, 1880, Palmer MSS, ISHS; John Bigelow to Tilden, August 10, 1884, Bigelow MSS, NYPL.

31. Clancy, *Presidential Election of 1880*, 122–56.

32. *ChDN*, October 29, 1883.

CHAPTER THREE

1. The standard works are Buck, *Road to Reunion*, 75–118, and Hirshson's excellent *Farewell to the Bloody Shirt*.

2. *Annapolis Maryland Republican*, June 23, 1883; *Norfolk Virginian*, October 31, 1883; Marszalek, *Sherman*, 472.

3. Jones, *John A. Logan*, 1–19; "A.C.B.," *BrE*, February 12, 1883.

4. *StJG*, July 25, 1884; Jones, *John A. Logan*, 33, 39.

5. Dearing, *Veterans in Politics*, 88–91, 127–33; *BrE*, March 17, 1884.

6. *ChDN*, October 29, 1883.

7. *Milan Exchange*, August 9, 1890; *NYH*, September 7, 1876.

8. *DMISR*, November 20, 1884; *SpR*, December 12, 1884; *Galena Daily Gazette*, October 10, 1884; *InJ*, July 3, October 7, 1884.

9. *WhIn*, January 4, 1884; Bensel, *Yankee Leviathan*, 405–12.

10. *Harper's Weekly*, March 1, September 27, 1879; *CiE*, February 12, 1878; *Nation*, April 3, 1879; *ChTr*, March 11, 1879; *ChTi*, January 3, 1888.

11. McConnell, *Glorious Contentment*, 85–98, 166–91; Wilson, *Baptized in Blood*.

12. McConnell, *Glorious Contentment*, 218–19.

13. Heywood T. Sanders, "Paying for the 'Bloody Shirt': The Politics of Civil War Pensions," in Rundquist, ed., *Political Benefits*, 137–59; Logue, "Union Veterans," 426–28.

14. *LoC*, May 27, 1879; *Crystal Springs Monitor*, August 12, October 28, 1882; Williamson, *Rage for Order*, 78–90.

15. *NYTr*, July 6, 1882; *Harper's Weekly*, January 4, February 1, 15, 1879.

16. Logan, *Betrayal of the Negro*, 167–94, 242–75; Chalfant, *Better in Darkness*, 397–400, 410, 806–9; Boskin, *Sambo*, 101–5.

17. *NYEP*, January 5, 1884.

18. Fairman, *Reconstruction and Reunion*, 2:560–87; *NYTr*, October 17, 1883.

19. *CoMo*, October 23, 1884; *Zanesville Daily Courier*, November 1, 1884; *DMISR*, October 1, 1884.

20. *NYTr*, July 6, 1882; *DMISR*, October 5, 1884.

21. Vazzano, "President Hayes," 25–34.

22. *Harper's Weekly*, March 29, April 5, 19, May 24, June 21, 1879.

23. *LoC-J*, June 24, 26, 27 (quote), 1879.

24. *Harper's Weekly*, April 19, May 10, 1879; August Belmont to Thomas F. Bayard, November 9, 1879, and Belmont to Benjamin H. Hill, November 9, 1879, BayM; J. H. Jordan to John Sherman, March 29, 1879, Sherman MSS, RBHML.

25. Dearing, *Veterans in Politics*, 185–289.

26. McConnell, *Glorious Contentment*, 138–46.

27. Richardson, *William E. Chandler*, 344–47.

28. Woodward, *Origins of the New South*, 100–103; Kirwan, *Revolt of the Rednecks*, 9–10; Barr, *Reconstruction to Reform*, 45–62; *Nation*, August 11, 1881; "S.H.C.," ibid., August 18, 1881.

29. Hyman, *Anti-Redeemers*, 172–75; John T. Hill to James R. Chalmers, December 29, 1882, and G. C. Chandler, J. B. Deason, and George C. McKee to William E. Chandler, March 1, 1883, ChaM.

30. Perman, *Road to Redemption*, 193–220; Maddex, *Virginia Conservatives*, 95–99, 258–59.

31. Maddex, *Virginia Conservatives*, 218–21, 233–75.

32. Ibid., 248–55; *ChTr*, June 4, 1884; *DMISR*, October 14, 1890.

33. Moore, *Two Paths to the New South*, 93–108; Degler, *Other South*, 279–82.

34. Moore, *Two Paths to the New South*, 101–4; *Norfolk Virginian*, June 13, 1883.

35. Barr, *Reconstruction to Reform*, 63–71; Wynne, *Continuity of Cotton*, 130–41.

36. Hyman, *Anti-Redeemers*, 167–91; James Longstreet to William Felton, January 23, 26, 1882, Box 1, Folder 13, and A. M. Franklin statement, August 5, 1882, Box 1, Folder 14, Felton MSS, University of Georgia Library, Athens.

37. Woodward, *Origins of the New South*, 86–92; Perman, *Road to Redemption*, 269–75; Hart, *Redeemers, Bourbons & Populists*, 46–72.

38. Schott, *Alexander H. Stephens*, 507–17; William Smythe to William E. Chandler, June 10, 1882, ChaM.

39. *Crystal Springs Monitor*, August 12, September 9, 1882; *Jackson Weekly Clarion*, October 4, 11, 1882; James R. Chalmers to William E. Chandler, November 6, 1882, H. C. Ware to Chandler, November 1882, and George C. McKee to Chandler, July 6, 1882 (quote), ChaM.

40. Moore, *Two Paths to the New South*, 105–6, 109–14; James E. Harvey to David Davis, May 27, 1883, Davis MSS, ISHS.

41. Moger, *Virginia*, 51–54; Moore, *Two Paths to the New South*, 114–16; *Norfolk Virginian*, October 28, November 4, 6, 1883.

42. Degler, *Other South*, 293–98; *Richmond Whig*, November 3, 4, 1883.

43. *StLP-D*, February 18, 1884.

CHAPTER FOUR

1. *NYS*, March 1, 1884.

2. See, for example, Josephson, *Politicos*; Dobson, *Politics in Gilded Age*, 64–67, 73; Ginger, *Age of Excess*, 100–101.

3. *ChTi*, April 15, 1879 (Morton); *NYTr*, November 3, 1879, and *SpR*, May 22, 1871 (Chandler); *NYH*, May 23, 24, 1876 (Cameron); Blankenburg, "Forty Years in the Wilderness," 113–19, 226–35; Kehl, *Boss Rule in Gilded Age*.

4. Jordan, *Roscoe Conkling*, 297–301.

5. Welch, *George Frisbie Hoar*; Hoar, *Autobiography*, 2:228–32; "Gath," *ChTr*, April 5, 1872.

6. Morgan, *From Hayes to McKinley*, 72; "Gath," *CiE*, February 27, 1884.

7. W. Harriman to Elihu Washburne, November 12, 1868, Washburne MSS, LC; "Gath," *NYGr*, April 20, 1876; "Gath," *ChTr*, March 23, 1871.

8. Muzzey, *James G. Blaine*, 110; Polakoff, *Politics of Inertia*, 16–17, 52–69.

9. Peskin, *Garfield*, 396; Beale, ed., *Letters of Mrs. Blaine*, 2:4, 16; Russell, *These Shifting Scenes*, 225; *SFAC*, July 13, 1884.

10. Summers, *Era of Good Stealings*, 54–58.

11. Muzzey, *James G. Blaine*, 87–97; *NYTr*, June 6, 1876.

12. Summers, *Era of Good Stealings*, 54–58.

13. Welch, *George Frisbie Hoar*, 90–91; for Blaine as Stalwart, see *Puck*, May 19, June 2, 1880; *LoC-J*, January 11, June 27, 1879.

14. Muzzey, *James G. Blaine*, 131–33; for the customary use of the term "Stalwart" referring to a critic of the "New Departure," see *LoC-J*, January 11, April 24, 30, June 26, 28, 1879; *Harper's Weekly*, April 12, May 17, 1879.

15. Muzzey, *James G. Blaine*, 130–34, 139–42; *Harper's Weekly*, January 4, 1879; *LoC-J*, June 26, 1879.

16. *Puck*, May 19, 1880.

17. L. P. Roberts to James O. Broadhead, May 4, 1880, Broadhead MSS, Missouri Historical Society, St. Louis; Marcus, *Grand Old Party*, 29–36.

18. William Henry Smith to W. W. Coleman, November 9, 1879, Box 10: Letterbooks, Smith MSS, OHS; Morgan, *From Hayes to McKinley*, 60–74, 84–96; Harrison, "Blaine and the Camerons," 165–69; Peskin, *Garfield*, 461–79; *CiG*, June 8, 11, 1880.

19. *StLG-D*, June 13, 1880; George C. Gorham, in *NYS*, December 2, 1884; Peskin, "Who Were the Stalwarts?" 703–16; Eidson, "Who Were the Stalwarts?" 235–61.

20. Reeves, *Gentleman Boss*, 208–10.

21. Muzzey, *James G. Blaine*, 128–30; Peskin, *Garfield*, 558–71; Henry L. Dawes to Electa Dawes, April 30, 1881, DawM.

22. Peskin, *Garfield*, 595–608.

23. *InS*, May 20, June 5, 1884; Thomas F. Bayard to Samuel L. M. Barlow, December 4, 1881, Barlow MSS, Huntington Library, San Marino.

24. *NYS*, December 21, 1884; *Philadelphia Times*, July 8, 1888; Jordan, *Roscoe Conkling*, 412–15.

25. Reeves, *Gentleman Boss*, 268–76; Benjamin H. Bristow to George F. Hoar, April 21, 1884, Bristow MSS, LC.

26. Beale, ed., *Letters of Mrs. Blaine*, 2:8; *InS*, June 5, 1884; Abram S. Hewitt to Samuel J. Randall, September 2, 1881, RanM.

27. Pletcher, *Awkward Years*, 42–56, 61, 72–73, 100; *NYS*, December 21, 1884.

28. Beale, ed, *Letters of Mrs. Blaine*, 1:309–10, 2:42; James G. Blaine to Whitelaw Reid, February 9, April 1, 29, 1882, ReiM.

29. William E. Chandler to James G. Blaine, October 2, 1882, ChaM; Blaine to Stephen B. Elkins, October 29, 1882, ElkM.

30. James E. Harvey to David Davis, June 18, 1883, Davis MSS, ISHS; Joseph S. Reynolds to Wayne MacVeagh, September 30, 1881, MacM; Jordan, *Roscoe Conkling*, 421.

31. Howe, *Chester A. Arthur*, 180–82; Wayne MacVeagh to Thomas L. James, August 27, 1881, MacM.

32. Reeves, *Gentleman Boss*, 299–304.

33. *NYTr*, July 7, 1882; *ClPD*, August 3, 1882; *ChDN*, April 9, 1884.

34. *NYTr*, July 30, August 1, 3, 1882; Reeves, *Gentleman Boss*, 280; *CR*, 47th Cong., 1st sess., app., 633.

35. *NYTr*, July 28, August 2, 3, 1882; Fred K. Brown to William D. Kelley, June 19, 1882, Kelley MSS, HSP; N. G. Ordway to William E. Chandler, August 5, 1882, ChaM(NH).

36. Rutherford B. Hayes to John Sherman, July 5, 1882, Sherman MSS, RBHML; Richardson, *William E. Chandler*, 342–47; *InS*, October 14, 1882.

37. Gillette, "Corrupt and Contented," 235–37; *NYH*, October 3, November 4, 5, 1882; *BoH*, November 7, 1882.

38. Thomas Brackett Reed to George Gifford, December 20, 1882, Reed MSS, Bowdoin College Library, Bowdoin.

39. Thoron, ed., *Letters of Mrs. Henry Adams*, 408; Skowronek, *Building a New American State*, 66–84.

CHAPTER FIVE

1. Term from *InS*, October 14, 1882.

2. *NYEP*, October 26, 1882; Kleppner, *Cross of Culture*, 35–69.

3. Jensen, *Winning of the Midwest*, 58–62; *Hocking Sentinel*, September 2, 1875; *Akron Summit County Beacon*, September 22, October 13, 1875.

4. *Akron Summit County Beacon*, October 6, 1875; Kleppner, *Third Electoral System*, 214–35; Green, "National Reform Association," 86–128.

5. *Ravenna Democratic Press*, October 7, 21, 28, 1875; Green, "National Reform Association," 82–91; McSeveney, "Religious Conflict," 18–44; Kleppner, *Third Electoral System*, 234–35; Marquis James, *Merchant Adventurer*, 154–58; Genen, "John Kelly," 244–50.

6. Jensen, *Winning of the Midwest*, 62–88; Kleppner, *Cross of Culture*, 69–91.

7. *Topeka Daily Capital*, October 15, 1886; *Atchison Daily Champion*, June 11, 13, October 1, 1886.

8. *Atchison Daily Champion*, October 24, 1886; *PoEA*, August 28, 1880.

9. *BrE*, April 7, 1884; the mind-set is explored succinctly in Hamm, *Shaping the Eighteenth Amendment*, 27–29.

10. *NYH*, October 23, November 15, 1877.

11. Gunther, *Inside U.S.A.*, 260.

12. Bader, *Prohibition in Kansas*, 30–60.

13. Ibid.; Champ Clark, *My Quarter Century*, 2:223.

14. Turner, "American Prohibition Movement," 236–40; Cherrington, *Evolution of Prohibition*, 204–18.

15. Turner, "American Prohibition Movement," 226, 276–77.

16. *Topeka Daily Capital*, October 20, 1886.

17. *NYH*, June 5, 12, August 14, 15, 1876.

18. *ClPD*, July 29, August 1, 1882; *StLG-D*, July 19, 1884.

19. *Leavenworth Evening Standard*, December 29, 1884 (first quote); James S. Clarkson to Cyrenus Cole, December 9, 1895 (second quote), Cole MSS, State Historical Society of Iowa, Iowa City.

20. *Lancaster Ohio Eagle*, October 26, 1882; *StPPP*, January 27, 1884.

21. *NYEP*, July 7, 1882; *Atchison Daily Champion*, October 31, 1886.

22. Bader, *Prohibition in Kansas*, 60–62, 72–74.

23. Jensen, *Winning of the Midwest*, 91–98; *ChTr*, November 2, 3, 8, 9, 1882; *InS*, October 11, 14, 21, 27, November 6, 1882.

New York's returns, though, should breed caution. The overall strength of the Prohibition Party in 1882 and 1884 stayed relatively stable: 25,783 votes in the first year, and 25,009 in the second (2.8 and 2.14 percent, respectively). But the places *casting* Prohibition ballots differed. Some of the difference certainly originated in varying levels of organization and the compulsion toward regularity in a presidential election year. But some, probably, had nothing to do with liquor. Many Republicans too angry to elect Folger governor, or to stay at home, would have been too Republican to support Grover Cleveland. Wyoming County, a western New York stronghold, cast 14.5 percent of its vote for the Prohibition ticket in 1882, and only 5.91 percent for John P. St. John in 1884; Allegany, just to its south, cast 16.78 and 9.46 percent respectively (which made it the banner Dry county both years); next-door Chautauqua gave 6.783 and 3.09 percent, and Cattaraugus gave 7.37 and 4.39 percent. In north-central New York, Cayuga 6.11 and 3.63 percent; Jefferson polled 7.31 and 3.79 percent; Herkimer (home of the Half-Breed boss, Senator Warner Miller) 6.58 and 2.76 percent.

For contemporary suggestions that Prohibition votes were often Republican protest votes, see A. C. Dodge to Elisha W. Keyes, November 6, 1882, and N. T. Martin to Keyes, November 7, 1882, Keyes MSS, SHSW.

24. *ClPD*, July 29, 1882.

25. George K. Nash to John Sherman, August 2, 1882, ShrM; *ClPD*, July 29, August 10, 1882.

26. *CiC*, July 9, 1882; *NYH*, September 4, 1882; *NYTr*, October 9, 12, 1882.

27. *CiC*, August 3, 1882.

28. J. C. F. Beyland to John Sherman, August 17, 1882, George K. Nash to Sherman, August 2, 1882, and Joseph H. Geiger to Sherman, August 13, 1882, ShrM; *ClPD*, August 1, 1882.

29. *CiE*, September 21, 1882; *NYTr*, October 10, 1882; *ClPD*, July 15, August 6, 9, 16, 1882.

30. *CiC*, September 1, October 13, 1882; *ClPD*, August 4, 5, 8, 1882; C. M. Keyes to John Sherman, August 25, 1882, and B. R. Cowen to Sherman, August 18, 1882, ShrM.

31. *Circleville Democrat and Watchman*, September 29, 1882; *ClPD*, July 10, 12 (quote), August 2, 3, 16, 18, 1882; *CiC*, September 24, 1882.

32. *ClPD*, August 10, 1882; John F. Oglevee to John Sherman, November 11, 1882, and Benjamin E. Hopkins to Sherman, October 14, 1882, ShrM; *Lancaster Ohio Eagle*, October 5, 1882; *Hocking Sentinel*, October 12, 1882.

33. *CiC*, October 11, 12 (quote), 1882; M. Boggs to John Sherman, October 13, 1882, ShrM; Rutherford B. Hayes to Carl Schurz, October 12, 1882, SchM.

34. *CiC*, October 13, 1882 (quoted).

35. George K. Nash to John Sherman, August 2, 1882, ShrM; Turner, "American Prohibition Movement," 253; *NYH*, June 27, 1883; *NYTr*, May 29, October 1, 1883.

36. John S. Jones to Charles L. Kurtz, May 28, 1883, Kurtz MSS, OHS.

37. *NYTr*, June 4, October 8, 12, 1883.

38. *NYH*, June 27, 1883; *ClPD*, June 27, 1883.

39. *NYTr*, October 11, 13, 1883.

40. *Bucyrus Journal*, October 5, 1883; *Georgetown Brown County News*, September 20, 1883; *Mount Gilead Morrow County Sentinel*, October 4, 1883; *NYTr*, October 2, 8, 9, 10, 1883.

41. William McKinley to Joseph B. Foraker, October 12, 1883, Foraker MSS, CHS; *NYTr*, October 11, 13, 16, 18, 1883.

42. *LoC-J*, July 13, 1882.

43. Morgan R. Wise to Samuel J. Randall, October 13, 1883, and L. Q. Washington to Randall, October 10, 1883, RanM.

44. John F. Coyle to Samuel J. Randall, October 12, 1883, RanM.

CHAPTER SIX

1. *Pittsburgh Post*, August 3, 1888.

2. *CR*, 48th Cong., 1st sess., app., 207; *SFAC*, July 10, 1884.

3. The fullest coverage of tariff arguments, albeit for a later election, is Reitano's *Tariff Question in the Gilded Age*. For the specific arguments assembled here, see George, *Protection or Free Trade*, esp. 208–15; J. S. Moore, "The Revision of the Tariff, Submitted before the Tariff Commission" (New York: n.p., 1882), 15–18, 22; Hartshorn, *Wages, Living, and Tariff*, 39–40, 50–51, 68; Roberts, *Government Revenue*, 181–93; John L. Hayes, "The Farmer's Question" (Cambridge: University Press, 1880), 23–24, 34–36; *CR*, 48th Cong., 1st sess., app., 9, 209, 211, 229, 234, 315.

4. *PhR*, October 10, 1884.

5. *CR*, 48th Cong., 1st sess., app., 211.

6. *Atchison Daily Champion*, October 24, 1886.

7. *CR*, 48th Cong., 1st sess., app., 229.

8. John Lambert, *Arthur Pue Gorman*, 87–88; *Lewiston Evening Journal*, February 1, 1882.

9. *Washington Post*, May 16, 1897 ("alkakange"); George, *Protection or Free Trade*, 168.

10. Taussig, *Tariff History of the United States*; Tarbell, *Tariff in Our Times*; Downey, "Rebirth of Reform," 128–72.

11. *Annapolis Maryland Republican*, June 16, 1883; *InS*, April 7, 1884.

12. Justin S. Morrill to James M. Swank, October 20, 1885, Swank MSS, HSP.

13. Doyle, *New Men, New Cities, New South*, 34–50, 136–58; Ingersoll, "City of Atlanta," 30–43; Gaston, *New South Creed*, 119–86; *Nation*, September 27, 1879, p. 190; *DMISR*, August 6, 1884.

14. *CR*, 48th Cong., 1st sess., app., 229 (May 5, 1884).

15. Crofts, "Blair Bill," 3–7, 140–46; Henry W. Blair to Whitelaw Reid, March 8, 1886, ReiM.

16. *InS*, October 27, 1882.

17. Hudson, *Random Recollections*, 112; James A. Garfield to John Sherman, September 25, 1880, ShrM; Jordan, *Winfield Scott Hancock*, 301–2; W. Wurts Dundas to Thomas F. Bayard, October 17, 1880, BayM.

18. Thomas G. Shearman to David Wells, November 23, 1880, Wells MSS, LC; Henry Philpott to William Graham Sumner, November 15, 1882, Sumner MSS, Sterling Memorial Library, Yale University, New Haven; Wall, *Henry Watterson*, 185.

19. *DtFP*, March 30, 1884; *Charleston News and Courier*, November 24, 1883; *StLP-D*, March 29, 1884.

20. Charles R. Randall (October 3, 1883), John E. Kenna (October 12, 1883), H. Clay Conde (March 10, 1883), Smith M. Weed (January 5, 9, 1883), Andrew H. Green (June 20, 1883), and John G. Priest (April 16, 1883), all to Samuel J. Randall, RanM.

21. *NYH*, July 9, 1884; *Charleston News and Courier*, November 24, 1883; Barnes, *John G. Carlisle*, 183.

22. *LoC*, December 1, 2, 1883.

23. John B. Haskin to S. S. Cox, December 16, 1883, Cox MSS, NYPL; *Richmond Dispatch*, December 5, 1883; Victor E. Piollet to Samuel J. Randall, December 4, 1883, and Rebecca Felton to Mrs. Randall, December 2, 1883, RanM.

24. *LoC*, December 2, 1883; *LoC-J*, November 29, December 3, 1883; W. W. H. Davis to Samuel J. Randall, December 2, 1883, and A. S. Colyar to Randall, December 5, 1883, RanM.

25. "Murray," *InN*, December 18, 1885; *Washington Critic*, January 28, 1890; *Portland Transcript*, June 11, 1884; Robbins, "William Ralls Morrison," 1–43.

26. "Gath," *CiE*, July 3, 1886; *NYEP*, March 19, 1884; *NYH*, March 24, 1884; Samuel J. Randall to George L. Miller, January 9, 1882, RanM.

27. Lester B. Faulkner to Samuel J. Randall, February 25, 1884, M. D. Hopkins to Randall, April 7, 1884, and H. H. Armstrong to Randall, April 14, 1884, RanM; Henry B. Payne to James R. Doolittle, April 10, 1884, Doolittle MSS, LC; *NYTr*, April 8, 1884; Theodore Lyman to Edward Atkinson, May 19, 1884, Atkinson MSS, MHS.

28. *NYEP*, January 9, 1884; David A. Wells to William R. Morrison, February 29, 1884, Morrison MSS, ISHS; *CiE*, March 1, 2, 7, 1884.

29. Charles Nordhoff to David A. Wells, February 16, 1884, Wells MSS, NYPL; Charles Durand to Samuel J. Randall, April 3, 1884, RanM.

30. Bryan Tyson to Samuel J. Randall, May 22, 1884, RanM; Hartshorn, *Wages, Living, and Tariff*, 72–73.

31. Frederick A. Claflin to John D. Long, May 12, 1884, Long MSS, MHS; *LoC-J*, March 27, 1884.

32. "G.F.D.," *BrE*, March 20, 29, 1884; *NYTr*, April 2, 4, 1884; *CiE*, April 8, 1884; *StLP-D*, March 18, 1884; William Morrison to David A. Wells, May 1, 1884, Marble MSS, LC; *Washington Post*, April 16, 1884.

33. *LoC-J*, May 3, 4, 5, 8, 1884.

34. *NYTr*, May 7, 1884.

35. *LoC-J*, May 10, 11, 13, 1884; *NYTr*, May 14, 1884.

36. *ChDN*, May 20, 1884.

37. *LoC-J*, May 8, 1884; Theodore S. Ransom to Samuel J. Randall, May 7, 1884, RanM.

38. *NYTr*, April 10, 1884.

39. McConnell, *Glorious Contentment*, 150; *CR*, 48th Cong., 1st sess., 2635 (April 5, 1884), 2678–86 (April 7, 1884); McPherson, *Abolitionist Legacy*, 128–29.

40. Dallas Sanders to Samuel J. Randall, March 1, 1884, and John B. Read to Randall, March 2, 1884, RanM.

41. William Morrison to David A. Wells, April 25, 1884, Marble MSS, LC; "G.F.," *BrE*, March 20, 1884; *NYEP*, April 4, 1884; "Gath," *CiE*, April 7, 1884.

CHAPTER SEVEN

1. Henry Ward to Samuel J. Randall, January 5, 1883, RanM; George F. Baer to Wayne MacVeagh, March 7, 1881, MacM; *PhR*, September 23, 28, 1886; Merrill, *Bourbon Democracy of the Middle West*, 139–66.

2. "Gath," *CiE*, December 13, 1878, and December 15, 1884.

3. *InJ*, September 10, 1884.

4. West, *Lincoln's Scapegoat General*, 373–76; Hammond, "'Beast' in Boston," 266–80.

5. James R. Collins to Allen G. Thurman, June 30, 1883, and Durbin Ward to Thurman, June 26, 1883, Thurman MSS, OHS; *CiE*, June 20, 23, 25, December 18, 19, 31, 1883, January 6, 7, 8, 9, 10, 1884; *ClPD*, January 10, 11, 18, 1884.

6. Myers, *Tammany Hall*, 211–49, 258, 265–66; Mushkat, *Reconstruction of New York Democracy*, 196–98, 237–40.

7. Grossman, *Democratic Party and the Negro*, 60–106; *Cleveland Gazette*, March 29, April 12, 1884; *Washington Bee*, September 6, 1884.

8. *NYTr*, October 2, 1882; Benson, *Merchants, Farmers and Railroads*, 150–86; Charles Folger to James B. Butler, September 11, 1882, Butler MSS, NYPL.

9. *Hocking Sentinel*, August 23, 1883; Williams, *Democratic Party and California Politics*, 19–51; Stephen M. White to Daniel Manning, April 23, 1885, and Barclay Henley to White, August 13, 1886, WhtM.

10. *InN*, August 20, September 1, 1884; *Dubuque Daily Herald*, September 12, 1886; *ClPD*, January 18, 1884.

11. John Lambert, *Arthur Pue Gorman*, 55–56, 367; *NYH*, October 28, 1888; *CiE*, January 23, 1885; *ClPD*, August 14, 1884; *ChTi*, May 3, 1878.

12. *NYH*, January 4, 1883.

13. *Philadelphia Inquirer*, July 6, 1883; McClure, *Old-Time Notes*, 2:542–47;

14. *Meriden Daily Republican*, January 9, 1884; *NYH*, January 17, June 14, 1883; *Newark Daily Advertiser*, April 18, 1884.

15. Henry Ward to Samuel J. Randall, May 31, 1883, January 5, 1884 [misdated 1883], RanM; *New York Herald*, January 24, 1884; *Newark Daily Advertiser*, April 1, 18, 1884; *Meriden Daily Republican*, January 9, 1884; *NYH*, January 4, 1883.

16. For a far more critical judgment, see Hammond, "'Beast' in Boston," 270–78.

17. "Gath," *CiE*, January 23, 1883.

18. Merrill, *Bourbon Leader*, 3–13; Armitage, *Grover Cleveland*, 42–64; Blodgett, "Emergence of Grover Cleveland," 134–45.

19. Merrill, *Bourbon Leader*, 14–23; *NYS*, March 12, 1885.

20. Nevins, *Grover Cleveland*, 127; "H.D.C.," *NYEP*, July 18, 1884; *NYH*, April 8, 1883.

21. Nevins, *Grover Cleveland*, 138–39, 143.

22. Ibid., 114–15.

23. *BrE*, May 1, 2, 5, 1883; Nevins, *Grover Cleveland*, 119–22.

24. Grover Cleveland to August Belmont, October 20, 1883, Belmont Family MSS, Columbia University, New York; *NYH*, October 23, 24, 25, 1883, July 10, 1884.

25. Nevins, *Grover Cleveland*, 140–41.

26. *NYEP*, July 18, 21, October 20, November 25, December 10, 16, 1884; *NYTi*, June 15, 1884; Nevins, *Grover Cleveland*, 142.

27. *BrE*, May 1, 1883; *NYEP*, March 18, 1884.

28. Nevins, *Grover Cleveland*, 116–18.

29. On labor laws, see the thorough coverage by "H.D.C.," *NYEP*, July 23, 1884.

CHAPTER EIGHT

1. Halstead, "Defeat of Blaine," 159–62; James G. Blaine to William T. Sherman, May 25, 1884, Sherman MSS, LC; Sherman to Blaine, May 28, 1884, BlaM.

2. Beale, ed., *Letters of Mrs. Blaine*, 2:90; *NYS*, May 11, 1884; Stoddard, *As I Knew Them*, 126; Halstead, "Defeat of Blaine," 168; *NYTr*, July 3, 4, 1881.

3. Hamilton, *James G. Blaine*, 564, 624; James G. Blaine to Whitelaw Reid, July 6, 1888, ReiM; *NYS*, December 21, 1884.

4. Chester A. Arthur to John A. Logan, May 8, 1884, LogM; Reeves, *Gentleman Boss*, 370.

5. *StLP-D*, February 7, 1884 (quote); Gresham, *Walter Quintin Gresham*, 495–96; Wayne MacVeagh to "my dear sir," May 23, 1884, MacM.

6. *NYS*, December 21, 1884; Reeves, *Gentleman Boss*, 372–74, 381.

7. A. K. Joy to John D. Long, June 2, 1884, Long MSS, MHS; Jerry Munn to John Sherman, May 16, 1884, ShM; Paul Strobach to William E. Chandler, April 18, 1884, and J. Martin to Chandler, May 28, 1884, ChaM.

8. Lodge, *Selections from the Correspondence*, 1:2; Wayne MacVeagh to "my dear sir," February 20, 1884, MacM; Whitelaw Reid to Edwin Cowles, May 16, 1884, ReiM; *CiCG*, March 7, 1884.

9. Robert H. Tyler to William E. Chandler, May 24, 1884, ChaM; John M. Gregory to Andrew D. White, May 12, 1884, and R. McMurdy to White, May 12, 1884, White MSS, Cornell University, Ithaca; *InN*, April 25, 1884 (quote).

10. Adler, "George F. Edmunds," 236–37, 270–71, 288–89; *CiC*, December 11, 1869; Perry Belmont to Thomas F. Bayard, January 11, 1875, BayM; *NYGr*, January 22, 1877; *NYTr*, April 4, 1886; Hoar, *Autobiography*, 1:388.

11. *InN*, January 8, 1885; *CinE*, August 13, 1883, May 14, 30 (headline), 1884; *NYH*, June 3, 1884 (quote).

12. *ChTr*, September 11, 1886; Dunn, *From Harrison to Harding*, 64; Adler, "George F. Edmunds," 275–80.

13. *StLG-D*, May 18, 1884; *NYEP*, March 17, 1884; *NYTr*, April 27, 1884; Horace White to William Henry Smith, May 6, 1884, Smith MSS, OHS.

14. Jones, *John A. Logan*, 158, 171–77; *NYH*, June 5, 1884 (quote).

15. Morgan, *From Hayes to McKinley*, 179–80; O. M. Nixon to Walter Q. Gresham, March 28, 1884, Gresham MSS, LC; John A. Logan to Mary Logan, April 4, 6, 1884, LogM; *ChDN*, May 10, 1884.

16. A. W. Jones to Charles L. Kurtz, April 17, 1884, Kurtz MSS, OHS; J. C. F. Beyland to William E. Chandler, May 27, 1884, ChaM.

17. James S. Clarkson to James G. Blaine, March 13, 1884, BlaM; Marcus, *Grand Old Party*, 62–64.

18. J. M. Hedrick to Walter Q. Gresham, March 27, 1884, Gresham MSS, LC.

19. C. L. Poorman to Charles L. Kurtz, March 27, 1884, Kurtz MSS, OHS; *CiCG*, April 25, 1884; H. C. Jones to John Sherman, April 25, 1884 (quote), and S. L. Johnson to Sherman, April 25, 1884, ShrM; Jones, *John A. Logan*, 171–76.

20. Marcus, *Grand Old Party*, 70–73; *NYS*, April 17, 23, 1884.

21. Whitelaw Reid to James G. Blaine, March 24, 1884, ReiM; *NYTi*, April 10, 11, 21, 1884; *NYS*, April 19, 1884.

22. *NYS*, April 23, 24, 25, 1884; *NYTr*, April 26, 1884.

23. *BrE*, April 24, 1884; Whitelaw Reid to John Hay, April 24, 1884, ReiM. Platt had favored accepting the Edmunds crowd's terms.

24. *NYTr*, April 30, 1884; *Nation*, May 8, 1884.

25. Adler, "George F. Edmunds," 250–54; *ChDN*, May 15, 1884 (quote); Blaine to Reid, April 27, May 1, 1884, Reid to Blaine, May 4, 1884, Reid to William W. Phelps, May 5, 1884, and Reid to S. M. Freeland, May 9, 1884, ReiM.

26. *NYH*, May 2, 1884.

27. Marcus, *Grand Old Party*, 80.

28. Ibid., 67–69, 79–80; D. P. Baldwin to Walter Gresham, May 22, 1884, E. B. Martindale to Gresham, May 19, 1884, and Carson Lake to J. H. Woodard, n.d., Gresham MSS, LC; *BrE*, June 3, 1884.

29. J. H. Wilson to Carl Schurz, May 28, 1884, SchM; Benjamin H. Bristow to Walter Q. Gresham, April 24, 1884, L. M. Brown to Gresham, March 28, 1884, Gresham MSS, LC; Gresham to Noble C. Butler, January 21, May 19, 1884, Butler MSS, ISL; *InN*, June 4, 1884 (quote).

30. *NYH*, June 2, 1884 (quote).

31. For wider press notice of the cartoons, see *CiE*, May 9, 10, 1884; *ChDN*, May 8, June 3, 1884; and *NYTi*, June 3, 1884. For impact on German Republicans, see J. C. Beyland to John Sherman, May 8, 1884, ShrM.

32. *Columbus Daily Times*, June 6, 1884; *StLP-D*, June 6, 1884; *NYH*, June 4, 1884; clipping, June 4, 1884, Carpenter MSS, LC; *BaC*, July 17, 1884.

33. Stone, *Fifty Years a Journalist*, 149–50; *NYH*, June 3, 4, 1884; Garraty, *Henry Cabot Lodge*, 78.

34. *NYTr*, June 3, 1884.

35. Stone, *Fifty Years a Journalist*, 150–51; Lynch, *Autobiography*, 281–83; *NYH*, June 4, 12, 1884; *NYTi*, June 4, 1884; Morris, *Rise of Theodore Roosevelt*, 263.

36. *Proceedings of the Eighth Republican National Convention*, 38–40; *NYH*, June 5, 1884; *StLP-D*, June 4, 5, 9, 1884.

37. Walter Q. Gresham to Benjamin H. Bristow, June 12, 1884, Bristow MSS, LC; Henry L. Dawes to Electa Dawes, June 8, 1884, DawM.

38. *StLP-D*, June 8, 1884; *StLG-D*, June 6, 1884; *NYW*, June 5, 1884; *NYH*, June 4, 6, 1884; *NYTr*, June 4, 6, 8, 1884; Garraty, *Henry Cabot Lodge*, 78.

39. Hoar, *Autobiography*, 1:407; *NYH*, June 4, 5, 1884; *StLP-D*, June 4, 1884.

40. *NYTr*, June 7, 1884; *NYH*, June 12, 1884; Morris, *Rise of Theodore Roosevelt*, 267 (quote); Edward F. Thayer to John D. Long, June 9, 1884, Long MSS, MHS; *StLP-D*, June 7, 1884.

41. *NYTr*, June 7, 1884; *NYH*, June 9, 1884 (first quote); Robinson, *Thomas B. Reed*, 100–101 (second quote).

CHAPTER NINE

1. *NYTi*, January 31, April 10, 1881; Samuel S. Cox, "Legislative Humors," *Harper's Monthly*, 52:273; column, June 7, September 26, 1885, and scrapbooks, Carpenter MSS, LC.

2. "D.P.," *CiC*, June 21, 1870; Horatio Pratt to Allen G. Thurman, June 16, 1883, Thurman MSS, OHS.

3. *StLP-D*, June 30, 1884.

4. Ibid. (quote); *InS*, April 17, 23, May 1, 1884.

5. George L. Miller to Samuel J. Randall, April 26, 1884, RanM; Daniel W. Voorhees to

John B. Stoll, July 18, 1883, Stoll MSS, ISL; *StLP-D*, July 8, 1884; Walter Q. Gresham to David Davis, February 11, 1884, Davis MSS, ISHS.

6. S. L. M. Barlow to Thomas Bayard, June 4, 1884, BayM; August Belmont to William C. Whitney, July 22, 1884, Whitney MSS, LC.

7. Pepper, *Henry Gassaway Davis*, 269; John Lambert, *Arthur Pue Gorman*, 97–98; William A. Wallace to Thomas F. Bayard, June 29, 1884, BayM.

8. *NYS*, June 16, 1884; *NYTr*, September 8, 1889.

9. John Bigelow, ed., *Letters and Memorials of Samuel J. Tilden*, 612–13; *CiE*, November 10, 1883, March 3, 1884; James S. Rollins to Andrew D. White, May 22, 1884, White MSS, Cornell University, Ithaca.

10. Nahum Capen to Samuel J. Tilden, May 30, 1884, Tilden MSS, NYPL; *NYH*, June 13, 1883.

11. John Read (May 4, June 2, 1884), Richard Vaux (June 16, 1884), Bob Randall (June 16, 1884), and Henry Ward (May 29, 1884), all to Samuel J. Randall, RanM; *Nation*, June 12, 1884.

12. Nevins, *Grover Cleveland*, 146–47.

13. *InN*, July 7, 1884; Hirsch, *William C. Whitney*, 227; *Nation*, June 19, 1884; C. F. Newman to Samuel J. Randall, June 11, 1884, RanM; W. B. Benson to John D. Long, May 8, 1884, Long MSS, MHS.

14. Nevins, *Grover Cleveland*, 146–47; Hirsch, *William C. Whitney*, 231–32; Bass, *"I Am a Democrat"*, 12–13; Henry Ward to Samuel J. Randall, June 22, 28, 1884, RanM; Merrill, *Bourbon Democracy of the Middle West*, 158–61.

15. *CiE*, July 11, 1884; *InN*, March 12, 1885; *Nation*, November 11, 1880.

16. Werner, *Tammany Hall*, 277–79.

17. *Nation*, November 11, 1880; *ChTr*, June 6, 1886; Genen, "John Kelly," 142–51, 186–88.

18. *NYH*, December 27, 1876; Hammack, *Power and Society*, 119–34; Mandelbaum, *Boss Tweed's New York*, 109–13, 131–35; Marquis James, *Merchant Adventurer*, 160–77.

19. Hirsch, *William C. Whitney*, 149–50, 160–73; *NYH*, September 21, 22, November 1, 6, 1882; *InN*, July 4, 1885.

20. John Kelly to James R. Doolittle, June 7, 1884, Doolittle MSS, SHSW; Manton Marble to Samuel J. Tilden, June 15, 1884, Marble MSS, LC; James E. Harvey to David Davis, July 2, 1884, Davis MSS, ISHS; *InJ*, July 2, 1884.

21. "Gath," *CiE*, May 9, 1884; J. P. Bryan to William A. Courtenay, August 28, 1884, Courtenay MSS, South Caroliniana Library, Columbia.

22. Samuel S. Cox to Worthington C. Ford, June 11, 1884, Cox MSS, NYPL; D. B. Saxton to Samuel J. Randall, June 10, 1884, and Richard R. McMahon to Randall, May 31, 1884, RanM; Flick, *Samuel Jones Tilden*, 483–84.

23. *NYS*, June 17, 18, 1884.

24. Ibid., June 19, 1884; *BrE*, June 19, 1884; John Read to Samuel J. Randall, June 23, 1884, and H. Clay Conde to Randall, June 24, 1884, RanM; *Troy Daily Press*, June 19, 1884; *NYTr*, August 1, 1886.

25. Stephen M. White to Daniel Manning, April 23, 1885, and White to G. W. Graves, May 16, 1885, WhtM.

26. *ClPD*, July 2, 1884; *NYTr*, July 7, 8, 1884; *InS*, July 9, 1884; *NYTi*, July 8, 1884.

27. Rathgeber, "Democratic Party in Pennsylvania," 129; *NYTi*, July 8, 1884; *Columbus Daily Times*, July 5, 1884.

28. *NYH*, July 3, 9, 11, 1884; *Official Proceedings of the National Democratic Convention*, 12–25, 177–78; *NYTr*, July 9, 10, 1884.

29. Tarbell, *Tariff in Our Times*, 140–41; *NYEP*, July 15, 1884; Samuel J. Randall to C. E. Sears, July 11, 1884, RanM; John G. Carlisle to David Wells, July 1, 1884, Wells MSS, NYPL; Edgar K. Apgar to Manton Marble, June 23, 1884, and Carlisle to Marble, April 7, June 17, June 25, 1884, Marble MSS, LC.

30. *ChTr*, July 11, 1884; *NYS*, September 19, 1884.

31. *InN*, July 17, September 6, 8, 1884; *NYTi*, July 12, 1884; *ChTr*, September 4, 1884; Merrill, *Bourbon Leader*, 51.

32. *ChTr, NYH, NYTr, NYTi*, all July 12, 1884.

33. *InN*, July 12, 1884; Pepper, *Henry Gassaway Davis*, 141; Perry Belmont to Thomas F. Bayard [n.d., but plainly spring 1879], BayM; A. M. Gibson to James G. Blaine, July 19, 1884, BlaM.

34. *Dayton Daily Democrat*, July 12, 1884; Stephen M. White to Charles A. Sumner, August 12, 1884, WhtM. The statement was not Cleveland's. Judge Thomas Cooley had used it in an article in 1877, and civil service reformer Dorman B. Eaton had borrowed it for his entry in an 1882 encyclopedia. See *NYS*, January 2, 5, 1889.

CHAPTER TEN

1. James S. Dawes to Henry L. Dawes, August 16, 1884, DawM.

2. *PoEA*, July 31, 1884.

3. *WhIn*, January 21, 1884; M. Woodruff to William E. Chandler, September 29, 1884, ChaM; Joseph S. Cannon to Edward McPherson, July 29, 1884, McPM.

4. Nevins, *Grover Cleveland*, 175–76; *NYEP*, August 20, 1884.

5. *Proceedings*, 192–93; Andrew D. White to William W. Phelps, June 16, 1884, and George M. Robeson to James G. Blaine, July 19, 1884, BlaM; *PoEA*, July 25, 1884.

6. Nevins, *Grover Cleveland*, 178–79.

7. *InJ*, September 2, 1884; James G. Blaine to Thomas C. Platt, July 5, 1884, Platt MSS, Sterling Memorial Library, Yale University, New Haven; Blaine to William Warland Clapp, July 26, 1884, Clapp MSS, Houghton Library, Harvard University, Boston.

8. *BrE*, August 6, 1884; *NYTr*, August 2, 1884.

9. Marcus, *Grand Old Party*, 85–86; James G. Blaine to Stephen B. Elkins, June 24, 1884, ElkM.

10. *BrE*, July 24, 1884; Marvin Bovee to William Vilas, July 19, 1884, Vilas MSS, SHSW.

11. *ChTr*, September 10, 1884; John Lambert, *Arthur Pue Gorman*, 103; *InJ*, November 16, 1884.

12. *NYTr*, April 18, 1886 (quote); John Lambert, *Arthur Pue Gorman*, 6–12, 22–24, 66–69.

13. John Lambert, *Arthur Pue Gorman*, 106; *BrE*, August 17, 18, 1884; but see the skeptical Blanton Duncan to Samuel J. Randall, November 26, 1888, RanM.

14. *NYTr*, September 14, 1884; B. B. Smalley to William Vilas, August 12, 16, 1884, and Arthur P. Gorman to the western subcommittee, October 24, 1884, Vilas MSS, SHSW; Lambert, *Arthur Pue Gorman*, 103; *BrE*, July 24, 1884; Marcus, *Grand Old Party*, 87–88.

15. *NYEP*, August 19, 27, 28, 1884; Benjamin F. Jones to John A. Logan, September 2, 1884 (first quote), and Shelby Cullom to Logan, July 31, 1884 (second quote), LogM; Almon M. Clapp to Edward McPherson, September 19, 1884, McPM.

16. J. B. Chaffee to Edward McPherson, October 8, 1884, and McPherson to John Roach, February 2, 1885, McPM; *CiE*, September 29, 1884; James S. Clarkson to William Loeb Jr., August 19, 1906, Roosevelt MSS, LC; Edward Bragg to William Vilas, November 15, 1884, Vilas MSS, SHSW.

17. Louis E. McComas to Edward McPherson, October 9, 1884, and A. H. Pettibone to McPherson, September 18, 1884, McPM.

18. *ClPD*, August 28, 1884; Sievers, *Benjamin Harrison*, 261–62; A. London Sowdue to Edward McPherson, August 27, 1884, Joseph Devens to McPherson, November 19, 1884, and Clarkson to McPherson, September 23, 1884, McPM; Whitelaw Reid to James G. Blaine, October 18, 1884, and Blaine to Reid, January 26, 1888, ReiM.

19. *HdTi*, October 6, 1884; Nevins, *Grover Cleveland*, 180–81; John Lambert, *Arthur Pue Gorman*, 103–4; Charles J. Canda to William C. Whitney, October 4, 24, 31, November 11, 1884, Whitney MSS, LC; *NYTr*, January 10, 1886; William R. Grace to Arthur P. Gorman, October 7, 1884, Grace MSS, Columbia University, New York.

20. William Barnum to William Vilas, November 11, 1884, and John L. Mitchell to Vilas, November 17, 1884, Vilas MSS, SHSW; John Kelly to Samuel L. M. Barlow, October 20, 1884, Barlow MSS, Huntington Library, San Marino; Louis Schade to Thomas F. Bayard, December 7, 1884, BayM; Hirsch, *William C. Whitney*, 238–39; Charles L. Lamberton to Samuel Randall, September 10, 1888, RanM.

21. *HdTi*, November 4, 1884; John T. Wait to John D. Long, November 2, 1884, Long MSS, MHS; Henry Ward to Samuel J. Randall, September 12, 1884, RanM; *CiE*, September 29, 1884.

22. James S. Clarkson to William Loeb Jr., August 19, 1906, Roosevelt MSS, LC; *BaW&C*, August 26, September 1, 1884; *BaC*, September 4, 1884.

23. *InN*, November 3, 1884; Marcus, *Grand Old Party*, 87; Reeves, *Gentleman Boss*, 387; *BaC*, August 25, 1884; Nevins, *Grover Cleveland*, 172.

24. *NYS*, December 21, 1884.

25. Richardson, *William E. Chandler*, 353; Calhoun, *Gilded Age Cato*, 82–83.

26. James Doyle to William E. Chandler, October 23, 1884, ChaM; James N. Tyner to James S. Clarkson, November 23, 1884, ClaM; Reeves, *Gentleman Boss*, 385.

27. John B. Hamilton to John A. Logan, August 26 1884, LogM; Howe, *Chester A. Arthur*, 265–66; *NYEP*, October 8, 1884.

28. *ChDN*, July 23, 1884 (first quote); Jones, *John A. Logan*, 193; *ChTr*, September 4, 5 (quote), 1884.

29. Peck, *Twenty Years of the Republic*, 42–43; Jones, *John A. Logan*, 193; John A. Logan to James G. Blaine, July 6, 17, 1884, BlaM; Stephen B. Elkins to Whitelaw Reid, October 13, 1884, ReiM; *ChDN*, October 2, 1884; *InN*, August 22, 1884; *CiE*, July 5, 1888.

30. *InJ*, August 29, 30, 31, 1884; *Mobile Register*, September 18, 1884; *InN*, September 19, 1884.

31. *NYTi*, September 12, 1884.

32. *InJ*, August 7, 1884.

33. *NYEP*, August 4, 1884.

34. *InJ*, July 29, 1884.

35. *Trenton Daily State Gazette*, November 4, 1884; M. Woodhull to William E. Chandler, September 16, October 7, 1884, ChaM; Russell, *Bare Hands and Stone Walls*, 39; Rathgeber, "Democratic Party in Pennsylvania," 132; *StJG*, November 16, 1884; Henry Ward to Samuel J. Randall, March 18, 1885, RanM.

36. *NYTi*, September 12, 1884; *ClPD*, September 22, 1884; *InS*, October 20, 1884; *LoC-J*, October 21, 1884; *HdTi*, October 4, 1884; Peck, *Twenty Years of the Republic*, 62.

37. *ChDN*, October 2, 8, 1884; *NYEP*, October 2, 11, 30, 31, 1884; Thomas Ewing to John Sherman, July 23, 1881, ShrM; James G. Blaine to William W. Phelps, August 25, 1884, and Reid to Blaine, June 25, 1884, ReiM; *ClPD*, August 28, 1884; *NYH*, September 2, 1884; *BoH*, September 13, 1884; *HdTi*, November 1, 3, 1884.

38. James G. Blaine to Whitelaw Reid, July 12, 1884, ReiM.

39. *St. Paul Dispatch*, September 25, 1884; Mary Logan to Dollie Logan, August 27, 1884, LogM.

40. *NYEP*, November 13, 1884.

41. *InS*, November 3, 1884; *CoMo*, October 25, 1884.

42. *InJ*, August 24, 1884; *CoMo*, October 25, 1884; *ChTr*, October 10, 1884; *Trenton Daily State Gazette*, November 4, 1884.

43. *NYEP*, October 28, 1884; R. W. Patterson to William E. Chandler, September 10, 1884, ChaM; *ChTr*, September 9, 1884; *PhR*, September 26, 1884.

44. D. P. Holt to A. L. Conger, October 2, 1884, Conger MSS, RBHML; Allie to her mother, October 31, 1884, Smith MSS, OHS.

45. *NYEP*, September 5, 1884; *NYTr*, August 29, 1884; Hudson, *Random Recollections*, 192; *InN*, July 24, 1884; Marcus, *Grand Old Party*, 86–87.

46. *NYEP*, August 20, 1884; *InS*, August 23, 1884.

47. *BrE*, September 28, 1884; *ChTi*, August 17, 1884; *NYEP*, August 26, 1884; *InN*, July 24, 1884; F. H. Marsh to William Vilas, July 18, 1884, Vilas MSS, SHSW.

CHAPTER ELEVEN

1. *Buffalo Evening Telegraph*, July 21, 1884.

2. Nevins, *Grover Cleveland*, 162–69; *Burlington Free Press*, August 9, 1884; Fuess, *Carl Schurz, Reformer*, 293–94. For Mugwumps' wavering, which lasted much longer than the story indicates, see Henry Ward Beecher to Carl Schurz, July 30, 1884, and George William Curtis to Schurz, July 31, 1884, SchM.

3. *Buffalo Evening Telegraph*, July 21, 1884.

4. *ChTr*, July 30, 1884; *Buffalo Express*, July 31, 1884.

5. *DMISR*, September 7, 19, 1884; *CoMo*, October 18, 1884.

6. *BaC*, September 8, 1884; "Journalist," *NYEP*, August 6, 1884.

7. *Buffalo Express*, August 14, 1884.

8. *Buffalo Courier*, August 11, November 3, 1884.

9. *NYEP*, August 11, 12, 1884; Nevins, *Grover Cleveland*, 164–66; *CiE*, August 12, 1884.

10. Sproat, *Best Men*, 130.

11. Swanberg, *Pulitzer*, 102; *Norton's Union-Intelligencer*, September 16, 1884.

12. *ChTi*, August 1, 1884; *ChDN*, July 24, August 2, 1884; *PoEA*, August 7, 1884; *StLG-D*, June 22, 1884.

13. *InS*, August 7, 8, 1884.

14. Sievers, *Benjamin Harrison*, 254–55; *DtFP*, August 21, 1884.

15. Muzzey, *James G. Blaine*, 264–65; "Ruhamah," *StLG-D*, June 22, 1884.

16. *LoC-J*, August 15, 1884; *BoH*, September 21, 1884.

17. *ChTr*, September 6, 1884; *NYTr*, August 29, 1884; *InJ*, August 12, 1884; *LoC-J*, August 14, 1884.

18. *ChTr*, September 24, 1884.

19. *InS*, October 4, 1884; *NYW*, September 24, 1884.

20. *BoH*, September 21, 24, 1884; *ChTi*, September 21, 23, 24, 1884.

21. *NYTi*, October 31, 1884; *InJ*, November 4, 1884.

22. *Poughkeepsie Daily Eagle*, August 21, 22, 23, 1884; *NYS*, October 26, 29, 1884; *DMISR*, October 2, 1884; *St. Paul Dispatch*, October 2, 1884.

23. *InS*, October 22, 1884.

24. "Gath," *ChTr*, July 20, 1868; *Marietta Register*, October 15, 1868.

25. *Nation*, October 10, 1872; William Henry Hurlburt to Manton Marble, December 1873, Marble MSS, LC; *CiE*, September 13, 18, 1876; *Springfield Illinois State Register*, August 6, 1868; *DMISR*, July 15, 16, 1880.

26. Barnes, *John G. Carlisle*, 158; Nevins, *Grover Cleveland*, 446; Dunn, *From Harrison to Harding*, 104–5.

27. Peskin, *Garfield*, 160–61; see *NYEP*, August 5, 1884, for hints on this score.

28. Reginald H. Williams to Carl Schurz, August 6, 1884, SchM.

29. William E. Chandler to Whitelaw Reid, September 25, 1884, ReiM.

30. *IW*, October 11, 1884; "Our Broadway Note-Book," *NYTr*, August 31, 1884; *Oneida Dispatch*, September 26, 1884; Robert M. Dolliver to Jonathan P. Dolliver, November 15, 1884, Dolliver MSS, State Historical Society of Iowa, Iowa City.

31. *InJ*, July 14, 1884; *Poughkeepsie Daily Eagle*, August 6, 1884; Charles E. Smith to James G. Blaine, August 4, 1884, BlaM.

32. Noble C. Butler to Walter Q. Gresham, September 28, 1884, Gresham MSS, LC; R. W. Patterson to James S. Clarkson, September 20, 1884, ClaM; *DtFP*, September 23, 1884, *ClPD*, September 20, 1884.

33. *Evansville Courier*, November 8, 1888; *StLG-D*, December 12, 1888.

34. *InJ*, August 24, 1884; *CoMo*, October 25, 1884; *Trenton Daily State Gazette*, October 16, 1884; *ChTi*, October 29, 1884.

35. Hudson, *Random Recollections*, 184–90; George Parker, *Recollections of Grover Cleveland*, 245–46; *ChTi*, October 31, November 3, 1884.

36. *Poughkeepsie Daily Eagle*, August 7, 15, 1884; *NYTr*, July 22–August 11, 1884; *Buffalo Express*, July 22, 1884; *Manchester Union*, August 1, 1884.

37. *NOP*, September 21, 1884; *Galena Daily Gazette*, September 30, 1884.

38. *Canajoharie Courier*, August 26, 1884; Jones, *John A. Logan*, 191; Charles Ingersoll to Robert Ingersoll, October 13, 1884, Ingersoll MSS, ISHS; *InN*, October 10, 1884.

39. *NYEP*, October 18, 1884; Charles A. Boutelle to Whitelaw Reid, August 4, 1884, ReiM; Carl Schurz to George Fred Williams, September 4, 1884, Charles E. Norton to Schurz, August 16, 1884, and Schurz to R. R. Bowker, September 10, 1884. SchM.

40. *PhP*, November 21, 1884; *Dayton Daily Democrat*, July 22, 1884.

1. *DMISR*, September 21, 1884.

2. A. M. Franz to Andrew D. White, June 13, 1884 (quote), White MSS, Cornell University, Ithaca; *InS*, June 11, 13, 14, 1884; *HdTi*, September 25, 1884.

3. Blodgett, *Gentle Reformers*, 1–8; Thomas Wentworth Higginson to John D. Long, June 10, 1884, Long MSS, MHS.

4. *NYH*, June 18, 1884; Paine, *Thomas Nast*, 497.

5. Armstrong, ed., *Gilded Age Letters of Godkin*, 315.

6. *NYEP*, August 6, 1884; *BoH*, October 25, 1884; *BoT*, November 1, 1884.

7. Cary, *George William Curtis*, 289–90; Paine, *Thomas Nast*, 490–93.

8. *DMISR*, September 21, 1884.

9. *BaW&C*, August 18, 1884; A. M. Gibson to James G. Blaine, July 19, 1884, and Charles Emory Smith to Blaine, August 4, 1884, BlaM; *InJ*, July 1, August 8, September 17, 19, 1884; *ChTr*, September 23, 1884; *HdC*, July 18, 1884; *NYEP*, October 15, 1884; Welch, *George Frisbie Hoar*, 129; *MnTr*, August 4, 1884.

10. *WhIn*, July 21, 1884.

11. *InJ*, July 14, 1884; Garraty, *Henry Cabot Lodge*, 78; *DtFP*, April 19, 1884; *NOP*, September 21, 1884.

12. *InS*, August 6, 1884; see also Joseph D. Foute to Leonidas C. Houk, July 5, 1884, Leonidas and John C. Houk MSS, Calvin M. McClung Historical Collection, Knox County Public Library, Knoxville.

13. *InJ*, July 3, 14, 1884; *ChTr*, September 10, 1884.

14. *StJG*, July 25, 1884; *NYEP*, August 8, 1884.

15. *HdTi*, October 20, 1884; Blodgett, *Gentle Reformers*, 46.

16. Benjamin H. Bristow to George Denny, September 18, 1884, Bristow MSS, LC; *NYEP*, October 28, 1884; Henry Ward to Samuel J. Randall, June 25, 1884, RanM.

17. John B. Henderson to Carl Schurz, July 1, 1884, and Schurz to Henderson, July 5, 1884, SchM.

18. *NYTi*, September 12, 1884; William C. Russell to Andrew D. White, November 14, 1884, White MSS, Cornell University, Ithaca.

19. *ChTr*, September 10, 12, 1884.

20. *NYEP*, August 26, September 15, 16, 17, 1884.

21. *ClPD*, October 28, 1884; Joseph Medill to James G. Blaine, June 13, 1884, BlaM; James M. Scovel to Walter Q. Gresham, June 12, 1884, Gresham MSS, LC; *ChDN*, April 26, 1884; *NYEP*, August 22, 29, 1884; *Hartford Times*, October 1, 1884; *Wilmington Every Evening*, September 25, 1884.

22. *LoC-J*, July 26, 1884; *StLP-D*, June 28, 1884; *Harper's Weekly*, July–November 1884.

23. *NYTr*, June 9, 10, September 3, 4, 6, 1884; *InS*, August 18, 1884; *Cazenovia Republican*, August 7, 1884; *CoMo*, September 13, October 27, 1884; *DMISR*, October 18, 1884; *NYTi*, September 11, 1884; John P. Foley to William E. Chandler, April 13, 1885, ChaM(NH).

24. George F. Williams to Carl Schurz, November 24, 1884, and George G. Wright to Horace C. Deming, September 6, 1884, SchM; *NYTi*, October 1, 7, 1884; *NYS*, January 18,

1885; Blodgett, *Gentle Reformers*, 8; *InS*, September 2, 1884, *NYTi*, October 7, 1884; *Meriden Daily Republican*, October 30, 1884; *CiE*, September 29, 1884.

25. Kinsley Twining to Carl Schurz, July 10, 1884, SchM; F. H. Miller to John D. Long, June 16, 1884, Long MSS, MHS; *ChTr*, September 27, 1884.

26. Morris, *Rise of Theodore Roosevelt*, 280, 289–90; *NYS*, October 12, 1884; Garraty, *Henry Cabot Lodge*, 78–83.

27. Nevins, *Grover Cleveland*, 178; *NYEP*, October 3, 1884; *ChTr*, September 24, October 11, 1884; George F. Edmunds to Justin S. Morrill, August 19, 1884, Morrill MSS, LC. On the potential third party, see Justin Smith Morrill letter to ?, n.d. [but clearly early summer 1884], Morrill MSS, LC.

28. *Nation*, November 11, 18, 1884; Henry Cabot Lodge to Carl Schurz, July 14, 1884, Lodge MSS, MHS. Later, much would be made of the Mugwumps' intemperate language against their old allies as a barrier to reconciliation. That was certainly true of Godkin, though it must be warned that his contempt for Hoar began years before the campaign. But many Mugwumps parted more in regret than rage. See Schurz to Lodge, July 12, 16, 1884, Rutherford B. Hayes to Schurz, June 23, 1884, and Albert H. Walker to Schurz, August 8, 1884, SchM; Moorfield Storey to Lodge, July 19, 1884, Lodge MSS, MHS; Schurz to Hayes, June 27, 1884, Hayes MSS, RBHML.

29. *NYEP*, August 8, 1884; Welch, *George Frisbie Hoar*, 124–28; George F. Hoar to Henry Cabot Lodge, November 18, 1884, Lodge MSS, MHS; *NYTr*, August 25, 1884; *InJ*, July 22, 1884; Russell, *Bare Hands and Stone Walls*, 37; Thomas M. Bayne to James G. Blaine, June 14, 1884, BlaM; McCall, *Thomas B. Reed*, 241 (quote).

CHAPTER THIRTEEN

1. *IW*, May 3, 1884.

2. Kleppner, *Third Electoral System*, 215–19, 234; *InS*, September 11, 12, 1884.

3. Brown, *Irish-American Nationalism*, 47–54, 65; Wharton Barker to Benjamin Harrison, June 4, 1888, Harrison MSS, LC; Dennis Clark, *Irish in Philadelphia*, 138–40.

4. Gordon, "Labor Boycott," 185–204; Foner, "Class, Ethnicity, and Radicalism," 6–43; *IW*, March 22, May 3, 1884 (quote).

5. *InJ*, September 3, 1884 (quote); *NYS*, October 21, 1884.

6. Brown, *Irish-American Nationalism*, 54–58, 64–83.

7. Ibid., 101–15; *BrE*, March 9, 1884.

8. John Devoy to Joseph Medill, July 26, 1884, BlaM.

9. Funchion, *Chicago's Irish Nationalists*, 78–88; *Boston Pilot*, August 23, 1884; *ChTr*, September 6, 1884.

10. G. Wrightson to John A. Logan, November 10, 1884, and George F. Dawson to Logan, October 8, 1884, LogM.

11. John Devoy to Joseph Medill, July 26, 1884, BlaM; *InS*, September 11, 12, 1884.

12. *IW*, November 8, 1884; Thomas Ewing Jr. to James G. Blaine, August 23, 1884, BlaM.

13. Paine, *Thomas Nast*, 249–50; *MnTr*, August 2, 1884.

14. *Auburn Daily Advertiser*, July 16, 1884; William E. Chandler to John C. Keenan, July 4, 1884, ChaM(NH); Anthony Higgins to Edward McPherson, October 7, 1884, McPM; *IW*, October 11, November 15, 1884; *Boston Pilot*, July 26, 1884.

15. *NYEP*, October 27, 1884.

16. A. E. Ford to James G. Blaine, n.d. [but probably early September 1884], and Patrick Ford to Blaine, October 18, 1884, BlaM.

17. *ClPD*, August 26, 1884; Jeremiah O'Donovan Rossa to Benjamin F. Butler, October 1, 1884, ButM.

18. *CoMo*, September 9, 1884; *Meriden Daily Republican*, October 6, 1884; *BaW&C*, October 27, 1884; *InJ*, October 17, 1884.

19. Henry Ward to Samuel J. Randall, June 25, 1884, RanM.

20. Walsh, "'A Fanatic Heart,'" 189–200; Kenny, "Molly Maguires," 360–76.

21. Kerby Miller, *Emigrants and Exiles*, 539–40; Brown, *Irish-American Nationalism*, 108–9; O'Grady, *Irish-Americans and Anglo-American Relations*, 87–92; *New York Irish-American*, January 23, 30, April 24, 1886.

22. Miller, *Emigrants and Exiles*, 495–97, 509–12, 528–35; Thernstrom, *Poverty and Progress*, 156–57, 177–78.

23. Thernstrom, *Poverty and Progress*, 174–84; Meager, "'Irish All the Time,'" 277–82.

24. Erie, *Rainbow's End*, 1–66.

25. Obituary, *IW*, February 23, 1884.

26. *DtFP*, August 1, 1884.

27. *Trenton Daily State Gazette*, October 1, 1884; *New York Irish-American*, October 11, 1884; *HdTi*, October 11, 1884.

28. *New York Irish-American*, October 11, 1884; *InJ*, July 1, 1884.

29. *Boston Pilot*, September 20, October 4, 11, 1884; *Milwaukee Sentinel*, October 25, 1884; John Devoy to Joseph Medill, July 26, 1884, BlaM; Funchion, *Chicago's Irish Nationalists*, 88.

30. Brown, *Irish-American Nationalism*, 157–58; Funchion, *Chicago's Irish Nationalists*, 88–119; *New York Irish-American*, January 30, April 3, 17, 1886.

31. H. L. Terrell to James G. Blaine, September 11, 1884, BlaM; *StLG-D*, September 28, October 23, 24, 1884.

32. *BrE*, October 25, 1884; Rebecca Edwards, "Gender in American Politics," 107–14.

CHAPTER FOURTEEN

1. *StLP-D*, May 30, 1884. The best, shrewdest study of Butler's campaign is Edward James, "Benjamin Butler Runs for President," 65–89.

2. *ChTr*, September 6, 10, 1884; *NYS*, October 19, 21, 1884.

3. *Dubuque Herald*, August 11, 1888; *ClPD*, September 3, 1884.

4. *ChDN*, October 1, 1884; *St. Paul Dispatch*, September 25, 1884.

5. Benjamin F. Butler to Henry Barnard, July 21, 1884, and Butler to Louis F. Post, July 31, 1884, ButM.

6. James G. Blaine to Stephen Elkins, July 27, 1884, ElkM; Whitelaw Reid to Warner Miller, July 21, 1884, ReiM; *ChTr*, September 11, 1884; Samuel Fessenden to Blaine, July 21, 1884, and Joseph Hawley to Blaine, n.d. [late July 1884], BlaM; *DtFP*, July 19, 1884.

7. West, *Lincoln's Scapegoat General*, 388–89, 394–96, 405–6; *NYEP*, August 22, 1884; *StLG-D*, October 26, 1884; Benjamin F. Butler to William E. Chandler, August 1, 1884, ButM.

8. West, *Lincoln's Scapegoat General*, 402–3; *NYS*, October 3, 19, 21, 22, 1884; *ChTr*, September 1, 29, 1884; *StLP-D*, September 13, 1884.

9. C. S. Hampton to N. A. Plympton, October 3, 1884, ButM; *InJ*, July 7, 1884.

10. James, "Benjamin Butler Runs for President," 80, 87; West, *Lincoln's Scapegoat General*, 392–93; Blanton Duncan to Benjamin F. Butler, October 5, 1884, ButM; Thomas V. Cooper to James G. Blaine, August 8, 1884, Edward McPherson to Blaine, August 28, 1884, and James S. Clarkson to Blaine, September 3, 1884, BlaM.

11. Terence V. Powderly to Wharton Barker, September 17, November 20, 1884, Barker to William Carroll, November 18, 1884, and Barker to Benjamin Harrison, November 21, 1884, Barker MSS, LC.

12. James, "Benjamin Butler Runs for President," 84; C. B. Smith to Benjamin F. Butler, September 20, 1884, J. S. Kalloch to N. A. Plympton, October 15, 1884, and William Nibel to Butler, October 27, 1884, ButM.

13. Benjamin F. Butler to William E. Chandler, September 24, 1884, ButM.

14. W. A. Fowler to Benjamin F. Butler, October 7, 1884, and N. A. Plympton to Butler, October 9, 10, 1884, ButM; James, "Benjamin Butler Runs for President," 81–82, 86.

15. *DMISR*, September 16, 1884.

16. James S. Clarkson to James G. Blaine, July 20, 1884, BlaM.

17. Stephen B. Elkins to Edward McPherson, October 11, 1884, McPM.

18. H. L. Terrell to James G. Blaine, September 11, 1884, BlaM.

19. *StLP-D*, January 9, 1885; *NYS*, January 10, 1885; Milton, *Age of Hate*, 619–20; William Moore diary, March 7, May 2, 1868, January 6, March 22, 1870, Johnson MSS, LC.

20. The full story of the negotiations, with letters reprinted, is in *NYTi*, January 14, 1885; *NYS*, January 10, 26, 1885; *ChTr*, January 10, 11, 13, 1885; and *StLP-D*, January 9, 13, 19, 20, 1885.

21. *ChTr*, January 12, 13, 1885; J. F. Legate to B. F. Simpson, October 10, 1884, Simpson to Legate, October 11, 1884, and W. H. Pearce to James S. Clarkson, January 28, 1885, ClaM.

22. Stephen B. Elkins to Edward McPherson, October 11, 1884, McPM; P. to R. C. Kerens, n.d. [October 1884], W. A. Johnson to R. C. Kerens, October 10, 1884, Aldridge [Stephen B. Elkins] to R. C. Kerens, October 14, 1884, and R. C. Kerens to Clarkson, January 2, 1885, ClaM; *ChTr*, January 13, 1885. On a possible diversion of Justice Department funds for St. John, see Lot Wright to James S. Clarkson, December 26, 1884, Kerens to Clarkson, December 31, 1884, January 2, 1885, and Fred Schaunte to Clarkson, January 3, 1885, ClaM.

23. "America" to *Cincinnati Commercial Gazette*, November 1884, Grosvenor MSS, Columbia University, New York.

24. *NYTr*, October 10, 11, 13, 14, 1884; *BrE*, October 25, 1884.

25. *NYTr*, October 13, 1884.

26. *NYTi*, January 14, 1885; *StLP-D*, January 19, 1885.

27. *CoMo*, October 24, 1884.

28. *BrE*, October 25, 1884.

29. Ibid., December 8, 1884; G. Wrightson to John A. Logan, November 10, 1884, LogM.

30. *BrE*, October 24, 1884.

31. Charles P. Button to Daniel S. Lamont, May 5, 1887, February 4, March 2, 1888, Cleveland MSS, LC.

32. *Omaha Republican*, August 31, September 3, 6, 18, 1888. George L. Miller issued a denial—of something entirely different. "I never told any one that Mr. St. John was bought by anybody in the campaign of 1884, and certainly not by Senator Gorman," he protested.

33. *ChTi*, October 4, 8, 1884; Polakoff, *Politics of Inertia*, 121–22; Thomas V. Cooper to James G. Blaine, August 8, 1884, BlaM; *NYS*, October 5, 1884.

34. *NYS*, January 18, 1885.

CHAPTER FIFTEEN

1. For awareness of the numbers, see *New York Age*, October 25, 1884.

2. The allusion was primarily classical: American politicians, never prouder than when they could be nicknamed "the old Roman," or "the American Cato," referred to the Punic Wars. For examples of its use, see *CiE*, October 4, 1883; *NYS*, October 8, 1888; and *Carson City Morning Appeal*, November 5, 1886.

3. *WhIn*, January 7, 1884.

4. Stephen H. Smith to Leonidas C. Houk, July 21, 1884, Leonidas and John C. Houk MSS, Calvin M. McClung Historical Collection, Knox County Public Library, Knoxville; Hirshson, *Farewell to the Bloody Shirt*, 123–26.

5. *Columbus Weekly Enquirer-Sun*, September 9, 1884.

6. Hyman, *Anti-Redeemers*, 21–22, 28–53.

7. Robert McKee to John T. Morgan, January 8, 1883, McKee MSS, Alabama Department of Archives and History, Montgomery. On Alabama's failings, see Rogers, "Agrarianism in Alabama," 100–102.

8. Hair, *Bourbonism and Agrarian Protest*, 107–19, 129–37.

9. T. P. Devereux to Edward McPherson, August 25, 1884, McPM; *WhIn*, January 7, 1884. On the limits of North Carolina Bourbonism, see Escott, *Many Excellent People*, 181–95.

10. *NYEP*, May 22, 1884.

11. W. H. Hidell to Rebecca Felton, September 29, 1884, Felton MSS, University of Georgia, Athens; Thomas Settle to John A. Logan, June 16, 1884, Settle MSS, Southern Historical Collection, Wilson Library, University of North Carolina, Chapel Hill; E. O. Locke to Edward McPherson, October 23, 1884, and Horatio Bisbee Jr. to McPherson, October 19, 1884, McPM; Lynch, *Facts of Reconstruction*, 225–26.

12. L. E. McComas to Edward McPherson, September 21, 1883, McPM; James E. Richardson to William E. Chandler, August 1, 1882, and J. R. G. Pitkin to Chandler, June 8, 1882, ChaM.

13. *NYEP*, May 22, 1884.

14. *Jacksonville Florida Times-Union*, October 14, 25, 1884; E. O. Locke to Edward McPherson, October 14, 1884, Louis E. McComas to McPherson, September 15, 1884, Joseph P. Evans to McPherson, September 24, 1884, and Joseph H. Sloss to McPherson, June 8, 1884, McPM; *Huntsville Gazette*, November 1, 1884 (quote).

15. William Mahone to Walter Q. Gresham, August 28, September 20, 1884, Gresham MSS, LC; *New York Age*, September 6, 1884; *Washington Grit*, March 29, April 26, 1884; *NYTr*, August 30, 1884; *NYEP*, August 28, 29 (quote), September 3, 1884.

16. *RN&O*, July 30, August 5, 1884; Bromberg, "Pure Democracy and White Supremacy," 97–100.

17. Currie-McDaniel, *Carpetbagger of Conscience*, 165–69, 174–75; *StLG-D*, May 2, 1884; interview with Postmaster McKee, Mississippi, fall 1884, in Southern notebooks, Folder B, BanM; *Washington Grit*, April 12, 1884; *New York Age*, August 16, 1884.

18. *Huntsville Gazette*, November 1, 1884; *Jacksonville Florida Times-Union*, September 11, 1884.

19. *Huntsville Gazette*, October 11, November 1, 1884.

20. Interview with Postmaster McKee, Mississippi, fall 1884, in Southern notebooks, Folder B, BanM (first quote); John R. Lynch to Edward McPherson, September 9, 1884, McPM; *Memphis Daily Appeal*, July 16, 20, August 30, 1884; *Huntsville Gazette*, September 20, October 11, November 1, 1884.

21. E. Clark, *Francis Warrington Dawson*, 120–22; *Richmond Dispatch*, August 14, 30, September 27, 1884; *New York Age*, August 4, 1884; *Jacksonville Florida Times-Union*, September 11, October 2, 1884; *NOT-D*, September 3, 1884.

22. Roush, "Aftermath of Reconstruction," 343–44; *Huntsville Gazette*, August 2, 1884; interview with President Pope of Tougaloo University and with Rev. Harris, both in Mississippi, fall 1884, Southern notebooks, Folder B, BanM.

23. *Huntsville Gazette*, August 2, 1884; E. Clark, *Francis Warrington Dawson*, 121–22, 196–98; see *Savannah Tribune*, September 24, 1892; Benjamin Butterworth to John Sherman, November 7, 1881, ShrM.

24. N. Dumont to Edward McPherson, October 11, 1884, McPM.

25. Interview, Wilson, black editor, *Greenville Republican*, fall 1884, Southern notebooks, Folder A, BanM.

26. Hair, *Bourbonism and Agrarian Protest*, 115; L. E. McComas to Edward McPherson, September 21, 1884, McPM.

27. *Columbus Weekly Enquirer-Sun*, September 30, 1884.

28. *RN&O*, June 27, 1884; *NYTr*, August 30, 1884.

29. See, for example, *AtC*, October 29, 1884; interview, Judge Millsaps, Mississippi, September 1884, Southern notebooks, Folder B, BanM.

30. *DMISR*, October 1, 1884 (first quote); *InJ*, October 7 (second quote), November 3, 1884; *SpR*, December 12, 1884; *CoMo*, September 10, 1884; *Meriden Daily Republican*, October 10, 27, 1884; *Cazenovia Republican*, July 17, 1884; *StLG-D*, October 27, 1884 (last quote).

31. "A Democrat" to Edward McPherson, July 20, 1884, McPM.

32. *Columbus Weekly Enquirer-Sun*, September 9, 23 (first quote), October 7 (second quote), 1884.

33. *Columbus Weekly Enquirer-Sun*, September 30, 1884.

34. *New York Age*, September 13, 1884; *Jacksonville Florida Times-Union*, November 14, 1884.

35. *Jackson Clarion*, October 15, 29, 1884; *Jacksonville Florida Times-Union*, September 11, October 26, 1884.

36. *Jacksonville Florida Times-Union*, September 11, 1884.

37. *New York Age*, September 27, 1884; *Cazenovia Republican*, September 25, 1884; *Washington Grit*, April 26, 1884; "Dunbar," "W.J.S.," *DtEN*, October 27, 31, November 2, 3, 1888.

38. Interview, Robert Smalls, South Carolina, Southern notebooks, Notebook E, BanM; *DtEN*, October 26, 27, 31, 1888; *Jacksonville Florida Times-Union*, October 2, 1884.

39. *Richmond Dispatch*, October 2, 1884.

40. *RN&O*, August 5, 8, 1884; *NYTr*, August 30, 1884; William S. Paico to Edward McPherson, September 3, 1884, and T. P. Devereux to McPherson, August 25, 1884, McPM.

41. *NOT-D*, October 22, 28, 31, 1884; *AtC*, October 29, 30, 1884; *Jacksonville Florida Times-Union*, October 24, November 2, 1884.

42. Horatio Bisbee Jr. to Edward McPherson, October 19, 1884, and E. O. Locke to McPherson, October 23, 1884, McPM; Thomas B. Keogh to John A. Logan, October 16, 1884 (quote), LogM.

43. *St. Louis Missouri Republican*, November 3, 1884; *NOP*, November 3, 1884; *New York Age*, November 8, 1884; *Washington Bee*, November 8, 1884.

44. Hirshson, *Farewell to the Bloody Shirt*, 126; *ChTi*, October 27, 1884.

CHAPTER SIXTEEN

1. "F.B.W.," *ChTi*, October 14, 1884.

2. *DMISR*, October 25, 1884; *ChTi*, October 14, 1884; *MnTr*, August 1, 1884 (quote).

3. *StJG*, November 2, 1884; *StLG-D*, July 19, 1884.

4. *StJG*, November 2, 1884.

5. *NYTr*, August 29, 1884; *ChTr*, September 8, 10, 1884; *StLP-D*, September 15, 1884; *StLG-D*, July 19, 1884.

6. *NYTi*, August 24, 25, September 10, 1884; A. Lindon Surdee to Edward McPherson, August 25, 1884, McPM; Benjamin F. Jones to John A. Logan, September 2, 1884, LogM; Benjamin Harrison to Eugene Hay, August 26, 1884, Harrison MSS, LC; *BaC*, August 27, 1884; *NYEP*, September 1, 2, 1884; B. B. Smalley to William Vilas, September 11, 1884, Vilas MSS, SHSW.

7. *ChTr*, September 10, 1884; John Roach to James G. Blaine, September 10, 1884, BlaM; George F. Dawson to Mrs. Logan, September 11, 1884, LogM.

8. Marcus A. Hanna to John Sherman, June 25, 1884, ShrM; Carson Lake to A. Conger, July 12, 1884, ConM; James S. Clarkson to James G. Blaine, August 28, 1884, BlaM.

9. C. L. Kurtz to John Sherman, September 8, 1884, Charles M. Grosvenor to Sherman, September 13, 1884, and J. C. Donaldson to Sherman, August 29, 1884, ShrM; John F. Oglevee to Samuel Fessenden, August 10, 1884, Homer C. Jones to A. Conger, August 22, 1884, and Albert M. Pratt to Conger, August 9, 1884, ConM.

10. *HdTi*, October 13, 1884; James S. Clarkson to James G. Blaine, August 31, 1884, BlaM.

11. J. C. Donaldson to John Sherman, August 29, 1884, ShrM; James S. Clarkson to James G. Blaine, August 28, 31, 1884, BlaM.

12. *StLP-D*, October 28, 1884; *LoC-J*, October 30, 1884; *InN*, October 20, 1884.

13. *StLP-D*, October 25, 1884 (first quote); John A. Logan to James G. Blaine, September 1, 1884, BlaM; James S. Clarkson to Blaine, July 22, 1884, and L. G. Dynes to Blaine, December 1, 1884 (third quote), BlaM; "B.," *NYEP*, October 9, 1884; *InN*, November 3, 8, 1884.

14. ? to Stephen B. Elkins, August 26, 1884, ElkM; *InN*, October 17, 1884 (first quote);

"B.," *NYEP*, October 9, 1884; James S. Clarkson to James G. Blaine, July 22, 31, August 28, 31, 1884, BlaM; C. L. Kurtz to John Sherman, September 11, 1884, ShrM; W. W. Dudley to Benjamin Harrison, August 14, 24, 1884, Harrison MSS, LC; Clarkson to A. Conger, September 1, 6, 1884, ConM.

15. Clinton Morrison (September 23, 1884), Charles Rawson (September 15, 1884), Charles Baird (September 13, 1884), George R. Haynes (September 12, 1884), H. C. Searles (September 13, 1884), O. W. Hale (September 12, 1884), George L. Barnes (September 26, 1884); Lewis T. Wolle (September 22, 1884), and William G. Park (September 16, 1884), all to Arthur L. Conger, ConM.

16. *StLP-D*, October 29, 1884; *LoC-J*, October 30, 1884; W. W. Dudley to Benjamin Harrison, August 14, 1884, Harrison MSS, LC; Benjamin Harrison to Wharton Barker, October 25, November 1, 1884, and Wharton Barker to Harrison, October 30, 1884, Wharton Barker MSS, LC.

17. H. L. Terrell to James G. Blaine, August 6, 1884, BlaM; *ChTr*, September 21, 24, 29, 1884; *HdC*, September 11, 1884; *ChTr*, September 26, 1884.

18. Joseph B. Foraker to R. McMurdy, August 1, 1884, Foraker MSS, CHS; Stephen B. Elkins to John Sherman, September 9, 1884, and Charles B. Foster to Sherman, April 15, 1884, ShrM; *ChTr*, September 25, 1884; John Sherman to Henry Cabot Lodge, September 5, 1884, Lodge MSS, MHS.

19. Jones, *John A. Logan*, 191–92; *ChTr*, September 25, 1884; *CiE*, October 16, 1884; *InN*, October 9, 1884.

20. Stephen B. Elkins to John Sherman, September 9, 1884, ShrM.

21. R. W. Patterson to James S. Clarkson, September 20, 1884, (quote), ClaM; W. M. Grosvenor to James G. Blaine, September 11, 1884, and H. L. Terrell to Blaine, September 14, 1884, BlaM.

22. *InN*, June 13, November 4, 1884; Murat Halstead to James G. Blaine, June 12, 1884, BlaM.

23. *ChTr*, September 22, 1884; *NYS*, September 20, 1884.

24. *Elmira Daily Advertiser*, October 28, 1884; *NYS*, September 25, 1884; *NYTr*, September 25, 1884; *ChTr*, September 27, 1884; *Wilmington Every Evening*, September 26, 1884; *ClPD*, October 1, 1884; John S. Long to Henry Cabot Lodge, October 7, 1884, Lodge MSS, MHS; John Hay to James G. Blaine, September 27, 1884, BlaM.

25. Charles Foster to John Sherman, April 15, 1884, and S. D. Cowden to John F. Oglevee, August 29, 1884, ShrM; *NYS*, September 29, 1884; *ChTr*, October 1, 9, 1884.

26. O. Jay to John Sherman, September 12, 1884, ShrM; Addison G. Harris to Walter Q. Gresham, August 13, 1884, Gresham MSS, LC; S. C. Harris to Robert S. Taylor, September 26, 1884, Taylor MSS, ISL; *StLP-D*, October 27, 1884; Theron Keator to Edward McPherson, August 16, 1884, McPM.

27. B. B. Smalley to William Vilas, September 11, 1884, E. B. Dickinson to Vilas, September 11, 1884, and Austin Brown to Vilas, September 24, 1884, Vilas MSS, SHSW.

28. *NYH*, October 13, 1884; *InN*, October 15, 1884; *ClPD*, October 20, 1884; Don M. Dickinson to William Vilas, October 1884, and William Barnum to Vilas, October 17, 1884, Vilas MSS, SHSW.

29. *DMISR*, October 16, 1884; *InN*, October 15, 17, 1884.

30. *CiE*, October 13, 1884 (quote); *NYH*, October 15, 16, 1884; *ClPD*, October 15, 20, 1884.

31. *WhIn*, April 8, May 31, September 1, 1884.

32. Warner Miller to James G. Blaine, September 9, 1884, BlaM; *ChTr*, September 29, October 6 (quote), 1884.

33. John W. Mason Diary, August–November 1884, O. G. Scofield to Mason, June 18, 1884, Charles Emory Smith to Mason, July 22, 1884, and W. J. W. Cowden to Mason, October 6, 1884, Mason MSS, WVUL; *WhIn*, September 3, 1884; Henry G. Davis to Lewis Baker, June 11, 1884, Davis MSS, WVUL.

34. *NYEP*, September 15, 1884; *WhIn*, August 15, 16, 1884.

35. *ChTr*, September 29, October 6, 1884; *WhIn*, July 29, August 2, 1884; B. B. Smalley to William Vilas, August 11, 1884, Vilas MSS, SHSW; Arthur Pue Gorman to Henry G. Davis, October 16, 1884, Davis MSS, WVUL.

36. *InN*, November 4, 1884.

37. *CiE*, June 24, 25, 1884; *InN*, June 24, 25, 26, 1884.

38. *InS*, August 9, 14, 15, 27, September 3, 13, October 3, 1884; *InJ*, September 10, 13, 1884; William H. Calkins to William E. Chandler, September 14, 1884, ChaM.

39. Benjamin Harrison to John Glover, September 19, 1884, Harrison MSS, LC; Schuyler Colfax to James G. Blaine, September 3, 1884, James S. Clarkson to Blaine, July 22, 1884, and L. G. Dynes to Blaine, December 1, 1884, BlaM; *InN*, June 18, September 24, 1884.

40. B. B. Plumb to Walter Q. Gresham, October 1, 1884, Gresham MSS, LC; "Creep" to James S. Clarkson, October 30, November 1 (telegram 56, telegram 214), 1884, W. W. Dudley to Clarkson, October 31, November 2, 1884, and John C. New to Clarkson, October 31, 1884, ClaM; James S. Clarkson to Benjamin Harrison, October 15, 1888, Harrison MSS, LC.

41. James N. Tyner to James S. Clarkson, November 23, 1884, ClaM; *InN*, November 4 (quote), 8, 1884.

42. H. L. Terrell to James G. Blaine, August 6, 1884, BlaM.

CHAPTER SEVENTEEN

1. J. B. Chaffee to James G. Blaine, June 10, 1884, BlaM; *NYS*, January 4, 1885.

2. Whitelaw Reid to Edwin Cowles, May 16, 1884, Reid to James G. Blaine, October 18, 1884, and Reid to M. H. DeYoung, October 31, 1884, ReiM; Titus Sheard to Blaine, July 22, 1884, BlaM.

3. Whitelaw Reid to J. M. Turner, June 19, 1884, ReiM; "Gath," *CiE*, November 15, 1884; *NYTr*, November 17, 1884; *DMISR*, August 1, 16, 1884; Stanwood, *James Gillespie Blaine*, 285.

4. *InJ*, July 1, September 8, 1884; George Davis to A. L. Conger, October 7, 1884, ConM; *InS*, October 24, 1884; *InN*, June 14, 1884.

5. Hudson, *Random Recollections*, 199–204; *NYTr*, November 17, 1884; Russell, *These Shifting Scenes*, 222–23; Peck, *Twenty Years of the Republic*, 42. For the original joke (clearly nothing more than rumor) ungussied with committees and visitations of prominent dignitaries, see *Richmond Dispatch*, September 19, 1884; *ChTi*, October 29, 1884.

6. Stone, *Fifty Years a Journalist*, 153 (first quote); *Dubuque Herald*, August 31, 1888.

7. Jordan, *Roscoe Conkling*, 421; James S. Clarkson to Stephen B. Elkins, February 2, 1887, ElkM; "Gath," *CiE*, January 21, 1885.

8. John B. Hamilton to John A. Logan, August 26, 1884, LogM; *NYTi*, June 25, 27, 1884; James D. Warren to James G. Blaine, July 1, November 29, 1884, Whitelaw Reid to Blaine, October 18, 1884, and Alonzo B. Cornell to Blaine, November 15, 1884, BlaM; "America" to the *CiCG*, November 1884, Grosvenor MSS, Columbia University, New York; *NYS*, January 4, 1885; Albert Daggett to William E. Chandler, September 17, 1884, ChaM.

9. For evidence that Kelly always meant to support the ticket eventually, see John Kelly to S. L. M. Barlow, July 16, 1884, Barlow MSS, Huntington Library, San Marino.

10. Nevins, *Grover Cleveland*, 170–71, 175; A. M. Gibson to James G. Blaine, July 19, 1884, and A. E. Ford to Blaine, n.d. [probably early September 1884], BlaM; *NYS*, November 29, 1884; John Kelly to David Bennett Hill, September 4, 1884, and Bourke Cockran to Hill, September 22, 1884, Hill MSS, NYSL; *NYEP*, September 29, 1884; *CiE*, October 1, 1884.

11. Nevins, *Grover Cleveland*, 170–71.

12. *NYEP*, September 29, 30, 1884.

13. *NYS*, October 1, 2, 22, 1884; "Gath," *CiE*, October 1, 25, 1884.

14. Marquis James, *Merchant Adventurer*, 196; *NYEP*, October 8, 20, November 17, 1884; *BrE*, October 21, 1884.

15. *BrE*, October 21, 1884; James Doyle to William E. Chandler, October 23, 1884, ChaM.

16. *NYTr*, March 21, 1886; George F. Dawson to John A. Logan, October 23, 1884, and John C. New to Logan, October 22, 1884, LogM; James G. Blaine to Whitelaw Reid, October 18, 1884, and Reid to Blaine, October 18, 1884, ReiM; Marcus, *Grand Old Party*, 96–98.

17. Muzzey, *James G. Blaine*, 316.

18. R. W. McMurdy to John A. Logan, August 23, September 2, 1884, LogM; *NYTr*, November 23, 1884; *NYS*, November 29, 1884; *NYW*, November 2, 1884.

19. *Meriden Daily Republican*, October 13, 1884; *BoT*, October 3, 1884; *InJ*, September 23, November 2, 1884; "Baptist Clergyman," *NYEP*, November 3, 1884; *ClPD*, October 20, 1884.

20. *BrE*, October 29, 31, 1884; *NYTr*, October 30, 1884.

21. *NYTr*, October 14, 30, 1884.

22. *ChTr*, October 30, 31, 1884; *Cedar Rapids Evening Gazette*, October 31, November 1, 1884.

23. *NYS*, November 29, 1884. Later, Blaine reportedly told a journalist that he selected Burchard himself, as a way out of the dispute. Hudson, *Random Recollections*, 211.

24. "Gath," *CiE*, November 6, 1884; *NYTr*, December 13, 1884.

25. "Kink," *InN*, March 14, 1885; obituary, *NYH*, September 26, 1891; *NYW*, November 2, 1884.

26. *ChTr*, October 30, 1884; Farrelly, " 'Rum, Romanism and Rebellion' Resurrected," 262–70.

27. For reports that Blaine *did* hear "Mormonism," see *BoT*, October 30, 1884; *ChDN*, November 14, 1884; and *NYS*, November 19, 1884.

28. *BrE*, October 29, 1884; Mack, " 'Rum, Romanism, and Rebellion,' " 1140–41; Harlan, "Phrase That Beat Blaine," 650; "Strategy of National Campaigns," 483–94; Hudson, *Random Recollections*, 212. For that quiet anti-Catholic suspicion of Blaine, see *Washington Grit*, May 17, 1884.

29. Mack, "'Rum, Romanism, and Rebellion,'" 1141.

30. Hudson, *Random Recollections*, 208–9.

31. *BrE*, October 29, 30, 31, November 1, 1884; *CiE*, October 30, 31, November 1, 1884; *ChDN*, October 29, 30, 31, November 1, 1884; *BoH*, October 30, 31, 1884.

32. *Cedar Rapids Evening Gazette*, October 29, 1884; *InJ*, October 30, November 1, 1884; *NYTr*, October 30, November 1, 2, 1884; *Trenton Daily State Gazette*, October 30, 1884; *DMISR*, October 30, 1884; Welch, *George Frisbie Hoar*, 132.

33. *NYW*, November 2, 1884; "Gath," *CiE*, November 6, 7, 1884.

34. *NYEP*, November 1, 1884; *InS*, November 1, 1884; *NYTr*, November 3, 1884; Mack, "'Rum, Romanism, and Rebellion,'" 1142; *SFAC*, November 3, 1884.

35. *ClPD*, November 3, 1884; "Gath," *CiE*, November 7, 1884; *NYTr*, November 21, 1884; G. Wrightson to John A. Logan, November 10, 1884, LogM; Joseph Medill to James G. Blaine, n.d. [but clearly early November 1884], BlaM.

36. *DtFP*, November 3, 1884.

37. Horace Porter to John A. Logan, October 25, 1884, LogM; *ClPD*, October 29, 1884; *NYTr*, October 30, 1884.

38. *NYW*, October 30, 1884.

39. *BrE*, October 26, 1884; Gribayedoff, "Pictorial Journalism," 480; Juergens, *Pulitzer and the World*, 100–105; *NYTr*, October 31, 1884.

40. Reeves, *Gentleman Boss*, 389; Marcus, *Grand Old Party*, 99; *BrE*, November 13, 1884.

41. *NYS*, October 22, 1884; "Gath," *CiE*, October 27, 1884; *BrE*, October 16, 1884; E. Edwards, "Tammany under John Kelly," 328.

42. Whitelaw Reid to W. B. Somerville, November 3, 1884, ReiM; *CiE*, June 23, 1886; *NYW*, November 2, 1888; the sources were two insiders in the New York machine, Al Daggett—who had seen the cash before it was delivered—and Colonel George Bliss. Possible confirmation for the story may be found in Jay Gould to James Clarkson, December 28, 1884, ClaM; for assertions that the sum was really $150,000, see *BaC*, September 10, 1888.

43. *NYTr*, December 7, 1884; *CiE*, September 24, 1891; for insiders' impressions, see Charles P. Button to Daniel S. Lamont, March 22, 1885, and John Kelly to Button, n.d., enclosed, in Cleveland MSS, LC.

CHAPTER EIGHTEEN

1. *Nation*, November 13, 1884; *NYS*, November 8, 19, 1884; *HdTi*, November 8, 1884; Theodore C. Ecclesine to Daniel Lamont, November 8, 1884, Lamont MSS, LC; *InN*, November 6, 8, 10, 1884; *PhP*, November 26, 1884.

2. J. N. Edwards to Samuel J. Randall, November 16, 1884 (quote), and F. J. Hearne to Randall, November 16, 1884, RanM; Michael F. Tarpey to Stephen M. White, January 11, 1885, WhtM; *NYEP*, November 14, 1884; Benson, *Toward the Scientific Study*, 26–35.

3. This means less than it seems, to be sure. Democrats *always* lost them. Buffalo had gone Republican in 1876 and 1880. Seven of the thirteen wards went against Tilden in 1876, eight against Hancock, seven against Cleveland. Cleveland more than halved the Republican margin from four years before, took a larger share of the vote of every ward but two, and ran much better in the most hopelessly Republican wards than Hancock had. Still, his 48.1 percent of the vote fell 1.3 points short of Tilden's margin.

It also should be warned that Republican losses in Buffalo came at Cleveland's hands, not at St. John's. Prohibition played miserably in a brewery-laden town. Citywide, the Dries cast one vote in forty. St. John carried more than 1 percent of the vote in just two wards, the Eleventh and Thirteenth. Adding his vote to Blaine's, Republican margins would still have been down in eleven wards and up in two—which, by no coincidence, were the only two where more than 20 percent of the inhabitants were Irish-born.

4. *NYEP*, November 14, 20, 1884; *InJ*, November 10, 1884. On Tammany and County Democracy's role, see *NYH*, November 6, 7, 8, 1884, *NYTr*, December 7, 1884, *NYS*, December 9, 17, 1884; R. W. McMurdy to W. Bickham, November 5, 1884, and W. to Logan, November 5, 1884, LogM. For Grace's own opinion, see William R. Grace to Dennis O'Brien, November 6, 1884, and Grace to William L. Brown, November 8, 1884, Grace MSS, Columbia University, New York.

5. In Troy, as a whole, Cleveland's percentage of the vote was down 3.71 points from Hancock's, and Blaine's had fallen by 1.73. With the Prohibition and People's Parties in the race, some decline was to be expected.

Similar patterns for the banner Irish wards can be found in Buffalo and Rochester as well, though in each the Irish made up a smaller share of the electorate to begin with.

6. *AtC*, October 11, 1888; C. S. Beardsley to David B. Hill, December 1, 1884, Hill MSS, NYSL; Wharton Barker to Levi P. Morton, August 13, 1888, Quay MSS, LC.

7. Thomas Sherman, *Twenty Years with Blaine*, 96; Stoddard, *As I Knew Them*, 136; Hoar, *Autobiography*, 1:408; Terence V. Powderly to W. L. Stark, April 7, 1892, Powderly MSS, Catholic University, Washington.

8. *NYS*, November 9, 10, 1884.

9. Ibid., November 7, 9, 1884.

10. Muzzey, *James G. Blaine*, 323–24.

11. *NYEP*, November 17, 19, 1884.

12. *DMISR*, November 19, 1884; G. Wrightson to John A. Logan, November 10, 1884, and A. L. Woodworth to Logan, November 8, 1884, LogM; James N. Tyner to James S. Clarkson, November 23, 1884, and R. C. Kerens to Clarkson, November 29, 1884, ClaM.

13. Pocock, "Wet or Dry?" 174–90; *NYS*, November 30, December 11, 1884. A thorough quantification of New York's returns can be found in Albert Parker, "Empire Stalemate," 374–76, 446. See also Albert Parker, "Beating the Spread," 76–78.

Rensselaer County's vote offers a revealing hint on the Prohibition-Republican relationship. With few exceptions, the worse Democrats did in a township, the higher St. John's share of the vote. At the same time, here as elsewhere, Prohibitionist defections cannot tell the full story. Even if every voter for St. John had voted for Blaine, the latter's share of the vote in fourteen of the eighteen cities, towns, and villages would have been less than Garfield's in 1880; in absolute terms, he still would have had fewer votes in ten places than Garfield had (Democrats cast fewer votes in six; adding Butler's vote to theirs would have given them an increase on 1880 turnout only in Troy itself).

14. Butler's showing in cities, outside of New York and Boston was particularly discouraging for the working-class candidate. He got just 333 votes in Providence (1.53 percent), 33 in Camden, New Jersey (0.21 percent), 778 in Philadelphia (0.45 percent), 117 in Buffalo (0.32 percent), 39 in Schenectady (1.1 percent), and 48 in Syracuse (0.35 percent). In some upstate New York cities he did a little better: 2.63 percent of the vote in Albany, 4.68 percent in Troy, 2.3 percent in Rochester. His showing in the coal country of

Pennsylvania, especially where the Greenbackers had done well, was sometimes respectable: 4.4 percent of the vote in Allegheny County (Pittsburgh) and 5.93 percent Schuylkill, but in the New Jersey metropoli, he did disappointingly: 1.41 percent of the votes in Essex County (Newark) and 1.67 percent in Hudson County (Jersey City). Thanks to fusion arrangements with the Democrats, his party carried 5.29 percent of the vote in Wayne County, Michigan (Detroit); but fusion arrangements in Missouri and Nebraska wiped him off the ballot entirely, and he got no votes in St. Louis or Omaha. In Cook County (Chicago), he won just 0.62 percent and in Marion County (Indianapolis), 1.58 percent. His failure was particularly telling in Ohio's three great cities: in Hamilton County (Cincinnati), 0.25 percent, in Cuyahoga (Cleveland), 0.73 percent, and 0.72 percent in Franklin (Columbus). Indeed, in some cities—notably Buffalo, Providence, Camden, and Philadelphia, and in the urban counties of Cook, Cuyahoga, Franklin, and Dane, St. John got more votes then Butler did.

15. *NYEP*, November 3, 1892; M. W. Valkenburg to John A. Logan, November 14, 1884, and G. Wrightson to Logan, November 10, 1884, LogM; W. W. Dudley to James S. Clarkson, November 12, 1884, ClaM; "Gath," *CiE*, July 17, 1886.

16. On Daniel Manning's promises to the McLaughlin machine, see *BrE*, July 10, August 6, 1885.

17. Paine, *Thomas Nast*, 507.

18. Nor, indeed, was it as comprehensive in Massachusetts as its supporters claimed later. See Baum, " 'Noisy but Not Numerous," 241–56.

19. *Poughkeepsie Daily Eagle*, November 21, 1884; *NYTr*, November 18, 20, 1884.

20. Bromberg, "Pure Democracy and White Supremacy," 101–2; William Mahone to James G. Blaine, November 16, 1884, BlaM; Gross, "Negro in Alabama Politics," 127; Barr, *Reconstruction to Reform*, 73–74.

21. *Washington Bee*, November 8, 1884; *DtEN*, October 27, 30, 31, 1888; *Jacksonville Florida Times-Union*, November 19, 20, 1884.

22. *Jacksonville Florida Times-Union*, November 22, 1884; Miller, " 'Let Us Die,' " 414–19.

23. E. W. Clarke to John A. Logan, November 8, 1884 (quote), LogM; *New York Age*, August 23, 1884; *Washington Bee*, November 8, 1884; Blanton Duncan to Samuel J. Randall, November 26, 1888, RanM; Duncan to Daniel Lamont, September 8, 1888, Daniel S. Lamont MSS, LC; Minot S. Morgan to Thomas F. Bayard, November 21, 1884, BayM.

24. "Kink," *InN*, March 14, 1885; *NYTr*, November 30, 1884; *CiE*, September 26, 1891; *NYH*, November 22, 1884; Harlan, "Phrase That Beat Blaine," 651.

25. Joseph D. Weeks to James S. Clarkson, December 15, 1884 (quote), ClaM; *StLP-D*, January 9, 10, 1885.

26. *StLP-D*, January 2, 9, 16, 22, 26, 1885; *NYS*, January 10, 1885; *Leavenworth Evening Standard*, December 19, 1884.

27. *NYTr*, April 18, 1886 (quote); George Fred Williams to Carl Schurz, November 24, 1884, Schurz to Williams, November 23, 1884, and R. R. Bowker to Schurz, November 9, 1884, SchM.

28. Halstead, "Defeat of Blaine," 159–72; Jones, *John A. Logan*, 197–98; *NYEP*, November 28, 1884.

29. Howe, *Chester A. Arthur*, 277–81; James G. Blaine to Whitelaw Reid, December 6,

1884, and Steven B. Elkins to Reid, December 17, 1884, ReiM; *NYTr*, December 20, 22, 26, 1884; for Blaine's possible forgiveness of Conkling, see Beale, ed., *Letters of Mrs. Blaine*, 2:203.

30. *NYS*, March 12, 1885; Blodgett, "Political Leadership of Grover Cleveland," 291–94.

CHAPTER NINETEEN

1. Richard Vaux to William A. Courtenay, November 7, 1884, Courtenay MSS, South Caroliniana Library, Columbia.

2. *DMISR*, November 20, 1884.

3. *InJ*, November 21, 1884; *Nation*, March 10, 1887.

4. Welch, *Presidencies of Grover Cleveland*, 57–60.

5. "Kink," *InN*, March 12, April 4, 1885; *ChTr*, June 6, 1886.

6. Hammack, *Power and Society*, 162–66; *NYH*, November 18, 19, 1892; *BrE*, November 17, 1892.

7. Hammack, *Power and Society*, 146–47; *NYEP*, November 5, 1890; *NYS*, January 23, 1886, November 1, 2, 3, 6, 1890; *NYW*, November 5, 1890; McCaffrey, *When Bosses Ruled Philadelphia*, 97–123.

8. Muzzey, *James G. Blaine*, 388–90.

9. Bass, *"I Am a Democrat"*, 115–20; Marcus, *Grand Old Party*, 148; Frederick W. Holls to Warner Miller, November 8, 1888, Holls MSS, Columbia University, New York.

10. Merrill, *Bourbon Democracy of the Middle West*, 190; Rathgeber, "Democratic Party in Pennsylvania," 206–13; Morgan, *William McKinley*, 131–45.

11. *New York Age*, March 10, 1888; *NOT-D*, September 3, 1888; *Baltimore American*, September 11, 1888; Nevins, *Grover Cleveland*, 332–34.

12. *Rochester Union and Advertiser*, October 15, 1894.

13. Merrill, *Bourbon Leader*, 147–65; Hollingsworth, *Whirligig of Politics*, 5–68.

14. Speech draft, May 10, 1893, ClaM; *NYEP*, November 13, 1884.

15. Speech draft, May 10, 1893, ClaM; Clarkson, "Permanent Republican Clubs," 249–64.

16. *NYH*, September 18, 1892.

17. *PhR*, November 4, 1892.

18. *PhP*, October 23, 1892; *NYEP*, October 12, 1892; *Pittsburgh Post*, September 8, 1892; McGerr, *Decline of Popular Politics*.

Bibliography

MANUSCRIPT COLLECTIONS

Albany, New York
  New York State Library
    David Bennett Hill MSS
Athens, Georgia
  University of Georgia Library
    Rebecca Felton MSS
Boston, Massachusetts
  Houghton Library, Harvard University
    William Warland Clapp MSS
  Massachusetts Historical Society
    Edward Atkinson MSS
    Henry Cabot Lodge MSS
    John D. Long MSS
Bowdoin, Maine
  Bowdoin College Library
    Thomas Brackett Reed MSS
Chapel Hill, North Carolina
  Southern Historical Collection, Wilson Library, University of North Carolina
    Elliott-Gonzales MSS
    Thomas Settle MSS
Cincinnati, Ohio
  Cincinnati Historical Society
    Joseph Benson Foraker MSS
    Murat Halstead MSS
    Alexander Long MSS
Columbia, Missouri
  State Historical Society of Missouri
    James S. Rollins MSS
Columbia, South Carolina
  South Caroliniana Library
    William A. Courtenay MSS
    Charles Spencer McCall MSS
Columbus, Ohio
  Ohio Historical Society
    Henry Van Ness Boynton MSS
    Samuel S. Cox MSS (on microfilm)
    Charles L. Kurtz MSS
    William Henry Smith MSS
    Allen G. Thurman MSS
Concord, New Hampshire
  New Hampshire Historical Society
    William E. Chandler MSS

Durham, North Carolina
  Duke University
    Francis Warrington Dawson MSS
    Alexander Stephens MSS
Fremont, Ohio
  Rutherford B. Hayes Memorial Library
    A. L. Conger MSS
    Rutherford B. Hayes MSS
    John Sherman MSS
Indianapolis, Indiana
  Indiana Historical Society
    Robert S. Taylor MSS
  Indiana State Library
    Noble C. Butler MSS
    John B. Stoll MSS
    Lucius B. Swift MSS
Iowa City, Iowa
  State Historical Society of Iowa
    Cyrenus Cole MSS
    Jonathan P. Dolliver MSS
Ithaca, New York
  Cornell University
    Kernan Family MSS
    Andrew D. White MSS
Knoxville, Tennessee
  Calvin M. McClung Historical Collection, Knox County Public Library System
    Leonidas and John C. Houk MSS
Madison, Wisconsin
  State Historical Society of Wisconsin
    James Rood Doolittle MSS
    Elisha W. Keyes MSS
    William F. Vilas MSS
Montgomery, Alabama
  Alabama Department of Archives and History
    Robert McKee MSS
Morganton, West Virginia
  West Virginia Collection, West Virginia University Library
    Henry G. Davis MSS
    Stephen Benton Elkins MSS
    John W. Mason MSS
New Haven, Connecticut
  Sterling Memorial Library, Yale University
    Thomas Collier Platt MSS
    William Graham Sumner MSS
New York, New York
  Columbia University

    Frederic Bancroft MSS
    Belmont Family MSS
    William R. Grace MSS
    William M. Grosvenor MSS
    Frederick W. Holls MSS
  New York Public Library
    John Bigelow MSS
    James B. Butler MSS
    Samuel S. Cox MSS
    Samuel Jones Tilden MSS
    David A. Wells MSS
Palo Alto, California
  Stanford University
    Stephen Mallory White MSS
Philadelphia, Pennsylvania
  The Historical Society of Pennsylvania
    Jay Cooke MSS
    William D. Kelley MSS
    Wayne MacVeagh MSS
    Painter Family MSS
    James Swank MSS
  Rare Book and Manuscript Library, University of Pennsylvania
    Samuel J. Randall MSS
St. Louis, Missouri
  Missouri Historical Society
    James O. Broadhead MSS
San Marino, California
  Huntington Library
    Thomas R. Bard MSS
    Samuel L. M. Barlow MSS
Springfield, Illinois
  Illinois State Historical Society
    David Davis MSS
    Ingersoll Family MSS
    William Ralls Morrison MSS
    John M. Palmer MSS
Washington, D.C.
  Catholic University
    Terence V. Powderly MSS
  Library of Congress
    William Allen MSS
    Wharton Barker MSS
    Bayard Family MSS
    James G. Blaine MSS
    Benjamin Helm Bristow MSS
    Benjamin Franklin Butler MSS

Frank Carpenter MSS
William E. Chandler MSS
James S. Clarkson MSS
Grover Cleveland MSS
Henry Laurens Dawes MSS
James Rood Doolittle MSS
Walter Q. Gresham MSS
Benjamin Harrison MSS
Andrew Johnson MSS
Daniel S. Lamont MSS
John A. Logan MSS
Edward McPherson MSS
Manton Marble MSS
Justin Smith Morrill MSS
Matthew Stanley Quay MSS
Whitelaw Reid MSS
Theodore Roosevelt MSS
Carl Schurz MSS
John Sherman MSS
William Tecumseh Sherman MSS
Elihu Washburne MSS
David A. Wells MSS
William C. Whitney MSS

NEWSPAPERS AND MAGAZINES OF OPINION

Akron Summit County Beacon
Annapolis Maryland Republican
Atchison Daily Champion
Atlanta Constitution
Auburn Daily Advertiser
Baltimore American
Bangor Commercial
Bangor Whig and Courier
Boston Evening Transcript
Boston Herald
Boston Morning Journal
Boston Pilot
Brooklyn Daily Eagle
Bucyrus Journal
Buffalo Commercial
Buffalo Courier
Buffalo Evening Telegraph
Buffalo Express
Burlington Free Press
Canajoharie Courier

Cazenovia (N.Y.) Republican
Cedar Rapids Evening Gazette
Charleston News and Courier
Chicago Daily News
Chicago Times
Chicago Tribune
Cincinnati Commercial
Cincinnati Commercial Gazette
Cincinnati Enquirer
Cincinnati Gazette
Circleville (Oh.) Democrat and Watchman
Cleveland Gazette
Cleveland Plain Dealer
Columbus (Ga.) Weekly Enquirer-Sun
Columbus (Oh.) Daily Times
Concord Monitor
Crystal Springs (Miss.) Monitor
Dayton Daily Democrat
Des Moines Iowa State Register
Detroit Evening News

Detroit Free Press
Dubuque Daily Herald
Elmira Daily Advertiser
Evansville Courier
Frankfort Tri-Weekly Kentucky Yoeman
Galena Daily Gazette
Georgetown Brown County News
Harper's Weekly
Hartford Courant
Hartford Times
Hocking Sentinel
Huntsville (Ala.) Gazette
Indianapolis Daily Sentinel
Indianapolis Journal
Indianapolis News
Irish World and American Industrial
    Laborer
Jackson Weekly Clarion
Jacksonville Florida Times-Union
Lancaster Ohio Eagle
Leavenworth Evening Standard
Lewiston Evening Journal
Louisville Commercial
Louisville Courier-Journal
Manchester Union
Marietta (Oh.) Register
Mechanicville (N.Y.) Mercury
Memphis Daily Appeal
Meriden Daily Republican
Milan (Tenn.) Exchange
Milwaukee Sentinel
Minneapolis Tribune
Mobile (Ala.) Register
Mount Gilead Morrow County Register
Nation
Newark Daily Advertiser
New Haven Register
New Orleans Daily Picayune
New Orleans Times-Democrat
New York Age
New York Evening Post
New York Graphic
New York Herald
New York Irish-American

New York Sun
New York Times
New York Tribune
New York World
Norfolk Virginian
Norton's Union-Intelligencer
Omaha Republican
Oneida Dispatch
Philadelphia Inquirer
Philadelphia Press
Philadelphia Record
Philadelphia Times
Pittsburgh Post
Portland (Me.) Eastern Argus
Portland (Me.) Transcript
Poughkeepsie Daily Eagle
Raleigh News and Courier
Ravenna (Oh.) Democratic Press
Richmond Dispatch
Richmond Whig
Rochester (N.Y.) Union and Advertiser
San Francisco Alta California
Sandusky (Oh.) Register
Saugerties (N.Y.) Telegraph
Savannah Tribune
Springfield (Ill.) State Register
Springfield (Mass.) Republican
St. Joseph Gazette
St. Louis Globe-Democrat
St. Louis Post-Dispatch
St. Paul Dispatch
St. Paul Pioneer Press
Topeka Daily Capital
Trenton Daily State Gazette
Troy Daily Press
Washington Bee
Washington Critic
Washington Grit
Washington Post
Watertown Daily Times
Wheeling Intelligencer
Wilmington Every Evening
Zanesville Daily Courier

Anderson, Eric. *Race and Politics in North Carolina, 1872–1901: The Black Second.* Baton Rouge: Louisiana State University Press, 1981.

Armitage, Charles H. *Grover Cleveland as Buffalo Knew Him.* Buffalo: Buffalo Evening News, 1926.

Armstrong, William M., ed. *The Gilded Age Letters of E. L. Godkin.* Albany: State University of New York Press, 1974.

Bader, Robert S. *Prohibition in Kansas: A History.* Lawrence: University Press of Kansas, 1986.

Barnes, James A. *John G. Carlisle, Financial Statesman.* New York: Dodd, Mead & Co., 1931.

Barr, Alwyn. *Reconstruction to Reform: Texas Politics, 1876–1906.* Austin: University of Texas Press, 1971.

Bass, Herbert J. *"I Am a Democrat": The Political Career of David B. Hill.* Syracuse: Syracuse University Press, 1961.

Beale, Harriet S. Blaine, ed. *Letters of Mrs. James G. Blaine.* 2 vols. New York: Duffield & Co., 1908.

Bensel, Richard F. *Yankee Leviathan: The Origins of Central State Authority in America, 1859–1877.* Cambridge: Cambridge University Press, 1990.

Benson, Lee. *Merchants, Farmers and Railroads: Railroad Regulation and New York Politics, 1850–1887.* Cambridge: Harvard University Press, 1955.

———. *Toward the Scientific Study of History.* Philadelphia: J. B. Lippincott, 1972.

Bigelow, John, ed. *Letters and Literary Memorials of Samuel J. Tilden.* 2 vols. New York: Harper, 1908.

Blodgett, Geoffrey. *The Gentle Reformers: Massachusetts Democrats in the Cleveland Era.* Cambridge: Harvard University Press, 1966.

Boskin, Joseph, *Sambo: The Rise and Demise of an American Jester.* New York: Oxford University Press, 1986.

Brann, William Cowper. *Brann the Iconoclast.* 10 vols. St. Louis: Phillips, 189-.

Brown, Thomas N. *Irish-American Nationalism, 1870–1890.* Philadelphia: J. B. Lippincott, 1966.

Buck, Paul H. *The Road to Reunion, 1865–1900.* New York: Random House, 1937.

Calhoun, Charles W. *Gilded Age Cato: The Life of Walter Q. Gresham.* Lexington: University of Kentucky Press, 1988.

Cary, Edward. *George William Curtis.* Boston: Houghton Mifflin, 1894.

Cashman, Sean D. *America in the Gilded Age.* New York: New York University Press, 1984.

Chalfant, Edward. *Better in Darkness: A Biography of Henry Adams: His Second Life, 1862–1891.* Hamden, Conn.: Archon, 1994.

Cherrington, Ernest H. *The Evolution of Prohibition in the United States of America.* Westerville, Oh.: American Issue Press, 1920.

Chidsey, Donald B. *Gentleman from New York: A Life of Roscoe Conkling.* New Haven: Yale University Press, 1935.

Clancy, Herbert S. *The Presidential Election of 1880.* Chicago: Loyola University Press, 1958.

Bibliography

Clark, Champ. *My Quarter Century of American Politics*. 2 vols. New York: Harper & Brothers, 1920.

Clark, Dennis. *The Irish in Philadelphia: The Generations of Urban Experience*. Philadelphia: Temple University Press, 1973.

Clark, E. Culpeper. *Francis Warrington Dawson and the Politics of Restoration: South Carolina, 1874–1899*. University: University of Alabama Press, 1980.

Congressional Quarterly's Guide to U.S. Elections. 3d. ed. Washington, D.C.: Congressional Quarterly, Inc., 1994.

Cooper, William. *The Conservative Regime: South Carolina, 1877–1890*. Baltimore: Johns Hopkins University Press, 1968.

Currie-McDaniel, Ruth. *Carpetbagger of Conscience: A Biography of John Emory Bryant*. Athens: University of Georgia Press, 1987.

Dearing, Mary. *Veterans in Politics: The Story of the GAR*. Baton Rouge: Louisiana State University Press, 1952.

Degler, Carl. *The Other South: Southern Dissenters in the Nineteenth Century*. New York: Harper & Row, 1974.

DeSantis, Vincent P. *Republicans Face the Southern Question: The New Departure Years, 1877–1897*. Baltimore: The Johns Hopkins University Press, 1959.

Dobson, John M. *Politics in the Gilded Age: A New Perspective on Reform*. New York: Praeger, 1972.

Doyle, Don H. *New Men, New Cities, New South: Atlanta, Nashville, Charleston, Mobile, 1860–1910*. Chapel Hill: University of North Carolina Press, 1990.

Dunn, Arthur Wallace. *From Harrison to Harding: A Personal Narrative Covering a Third of a Century, 1888–1921*. 2 vols. New York: G. P. Putnam's Sons, 1922.

Erie, Steven P. *Rainbow's End: Irish-Americans and the Dilemmas of Urban Machine Politics, 1840–1985*. Berkeley: University of California Press, 1988.

Escott, Paul D. *Many Excellent People: Power and Privilege in North Carolina, 1850–1900*. Chapel Hill: University of North Carolina Press, 1985.

Fairman, Charles. *Reconstruction and Reunion*. New York: Macmillan, 1987.

Flick, Alexander C. *Samuel Jones Tilden: A Study in Political Sagacity*. New York: Dodd, Mead & Co., 1939.

Foner, Eric. *Reconstruction: America's Unfinished Revolution, 1863–1877*. New York: Harper & Row, 1988.

Foraker, Julia B. *I Would Live It Again: Memories of a Vivid Life*. New York: Harper & Brothers, 1932.

Fuess, Claude M. *Carl Schurz, Reformer*. New York: Dodd, Mead & Co., 1932.

Funchion, Michael F. *Chicago's Irish Nationalists, 1881–1890*. New York: Arno Press, 1976.

Garraty, John. *Henry Cabot Lodge: A Biography*. New York: Knopf, 1953.

Gaston, Paul. *The New South Creed: A Study in Southern Mythmaking*. New York: Knopf, 1970.

George, Henry. *Protection or Free Trade: An Examination of the Tariff Question, with Especial Regard to the Interests of Labor*. New York: Robert Schalkenbach Foundation, 1944.

Gillette, William. *Retreat from Reconstruction, 1869–1879*. Baton Rouge: Louisiana State University Press, 1979.

Ginger, Ray. *Age of Excess.* New York: Macmillan, 1965.

Goodwyn, Lawrence. *Democratic Promise: The Populist Moment in America.* New York: Oxford University Press, 1976.

Gresham, Matilda. *Life of Walter Quintin Gresham, 1832–1895.* 2 vols. Chicago: Rand McNally & Co., 1919.

Grossman, Lawrence. *The Democratic Party and the Negro: Northern and National Politics, 1868–1892.* Urbana: University of Illinois Press, 1976.

Gunther, John. *Inside U.S.A.* New York: Harper & Brothers, 1947.

Hair, William I. *Bourbonism and Agrarian Protest: Louisiana Politics, 1877–1900.* Baton Rouge: Louisiana State University Press, 1969.

Hamilton, Gail. *Biography of James G. Blaine.* Norwich: Henry Bill Publishing Co., 1895.

Hamm, Richard F. *Shaping the Eighteenth Amendment: Temperance Reform, Legal Culture, and the Polity, 1880–1920.* Chapel Hill: University of North Carolina Press, 1995.

Hammack, David C. *Power and Society: Greater New York at the Turn of the Century.* New York: Columbia University Press, 1987.

Harlan, Abram D. *Pennsylvania Constitutional Convention, 1872 and 1873; Its Members and Officers and the Result of Their Labors.* Philadelphia, 1873.

Hart, Roger L. *Redeemers, Bourbons & Populists: Tennessee, 1870–1896.* Baton Rouge: Louisiana State University Press, 1975.

Hartshorn, Edwin A. *Wages, Living, and Tariff.* Troy, N.Y.: William H. Young, 1884.

Hirsch, Mark D. *William C. Whitney: Modern Warwick.* New York: Dodd, Mead & Co., 1948.

Hirshson, Stanley P. *Farewell to the Bloody Shirt: Northern Republicans and the Southern Negro, 1877–1893.* Bloomington: Indiana University Press, 1962.

Hoar, George F. *Autobiography of Seventy Years.* 2 vols. New York: Charles Scribner's Sons, 1903.

Hollingsworth, J. Rogers. *The Whirligig of Politics: The Democracy of Cleveland and Bryan.* Chicago: University of Chicago Press, 1963.

Hoogenboom, Ari. *Outlawing the Spoils: A History of the Civil Service Reform Movement, 1865–1883.* Urbana: University of Illinois Press, 1968.

——. *Rutherford B. Hayes: Warrior and President.* Lawrence: University Press of Kansas, 1995.

Howe, George F. *Chester A. Arthur: A Quarter-Century of Machine Politics.* New York: Dodd, Mead & Co., 1934.

Hudson, William C. *Random Recollections of an Old Political Reporter.* New York: Cupples & Leon, 1911.

Hyman, Michael R. *The Anti-Redeemers: Hill Country Political Dissenters in the Lower South from Redemption to Populism.* Baton Rouge: Louisiana State University Press, 1990.

James, Marquis. *Merchant Adventurer: The Story of W. R. Grace.* Wilmington, Del.: Scholarly Resources, Inc., 1993.

Jensen, Richard. *The Winning of the Midwest: Social and Political Conflict, 1888–1896.* Chicago: University of Chicago Press, 1971.

Jones, James P. *John A. Logan, Stalwart Republican from Illinois.* Tallahassee: Florida State University Press, 1982.

Bibliography

Jordan, David. *Roscoe Conkling of New York: Voice in the Senate*. Ithaca: Cornell University Press, 1971.

———. *Winfield Scott Hancock: A Soldier's Life*. Bloomington: Indiana University Press, 1988.

Josephson, Matthew. *The Politicos, 1865–1896*. New York: Harcourt, Brace, 1938.

Juergens, George. *Joseph Pulitzer and the New York World*. Princeton: Princeton University Press, 1966.

Kehl, James. *Boss Rule in the Gilded Age: Matt Quay of Pennsylvania*. Pittsburgh: University of Pittsburgh Press, 1981.

Keller, Morton. *Affairs of State: Public Life in Late Nineteenth Century America*. Cambridge, Mass.: Belknap Press, 1977.

Kirwan, Albert. *Revolt of the Rednecks: Mississippi Politics, 1876–1925*. Lexington: University of Kentucky Press, 1951.

Kleppner, Paul. *The Cross of Culture: A Social Analysis of Midwestern Politics, 1850–1900*. New York: The Free Press, 1970.

———. *The Third Electoral System, 1853–1892: Parties, Voters, and Political Cultures*. Chapel Hill: University of North Carolina Press, 1979.

Lambert, John R. *Arthur Pue Gorman*. Baton Rouge: Louisiana State University Press, 1953.

Lambert, Oscar Doane. *Stephen Benton Elkins*. Pittsburgh: University of Pittsburgh Press, 1955.

Lodge, Henry Cabot, ed. *Selections from the Correspondence of Theodore Roosevelt and Henry Cabot Lodge, 1884–1918*. 2 vols. New York: Scribner's, 1925.

Logan, Rayford W. *The Betrayal of the Negro*. New York: Collier, 1965.

Lynch, John Roy. *The Facts of Reconstruction*. New York: Neale Publishing Co., 1913.

———. *Reminiscences of an Active Life: The Autobiography of John Roy Lynch*. Edited by John Hope Franklin. Chicago: University of Chicago Press, 1970.

McCaffrey, Peter. *When Bosses Ruled Philadelphia: The Emergence of the Republican Machine, 1867–1933*. University Park: Pennsylvania State University Press, 1993.

McCall, Samuel W. *The Life of Thomas B. Reed*. New York: Houghton Mifflin, 1914.

McClure, Alexander K. *Old-Time Notes of Pennsylvania*. 2 vols. Philadelphia: John C. Winston Co., 1905.

McConnell, Stuart. *Glorious Contentment: The Grand Army of the Republic, 1865–1900*. Chapel Hill: University of North Carolina Press, 1992.

McElroy, Robert M. *Grover Cleveland, the Man and the Statesman*. New York: Harper, 1923.

McFarland, Gerald. *Mugwumps, Morals and Politics*. Amherst: University of Massachusetts Press, 1975.

McGerr, Michael E. *The Decline of Popular Politics: The American North, 1865–1928*. New York: Oxford University Press, 1986.

McKinney, Gordon B. *Southern Mountain Republicans, 1865–1900: Politics and the Appalachian Community*. Chapel Hill: University of North Carolina Press, 1978.

McPherson, James M. *The Abolitionist Legacy: From Reconstruction to the NAACP*. Princeton: Princeton University Press, 1975.

Maddex, Jack P. *The Virginia Conservatives, 1867–1869*. Chapel Hill: University of North Carolina Press, 1970.

Mandelbaum, Seymour J. *Boss Tweed's New York.* New York: John Wiley and Sons, 1965.

Marcus, Robert. *Grand Old Party: Political Structure in the Gilded Age, 1880–1896.* New York: Oxford University Press, 1971.

Marszalek, John F. *Sherman: A Soldier's Passion for Order.* New York: Free Press, 1993.

Mencken, Henry L. *The American Language.* 4th ed. New York: Knopf, 1937.

Merrill, Horace Samuel. *Bourbon Democracy of the Middle West, 1865–1896.* Seattle: University of Washington Press, 1953.

——. *Bourbon Leader: Grover Cleveland and the Democratic Party.* Boston: Little, Brown and Co., 1957.

Miller, Kerby. *Emigrants and Exiles: Ireland and the Irish Exodus to North America.* New York: Oxford University Press, 1985.

Milton, George Fort. *The Age of Hate: Andrew Johnson and the Radicals.* New York: Coward-McCann, 1930.

Mitchell, Edward P. *Memoirs of an Editor.* New York: Charles Scribner's Sons, 1924.

Moger, Allen W. *Virginia: Bourbonism to Byrd, 1870–1925.* Charlottesville: University Press of Virginia, 1968.

Moore, James Tice. *Two Paths to the New South: The Virginia Debt Controversy, 1870–1883.* Lexington: University Press of Kentucky, 1974.

Morgan, H. Wayne. *From Hayes to McKinley: National Party Politics, 1877–1896.* Syracuse: Syracuse University Press, 1969.

——. *William McKinley and His America.* Syracuse: Syracuse University Press, 1963.

——, ed., *The Gilded Age: A Reappraisal.* Syracuse: Syracuse University Press, 1970.

Morris, Edmund. *The Rise of Theodore Roosevelt.* New York: Coward, McCann and Geoghegan, 1979.

Murphy, James B. *L. Q. C. Lamar: Pragmatic Patriot.* Baton Rouge: Louisiana State University Press, 1973.

Mushkat, Jerome. *The Reconstruction of the New York Democracy, 1861–1874.* Rutherford: Fairleigh Dickinson Press, 1981.

Muzzey, David Saville. *James G. Blaine: A Political Idol of Other Days.* New York: Dodd, Mead & Co., 1934.

Myers, Gustavus. *Tammany Hall.* New York: Boni & Liveright, 1917.

Nevins, Allan. *Grover Cleveland: A Study in Courage.* New York: Dodd, Mead & Co., 1948.

Norton, Mary Beth, David M. Katzman, Paul D. Escott, Howard P. Chudacoff, Thomas G. Paterson, and William Tuttle Jr. *A People and a Nation,* 4th ed. Boston: Houghton Mifflin, 1994.

Official Proceedings of the National Democratic Convention, Held in Chicago, Ill., July 8th, 9th, 10th, and 11th, 1884. New York: Douglas Taylor's Democratic Printing House, 1884.

O'Grady, J. P. *Irish-Americans and Anglo-American Relations, 1880–88.* New York: 1976.

Paine, Albert Bigelow. *Thomas Nast: His Period and His Pictures.* New York: Harper and Brothers, 1904.

Parker, George F. *Recollections of Grover Cleveland.* New York: The Century Co., 1909.

Peck, Harry T. *Twenty Years of the Republic, 1885–1905.* New York: Dodd, Mead & Co., 1907.

Pepper, Charles M. *The Life and Times of Henry Gassaway Davis, 1823–1916.* New York: The Century Co., 1920.

Perman, Michael. *The Road to Redemption: Southern Politics, 1869–1879.* Chapel Hill: University of North Carolina Press, 1984.

Peskin, Allan. *Garfield: A Biography.* Kent, Ohio: Kent State University Press, 1978.

Platt, Thomas C. *The Autobiography of Thomas Collier Platt.* New York: Charles Scribner's Sons, 1925.

Pletcher, David M. *The Awkward Years.* Columbia: University of Missouri Press, 1962.

Polakoff, Keith Ian. *The Politics of Inertia: The Election of 1876 and the End of Reconstruction.* Baton Rouge: Louisiana State University Press, 1973.

Proceedings of the Eighth Republican National Convention Held at Chicago, Illinois, June 3, 4, 5, and 6, 1884. Chicago: Rand McNally & Co., 1884.

Rabinowitz, Howard N. *Race Relations in the Urban South, 1865–1890.* Urbana: University of Illinois Press, 1980.

Reeves, Thomas C. *Gentleman Boss: The Life of Chester Alan Arthur.* New York: Knopf, 1975.

Reitano, Joanne. *The Tariff Question in the Gilded Age: The Great Debate of 1888.* University Park: Pennsylvania State University Press, 1994.

Richardson, Leon B. *William E. Chandler, Republican.* New York: Dodd, Mead & Co., 1940.

Roberts, Ellis H. *Government Revenue: Especially the American System.* Boston: Houghton Mifflin, 1883.

Robinson, William A. *Thomas B. Reed, Parliamentarian.* New York: Dodd, Mead & Co., 1930.

Rundquist, Barry S., ed. *Political Benefits: Empirical Studies of American Public Programs.* Lexington, Mass.: 1980.

Russell, Charles E. *Bare Hands and Rock Walls: Some Recollections of a Side-Line Reformer.* New York: Scribner's, 1933.

———. *These Shifting Scenes.* New York: Hodder & Stoughton, 1914.

Ryan, Mary P. *Women in Public: Between Banners and Ballots, 1825–1880.* Baltimore: Johns Hopkins University Press, 1990.

Schott, Thomas E. *Alexander H. Stephens of Georgia: A Biography.* Baton Rouge: Louisiana State University Press, 1988.

Sherman, John, *Recollections of Forty Years in the House, Senate, and Cabinet.* Chicago: Werner, 1895.

Sherman, Thomas H. *Twenty Years with Blaine.* New York: Grafton Press, 1928.

Sievers, Harry J. *Benjamin Harrison: Hoosier Statesman: From the Civil War to the White House, 1865–1888.* New York: University Publishers, Inc., 1959.

Silbey, Joel. *The American Political Nation, 1838–1893.* Stanford: Stanford University Press, 1991.

Skowronek, Stephen. *Building a New American State: The Expansion of National Administrative Capacities.* Cambridge: Cambridge University Press, 1982.

Sproat, John G. *The Best Men: Liberal Reformers in the Gilded Age.* New York: Oxford University Press, 1968.

Stanwood, Edward. *American Tariff Controversies in the Nineteenth Century.* Boston: Houghton Mifflin, 1903.

—. *James Gillespie Blaine*. Boston: Houghton Mifflin, 1905.

Stealey, Orlando O. *Twenty Years in the Press Gallery: A Concise History of Important Legislation from the 48th to the 58th Congress*. New York: Orlando O. Stealey, 1906.

Stoddard, Henry L. *As I Knew Them: Presidents and Politics from Grant to Coolidge*. New York: Harper and Brothers, 1927.

Stone, Melville E. *Fifty Years a Journalist*. Garden City, N.Y.: Doubleday, 1921.

Summers, Mark. *The Era of Good Stealings*. New York: Oxford University Press, 1993.

—. *The Press Gang: Newspapers and Politics, 1865–1878*. Chapel Hill: University of North Carolina Press, 1994.

Swanberg, W. A. *Pulitzer*. New York: Scribner's, 1967.

Tarbell, Ida. *The Tariff in Our Times*. New York: Macmillan, 1912.

Taussig, Frank W. *The Tariff History of the United States*. New York: G. P. Putnam's Sons, 1931.

Thernstrom, Stephan. *Poverty and Progress: Social Mobility in a Nineteenth Century City*. Cambridge: Harvard University Press, 1964.

Thomas, Harrison Cook. *The Return of the Democratic Party to Power in 1884*. New York: Columbia University, 1919.

Thompson, E. Bruce. *Matthew Hale Carpenter: Webster of the West*. Madison: State Historical Society of Wisconsin, 1954.

Thoron, Ward, ed. *Letters of Mrs. Henry Adams, 1865–1883*. Boston: Little, Brown and Co., 1936.

Tribune Almanac, 1875–1889. New York: Tribune Publishing Co., 1875–89.

Van Deusen, Glyndon. *Horace Greeley, Nineteenth Century Crusader*. New York: Hill & Wang, 1953.

Villard, Oswald Garrison. *Fighting Years: Memoirs of a Liberal Editor*. New York: Harcourt, Brace & Co., 1939.

Wall, Joseph F. *Henry Watterson: Reconstructed Rebel*. New York: Oxford University Press, 1956.

Welch, Richard E. *George Frisbie Hoar and the Half Breed Republicans*. Cambridge, Mass.: Harvard University Press, 1971.

—. *The Presidencies of Grover Cleveland*. Lawrence: University Press of Kansas, 1988.

Werner, M. L. *Tammany Hall*. Garden City, N.Y.: Garden City Publishing Co., 1932.

West, Richard S. *Lincoln's Scapegoat General: A Life of Benjamin F. Butler, 1818–1893*. Boston: Houghton Mifflin, 1965.

—. *Satire on Stone: The Political Cartoons of Joseph Keppler*. Urbana: University of Illinois Press, 1988.

White, Leonard. *The Republican Era: A Study in Administrative History*. New York: Macmillan, 1958.

White, William Allen. *Masks in a Pageant*. New York: Macmillan, 1928.

William, Charles R., ed. *Diary and Letters of Rutherford B. Hayes*. 4 vols. Columbus: Ohio State Archives and Historical Society, 1924.

Williams, R. Hal. *The Democratic Party and California Politics, 1880–1896*. Stanford: Stanford University Press, 1973.

Williamson, Joel. *A Rage for Order: Black-White Relations in the American South since Emancipation*. New York: Oxford University Press, 1986.

Wilson, Charles Reagan. *Baptized in Blood: The Religion of the Lost Cause, 1865–1920.* Athens: University of Georgia Press, 1980.

Woodward, C. Vann. *Origins of the New South, 1877–1913.* Baton Rouge: Louisiana State University Press, 1951.

——. *Reunion and Reaction: The Compromise of 1877 and the End of Reconstruction.* Boston: Little, Brown and Co., 1951.

Wynne, Lewis N. *The Continuity of Cotton: Planter Politics in Georgia, 1865–1892.* Macon: Mercer University Press, 1986.

ARTICLES AND UNPUBLISHED PAPERS

Adler, Selig. "The Senatorial Career of George F. Edmunds, 1866–1891." Ph.D. diss., University of Illinois, 1934.

Altschuler, Glenn C., and Stuart M. Blumin. "Limits of Political Engagement in Antebellum America: A New Look at the Golden Age of Participatory Democracy." *Journal of American History* 84 (December 1997): 855–85.

Armstrong, William M. "Godkin's *Nation* as a Source of Gilded Age History: How Valuable?" *South Atlantic Quarterly* 72 (Autumn 1973): 476–93.

Baker, Paula. "The Culture of Politics in the Late Nineteenth Century: Community and Political Behavior in Rural New York." *Journal of Social History* 18 (Winter 1984): 167–94.

Baum, Dale. " 'Noisy but Not Numerous': The Revolt of the Massachusetts Mugwumps." *Historian* 4 (February 1979): 241–56.

Benedict, Michael Les. "Southern Democrats in the Crisis of 1876–1877: A Reconsideration of *Reunion and Reaction.*" *Journal of Southern History* 46 (November 1980): 489–524.

Blankenburg, Rudolph, "Forty Years in the Wilderness." *Arena* 33 (1905): 113–19.

Blodgett, Geoffrey. "The Emergence of Grover Cleveland: A Fresh Appraisal." *New York History* (April 1992): 133–68.

——. "The Mugwump Reputation, 1870 to the Present." *Journal of American History* 66 (March 1980): 867–87.

——. "The Political Leadership of Grover Cleveland." *South Atlantic Quarterly* 82 (Summer 1983): 288–99.

Bromberg, Alan. "Pure Democracy and White Supremacy: The Redeemer Period in North Carolina, 1876–1894." Ph.D. diss., University of Virginia, 1977.

Clarkson, James S. "Permanent Republican Clubs." *North American Review* 146 (March 1888): 249–64.

Crofts, Daniel W. "The Blair Bill and the Elections Bill: The Congressional Aftermath to Reconstruction." Ph.D. diss., Yale University, 1968.

Downey, Matthew T. "The Rebirth of Reform: A Study of Liberal Reform Movements, 1865–1872." Ph.D. diss., Princeton University, 1963.

Edwards, E. J. "Tammany under John Kelly," *McClure's* 5 (September 1895): 325–29.

Edwards, Rebecca B. "Gender in American Politics, 1880–1900." Ph.D. diss., University of Virginia, 1995.

Eidson, William G. "Who Were the Stalwarts?" *Mid-America* 52 (October 1970): 235–61.

Farrelly, David G. "'Rum, Romanism and Rebellion' Resurrected." *Western Political Quarterly* 8 (June 1955): 262–70.

Foner, Eric. "Class, Ethnicity, and Radicalism in the Gilded Age: The Land League & Irish America." *Marxist Perspectives* 1 (Summer 1978): 6–43.

Fram, Steven J. "Purifying the Ballot? The Politics of Electoral Procedure in New York State, 1821–1871." M.A. Thesis, Cornell University, 1983.

Genen, Arthur. "John Kelly, New York's First Irish Boss." Ph.D. diss., New York University, 1971.

Gillette, Howard F. "Corrupt and Contented: Philadelphia's Political Machine, 1865–1887." Ph.D. diss., Yale University, 1970.

Gordon, Michael A. "The Labor Boycott in New York City, 1880–1886." *Labor History* 16 (Spring 1975): 185–204.

Green, Stephen K. "The National Reform Association and the Religious Amendments to the Constitution, 1864–1876." M.A. thesis, University of North Carolina, 1987.

Gribayedoff, Valerian. "Pictorial Journalism." *Cosmopolitan* 11 (August 1891): 471–79.

Gross, Jimmie F. "The Negro in Alabama Politics, 1874–1901." Ph.D. diss., University of Georgia, 1969.

Halstead, Murat. "The Defeat of Blaine for the Presidency." *McClure's* 6 (January 1896): 159–72.

Hammond, Richard. "'The Beast' in Boston: Benjamin F. Butler as Governor of Massachusetts." *Journal of American History* 55 (September 1986): 266–80.

Harlan, Richard D. "The Phrase That Beat Blaine: An Inside Story of a Decisive Incident in American Politics." *Outlook* 126 (December 8, 1920): 650–52.

Harrison, Robert. "Blaine and the Camerons: A Study in the Limits of Machine Power." *Pennsylvania History* 49 (July 1982): 165–69.

Hoogenboom, Ari. "The Pendleton Act and the Civil Service." *American Historical Review* 64 (January 1959): 301–18.

Ingersoll, Ernest. "The City of Atlanta." *Harper's* 60 (December 1879): 30–43.

James, Edward T. "Benjamin Butler Runs for President: Labor, Greenbackers and Anti-Monopolists in the Election of 1884." *Essex Institute Historical Collections* 113 (April 1977): 65–89.

Kelley, Robert. "Presbyterianism, Jacksonianism, and Grover Cleveland." *American Quarterly* 18 (1966): 615–36.

——. "The Thought and Character of Samuel J. Tilden: The Democrat as Inheritor." *Historian* 26 (February 1964): 176–205.

Kenny, Kevin. "The Molly Maguires and the Catholic Church." *Labor History* 37 (Summer 1995): 360–76.

Logue, Larry M. "Union Veterans and Their Government: The Effect of Public Policies on Private Lives." *Journal of Interdisciplinary History* 22 (Winter 1992): 411–34.

McFarland, Gerald. "The New York Mugwumps of 1884: A Profile." *Political Science Quarterly* 78 (March 1963): 40–58.

Mack, Frank W. "'Rum, Romanism, and Rebellion': How James G. Blaine was Defeated by a Phrase." *Harper's Weekly* 48 (July 23, 1904): 1140–42.

McSeveney, Samuel T. "Religious Conflict, Party Politics, and Public Policy in New Jersey, 1874–1875." *New Jersey History* 110 (Spring/Summer 1992): 18–44.

Meager, Timothy J. "'Irish All the Time': Ethnic Consciousness among the Irish in

Worcester, Massachusetts, 1880–1905." *Journal of Social History* 19 (Winter 1985): 273–304.

Miller, Clark L. "Let Us Die to Make Men Free": Political Terrorism in Post-Reconstruction Mississippi, 1877–1896." Ph.D. diss., University of Minnesota, 1983.

Parker, Albert C. E. "Beating the Spread: Analyzing American Election Outcomes." *Journal of American History* 67 (June 1980): 61–87.

——. "Empire Stalemate: Voting Behavior in New York State, 1860–1892." Ph.D. diss., Washington University, 1975.

Peskin, Allan. "Who Were the Stalwarts? Who Were Their Rivals? Republican Factions in the Gilded Age," *Political Science Quarterly* 99 (Winter 1984–85): 703–16.

Pocock, Emil. "Wet or Dry? The Presidential Election of 1884 in Upstate New York." *New York History* 54 (April 1973): 174–90.

Rathgeber, Lewis R. "The Democratic Party in Pennsylvania, 1880–1896." Ph.D. diss., University of Pittsburgh, 1955.

Reeves, Thomas C. "Chester A. Arthur and Campaign Assessments in the Election of 1880." *The Historian* 31 (August 1969), 573–82.

Reynolds, John F., " 'The Silent Dollar': Vote Buying in New Jersey," *New Jersey History* (Fall–Winter 1980): 191–211.

Reynolds, John F., and Richard L. McCormick. "Outlawing 'Treachery': Split Tickets and Ballot Laws in New York and New Jersey, 1880–1914." *Journal of American History* 72 (March 1986): 835–58.

Robbins, David Earl. "The Congressional Career of William Ralls Morrison." Ph.D. diss., University of Illinois, 1963.

Rogers, William W. "Agrarianism in Alabama, 1865–1896." Ph.D. diss., University of North Carolina at Chapel Hill, 1959.

Roush, Gerald L. "Aftermath of Reconstruction: Race, Violence and Politics in Alabama, 1874–1884." M.A. thesis, Auburn University, 1973.

"The Strategy of National Campaigns." *McClure's* 15 (October 1900): 483–94.

Turner, James Ross. "The American Prohibition Movement, 1865–1897." M.A. thesis, University of Wisconsin, 1972.

Vazzano, Frank P. "President Hayes, Congress and the Appropriations Riders Vetoes." *Congress and the Presidency* 20 (Spring 1993): 25–34.

Walsh, Victor A. " 'A Fanatic Heart': The Cause of Irish-American Nationalism in Pittsburgh during the Gilded Age." *Journal of Social History* 15 (Winter 1981): 189–200.

Watson, Harry L. "Humbug? Bah! Altschuler and Blumin and the Riddle of the Antebellum Electorate." *Journal of American History* 84 (December 1997): 886–93.

Index

Abbett, Leon, 113, 115
Adams, Charles Francis, 198
Adams, Henry, 46
Adams, Marian Hooper (Mrs. Henry), 75
Alabama, 50, 53, 102, 153, 242, 245–47, 257
Albany Argus, 148
Alkakange, 94
Allen, William, 79
Allison, William Boyd, 137
American Land League, 217
American Political Alliance, 237
Andrew, John F., 207
Andrews, William S., 177
Anti-Catholicism, 78–79, 80, 83, 192, 203, 206, 216–17, 281–84
Apgar, Edward, 9
Apollo Hall, 151
Arizona, 249
Arkansas, 50
Arthur, Chester Alan, 7, 37, 169, 170, 191, 273–74, 294; ailing, 4; Southern policy, 50–51, 243–45; administration, 67–76; and 1884 nomination, 125–27, 131–34, 137–41; death, 303
Assessments, 73, 74, 75–76, 164–65, 167
Associated Press, 10, 282–83
Atlanta Constitution, 96

Baer, George, 108
Ball, George H., 180–83
Baltimore & Ohio Railroad, 268
Barker, Wharton, 211, 228, 262
Barnum, William H., 164, 168, 173
Bayard, Thomas F., 68, 106, 287, 301; character, 109, 110; and 1876 election, 36, 152; presidential boom, 145–46, 152, 155–57, 159
Beaver Island Club, 180, 182
Beecher, Henry Ward, 4, 108, 193, 198, 305
Belmont, August, 146

"Belshazzar's Feast." *See* Delmonico's banquet
Big Divide, 73
Birmingham, 96
Bisbee, Horace, 247, 251
Bissell, Wilson S., 166
Blaine, Harriet Stanwood, 5, 12, 70, 71, 186–89, 193, 303
Blaine, James G., xi, 1, 61–71, 76, 79, 237; corruption, xi, 4, 5, 62–63, 173, 192, 205; character, 3–4, 61–64; and election returns, 6–12, 289–303; in *Democracy*, 46; and bloody shirt, 61, 64–65, 254, 256, 270, 303; and tariff, 96–98; and 1884 nomination, 124–26, 128–30, 132–42, 144; and 1884 campaign management, 169–79 passim; marriage scandal, 183–89, 190–95; Mugwumps resist, 197–200, 202–9; and Irish vote, 212–17, 219–21; and Butler problem, 225–26, 228, 238; and Prohibition problem, 230, 232, 235, 256–57; appeal to the South, 243–45, 249; and Maine election, 258–59; and Ohio election, 259–61, 263–67; stumps Midwest, 264–65, 270–71, 278; and New York Stalwarts, 272–75; stumps New York, 278–88; Burchard incident, 281–83
Blaine marriage, 183–89
Blair, Henry W., 97
Blair bill, 97, 106, 129, 243, 246, 306
Bloody shirt, 36, 41–50, 56–58, 63, 65, 170, 176, 250, 256, 297, 310
Boston Journal, 180–81
Bowker, R. R., 198
Brady, Thomas J., 69, 72
Bragg, Edward, 157
Bristow, Benjamin H., 137
Brooklyn Eagle, 177, 219
Brown, Joseph E., 53, 108
Buchanan, James, 191
Buffalo Evening Telegraph, 179–81, 182, 184, 196

Burchard, Rev. Samuel, 281–83, 296, 297, 301, 303, 307
Burrows, Roswell, 183–84
Butler, Benjamin F., 11, 169, 176, 203, 213, 215–16, 276–77, 289, 306, 307; character, 2–3, 109–10; elected governor, 75, 110–11; as governor, 109–11, 115–16; at Democratic convention, 156–58, 159, 160; campaigns, 223–29, 233, 237–39; and 1884 election, 293, 295–96

California, 102, 104, 114, 155, 156, 157, 161, 228–29
Calkins, William H., 261, 269
Cameron, J. Donald, 60, 66, 164; faces 1882 revolt, 74, 131; and Blaine nomination, 126, 131, 137
Cannon, Joseph, 163
Carlisle, John G., 98–106, 145, 191, 309
Carpenter, Matthew, 60, 66
Carroll, William, 210, 211, 220
Catholic Workingmen's Society, 217
Chaffee, Jerome B., 253
Chalmers, James R., 50, 55, 267
Chandler, William E., 169–70, 294; fixes Butler, 227, 229
Chandler, Zachariah, 60, 66
Chesapeake & Ohio Canal, 165
Chesapeake & Ohio Railroad, 268
Chicago Daily News, 40, 43, 104, 124, 129, 135, 198
Chicago Times, 185, 190, 193, 194
Chicago Tribune, 176–77, 213, 302
Cipher dispatches, 38
Civil rights cases (1883), 47
Civil service reform, 64, 75–76, 111, 115, 118, 146, 163, 172, 204–5, 208, 297–98
Clan na Gael, 211–12
Clarkson, James S., 167, 228, 230, 259, 260–61, 270, 311, 312, 314; on Prohibitionism, 83; and Legate intrigue, 232–34, 236, 239, 301–2
Clay, Henry, 5, 6, 92
Clayton, Powell, 137–38
Cleveland, Grover, xi–xii, xiv, 4, 6–12, 238, 249, 250, 259; and sex scandals,

xi, 171–73, 177–84, 187, 189, 192–96, 265, 270, 280–81, 285, 286; character, 6, 116–17; elected governor, 70, 75, 112, 118, 152; as governor, 118–23; presidential boom, 145, 148–49, 152–61; letter of acceptance, 163; campaign management by, 164, 166, 168; Mugwumps support, 201, 203–4, 207; and Irish vote, 211, 214, 220, 292, 296; Tammany accepts, 277, 278, 287; election analyzed, 289–303
Cleveland Plain Dealer, 86
Coal-Oil Gang, 111, 155, 263
Committee of One Hundred, 182
Cobden Club, 168, 191, 312
Collins, Patrick, 217
Conaty, Thomas J., 221
Confederate bonds, 41–42
Conger, Arthur L., 262
Conger, Omar, 102
Conkling, Roscoe, 22, 172; character, 60, 61; feud with Blaine, 64–67, 204, 272–74; in 1880 campaign, 65–66, 71, 139, 273; downfall, 67–68; on Arthur, 67–69; on Thurman, 143; and Halpin scandal, 196, 273; in 1884 campaign, 272–74, 294, 295, 303
Connecticut, 98, 113, 115, 165, 173, 228, 240, 257, 289
Converse, George, 104
Cooke, Jay, 63
Copiah killings, 57–58
Cornell, Alonzo, 67; denied renomination, 69, 113; aids Blaine, 132, 272–73
Corruption, 14–16, 22–23, 29–33, 38, 62, 63, 71–73, 74, 78, 98, 112, 117, 120, 126–27, 135, 203, 205, 232–37, 248–49, 309. See also Mulligan letters; Vote fraud
County Democracy, 120–21; and Cleveland boom, 149–50, 152, 154; in 1884 mayoral race, 275, 277–78; demise, 306–7
Cox, Samuel S., 93, 98–100
Craig, George, 247
Credit Mobilier scandal, 25

Crisp, Charles, 34–35
Croker, Richard, 306
Cullom, Shelby, 131, 166
Curtis, George William, 111, 137, 305; at
    Republican convention, 139, 141; sup-
    ports Cleveland, 198–201, 202

Daggett, Albert, 294
Dana, Charles A., 225, 226
Davis, David, 128, 146
Davis, Henry Gassaway, 146, 157, 160–61,
    268
Dawes, Henry L., 60
Delaware, 14, 244
Delmonico's banquet: "soap" (1881), 73;
    "Belshazzar's Feast" (1884), 278–79,
    285–87
Democratic Party, 108–23, 143–61
Depew, Chauncey, 199
Devoy, John, 210–14, 217, 220–21
Disfranchisement, 16, 30–33, 34–35, 47,
    50–51, 248–49, 252, 299–301, 309–10
Dodge, Mary A., 65
Dorsey, Stephen W., 4, 37, 69, 72, 199
Douglass, Frederick, 47, 129, 252
Dow, Neal, 84
"Dudes," 176, 201–2
Dudley, William W., 10, 169, 296; man-
    ages Indiana, 261–62, 270

Edmunds, George F., 191, 303; character,
    127–28; presidential boom, 127–29,
    132–37, 140; backs Blaine coolly,
    207–8, 258
Edson, Franklin, 121, 151
Egan, Patrick, 218, 221
Elections, 13–17; of 1856, 190–91; of 1872,
    79; of 1874, 28; of 1875, 79; of 1876,
    10–11, 22, 27–30, 36, 37, 42, 110, 145,
    146, 147, 150, 158, 169, 191, 198, 237,
    273, 289–91, 295–96, 300; of 1878,
    31–33, 50, 81, 151; of 1879, 38, 51, 110,
    111; of 1880, 22, 35, 36–37, 39–40, 49,
    54, 65–66, 72, 79, 81, 94, 98, 125, 138–
    39, 145, 146, 151, 158, 191, 198, 211,
    228, 257–59, 270, 273, 289–91, 293,

295, 297; of 1881, 51, 66–67, 84–85,
    117; of 1882, 42–55, 73–75, 84–87, 98,
    111–14, 118, 127, 152, 223, 274, 292;
    of 1883, 57–59, 87–90, 111, 116, 119;
    of 1888, 193, 296, 303, 307, 308–10; of
    1890, 307, 309; of 1892, 306, 312; of
    1896, 312
Elkins, Stephen B., 10, 165–66, 167, 174,
    183, 216, 225, 264, 273, 275, 278; man-
    ages Blaine boom, 130–31; and West
    Virginia politics, 267–68
Ellsworth, William, 237
Equal Suffrage Association, 222
Evarts, William Maxwell, 137, 189

Farmers' Alliance, 222
Felton, Rebecca, 52–54
Fenian movement, 211
Fessenden, Samuel, 8
Field, Cyrus W., 174, 175, 285–86
Field, Stephen, 143–45, 155, 156
Finch, John B., 236
Fisher, Warren, 62–63, 205
Five-cent fare veto, 121–22, 152
Flanagan, Webster, 35
Flower, Roswell B., 148, 155, 156
Folger, Charles, 169–70; and 1882 elec-
    tion, 70, 114, 118, 127, 274
Folsom, Frances, 193
Folsom, Oscar, 180, 182
Foraker, Joseph B., 89, 259
Foran, Martin, 267
Ford, Patrick, 210–12, 214, 217, 218, 220,
    222
Foster, Charles, 41, 259; and temperance
    issue, 84–89, 308
Foster, J. Ellen, 221
Fourteenth Amendment, 47

Garfield, James A., 8, 60, 66–68, 191,
    198, 264, 286; administration, 66–68;
    Blaine and, 66–68, 70–71, 125–27, 131;
    assassination, 67–68, 73, 125, 126, 127;
    and Star Routes, 71–72; tariff elects,
    98; election results compared, 289,
    290, 292

Gas Trust, 74

George, Henry, 35, 52, 53, 240, 242, 246

Georgia, 52–54, 109

Gibson, Eustace, 268

Gillam, Bernhard, 18, 74, 105, 110, 117, 187, 206, 276, 310; "tattooed man" cartoons, 136, 137

Gillette, E. C., 256

Gleason, Patrick, 292

Glick, George, 84

Godkin, Edwin L., 23–24, 111, 198, 205, 208, 214, 307

Gorman, Arthur Pue, 146, 168, 173, 177; character, 165–66; funds Prohibitionists, 237; and Burchard, 283

Gougar, Helen, 222

Gould, Jay, 3, 11, 69, 113–14, 199, 266, 286–89; campaign whipping boy, 174–75, 286–87; at Delmonico's, 286–87

Grace, William, 79, 151; 1884 mayoral candidate, 277–78, 287, 292, 297

Grady, Henry, 96

Grady, Thomas, 119, 152, 156, 157, 277

Grand Army of the Republic, 42–45, 309

Grant, Hugh, 277–78, 292

Grant, Ulysses S., 69, 71, 95, 190, 191, 264; administration, 28, 68, 203; and third term, 49, 65

Gray, Isaac, 269

Greeley, Horace, 191, 264

Greenbackers, 2, 22, 50–51, 52, 54, 114, 174, 223–29, 237–38, 256, 295, 309, 311, 314

Gresham, Walter Q., 136, 139, 169, 170, 261, 270, 303

Grimes, Thomas, 250

Guiteau, Charles, 67, 125

Half-Breeds, xii, 59–61, 63–64, 274

Halpin, Maria, xi, 179–84, 187, 263

Halpin scandal, xi, 159, 179–84, 187, 189–93, 194–96, 263, 267, 270, 273–76, 279–81, 285

Halstead, Murat, 86, 87, 124–25, 303

Hamilton, Alexander, 6, 92

Hamilton, Gail, 65

Hampton, Wade, 53, 157

Hancock, Winfield Scott, 40, 79, 191, 292; and tariff, 94, 98

Hanna, Marcus Alonzo, 259

Haralson, Jere, 247

Harper's Weekly, 46, 49, 133, 198–99, 200, 205–6, 305

Harris, Joel Chandler, 46

Harrison, Benjamin, 261–62, 307, 309; presidential boom, 127, 133, 135, 137; libel suit, 185

Harrison, Carter, 155, 157

Hawley, Joseph, 136

Hay, John, 265

Hayes, Rutherford B., 40, 60, 87, 198, 264; election, 29–30; New Departure policy, 30–33, 35–39, 45–46, 64, 237, 244; and army appropriations bills, 48–49; Blaine warns, 64

Henderson, John, 139, 140, 204

Hendricks, Thomas, 11, 163, 275–76, 288; presidential boom, 143, 145, 147, 156–57, 159–61; as vice presidential nominee, 170–73, 176

Hewitt, Abram S., 73, 104, 106, 145, 147, 151, 168

Hill, David Bennett, 149, 154, 276–77, 308

Hill, James J., 54, 109, 149

Hiscock, Frank, 102

Hoadly, George, 111, 113; elected governor, 89; presidential boom, 143, 145, 156, 160

Hoar, Ebenezer R., 200

Hoar, George F., 61, 207, 208

Hocking Valley troubles, 174–75, 205

Home Rule (Ireland), 212, 215, 217, 220

Homestead strike, 312

Hoopla, xi, 4, 18–21, 175–78, 264–65, 288, 311–12

Hopkins, John P., 219

Howells, William Dean, 184

Hubbell, Jay, 73, 74

Hudson, William C., 12, 177

Hurd, Frank, 158, 267
Husted, James M., 199

Independent, 182
Independents. *See* Mugwumps
Indiana, 14, 102, 114, 168, 257; in 1882 election, 84; and Republican nomination, 127, 129, 133, 135, 136, 137, 139; and Democratic nomination, 143, 145, 147, 156–57, 160–61; in 1884 campaign, 171–73, 256, 257, 260–62, 269–70, 289, 290, 296
Indianapolis Journal, 10, 216, 261, 284
Indianapolis Sentinel, 73, 97, 185–86, 190, 193, 194, 284–85
Ingalls, John J., 17, 83
Ingersoll, Robert G., 61, 195, 199, 252
Internal Revenue system, 75–76, 80, 96, 103
Interstate Commerce Commission, 306
Iowa, xiii, 83, 84, 98, 256–57, 289
Irish Land League, 221
Irish Nation, 220
Irish National League, 212
Irish World, 210, 212, 217
Irving Hall, 17, 151

Jackson, Andrew, 7
James, Henry, 46
James, Thomas, 72
Jefferson, Thomas, 7
Jingo, 206
Johnson, Andrew, 232, 264
Jones, Benjamin F., 10, 164–67, 293
Jones, George, 305
Judge, xii, 201, 206

Kansas, 81–84, 240, 256
Kansas State Temperance Union, 31
Kearney, Dennis, 211
Keifer, J. Warren, 72–73
Kelley, William Darrah, 92, 94, 105
Kellogg, William Pitt, 174
Kelly, John, 18, 28, 38, 136, 111–12, 119–20, 160, 161, 172, 292, 295, 314; fights Cleveland's nomination, 149–58; sup-

ports Cleveland, 275–78, 287–88; death, 306
Kentucky, 14, 16, 98, 241
Keppler, Joseph, 18, 69, 136, 153, 174, 199, 226, 305
Kerens, R. C., 234
Kerwin, Michael, 212
Key, David M., 64
Kinsella, Michael, 219
Knights of Labor, 97, 211, 228, 292, 293, 309
Know-Nothings, 214–15, 269

Labor Party, 144, 309, 311
Lamar, Lucius Q. C., 43, 244
Lamont, Daniel, 9, 16, 118, 119, 149, 163
Lapham, Elbridge, 137
Legate, James F., 232–36, 302
LeMoyne, John V., 188
Lincoln, Abraham, 92, 180
Lincoln, Robert, 124, 127
Little Rock & Fort Smith Railroad, 62–63, 134–36, 205
Lockwood, Belva, 1, 16–17, 189
Lodge, Henry Cabot, 138, 140, 202, 207–9, 265
Logan, John A., 7, 166, 213, 235, 260; character, 42–43; Stalwart leader, 60, 65–66, 68, 69; presidential boom, 126, 129–30, 137, 140–42; nominated, 142; as vice presidential nominee, 170–72, 263, 265, 279; relationship with Blaine, 171; and Delmonico's dinner, 279, 287; on defeat, 303
Long, John D., 207, 265
Longstreet, James, 45, 246
Louisiana, 13, 31, 33, 94, 96, 242; in 1884 campaign, 248–49, 253–54, 299
Louisville Courier-Journal, 49, 98

McDonald, Joseph, 106, 145–47, 156, 158, 159
McDougall, Walt, 199, 286–87
McEnery, Samuel, 243
Mack, Frank, 282–83
McKane, John Y., 292

McKinley Tariff, 309, 312

McLaughlin, Hugh, 119, 122, 219, 313; and Cleveland boom, 152, 154, 155, 156; delivers Brooklyn, 296

McLean, John, 263

McManes, James, 74, 132

McMurdy, R. W., 7, 279–80, 284

McPherson, Edward, 250

McVeagh, Wayne, 72–73

Magee, Christopher, 132

Mahone, William, 51–57, 66, 73, 74; in 1884 campaign, 245, 250, 289–90, 299, 301

Maine, 22, 168, 228, 257, 258–59, 289

Manning, Daniel, 8, 11, 118, 166, 168; manages Cleveland boom, 148, 149, 153–56, 158

Manson, Mahlon D., 269

Maryland, 14, 165–66, 249

Massachusetts, 82, 289

Medill, Joseph, 176–77, 199

Michigan, 82, 102, 168, 204, 289

Miller, George, 237

Miller, Warner, 67, 308; and Blaine's nomination, 132–33, 137

Milliken, Seth, 295

Mills, Roger Q., 309

Minneapolis Tribune, 256

Minnesota, 240, 257

Mississippi, 43, 50, 54–55, 57, 58, 241, 242, 247, 252, 299, 300

Missouri, 94, 241, 256, 290

Mitchell, Alexander, 149, 168

Mollie Maguires, 211, 218–19

Money, campaign finance, 36–37, 73, 166–69, 227, 230–37, 244, 245, 257, 259–63, 268, 270, 278–79, 285–88, 298–99, 313–14

Morgan, John T., 106

Mormonism, 78, 128, 281, 283

Morrison, William R., 101–6, 145, 155, 158, 309

Morrison tariff bill, 102–6, 107, 173

Morton, Levi P., 266, 278

Morton, Oliver P., 59–60

Mossbacks, 155

Mott, John J., 243

Mugwumps, xi, xiv, 22–24, 45, 148, 149, 161, 172, 179, 192, 197–209, 222, 266, 270, 275, 289, 295, 296–98, 302, 306, 313

Mulligan, James, 62–63, 205

Mulligan letters, 62, 63, 135, 205

Nast, Thomas, 3, 18, 32, 40, 63, 112, 130, 286, 296–97; joins Mugwumps, 199, 201–2; scores Irish, 214, 215

Nation, 21, 111, 148, 208, 214

Nebraska, 34, 98, 256, 257, 289

New, John C., 261

New Departure, 30–31, 64

New Hampshire, 14, 257

New Jersey, 14, 35, 98, 113, 115, 168, 173, 255

New Orleans Picayune, 194–95, 202

New York (city), 14, 16, 17, 23, 79, 120–21, 149–54, 260, 275, 277–78, 294, 306–8. *See also* Tammany Hall

New York (state), 8–12, 35, 84, 94, 98, 168; Republican factionalism, 66–67, 70–71; in 1882 election, 70, 73–75, 113–14, 118; and Republican nomination, 132–33; in Republican convention, 138–41; and Democratic nomination, 144–45, 146–55; in Democratic convention, 156–60; in fall campaign, 173, 271, 272–88; and 1884 election results, 289, 290, 297, 298

New York Central Railroad, 113, 117

New York Evening Post, 23, 135, 198, 215, 302

New York Herald, 102–3, 151, 198

New York State Temperance Alliance, 234

New York Sun, 151, 225–26, 297

New York Tablet, 212

New York Tribune, 64–65, 70, 108, 130, 134–35, 137, 151, 174–75, 199, 297, 302, 310, 311

New York World, 4, 151, 273; "Belshazzar's Feast," 286–87, 297

North Carolina, 14, 31, 43, 50, 52, 96,

241; in 1884 campaign, 242–45, 248, 252–53; Republican defeat, 299

O'Brien, Hugh, 219
O'Brien, Johnny, 275, 288, 294
O'Day, John, 159
Ohio, 14, 168, 204, 290; temperance politics, 84–90; tariff issue, 90, 98, 100, 102–4; and Republican nomination, 129, 131, 135; 1884 campaign, 171, 257–70 passim
O'Reilly, John Boyle, 218
Othello, 195
Ottendorfer, Oswald, 168

Pacific Mail Steamship Company, 114
Parades. *See* Hoopla
Parnell, Charles Stewart, 217, 220, 221
Parsons, Henry, 242
Partisanship, 6–7, 15–22, 34, 41–43, 59–60, 77–78, 173–78, 202–3, 208–9, 213–14, 220–22, 239, 264–65, 310–13
Payne, Henry B., 111, 262, 263; presidential boom, 144–45, 147, 149
Pelton, William F., 38
Pendleton, George, 111
Pendleton Act, 75–76, 111, 163, 164, 204. *See also* Civil service reform
Pension Bureau, 261
Pensions, 43, 45, 49–50, 309
People's Party, 159, 213, 223–29, 237–39
Pepper, George, 211
Phelps, William Walter, 134–35, 174, 188
Platt, Thomas Collier, 67, 69, 132, 199, 279
Plumb, Preston B., 232
Plumed Knight, xi, 61, 279. *See also* Blaine, James G.
Political culture. *See* Hoopla
Pomeroy, Samuel S., 232
Pond Act, 85–87, 88
Populists, 222, 314
Porter, Horace, 200
Powderly, Terence V., 211, 228, 292
Prohibition movement, 45, 47, 50, 80–90, 96, 121, 172, 192, 257–59, 308

Prohibition Party, 2–3, 189, 192, 204, 221, 256–58, 269, 294, 295, 308
Puck, 5, 18, 39, 53, 57, 69, 74, 105, 110, 117, 120, 258, 276, 297, 305, 310; tattooed man, 136–37, 153; and sex scandals, 174, 183, 187; aids Mugwumps, 199, 201; roasts Irish, 213, 214; on St. John, 226; on Butler, 231
Pudding tickets, 14
Pulitzer, Joseph, 4

Quay, Matthew S., 60, 126, 131
Quincy, Josiah, 198

Randall, Samuel J., 36, 173, 290, 310; Speakership race, 98–100; stymies Morrison tariff bill, 100–106, 107; downfall, 105–6, 308–9; and 1884 nomination, 106–7, 143, 145, 147, 155, 157, 158, 160; cajoles Butler, 227
Readjuster movement, 51–52, 55–57
Redemption (Southern), 31–36, 41–42, 243
Reed, Thomas Brackett, 75, 142, 208
Reform, xi, xiv, 2–3, 22–25, 30, 38, 43, 45, 59–60, 64, 68, 73–76, 78–79, 92–94, 101–4, 113–24, 146, 148, 163, 172, 175, 197–209, 223–25, 242–44, 297–98, 304–7
Reid, Whitelaw, 18, 70, 130, 137, 174–75, 199, 266, 274, 278–79, 284, 310
Republican National Committee, 165–67, 170, 177–78, 195, 213, 253, 259–62
Republican Party, xi, xiii, 1–4, 11, 13–26 passim, 27, 59–90, 117–18, 162–78 passim, 191–92, 194–96; and 1876 election, 29–33, 34–36; and South, 36, 41–50, 56–58, 63, 65, 170, 176, 243–54, 256; and Prohibitionists, 80–90, 229–36; and tariff, 95–98; and 1884 nomination, 124–42; and Mugwumps, 197–209; and Irish, 210–17; and Butler movement, 225–29; and nativists, 237; and election results, 289–303. *See also* Blaine, James G.; Conkling, Roscoe;

Elections; Hayes, Rutherford B.; Tariff
  issue
Rhode Island, 13, 257
Rice, William G., 9
Richmond Whig, 54
Riddleberger, Harrison H., 157–58
Roach, John, 174
Robertson, William H., 67, 76, 137
Robeson, George, 18, 72–73, 74, 174
Robinson, George D., 207
Robinson, John, 248
Robinson, William S. "Richelieu," 220
Rockefeller, John D., 230–32
Roosevelt, Theodore, 23, 121, 127, 297;
  opposes Blaine, 130, 133, 138; and
  Mugwumps, 202, 207–8
Rossa, Jeremiah O'Donovan, 212, 216,
  218, 220
"Rum, Romanism, and Rebellion," xi, 80,
  279–85, 287, 296, 297, 301

Sage, Russell, 174
St. John, John P., 3, 221, 224, 225, 227,
  230–37, 257, 272, 307; dries up Kansas,
  81–84; marriage scandal, 189, 281;
  apparently for sale, 232–37, 239, 301–2;
  effect on New York's results, 295, 297,
  302
St. Joseph Gazette, 257
St. Louis, 15
St. Louis Globe-Democrat, 302
St. Louis Post-Dispatch, 144
St. Paul Dispatch, 175
Salisbury prison, 43–44
San Francisco *Alta California*, 156
Sawyer, Philetus, 102
Scales, Alfred, 249–50, 252–53
Scandals. *See* Blaine marriage; Halpin
  scandal; Mulligan letters
Schurz, Carl, 64, 111, 137, 146, 173, 177,
  196, 200, 204, 205–6, 230, 297, 305,
  306
Scott, Thomas, 62–63
Scott, William L., 168, 309
Scott Law, 87–89
Seymour, Horatio, 190

Shanahan, James, 119
Sheridan, Philip, 127
Sherman, John, 57, 96, 263–65; Half-
  Breed leader, 60, 65–66; and Ohio
  politics, 86, 89; presidential boom, 127,
  129, 131, 135, 137
Sherman, William Tecumseh, 42, 96,
  124–25, 141
Shoemaker, John C., 185
Skirmishing Fund, 212
Smith, William H., 246
Smith Act, 85–87
"Soap," 37
Solid South, xiv-xv, 10, 31–36, 95,
  240–54, 289, 304, 310, 313
South Carolina, 31–35, 241, 248, 299
Southern Pacific Railroad, 114
Speer, Emory, 250
Springer, William M., 57
Stalwarts, xii, 4, 49, 164, 170, 314; lead-
  ers, 59–60; issues, 63–70; and 1882
  elections, 73–74, 76; and 1884 nomina-
  tion, 125, 126, 129–35; in campaign,
  272–75, 295, 297
Standard Oil, 112, 230–32
Stanwood, Edward, 294
Star Route frauds, 71–72, 199
Stephens, Alexander, 52–54
Stolen election (1876), 29–31, 37–38, 40
Strobach, Paul, 246
Sullivan, Alexander, 218, 221
Swallowtails, 108, 151, 314

Talmadge, DeWitt, 80
Tammany Hall, 8, 28, 111–13, 119–20,
  122, 172, 204, 219, 225, 238, 243, 292,
  297, 306, 307, 314; opposes Cleveland's
  nomination, 146, 149–58; in 1884 campaign, 275–78, 287–88
Tariff issue, 48, 75–76, 89–90, 91–107,
  144–46, 163, 172–73, 176, 178, 241–42,
  250, 255–56, 264–65, 268, 288, 297; in
  Democratic platform, 157–59; Butler
  and, 157–59, 225, 228; Mugwumps and,
  208; appeal to Irish, 214–15; after 1884
  campaign, 309–11

Temperance. *See* Prohibition movement

Tennessee, 50, 242, 244

Tenniel, John, 214

Texas, 35, 50, 52, 242, 249

Texas & Pacific Railroad, 62–63, 205

Thompson, Hubert O., 120–21, 151, 306. *See also* County Democracy

Thompson, John G., 263

Thurman, Allen, 36, 128, 143–45, 155–59, 191, 207, 287

Thurman Pacific Railroad Funding Act, 128, 144

Tilden, Samuel J., 89, 110, 114, 161, 173, 191, 198, 204, 236, 290; character, 26–29, 37–38, 40; in 1876 election, 27–30, 37–38; seeks 1880 nomination, 38–40; and tariff issue, 99, 106–7; declines 1884 race, 145–53, 155, 157; death, 306

Tracey, John, 283–84

Turner, George, 240

Turner, Henry, 34

Twain, Mark, 184

Tweed, William M., 112, 150, 206, 219

Twining, Kinsley, 182, 184

Typographical Union, 175

United Irishman, 216, 220

Utah, 16, 249

Vanderbilt, William, 69, 97, 113, 199, 286–87

Vaux, Richard, 304

Virginia, 14, 96, 241, 245, 250, 252, 267, 290, 299; Readjuster movement, 51–58

Voorhees, Daniel W., 114, 160, 173

Vote fraud, 10–11, 14–16, 22–23, 29–33, 38, 237–38, 248–49, 270, 293–94, 299–300, 309

Wall, E. C., 178

Wallace, William A., 146

Waller, Thomas, 113, 115, 173

Walls, Josiah, 247

Warner, Willard, 246

Watterson, Henry, 43, 49, 98, 147, 158

Weaver, James B., 228, 295

Webster, Daniel, 92

Weed, Smith M., 149, 236

Wells, David A., 104

West Virginia, 14, 131, 174, 195–96, 241, 242, 256, 257; in 1884 election, 262, 267–68

Wheeler, Clint, 294

Wheeler, Everett P., 198

Wheeling Intelligencer, 268

Whiskey Ring, 96, 100, 135

White, Andrew D., 128, 163

White, Horace, 135

Whitney, William C., 166, 168; and Tilden, 28–29; and Cleveland boom, 149, 151; bankrolls Prohibition Party, 236, 239

Willard, Frances, 221, 224

Wilson, E. Willis, 268

Wisconsin, 66, 84, 102, 290

Wise, John S., 241

Woman's Crusade, 80–81

Woman's Rights Party, 16–17, 189

Woman suffrage, 16–17

Women's Christian Temperance Union (WCTU), 2, 80–81, 89, 97, 257; divides, 221–22

Workingmen's Party, 114, 211, 228, 229

Workingmen's Assembly, 122

Wyoming, 16

York, Tyre, 249–50, 252–53, 299